# Applied Machine Learning III

# Applied Machine Learning III

Guest Editor

**Grzegorz Dudek**

MDPI

Basel • Beijing • Wuhan • Barcelona • Belgrade • Novi Sad • Cluj • Manchester

*Guest Editor*
Grzegorz Dudek
Department of Automatic
Control, Electrical
Engineering and
Optoelectronics
Częstochowa University
of Technology
Częstochowa
Poland

*Editorial Office*
MDPI AG
Grosspeteranlage 5
4052 Basel, Switzerland

This is a reprint of the Special Issue, published open access by the journal *Applied Sciences* (ISSN 2076-3417), freely accessible at: https://www.mdpi.com/journal/applsci/special_issues/P04T24PV0Q.

For citation purposes, cite each article independently as indicated on the article page online and as indicated below:

| Lastname, A.A.; Lastname, B.B. Article Title. *Journal Name* **Year**, *Volume Number*, Page Range. |
|---|

**ISBN 978-3-7258-7268-8 (Hbk)**
**ISBN 978-3-7258-7269-5 (PDF)**
**https://doi.org/10.3390/books978-3-7258-7269-5**

# Contents

# About the Editor

**Grzegorz Dudek**

Grzegorz Dudek received his PhD in Electrical Engineering from Czestochowa University of Technology, Poland, in 2003, and completed his habilitation in Computer Science at Lodz University of Technology, Poland, in 2013. In 2023, he was appointed as a full professor. His research primarily focuses on machine learning and artificial intelligence, with a strong emphasis on their applications in classification, regression, forecasting, and optimization. He has authored and co-authored 4 books and over 140 scientific papers in these areas.

# Preface

This Reprint is devoted to recent advances in machine learning, with particular emphasis on emerging methods and their application to complex real-world problems. Machine learning has become a central pillar of contemporary applied science, enabling data-driven discovery, prediction, and decision support across a wide range of disciplines. The rapid growth of data availability, computational power, and algorithmic sophistication has created both new opportunities and new methodological challenges, motivating continued research into robust, interpretable, and application-oriented learning frameworks.

The scope of this Reprint encompasses methodological developments as well as practical implementations of machine learning techniques. The collected articles address topics such as data preprocessing and imputation, nonlinear and hybrid modeling, feature selection and optimization, deep learning architectures, and explainable artificial intelligence. These methods are examined and validated in diverse application contexts, including environmental and climate modeling, wearable sensing and human movement analysis, clinical risk prediction, financial time series forecasting, and intelligent manufacturing systems. Together, the contributions illustrate how machine learning methods are adapted and extended to meet the demands of real-world data characterized by uncertainty, heterogeneity, and dynamic behavior.

The primary aim of this Reprint is to provide a coherent overview of current research directions that bridge methodological innovation and applied impact. Rather than focusing on a single domain, the Reprint highlights cross-cutting themes that recur across disciplines, such as the importance of data quality, the integration of domain knowledge into learning models, and the growing need for transparent and interpretable predictive systems. By presenting rigorously reviewed studies that demonstrate measurable improvements over existing approaches, the Reprint seeks to support the transfer of advanced machine learning techniques from theory to practice.

This Reprint is intended for researchers, engineers, and practitioners working in applied sciences who seek a consolidated perspective on contemporary machine learning research. It is also relevant to graduate students and early career scientists looking to understand how modern learning methods are designed, evaluated, and deployed in real-world settings. By bringing together contributions from different fields under a shared methodological framework, the Reprint aims to foster interdisciplinary dialogue and to encourage further innovation at the intersection of machine learning and applied science.

**Grzegorz Dudek**
*Guest Editor*

applied sciences

MDPI

Editorial

# Advances in Machine Learning: Emerging Methods and Real-World Applications

**Grzegorz Dudek**

Department of Electrical Engineering, Częstochowa University of Technology, 42-200 Częstochowa, Poland; grzegorz.dudek@pcz.pl

## 1. Introduction

Machine learning has evolved into a pivotal discipline within contemporary computation, driving innovation across an expanding range of scientific, industrial, and societal domains. Its rapid development over recent decades has enabled the creation of data-driven solutions that address increasingly complex real-world problems. Today, machine learning techniques underpin advances in engineering, manufacturing, finance, medicine, environmental science, and numerous other fields. This progress is supported by a diverse methodological landscape that spans long-established models—such as linear regression, k-nearest neighbors, decision trees, support vector machines, and classical neural networks—as well as modern, high-capacity approaches including deep learning architectures, transformers, and ensemble-based boosted methods.

Despite remarkable achievements, several methodological challenges remain central to the advancement of machine learning. Identifying suitable model architectures, designing efficient training procedures, and tuning hyperparameters continue to be demanding tasks that significantly influence predictive accuracy and generalization. Additionally, machine learning workflows frequently contend with large-scale, incomplete, noisy, or uncertain data, which require robust preprocessing strategies and specialized modeling techniques. Another enduring priority is interpretability: the ability to articulate how and why a model arrives at its predictions is essential for ensuring transparency, trustworthiness, and responsible deployment in high-stakes environments.

This Special Issue brings together contributions that address these challenges from complementary perspectives. Following rigorous peer review, nine high-quality papers were selected from twenty-five submissions. Collectively, these works encompass diverse problem formulations, data representations, feature engineering strategies, learning algorithms, and performance evaluation methodologies. They additionally highlight the importance of measurable improvements over existing techniques and of the clear interpretation of empirical results. Through this curated selection, the Special Issue seeks to illustrate not only the breadth of machine learning applications but also the methodological innovations that support continued progress in the field.

The research contributions collected in this Special Issue reflect the accelerating evolution of data-driven science, in which machine learning, hybrid computational modeling, environmental monitoring, wearable systems, predictive analytics, and industrial intelligence converge to address a diverse array of scientific and societal challenges. Although the nine articles under consideration originate from distinct disciplinary backgrounds, they share a conceptual foundation in the rigorous treatment of data irregularities, the exploitation of nonlinear learning architectures, the infusion of domain knowledge into computational models, and the pursuit of interpretable yet high-performing predictive systems. This editorial aims to integrate these contributions into a cohesive scientific narrative, providing enough depth, contextualization, and analytical synthesis to serve as a substantive reference for researchers across fields as diverse as hydrology, atmospheric chemistry, pediatric motor development, nephrology, evolutionary computation, commodities forecasting, and production logistics.

## 2. Summary of the Contributions

The editorial begins by examining contributions focused on environmental modeling, highlighting how agricultural yield prediction, rainfall reconstruction, and ozone forecasting share a reliance on robust imputation and nonlinear machine learning architectures for handling variability induced by climate dynamics and anthropogenic pressures. It then transitions to wearable sensor analytics, where studies of gait irregularity detection and schoolchildren's motor competence demonstrate how pervasive sensing technologies enable novel forms of physiological and biomechanical assessment. From there, the analysis moves to clinical machine learning for mortality prediction among hemodialysis patients, illustrating the complexities of prognostics in multivariate biomedical domains and the need for standardized predictive feature sets. The editorial then explores computational optimization and its applications to feature selection and financial modeling, before concluding with an examination of data-driven decision support in manufacturing environments. Throughout, the aim is not merely to summarize each study but to clarify how they collectively illuminate broader scientific patterns, methodological tensions, and conceptual advancements.

### 2.1. *Environmental and Climate-Oriented Modeling*

The first cluster of articles addresses the pervasive challenge of irregular, incomplete, or noisy environmental data. The article by Călin, Coroiu, and Mureșan situates itself at the nexus of agronomy, climate modeling, and computational data analysis by examining machine learning-based crop yield prediction [1], with a specific focus on sunflower yield under conditions of climatic variability. Sunflower crops grown without irrigation are especially sensitive to fluctuations in precipitation, temperature, timing of sowing, and the accumulated stress of extreme weather conditions. These variables seldom conform to the structured, dense datasets favored by traditional statistical modeling; instead, agronomic datasets frequently include missing entries across key meteorological variables. The authors therefore treat missing data imputation not as a mundane preprocessing step but as an essential methodological challenge that fundamentally shapes the performance of downstream predictive models.

Their analysis includes a comparison among mean value imputation, similarity-based approaches, deterministic interpolation techniques such as linear and spline interpolation, and predictive imputation based on linear regression, Random Forest, extreme gradient boosting, and histogram gradient boosting. Critically, the authors also examine four unsupervised outlier removal methods to investigate how anomalous observations interact with imputation strategies. Their experiments reveal that Random Forest-based imputation combined with One-Class SVM outlier removal delivers a substantial improvement in predictive accuracy, raising the coefficient of determination from 0.723 to 0.938. This finding should be interpreted within the broader global literature, which increasingly recognizes that ensemble-based imputers capture nonlinear co-variations within environmental variables more effectively than deterministic approaches [2]. The longitudinal, seasonal, and meteorological dependencies inherent to agricultural yield formation are particularly difficult to reconstruct through simple interpolation because such methods implicitly assume smooth temporal progression rather than variable responses to rainfall

https://doi.org/10.3390/app16010443

anomalies, heat stress, and soil moisture dynamics. The study therefore serves as an important demonstration of why predictive imputation must be treated as an integral component of agronomic modeling pipelines, especially as climate change intensifies variability and disrupts data continuity.

The second article in this cluster, authored by Saubhagya, Tilakaratne, Lakraj, and Mammadov, extends the challenge of missing data reconstruction into the domain of hydrology. Rainfall data are notoriously prone to missingness, often due to equipment malfunction in extreme weather, accessibility limitations in mountainous terrain, or prolonged periods during which manual gauge measurements cannot be performed. The Ratnapura region of Sri Lanka, characterized by diverse topography and exposure to monsoon dynamics, presents an especially challenging dataset containing extended periods of missing values at multiple stations distributed across five years.

The authors propose a hybrid imputation model integrating temporal modeling via multilayer perceptrons with spatial interpolation via kriging. Their innovation lies in the optimal combination of the two components, recognizing that rainfall exhibits nonlinear temporal patterns influenced by seasonal cycles, but also spatial coherence shaped by orographic effects and localized convective behavior. By assigning optimal weights to chemical-based predictions and kriging-based estimates, the hybrid model outperforms standalone approaches, including spatiotemporal kriging. This suggests that rainfall imputation benefits from deep learning's ability to capture high-frequency temporal anomalies and kriging's ability to express spatial continuity. Their contribution reflects a broader scientific trend in hydrological modeling where hybrid models increasingly replace monolithic statistical approaches [3]. As climate change alters rainfall distribution patterns, such models may become essential for flood forecasting, reservoir management, and the calibration of hydrological simulations that depend on complete rainfall datasets.

The third article in this section, by Domínguez-García and Arellano-Vázquez, examines ozone concentration forecasting in Mexico City. The metropolitan valley, marked by high population density, mountainous topography, vehicular traffic, and intense solar radiation, presents a complex atmospheric environment where ozone formation stems from nonlinear chemical interactions among nitrogen oxides, volatile organic compounds, and meteorological factors. Forecasting ozone levels twenty-four hours ahead has profound implications for public health because ozone exacerbates respiratory conditions and contributes to acute and chronic health burdens [4].

The authors compare Random Forests, Support Vector Regression, and gradient boosting, demonstrating superior performance of ensemble-based models. Their results accord with international atmospheric modeling research, which has repeatedly shown that gradient boosting techniques outperform linear and kernel-based models in capturing the complex relationships underlying tropospheric ozone formation. This study also underscores the limitations of relying exclusively on chemical transport models, which, while physically grounded, often require substantial computational resources and extensive tuning. The authors' findings confirm that machine learning, when supported by high-quality meteorological inputs, can provide accurate short-term ozone forecasts that enhance environmental decision-making and contextualize real-time air quality alerts.

### *2.2. Wearable Sensing and Human Movement Analysis*

The next thematic grouping concerns wearable sensor analytics and its application to human movement, walkability, and pediatric motor development. The ability to detect subtle changes in gait or walking environments using accelerometer data has major implications for urban planning, fall prevention, rehabilitation, and physical activity monitoring [5].

https://doi.org/10.3390/app16010443

Ng, Zhong, Nam, and Youn contribute a study on detecting irregular walking surfaces using LSTM networks trained on data recorded from a single wearable accelerometer. Detecting uneven surfaces is essential for understanding walkability, which influences mobility behaviors, accessibility, and pedestrian risk. Traditional walkability surveys rely heavily on human inspectors or subjective scoring systems, which limits their reproducibility and scalability. The authors propose a classifier that processes raw accelerometer sequences as well as stride-level features extracted from the signal. They find that models trained on multi-stride feature sets achieve the highest area under the curve, although raw-signal models retain advantages in capturing micro-perturbations.

This study belongs to a growing global body of research using wearable sensors to map environmental conditions indirectly through physiological signatures [6]. The LSTM architecture is particularly well-suited to capturing the temporal dependencies in gait dynamics, where surface irregularities cause subtle variations in step timing, acceleration, and impact absorption. The recent literature in movement science has shown that temporal deep learning models outperform classical machine learning in detecting gait abnormalities, early neurodegenerative signs, and fall-risk indicators [7]. The authors' work therefore contributes directly to methodological advances in computational gait analysis, while also offering practical opportunities for low-cost urban walkability monitoring.

Sulla-Torres, Calla Gamboa, Avendaño Llanque, Angulo Osorio, and Zúñiga Carnero extend wearable analytics into pediatric evaluation by examining motor competence among schoolchildren in Arequipa. Motor competence, encompassing walking, running, balance, coordination, and dynamic mobility, has long been associated with physical health trajectories and developmental outcomes [8]. However, traditional assessment methods often rely on trained evaluators or laboratory-based equipment, which limits accessibility in low-resource settings.

The authors employ smart bands to collect data on cadence, stride, heart rate, and energy expenditure during six-minute walking and running tests administered to more than 760 children. They apply the LMS method to generate normative percentile curves and use a wide range of machine learning models to classify motor competence levels. The gradient boosting model produces the highest performance, illustrating that nonlinear relationships across physiological features are critical for accurate classification. By validating a software prototype designed to implement their classification model in educational settings, the authors bridge the gap between research and applied practice. Their work adds to international research emphasizing the importance of culturally and geographically tailored motor competence assessment using affordable digital tools.

### *2.3. Predictive Nephrology and Clinical Risk Modeling*

Hemodialysis mortality prediction forms a distinct thematic axis in this Special Issue. The systematic review by Motofelea, Mihaescu, Olariu, Marc, Chisavu, Pop, Crintea, Jura, Ivan, Apostol, and Schiller examines machine learning models used to predict mortality among hemodialysis patients, offering a rigorous synthesis guided by PRISMA principles. Hemodialysis patients exhibit 10-20 times higher mortality rates than the general population, due to the high burden of comorbidities, chronic inflammation, cardiovascular deterioration, and the physiological instability inherent to dialysis sessions.

The authors identify logistic regression, Random Forest, and XGBoost as the most frequently employed prediction models. Their meta-analysis finds that Random Forest achieves the highest average AUC, particularly at three-year follow-up horizons, although logistic regression frequently performs comparably despite its relative simplicity. This result is significant because it challenges the assumption that high model complexity necessarily

https://doi.org/10.3390/app16010443

leads to superior performance in clinical prognostics. Instead, model performance depends as much on the quality and structure of input features as it does on algorithmic complexity.

A major insight from the review is that predictor heterogeneity across studies greatly limits model generalization. Some studies rely heavily on biochemical indicators, whereas others emphasize comorbidity indices or dialysis-specific parameters such as ultrafiltration volume, interdialytic weight gain, or heart rate variability. This inconsistency hinders the development of standardized prognostic frameworks. The authors argue that future progress requires the harmonization of predictive feature sets, longitudinal study designs, and robust interpretability mechanisms. Their emphasis on interpretability echoes global trends in clinical machine learning, where black-box models face increasing scrutiny and where transparent, clinically actionable features remain essential for adoption in patient care [9].

### 2.4. Other Topics: Evolutionary Optimization, Financial Modeling, and Smart Manufacturing

Zhou, Zheng, Li, Hao, Zhang, Gao, and Wang present a knowledge-guided competitive co-evolutionary algorithm designed for feature selection in high-dimensional datasets. Feature selection plays a crucial role in machine learning, particularly in domains where interpretability, efficiency, and dimensionality reduction are essential [10]. In many applications, including biomedical modeling, industrial diagnostics, remote sensing, and financial forecasting, the input feature space is vast, and correlations among features can significantly influence model performance. The authors introduce a co-evolutionary mechanism that incorporates correlation-based domain knowledge to guide the search process, enhancing the ability of the algorithm to find meaningful and non-redundant feature subsets.

Their competitive–cooperative evolutionary architecture improves convergence speed while maintaining diversity among solutions, addressing a classical challenge in evolutionary computation. Traditional multi-objective evolutionary algorithms often suffer from premature convergence, or stagnation in local optima, especially when dealing with complex feature landscapes. By integrating correlation awareness into evolutionary dominance relationships, the authors demonstrate that feature selection becomes more efficient and yields subsets that contribute to higher predictive quality and more interpretable downstream models. This approach resonates with the emerging trend of hybrid optimization strategies in which domain-specific information is infused into evolutionary search, thereby reducing the randomness inherent in traditional population-based algorithms and enabling more refined exploration of the solution space [11].

Financial time series prediction represents another area where hybrid machine learning models increasingly prove advantageous. The study by Huo, Xie, and Li proposes a deep learning-based futures price prediction system supported by a chaotic-mapping artificial bee colony algorithm. Futures markets are characterized by volatility, abrupt regime shifts, nonlinear temporal dependencies, and sensitivity to geopolitical or macroeconomic fluctuations. The LSTM architecture is well-suited for modeling long-term dependencies within such time series [12], yet LSTM performance is heavily influenced by hyperparameter choices that define network size, learning rates, dropout proportions, and internal gating behavior. Hyperparameter tuning becomes particularly challenging in financial contexts, where overfitting is common and model generalization requires careful balancing of complexity and regularization.

The authors incorporate chaotic mapping into the artificial bee colony algorithm to enhance search diversity and counteract premature convergence. Chaotic sequences generate quasi-random oscillations that improve the exploration of the hyperparameter space, thereby enabling the optimization method to escape local minima. Through backtesting on gold and natural gas futures, the authors demonstrate that the chaotic bee colony-

https://doi.org/10.3390/app16010443

enhanced LSTM exhibits superior performance across error metrics compared to models optimized through conventional heuristic methods. This result reflects a broader shift in computational finance toward hybrid architectures that marry recurrent neural networks with swarm intelligence or evolutionary tuning. Recent research indicates that financial forecasting benefits greatly from models capable of capturing nonlinear patterns while maintaining adaptability in unstable markets [13]. The hybrid system proposed in this study illustrates how computational intelligence can complement deep learning to address the intrinsic unpredictability of financial data.

In the domain of industrial analytics, Çağlayan and Aksoy investigate the use of machine learning to support the selection of material feeding systems in modern manufacturing. Material feeding strategies determine how components are delivered to assembly lines and directly influence cost efficiency, production stability, lead time, and material handling overhead. Conventional selection methods typically rely on engineering heuristics, rule-of-thumb guidelines, or expert judgment. These approaches become increasingly inadequate as modern manufacturing systems grow more dynamic, with greater variation in product types, material dimensions, demand profiles, and process constraints.

The authors construct a large dataset of more than two thousand materials, each represented by attributes such as usage frequency, storage constraints, handling characteristics, and consumption rates. They train several classification models, ultimately demonstrating the superior performance of artificial neural networks for predicting optimal feeding strategies. A particularly noteworthy aspect of their work is the use of Shapley value analysis, which provides a transparent explanation of feature contributions to the model's decisions. This step is crucial in industrial contexts, where interpretability not only increases trust but also enables practitioners to integrate model recommendations into existing engineering workflows. Their system shows how machine learning can enhance the adaptability and intelligence of production systems, aligning with global Industry 4.0 trends [14] toward data-driven automation, resource optimization, and real-time decision-making.

## 3. Cross-Domain Themes and Conceptual Integration

The diverse contributions summarized above exhibit several overarching scientific themes. One prominent theme is the centrality of high-quality data preprocessing. Whether reconstructing missing agricultural records, rainfall gaps, or inconsistent hemodialysis datasets, many of the studies emphasize that the quality of the input data often determines the attainable predictive performance more than model architecture alone. This observation aligns with the growing movement toward data-centric approaches in machine learning, which argue that computational models reach their full potential only when the structure, continuity, and resolution of input data are sufficiently refined [15].

Another theme concerns the growing reliance on hybrid approaches [16]. Hydrological modeling in the Special Issue combines neural networks with geostatistics; futures forecasting merges LSTM networks with swarm intelligence; feature selection fuses evolutionary search with correlation-based knowledge; and wearable analytics blends handcrafted features with deep recurrent architectures. These hybrid models illustrate the advantages of synthesizing domain knowledge with algorithmic flexibility. Rather than choosing between physically grounded models and data-driven models, the articles demonstrate how the combination of both can outperform either approach alone. This reflects a broader epistemological shift in applied sciences, where hybridization increasingly becomes the default expectation rather than a methodological exception.

Interpretability constitutes a third cross-domain theme [17]. Several articles explicitly incorporate interpretability mechanisms, such as Shapley values, or emphasize the need for transparent feature selection and clinically meaningful predictors. This focus reflects

https://doi.org/10.3390/app16010443

growing recognition that black-box outputs cannot be adopted uncritically in medical, industrial, or policy-relevant applications. Interpretability enables expert validation, fosters trust, and supports ethical decision-making. In manufacturing and clinical settings, where practitioners must justify model recommendations, explainable AI is no longer optional but fundamental.

## 4. Conclusions

This Special Issue highlights significant advances in data-driven modeling across environmental sciences, human health, financial analytics, and industrial decision support. The nine articles collectively demonstrate that the integration of machine learning, hybrid optimization, and wearable sensing is reshaping predictive science. As these fields continue converging, interdisciplinary collaboration and methodological transparency will remain essential to sustaining scientific progress.

**Funding:** This research received no external funding.

**Conflicts of Interest:** The author declares no conflicts of interest.

**List of Contributions**

1. Călin, A.; Coroiu, A.; Mureşan, H. Analysis of Preprocessing Techniques for Missing Data in the Prediction of Sunflower Yield in Response to the Effects of Climate Change. *Appl. Sci.* **2023**, *13*, 7415. https://doi.org/10.3390/app13137415.
2. Saubhagya, S.; Tilakaratne, C.; Lakraj, P.; Mammadov, M. A Novel Hybrid Spatiotemporal Missing Value Imputation Approach for Rainfall Data: An Application to the Ratnapura Area, Sri Lanka. *Appl. Sci.* **2024**, *14*, 999. https://doi.org/10.3390/app14030999.
3. Domínguez-García, R.; Arellano-Vázquez, M. Evaluation of Machine Learning Models for Ozone Concentration Forecasting in the Metropolitan Valley of Mexico. *Appl. Sci.* **2024**, *14*, 1408. https://doi.org/10.3390/app14041408.
4. Ng, H.; Zhong, X.; Nam, Y.; Youn, J. Deep-Learning-Based Approach for Automated Detection of Irregular Walking Surfaces for Walkability Assessment with Wearable Sensor. *Appl. Sci.* **2023**, *13*, 13053. https://doi.org/10.3390/app132413053.
5. Sulla-Torres, J.; Calla Gamboa, A.; Avendaño Llanque, C.; Angulo Osorio, J.; Zúñiga Carnero, M. Classification of Motor Competence in Schoolchildren Using Wearable Technology and Machine Learning with Hyperparameter Optimization. *Appl. Sci.* **2024**, *14*, 707. https://doi.org/10.3390/app14020707.
6. Motofelea, A.; Mihaescu, A.; Olariu, N.; Marc, L.; Chisavu, L.; Pop, G.; Crintea, A.; Jura, A.; Ivan, V.; Apostol, A.; Schiller, A. Machine Learning Models for Predicting Mortality in Hemodialysis Patients: A Systematic Review. *Appl. Sci.* **2025**, *15*, 5776. https://doi.org/10.3390/app15105776.
7. Zhou, J.; Zheng, H.; Li, S.; Hao, Q.; Zhang, H.; Gao, W.; Wang, X. A Knowledge-Guided Competitive Co-Evolutionary Algorithm for Feature Selection. *Appl. Sci.* **2024**, *14*, 4501. https://doi.org/10.3390/app14114501.
8. Huo, L.; Xie, Y.; Li, J. An Innovative Deep Learning Futures Price Prediction Method with Fast and Strong Generalization and High-Accuracy Research. *Appl. Sci.* **2024**, *14*, 5602. https://doi.org/10.3390/app14135602.
9. Çağlayan, M.; Aksoy, A. Integrating Machine Learning and Material Feeding Systems for Competitive Advantage in Manufacturing. *Appl. Sci.* **2025**, *15*, 980. https://doi.org/10.3390/app15020980.

## References

1. van Klompenburg, T.; Kassahun, A.; Catal, C. Crop yield prediction using machine learning: A systematic literature review. *Comput. Electron. Agric.* **2020**, *177*, 105709. https://doi.org/https://doi.org/10.1016/j.compag.2020.105709.
2. Everingham, Y.; Smyth, C.; Inman-Bamber, N. Ensemble data mining approaches to forecast regional sugarcane crop production. *Agric. For. Meteorol.* **2009**, *149*, 689–696. https://doi.org/https://doi.org/10.1016/j.agrformet.2008.10.018.

3. Anuradha, T.; Aruna Sri Formal, P.; RamaDevi, J. Hybrid model for rainfall prediction with statistical and technical indicator feature set. *Expert Syst. Appl.* **2024**, *249*, 123260. https://doi.org/https://doi.org/10.1016/j.eswa.2024.123260.
4. Rojas-Martinez, R.; Perez-Padilla, R.; Olaiz-Fernandez, G.; Mendoza-Alvarado, L.; Moreno-Macias, H.; Fortoul, T.; McDonnell, W.; Loomis, D.; Romieu, I. Lung function growth in children with long-term exposure to air pollutants in Mexico City. *Am. J. Respir. Crit. Care Med.* **2007**, *176*, 377–384. https://doi.org/10.1164/rccm.200510-1678OC.
5. Otamendi, J.; Zubizarreta, A.; Portillo, E. Machine learning-based gait anomaly detection using a sensorized tip: an individualized approach. *Neural Comput. Appl.* **2023**, *35*, 17443–17459. https://doi.org/10.1007/s00521-023-08601-1.
6. Dion, G.; Tessier-Poirier, A.; Chiasson-Poirier, L.; Morissette, J.-F.; Brassard, G.; Haman, A.; Turcot, K.; Sylvestre, J. In-sensor human gait analysis with machine learning in a wearable microfabricated accelerometer. *Commun. Eng.* **2024**, *3*, 48. https://doi.org/10.1038/s44172-024-00193-5.
7. Zheng, X.; Wilhelm, E.; Otten, E.; Reneman, M.F.; Lamoth, C.J. Age-related gait patterns classification using deep learning based on time-series data from one accelerometer. *Biomed. Signal Process. Control* **2025**, *104*, 107406. https://doi.org/https://doi.org/10.1016/j.bspc.2024.107406.
8. Hill, P.J.; McNarry, M.A.; Mackintosh, K.A.; Murray, M.A.; Pesce, C.; Valentini, N.C.; Getchell, N.; Tomporowski, P.D.; Robinson, L.E.; Barnett, L.M. The Influence of Motor Competence on Broader Aspects of Health: A Systematic Review of the Longitudinal Associations Between Motor Competence and Cognitive and Social-Emotional Outcomes. *Sport. Med.* **2024**, *54*, 375–427. https://doi.org/10.1007/s40279-023-01939-5.
9. Akbilgic, O.; Obi, Y.; Potukuchi, P.K.; Karabayir, I.; Nguyen, D.V.; Soohoo, M.; Streja, E.; Molnar, M.Z.; Rhee, C.M.; Kalantar-Zadeh, K.; et al. Machine Learning to Identify Dialysis Patients at High Death Risk. *Kidney Int. Rep.* **2019**, *4*, 1219–1229. https://doi.org/10.1016/j.ekir.2019.06.009.
10. Dhal, P.; Azad, C. A comprehensive survey on feature selection in the various fields of machine learning. *Appl. Intell.* **2022**, *52*, 4543–4581. https://doi.org/10.1007/s10489-021-02550-9.
11. da S. Bohrer, J.; Dorn, M. Enhancing classification with hybrid feature selection: A multi-objective genetic algorithm for high-dimensional data. *Expert Syst. Appl.* **2024**, *255*, 124518. https://doi.org/https://doi.org/10.1016/j.eswa.2024.124518.
12. Zhang, J.; Liu, H.; Bai, W.; Li, X. A hybrid approach of wavelet transform, ARIMA and LSTM model for the share price index futures forecasting. *N. Am. J. Econ. Financ.* **2024**, *69*, 102022. https://doi.org/https://doi.org/10.1016/j.najef.2023.102022.
13. Sezer, O.B.; Gudelek, M.U.; Ozbayoglu, A.M. Financial time series forecasting with deep learning : A systematic literature review: 2005–2019. *Appl. Soft Comput.* **2020**, *90*, 106181. https://doi.org/https://doi.org/10.1016/j.asoc.2020.106181.
14. Wang, B.; Tao, F.; Fang, X.; Liu, C.; Liu, Y.; Freiheit, T. Smart Manufacturing and Intelligent Manufacturing: A Comparative Review. *Engineering* **2021**, *7*, 738–757. https://doi.org/https://doi.org/10.1016/j.eng.2020.07.017.
15. Golazad, S.; Mohammadi, A.; Rashidi, A.; Ilbeigi, M. From raw to refined: Data preprocessing for construction machine learning (ML), deep learning (DL), and reinforcement learning (RL) models. *Autom. Constr.* **2024**, *168*, 105844. https://doi.org/https://doi.org/10.1016/j.autcon.2024.105844.
16. Azevedo, B.F.; Rocha, A.M.A.C.; Pereira, A.I. Hybrid approaches to optimization and machine learning methods: A systematic literature review. *Mach. Learn.* **2024**, *113*, 4055–4097. https://doi.org/10.1007/s10994-023-06467-x.
17. Xu, B.; Yang, G. Interpretability research of deep learning: A literature survey. *Inf. Fusion* **2025**, *115*, 102721. https://doi.org/https://doi.org/10.1016/j.inffus.2024.102721.

*applied sciences*

MDPI

*Article*

# Analysis of Preprocessing Techniques for Missing Data in the Prediction of Sunflower Yield in Response to the Effects of Climate Change

**Alina Delia Călin *,†, Adriana Mihaela Coroiu † and Horea Bogdan Mureşan †**

Department of Computer Science, Babeş Bolyai University, Mihail Kogalniceanu 1, 400084 Cluj-Napoca, Romania; adriana.coroiu@ubbcluj.ro (A.M.C.); horea.muresan@ubbcluj.ro (H.B.M.)

* Correspondence: alina.calin@ubbcluj.ro; Tel.: +40-741-687-448

† These authors contributed equally to this work.

**Featured Application: The application of this research in agriculture is related to the rapid progression of climate change, which has drastic effects on crops. We can build an accurate and robust model that can help identify the optimum planting day to maximise the crop yield, based on the weather forecast and meteorological conditions of the region. This can support farmers in their agricultural activity planning and help minimise the impact of weather anomalies.**

**Abstract:** Machine learning is often used to predict crop yield based on the sowing date and weather parameters in non-irrigated crops. In the context of climate change, regression algorithms can help identify correlations and plan agricultural activities to maximise production. In the case of sunflower crops, we identified datasets that are not very large and have many missing values, generating a low-performance regression model. In this paper, our aim is to study and compare several approaches for missing-value imputation in order to improve our regression model. In our experiments, we compare nine imputation methods, using mean values, similar values, interpolation (linear, spline, pad), and prediction (linear regression, random forest, extreme gradient boosting regressor, and histogram gradient boosting regression). We also employ four unsupervised outlier removal algorithms and their influence on the regression model: isolation forest, minimum covariance determinant, local outlier factor and OneClass-SVM. After preprocessing, the obtained datasets are used to build regression models using the extreme gradient boosting regressor and histogram gradient boosting regression, and their performance is compared. The evaluation of the models shows an increased $R^2$ from 0.723 when removing instances with missing data, to 0.938 for imputation using Random Forest prediction and OneClass-SVM-based outlier removal.

**Keywords:** imputation; crop yield; regression; prediction; outlier detection; climate change; sowing date

## 1. Introduction

In the context of climate change, experts project major anomalies in precipitation rates and spread, and an increase in average soil temperature, which will affect food crops [1]. There is a focus on developing agro-meteorological decision systems to mitigate these problems and ensure food production is sustained for sensible crops [2,3] and continued for those found to be more resilient to changes [4].

Applied artificial intelligence and machine learning models demonstrate successful approaches to solving the current agricultural challenges. They can automate agricultural processes, build prediction models from phenology information and crop interventions [5,6], detect diseases early on, identify factors to maximise production with minimal investment, assess the impact of climate change [7], and forecast crop and meteorological trends [8].

The problem of optimising the planting window (which is very extensive, up to 60 or even 90 days) has been approached by researchers, considering factors such as climate or soil composition, hybrid type, and region [9,10]. For example, a case study on Romanian crops in 2019–2021 revealed that a delay of 15 days on the sowing day resulted in a decrease in yield, with 45–51% for several hybrids as presented by [11].

Our main research objective is to optimise sunflower crop production by modelling a yield prediction based on the planting or sowing day, given a weather forecast for a specific region. We use information about crops, planting day, crop type, location, and yield, combined with meteorological parameters (precipitation, temperature) to build a regression model that can accurately predict yield.

However, one problem encountered in this type of data is missing information. In our case, 80% of the data do not have information on the planting day. This feature is relevant for our objective to identify the correlation between planting day and yield, considering a given meteorological context. Thus, in this paper, we have explored different approaches for data preprocessing that can be used to build reliable prediction models. We compare the performance of several methods to fill in the missing data: mean values, interpolation, prediction (using several machine learning algorithms), removal, and similar fill.

Another important aspect of the data collected in a non-controlled environment is that it is error prone. In this regard, the selection and elimination of outliers can help improve the model. For this reason, we applied several unsupervised outlier removal algorithms and measured how they impact the performance of the supervised machine learning models built for the prediction of sunflower crop yield estimation, based on crop information (including sowing date) and meteorological data.

The main novel contributions of this paper consist of demonstrating the feasibility of using combined preprocessing techniques to build a robust model based on a small dataset with 80% of the instances having missing data, by increasing model performance from 0.723 to 0.938 (for the coefficient of correlation). This model can be used to simulate crop yield values based on sowing dates and meteorological forecast, thus helping farmers select the best planting window to maximise production.

In Section 2, we present a literature review. Section 3 details the methods used, from data collection, cleaning, preprocessing, to train and test the model. In Section 4, we present the results obtained, followed by Section 5 for discussion, and then Section 6 with conclusions.

## 2. Background

There is an active interest among researchers in using machine learning to find solutions to problems in the agricultural domain. One major advantage of using regression algorithms, as opposed to pure classical statistical mathematical approaches, is the fact that they allow the exploration of a combination of factors, instead of a single independent variable [5,12]. Moreover, data preprocessing and augmentation techniques, such as value imputation or outlier detection, can help build more robust and complex models [13]. In this section, we analyse the state-of-the-art techniques related to the yield prediction of crops, with special emphasis on building models based on the sowing date and meteorological input, and a focus on preprocessing techniques.

For the purpose of evaluating the risk of climate change for sunflower sowing dates, Aparecido et al. used artificial neural networks to build a tool for agricultural zoning climate risk in Brazil [14]. Climate data (air temperature, rainfall, relative air humidity, solar radiation, and wind velocity) were selected and used to model the sowing of sunflower on different dates. The model identified the largest viable areas for spring and summer planting according to the required conditions (58.13% and 64.36% of the suitable areas, respectively). They also obtained a correlation coefficient of 0.9936, 0.7472 and 0.8170 for air temperature (T), rainfall (P), and cycle soil water deficit (DEF), respectively. This result is based on the input characteristics and does not include historical planting dates in the model.

A summary of the most relevant related work in the prediction of yield based on crop and phenology data, such as planting day and meteorological data, is presented in Table 1. We note that the most utilised methodologies involve regression, forecasting or crop production, while one study employed the classification of sowing dates into early, mid or late. Regarding the metrics used specifically for regression, we note that the most utilised are $R^2$ (coefficient of determination), $MAE$ (mean absolute error), and $MAPE$ (mean absolute percentage error). The most explored crops are maize, soybean, wheat, and corn crops, which present a generous amount of data ($n = 10 - 25k$) around the world, with results up to 0.94 for $R^2$ [5] and an $MAPE$ of 7.6% [15].

**Table 1.** Related work for yield prediction using the planting date and weather information.

| Paper | Crop | Prediction Model | Dataset and Size | Metrics and Results |
|---|---|---|---|---|
| [16] | soybean, maize | Recurrent neural network | 1500 cities in Brazil and USA | $R^2 = 0.55$ for soybean in Brazil, $R^2 = 0.75$ for soybean in US and $R^2 = 0.71$ for maize in US |
| [17] | wheat | Random forest, multiple linear regression | 29 study sites in Australia | Forecast: 35 days before harvest $r = 0.85$, $MAPE = 17.6\%$; 60 days before harvest $r = 0.62$, $MAPE = 27.1\%$. |
| [18] | wheat | Decision trees, k-NN, SVM | 53 years data from Sanliurfa city, 1965–2017 | Accuracy for classifying into early, mid and late sowing dates: k-NN = 0.921; decision tree = 0.862; SVM = 0.470 |
| [5] | maize, soybean | XGBT | Maize ($n$ = 17,013) and soybean ($n$ = 24,848), 28 US states, 2014–2018 (USDA) | $MAE = 4.7$, $R^2 = 0.94$ for maize, and $MAE = 6.4$, $R^2 = 0.92$ for soybean |
| [19] | corn | Linear regression, LASSO, random forest, XGBT | Corn Belt US States ($n$ = 10,016), 1984–2018 (USDA and APSIM) | $R^2\% = 71.9$ for LASSO, $R^2\% = 72.5$ for Average, $R^2\% = 66.5$ for random forest |

Due to the lack of sufficient data on plant phenology on a large scale, there is limited research on the impact of the sowing date on the production of specific crops, such as sunflower. With limited and/or incomplete data available, the perspectives are much reduced. In an attempt to supplement this data scarcity, one approach aimed to use satellite image processing, such as Sentinel-1 SAR [20]. The work managed to approximate the sowing date with up to 85% accuracy [21]. In this case, the limitations are posed by visibility issues due to meteorological conditions.

Our approach in this study is to make the most of limited or incomplete data by applying and comparing preprocessing imputation techniques to fill in the blanks of non-available data, in order to create robust prediction models. The research literature of this area contains some comparative studies and imputation methods with great potential on various types of data, such as statistical, mean values, hot deck (similar values), regression (decision trees, random forest), k-NN, and clustering, applied on datasets with various missing rates (below 30%, 30 to 50%, and above 50%) [13]. The performance of these methods depends on the dataset type, size, and the randomness and rate of missing data [22].

The literature reveals various techniques for missing data, as an important step before data analysis, especially when there is a large amount of gaps in the dataset [23]. This can arise from human error, at the collection phase, drop-out in studies or merging unrelated datasets into one, as is in our case (the crop data were separated into one phenology dataset and one yield dataset). One approach often found in the literature is the deletion of instances with missing data; however, this can lead to biased, misinformed analysis, or errors in the regression model [24].

Computerised imputation (completion of missing values with potential or estimated ones) is an alternative to statistical or manual imputation methods when large amounts of data are involved, and can involve using mean values, regression (support vector machine, decision tree, random forest), ensemble based, k-NN, multiple imputation or similar values (hot-deck imputation) [13,22,23].

Furthermore, when data collection is not performed in a controlled environment, anomalies and outliers are often present. This poses a new challenge in building robust regression models, as each data point can greatly influence the result [25]. In this context, a study compared nine representative outlier detection (OD) models applied on eight regression datasets, to evaluate their performance [26]. The supervised regression models used to validate the unsupervised OD model performance are Ridge and Huber regression, and multi-layer perceptron regressor, with the evaluation metric being the $MAE$. The results showed that the minimum covariance determinant and isolation forests algorithms perform best, while principal components analysis, histogram-based outlier detection and local outlier factor are to be considered second, especially as they are faster computationally. A similar comparison was performed by Belhaouari et al. [25], showing a proposed box plot adjustment using the D-k-NN method performing well in terms of $MAE$ and computational efficiency, together with local outlier factor and minimum covariance determinant.

## 3. Materials and Methods

### 3.1. Data Collection and Aggregation

The data used in this research consist of historical yield and sowing information about sunflower crops in several US states (see Figure 1) and the corresponding meteorological parameters (temperature, precipitation) for each year and state in the dataset.

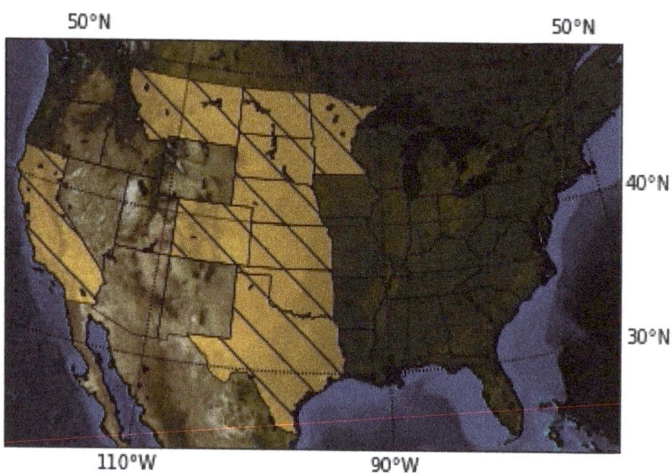


**Figure 1.** The map highlights in yellow the states contained in the dataset.

Crop data have been extracted from the US National Agricultural Statistics Service [27], and contain information on 10 states from 1950 to 2021 (with missing years), including the sunflower yield obtained for different types of non-irrigated crops (oil-type, non-oil-type, and total). We have selected all available data for the sunflower crop yield (as commodity), selecting the yield category, and all data items available which are measured in lb/acre, on the state geographical level, for all states and years. From the same source, we also identified and extracted, selecting the category progress, information on plant phenology, selecting the data item referring to the progress measured in percentage planted. This information was only available for 312 instances of the 1088 entries extracted in the first phase representing yield. These phenology data contained information regarding the planting date, in the form of the percentage of the planted area for that state by each week of the year. The cumulative percentages ran for a window of several weeks, up to 2–3 months, for which reason we decided to compute a new feature, representing an average planting week of the year, later translated into day of the year denoted with $D$ in the equation and named $AVGWeek$ as an attribute in the dataset (with 1 January being the first day of the year). This feature was calculated as a weighted average based on the weekly non-cumulative percentage. Let $d_i$ be the planting day and $w_i$ the cumulative weekly percentage planted to day $d_i$, initialising $w_0 = 0$ we obtain Equation (1):

$$D = \frac{1}{n}\sum_{i=1}^{n} d_i(w_i - w_{i-1}) \quad (1)$$

Meteorological data was obtained from the Daymet Online source [28] containing information complementing the existing entries in the sunflower crop dataset. The daily weather data from this source is reasonably accurate when computing monthly averages. It is provided by Oak Ridge National Laboratory and supported by NASA, and has been used by other studies for this purpose [5]. The Daymet Python API was used to download the data (with the support of the daymetpy Python library version 1.0.0 developed by Koen Hufkens and Colin Talbert, under the GNU Affero General Public License v3). Based on geolocation coordinates, for each state and year pair, we extracted the fields: daily precipitation, maximum temperature, and minimum temperature. After extraction, the data were aggregated into monthly averages for the temperature and cumulative monthly precipitation. The 12 months of weather information for each year was merged with the crop yield entries. The available meteorological data were from 1980 to 2021, resulting in the removal of the crop data from 1950 to 1979 from the initial dataset, as these were irrelevant to our research aim which focuses on more recent climate and crop information.

The 41 resulting features are the following: year (1980 to 2021), state ANSI (10 US States), crop type (oil, non-oil, all sunflower reported), yield (in lb/ac), planting day (day of year), and for each month × (from January—M1 to December—M12) the values for TMax-Mx (the monthly average maximum temperature in degrees Celsius), TMin-Mx (the monthly average minimum temperature in degrees Celsius), Prec-Mx (the cumulative monthly precipitations in mm).

### 3.2. Data Preprocessing

After data cleaning and non-valid data removal, our data comprises 984 instances and 41 features, of which only 312 are complete, and the other 796 (representing 80.89% of the total instances) are missing information on the AVGWeek feature or planting day. To handle the missing values, we experimented with several approaches and analysed the impact. Furthermore, we identified outliers and trained the models both with and without them. The entire process is described in the conceptual study process in Figure 2.

The approach, however, has its own limitations due to the particularities of the dataset. Data were collected by third parties for other purposes. We have limited information on the collection process and methodology or the validity of the information provided and how it was ensured. Missing data and errors in the values collected are challenges that we aim to address by using preprocessing techniques, to some extent, as described in the following. However, some issues cannot be fully addressed and the final model will be somewhat influenced by data inconsistencies. For example, the weekly percentage of land planted is a very general description and does not address particular cases such as replanting of an area because previous sowing failed a few weeks before (for example, affected by frost). Such an issue would change the average planting day feature and therefore influence the model. All these issues could be exacerbated by human error, at the collection phase, or lack of validation of the data.

The models were implemented using the scikit-learn 1.1.2 Python package. The average execution time for building and evaluating the model was approximately between 20 and 40 min for each of the algorithms and combination of the preprocessing techniques, on a computer with an Intel(R) Core(TM) i7-10510U CPU@1.80 GHz–2.30 GHz processor and 16.0 GB RAM.

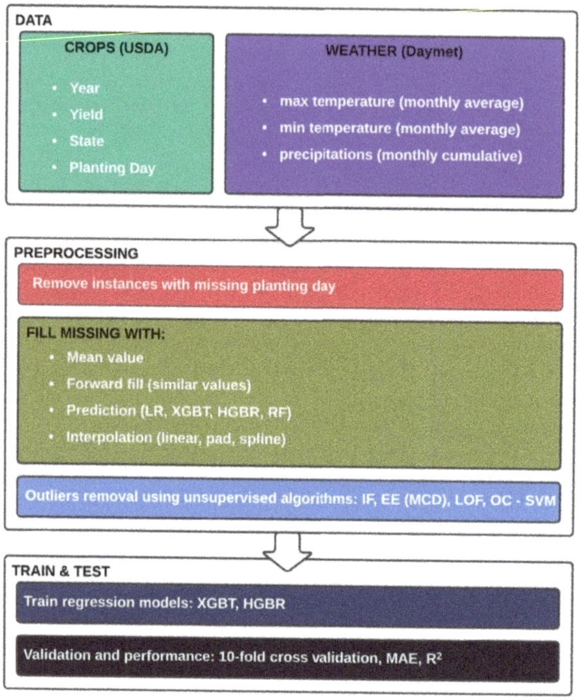


**Figure 2.** Conceptual framework of the experimental study.

#### 3.2.1. Handling Missing Values for the Planting Day

For the purpose of handling the approximately 80% of missing planting day data (14.3% of the initial crop data), we experimented with several approaches for random missing data, as described below. Considering very few studies handle large data missing rates, and the literature reveals that results depend on the dataset characteristics, pattern of missing data and data size, we used a variety of methods selected based on our literature review (Section 2). We chose five different approaches, and up to three different methods for each (where possible) that have been used with similar datasets for univariate imputation [13]. In Figures 3 and 4 we visualise the value distribution graph for the planting day feature after using each method.

The first method involves the removal of incomplete instances from the dataset. While this is one of the most common approaches with incomplete data, it results in our case with the loss of 80% of our dataset, with very few remaining instances to train the models. Since the sowing day is central to our experiments in predicting the crop yield, we also considered other approaches.

The second approach is to fill the null values with adjacent ones. For this method, the forward fill ($ffill$) Pandas DataFrame algorithm was used. Given that the data was sorted by state, the missing values were completed with similar values of planting day for the same state, by duplicating the last existing value for that state. This method is also called hot-deck imputation. Although the values would closely correspond to real planting days for that state, given its specific climate context, the risk is that we might introduce inconsistencies corresponding with the meteorological data and yearly variations occurring that interfere with the planting day.

The third approach is to complete with mean values. For this method, we complete all missing values with the overall mean value of the planting day from the dataset. This method is commonly applied as it has the advantage of not introducing statistical changes. However, a great disadvantage is that it cannot simulate seasonality or trends.

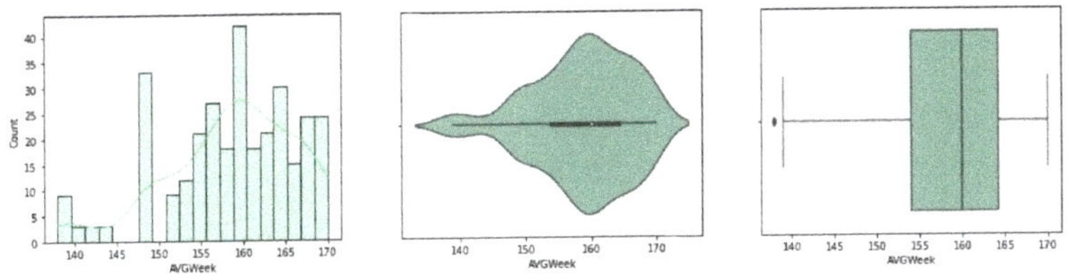

(**a**) Remove instances with missing planting day.

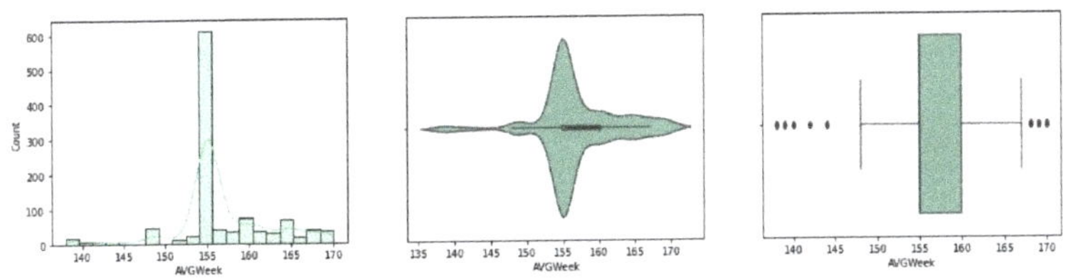

(**b**) Similar fill of values.

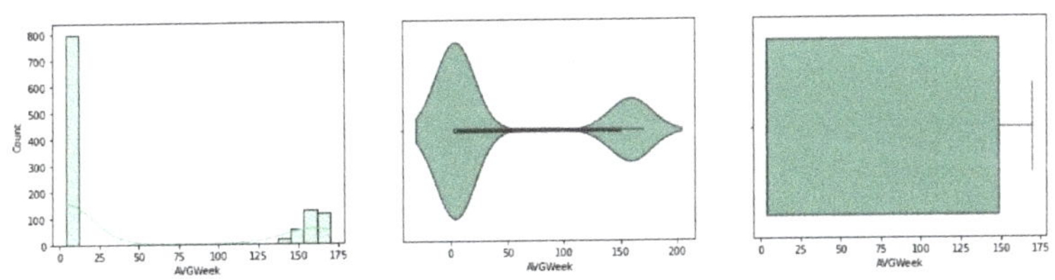

(**c**) Fill in with mean values.

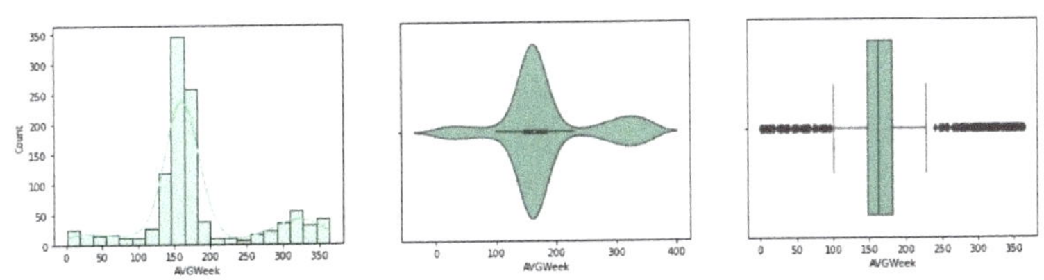

(**d**) Use predicted values generated with HGBR.

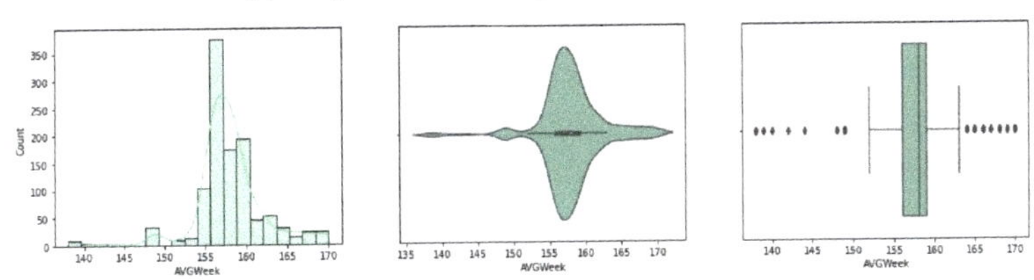

(**e**) Use predicted values generated with LR.

**Figure 3.** Planting day values after preprocessing.

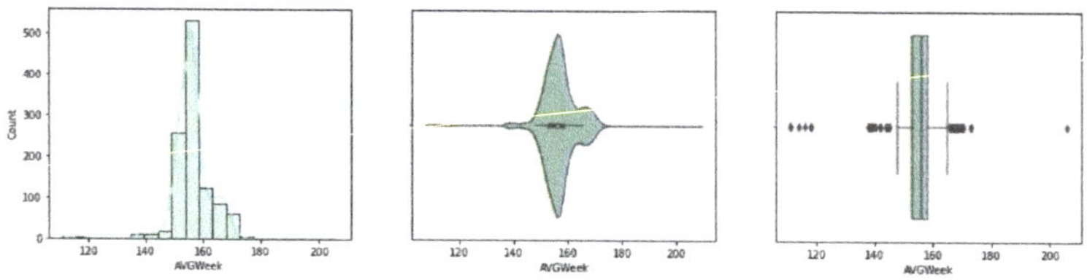


(**a**) Use predicted values generated with RF.

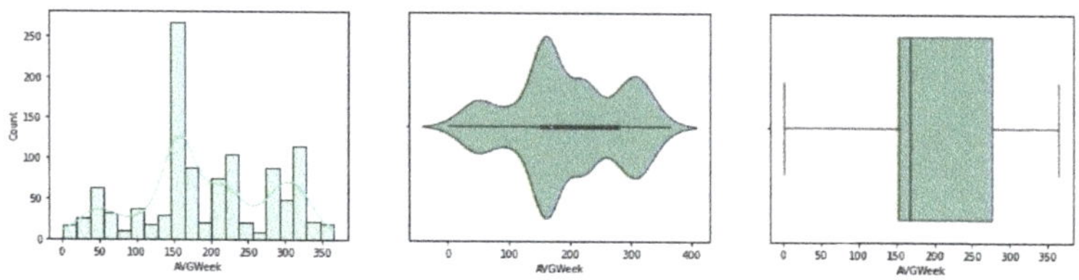


(**b**) Use predicted values generated with XGBT.

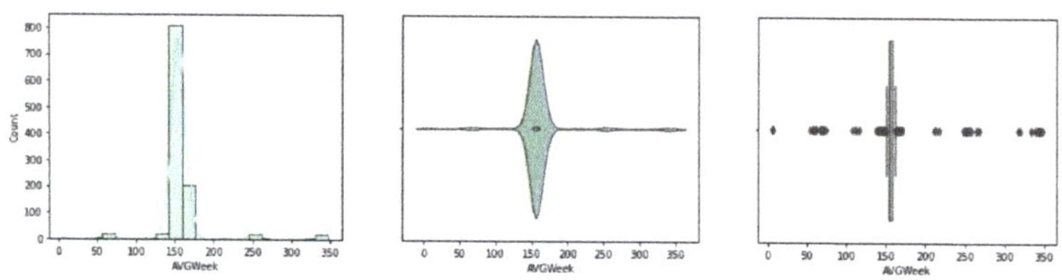


(**c**) Complete by linear interpolation.

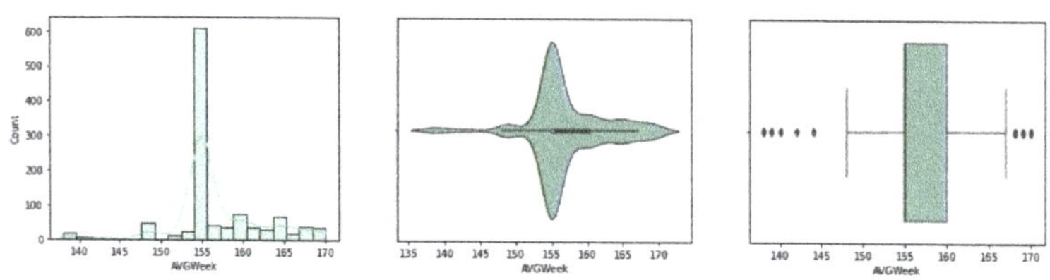


(**d**) Complete by similar values interpolation.

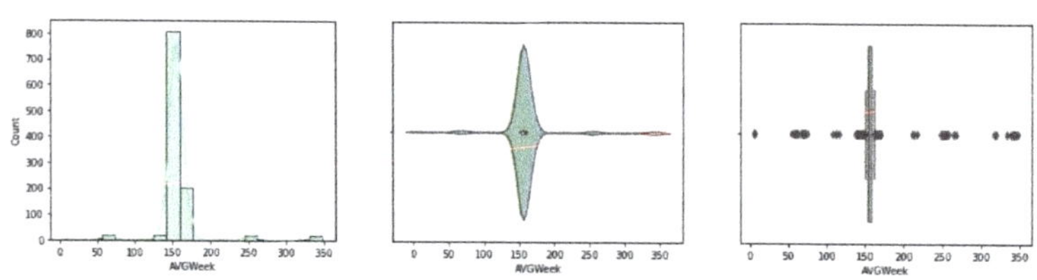


(**e**) Complete by spline interpolation.

**Figure 4.** Planting day after preprocessing: histogram, violin plot and box plot.

For the fourth approach we use prediction to fill in the missing data. Several algorithms have been used to generate univariate prediction models for missing values, informed by the literature review, to perform effectively on similar data and missing data rates [13], including (1) linear regression (LR), (2) histogram gradient boosting regressor (HGBR), (3) extreme gradient boosting tree regressor (XGBT), and (4) random forest (RF). In our case, this approach is expected to be better than using the mean values, provided that the models can predict based on all other features, with more accuracy, based on a trend expected to influence the data.

For this purpose, we have split the dataset in two: dataset $A$ containing the instances missing the value for the planting day, and dataset $B$ containing the complete rows. Next, we created a prediction model using dataset $B$ for training, based on the attributes year, state ANSI, crop type and yield, with target planting day. In the next step, this model was used on dataset $A$ to predict all the missing values for the planting day. Finally, the two datasets were joined again to be used further, together with meteorological data, to predict the yield.

The fifth method consists in the use of an interpolation method. In this approach, the null values of the planting day have been filled using interpolation. This is a statistical method for estimating unknown values based on several known points. The estimation refers to points in between the known values. Here, we used linear interpolation, which estimates a linear polynomial for curve fitting. The pad method was also used, which fills the dataset in with existing values (similar to a hot-deck imputation method). A third interpolation method is spline, which involves fitting the data to several low-degree polynomials. The implementations used in this study are part of the Python Sklearn interpolate() method, with each of the three options.

#### 3.2.2. Handling Outliers

The purpose of outlier detection (OD) is to identify and separate outliers in a sample (anomalies from usual data) from normal data (also called inliers). This is usually an unsupervised problem, as there is not enough knowledge about the data patterns. The general scope of OD algorithms is to allow for the identification of outliers, as their removal from the dataset can be crucial to improving model performance [26].

The crop data involved in the study contained self-reported information filled in by the farmers in a national statistics information platform. A first analysis of the data showed a small percentage (5–10%) of inconsistent or incomplete data (for example, the percentage of planting per week was not filled in for all weeks). This is normal for data collected in an uncontrolled manner. Furthermore, the missing data on planting day were completed using various methods, generating values for 80% of the instances. This is likely to have either introduced or exacerbated anomalies in the dataset.

Given these reasons, we analysed the impact of removing outliers from our data to create the prediction models. In this sense, we applied and compared the unsupervised algorithms for anomaly detection described below, chosen based on the robustness and computation requirements for the regression tasks, as found in the literature.

Isolation forest (IF) uses isolation trees to separate each instance from the rest, and compute the anomaly score from the expected path length $E(h(x))$ of each instance, with $h(x)$ as the average estimation path length and $c(n)$ defined based on $H(i)$, the harmonic number.

$$c(n) = 2H(n-1) - 2(n-1)/n \tag{2}$$

$$s(x,n) = 2^{-E(h(x))/c(n)} \tag{3}$$

This method is very flexible, as it has been proven to work well even in high-dimensional problems (even for a large number of irrelevant attributes), or in the case where the training set does not contain anomalies [29]. It can be configured by the number of trees and contamination rate (expected rate of outliers in the dataset).

Minimum covariance determinant (MCD) uses a statistical covariance distance to compute a tolerance ellipse, defined as the set of $p$-dimensional points $x$ whose Mahalanobis distance

$$MD(x) = d(x, \bar{x}, Cov(X)) = \sqrt{(x-\bar{x})' Cov(X)^{-1} (x-\bar{x})} \tag{4}$$

describes the distance from the centre of the data cloud to $x$ [30]. The elliptic envelope (EE) implementation in Sklearn was used in our case, as described by [31], and requires setting the contamination rate parameter.

The Local outlier factor (LOF) approach defines LOF of an instance $p$ as

$$LOF_{MinPts}(p) = \frac{\sum_{o \in N_{MinPts}(p)} \frac{lrd_{MinPts}(o)}{lrd_{MinPts}(p)}}{N_{MinPts}(p)} \tag{5}$$

the degree to which we call $p$ an outlier, calculated as the average of the ratio of the local reachability density of $p$ (that is, the average reachability distance based on the MinPts-nearest neighbours of $p$) and those of $p$'s MinPts-nearest neighbours. The reachability distance of object $p$ with respect to object $o$ is calculated as the distance between an object and the k-neighbourhood of $p$:

$$reachdist_k(p,o) = max\{kdistance(o), d(p,o)\} \tag{6}$$

OneClass-SVM (OC-SVM) is a kernel-based algorithm focused on estimating the density function of the input data (K) in order to define a binary function that decides if a point is an outlier or inlier based on an anomaly detection sensitivity [32]. In short, this involves solving a dual optimisation problem, defined formally as:

$$\min_{\alpha \in R^n} \{\frac{1}{2}\alpha^{\gamma} K\alpha\} s.t. \{\alpha^{\gamma} 1 = 1, 0 \leq \alpha \leq \frac{1}{\nu N}\} \tag{7}$$

where $K$ is a Gaussian kernel function, $\gamma$ is the kernel scale, and $\nu \in (0,1]$ measures the anomaly detection sensitivity [26]. The $\nu$ hyperparameter needs to be optimised, considering a low value involves a small chance for a point to be an anomaly.

Figures 5 and 6 show the model variation for each outlier removal method with contamination rates from $c = 0.05$ to $c = 0.5$, when using the prediction with RF as the imputation method, and the XBGT model, HGBR, for evaluation. The metric used for evaluation is $R^2$. The number of instances remaining in the dataset for each contamination rate applied, further used in model training, is presented in Table 2. The research problem in this case is to identify the smallest contamination rate to avoid model overfitting while obtaining the best model performance.

Looking at Figure 5 for the XGBT model, we notice that IF increases the performance constantly as the contamination rate increases, suggesting an overfitting trend, and a specialisation of the algorithms to select outliers to specialise the model. EE produces a similar variation, with the exception of a local maximum for $c = 0.1$, suggesting that this is a good choice of the anomaly rate. On the other hand, LOF presents a local maximum for $c = 0.2$, and then performance decreases for higher contamination rates, meaning higher contamination rates will lead to a loss of relevant information for the model. OC-SVM is similar with LOF, with the exception that the local maximum is at $c = 0.3$. Figure 6 presents very similar patterns for the HGBR model to those expressed in Figure 5.

For each of the algorithms presented above, we used the Python Sklearn implementations: IF, LOF, EE (for MCD) and OC-SVM. Considering the experiments with different contamination rates and their impact on the model, the proposed candidates for the best results were 0.1, 0.2 and 0.3. Considering the literature recommendations for the contamination rate to avoid model overfitting and the limited data available in our case, we decided on the value $c = 0.1$ for our future experiments. For larger datasets of this type, a better choice could be $c = 0.2$, provided it was collected similarly in an uncontrolled environment without specific validation.

**Table 2.** Number of instances remaining in the dataset corresponding to each contamination rate applied.

| Contamination | 0.05 | 0.1 | 0.2 | 0.3 | 0.4 | 0.5 |
|---|---|---|---|---|---|---|
| $n$ | 934 | 885 | 787 | 689 | 590 | 492 |

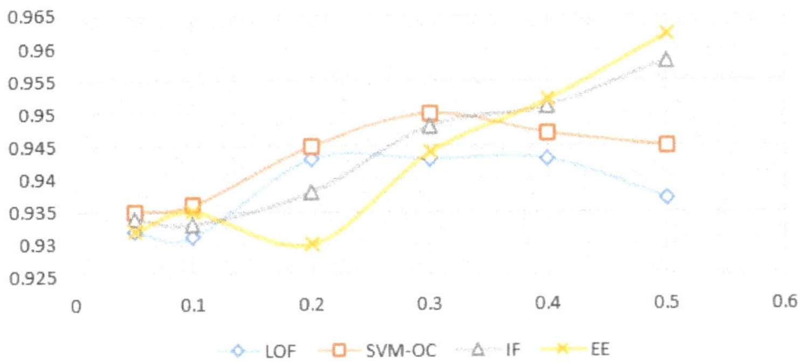


**Figure 5.** Variation for imputation prediction with RF, for each contamination rate used ($X$ axis) and evaluation model XGBT ($R^2$ results on the $Y$ axis).

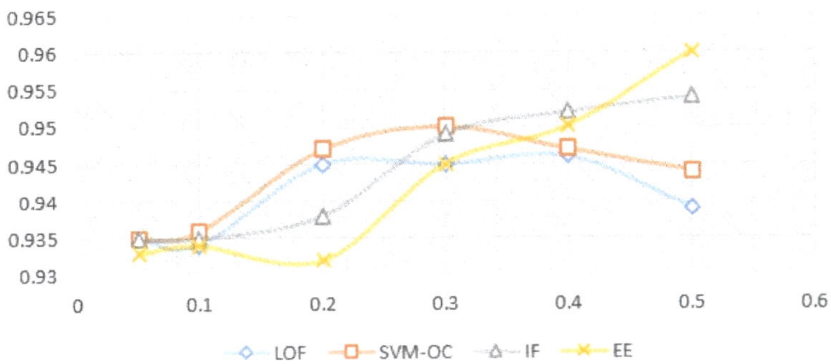


**Figure 6.** Variation for imputation prediction with RF, for each contamination rate used ($X$ axis) and evaluation model HGBR ($R^2$ results on the $Y$ axis).

### 3.3. *Training and Testing*

After data preprocessing, involving each of the 10 different approaches for handling missing values for the planting day, the crop data were aggregated with the meteorological data, resulting in 41 features. The dataset was used to train several regression models using a selection of algorithms suitable for this purpose, as exhibited by the state-of-the-art methods and our previous experiments on similar data [33]. The target was chosen to be the yield value field, while all the other 40 features were used as the input.

#### 3.3.1. Histogram Gradient Boosting Regressor

The HGBR is based on ensemble decision trees. The algorithm adds new corrective models in a greedy stepwise manner to improve performance by reducing the square error loss function until it is acceptable [34]. The histogram is an efficient data structure used by the tree-building algorithm to accelerate the process.

#### 3.3.2. Extreme Gradient Boosting Regressor

The XGBT is also a tree-based algorithm. By using a scalable end-to-end gradient boosting tree system, it optimises resource use, introducing cache access patterns, data compression, and block sharding [35].

#### 3.3.3. Hyperparameter Fine-Tuning

The hyperparameters were fine-tuned by experimenting with ranges of significant values, while also balancing the computation time. The best results for the XBGT were obtained using 700 estimators, a maximum depth of 10 and a learning rate of 0.01. For the HGBR we selected a learning rate of 0.002, the maximum number of iterations to be 5000 and the Poisson loss function.

### 3.4. Validation Metrics

Several metrics have been used to validate and compare the models, based on literature recommendations: the coefficient of determination $R^2$ (considered among the most reliable metrics for regression), the $MAE$, and the $MAE\%$ defined below [36].

The coefficient of determination $R^2$ measures the variation in the $y$ observed values, where $\bar{y}$ is the mean, and is calculated using the equation below [37,38]:

$$R^2 = 1 - \frac{\sum_{i=1}^{n}(y_i - \hat{y}_i)^2}{\sum_{i=1}^{n}(y_i - \bar{y})^2} \tag{8}$$

The $MAE$ represents an average of the absolute prediction error with $y_i$ as the observed value and $\hat{y}_i$ as the predicted value, as computed in Equation [38]:

$$MAE = \frac{1}{n}\sum_{i=1}^{n} abs(y_i - \hat{y}_i) \tag{9}$$

Another metric used is the $MAE\%$ or median absolute percentage error ($MdAPE$) [36], which measures $MAE$ as a percentile from the mean of the $y$ values, as in Equation:

$$MAE\% = \frac{MAE}{\frac{1}{n}\sum_{i=1}^{n} y_i} \times 100 \tag{10}$$

We used repeated k-fold cross validation with $k = 10$, computing the mean and standard deviation for five repeats, for each of the metrics $R^2$ and $MAE$.

## 4. Results

Table 3 shows the comparison between several metrics obtained by the selected algorithms, when using each of the five approaches (presented in the Section 3) in dealing with missing data regarding the planting date. In our case, we are dealing with 984 instances with 41 attributes, of which 80% of the instances are only missing the planting date attribute, and was completed using imputation methods. In this table, we also included the evaluation of the model for the case when the instances with missing data were removed ($n = 312$). The mean yield value is 1093.053, meaning the $MAE$ of 87.628 represents a percentile error of $MAE\%$ = 8.01%, and all $MAE$ values under 100 have a corresponding $MAE\%$ under 10%.

We notice that the $R^2$ values increase when imputation is used as opposed to removing incomplete data instances: from 0.723 for XBGT and 0.740 for HGBR to values in the range of 0.918–0.929 for the different imputation utilised methods. Accordingly, the $MAE$ was reduced from 111.645 for XGBT (remove missing) to 81.483–91.202, meaning a reduction in $MAE\%$ from 10.2% to 7.44% in the best case. Therefore, the first important result is that the imputation step greatly improves our model, regardless of the approach used. However, it can still be further fine-tuned and improved.

The next step was to handle outliers in our data. Tables 4–7 show the results obtained after using each of the four outlier removal methods. The notations used in these tables are as explained in Table 3.

**Table 3.** Comparative results of using different preprocessing imputation methods for handling missing values, including all data in training (without removing outliers).

| Method | XGBT $R^2$ | XGBT $MAE$ | HGBR $R^2$ | HGBR $MAE$ |
|---|---|---|---|---|
| Remove missing | 0.723 (0.127) | 111.645 (20.084) | 0.740 (0.142) | 107.288 (21.944) |
| Similar fill | 0.918 (0.024) | 90.300 (10.402) | 0.922 (0.023) | 87.315 (10.608) |
| Mean values | 0.915 (0.027) | 91.202 (9.206) | 0.919 (0.027) | 87.669 (9.091) |
| Predict (LR) | 0.920 (0.025) | 88.667 (10.325) | 0.922 (0.025) | 86.593 (10.464) |
| Predict (HGBR) | 0.925 (0.024) | 85.395 (9.903) | 0.927 (0.023) | 84.427 (10.156) |
| Predict (XGBT) | 0.926 (0.022) | 84.052 (8.762) | 0.928 (0.022) | 83.031 (9.039) |
| Predict (RF) | 0.929 (0.023) | 82.050 (9.385) | 0.929 (0.022) | 81.483 (9.387) |
| Interpolation (L) | 0.918 (0.024) | 90.685 (10.332) | 0.922 (0.022) | 87.687 (10.339) |
| Interpolation (P) | 0.918 (0.024) | 90.300 (10.402) | 0.922 (0.023) | 87.315 (10.608) |
| Interpolation (S) | 0.918 (0.024) | 90.685 (10.332) | 0.922 (0.022) | 87.687 (10.339) |

The numbers in the table represent the mean values, with the standard deviation (SD) value in parenthesis, calculated from five repetitions of the 10-fold cross validation. For example, the $R^2$ when we remove the instances containing missing values is 0.687 (0.119), that is: the mean value is 0.687 with $SD = 0.119$. Method notations: LR—linear regression; RF—random forest; L—linear; P—pad; S—spline.

**Table 4.** Comparative results of using different preprocessing methods for missing values, after removing outliers with Isolation Forest.

| Method | XGBT $R^2$ | XGBT $MAE$ | HGBR $R^2$ | HGBR $MAE$ |
|---|---|---|---|---|
| Remove missing | 0.743 (0.167) | 106.242 (19.641) | 0.752 (0.163) | 102.309 (17.622) |
| Similar fill | 0.928 (0.019) | 88.156 (10.262) | 0.927 (0.024) | 86.301 (10.678) |
| Mean values | 0.928 (0.022) | 85.868 (10.136) | 0.930 (0.022) | 83.769 (10.009) |
| Predict (LR) | 0.930 (0.020) | 85.632 (10.274) | 0.930 (0.021) | 85.126 (9.833) |
| Predict (HGBR) | 0.933 (0.021) | 82.086 (7.851) | 0.934 (0.020) | 81.156 (7.867) |
| Predict (XGBT) | 0.937 (0.017) | 81.038 (9.599 | 0.936 (0.018) | 81.195 (9.896) |
| Predict (RF) | 0.937 (0.018) | 80.106 (9.159) | 0.934 (0.019) | 81.414 (8.320) |
| Interpolation (L) | 0.927 (0.022) | 88.607 (10.667) | 0.930 (0.021) | 86.025 (9.692) |
| Interpolation (P) | 0.928 (0.020) | 86.998 (9.626) | 0.929 (0.020) | 85.743 (9.561) |
| Interpolation (S) | 0.932 (0.042) | 80.357 (13.635) | 0.932 (0.041) | 80.123 (13.238) |

**Table 5.** Comparative results of using different preprocessing methods for missing values, after removing outliers with local outlier factor.

| Method | XGBT $R^2$ | XGBT $MAE$ | HGBR $R^2$ | HGBR $MAE$ |
|---|---|---|---|---|
| Remove missing | 0.727 (0.130) | 108.730 (17.376) | 0.753 (0.118) | 103.766 (16.987) |
| Similar fill | 0.925 (0.019) | 88.245 (9.865) | 0.928 (0.017) | 85.205 (9.155) |
| Mean values | 0.927 (0.022) | 87.068 (10.362) | 0.929 (0.022) | 84.388 (10.372) |
| Predict (LR) | 0.926 (0.022) | 86.516 (10.893) | 0.928 (0.023) | 84.766 (11.757) |
| Predict (HGBR) | 0.930 (0.024) | 84.503 (10.754) | 0.931 (0.023) | 84.027 (10.103) |
| Predict (XGBT) | 0.931 (0.032) | 81.576 (10.299) | 0.934 (0.030) | 79.629 (10.327) |
| Predict (RF) | 0.934 (0.022) | 78.954 (10.882) | 0.936 (0.021) | 78.223 (11.116) |
| Interpolation (L) | 0.921 (0.018) | 91.107 (9.300) | 0.925 (0.018 | 87.509 (8.895) |
| Interpolation (P) | 0.925 (0.019) | 88.245 (9.865) | 0.928 (0.017) | 85.205 (9.155) |
| Interpolation (S) | 0.921 (0.018) | 91.107 (9.300) | 0.925 (0.018) | 87.509 (8.895) |

**Table 6.** Comparative results of using different preprocessing methods for missing values, after removing outliers with MCD.

| Method | XGBT | | HGBR | |
|---|---|---|---|---|
| | $R^2$ | $MAE$ | $R^2$ | $MAE$ |
| Remove missing | 0.739 (0.111) | 109.408 (20.823) | 0.749 (0.103) | 106.983 (20.386) |
| Similar fill | 0.924 (0.023) | 89.103 (9.608) | 0.926 (0.021) | 86.565 (9.551) |
| Mean values | 0.925 (0.020) | 90.240 (9.794) | 0.929 (0.018) | 86.750 (9.041) |
| Predict (LR) | 0.927 (0.023) | 87.129 (11.312) | 0.927 (0.024) | 85.118 (11.361) |
| Predict (HGBR) | 0.929 (0.025) | 85.901 (11.576) | 0.930 (0.025) | 84.633 (11.123) |
| Predict (XGBT) | 0.930 (0.024) | 83.389 (11.251) | 0.931 (0.023) | 83.619 (11.172) |
| Predict (RF) | 0.935 (0.027) | 78.590 (11.139) | 0.935 (0.027) | 78.853 (11.647) |
| Interpolation (L) | 0.927 (0.016) | 89.823 (8.578) | 0.930 (0.016) | 85.956 (8.972) |
| Interpolation (P) | 0.922 (0.026) | 90.298 (10.035) | 0.925 (0.025) | 87.253 (10.146) |
| Interpolation (S) | 0.924 (0.021) | 90.676 (10.070) | 0.929 (0.020) | 86.279 (10.069) |

**Table 7.** Comparative results of using different preprocessing methods for missing values, after removing outliers with OC-SVM.

| Method | XGBT | | HGBR | |
|---|---|---|---|---|
| | $R^2$ | $MAE$ | $R^2$ | $MAE$ |
| Remove missing | 0.750 (0.100) | 105.738 (19.072) | 0.766 (0.103) | 101.952 (20.124) |
| Similar fill | 0.928 (0.019) | 86.783 (9.188) | 0.931 (0.018) | 83.636 (9.205) |
| Mean values | 0.929 (0.020) | 86.062 (9.985) | 0.932 (0.019) | 83.714 (9.608) |
| Predict (LR) | 0.928 (0.019) | 86.347 (9.696) | 0.929 (0.019) | 84.630 (9.602) |
| Predict (HGBR) | 0.934 (0.022) | 82.611 (10.374) | 0.934 (0.021) | 82.107 (9.662) |
| Predict (XGBT) | 0.935 (0.020) | 81.085 (10.845) | 0.936 (0.019) | 80.581 (9.695) |
| Predict (RF) | 0.937 (0.017) | 77.262 (8.176) | 0.938 (0.017) | 77.689 (7.980) |
| Interpolation (L) | 0.925 (0.021) | 88.573 (8.675) | 0.927 (0.020) | 85.441 (8.142) |
| Interpolation (P) | 0.928 (0.019) | 86.783 (9.188) | 0.931 (0.018) | 83.636 (9.205) |
| Interpolation (S) | 0.925 (0.021) | 88.573 (8.675) | 0.927 (0.020) | 85.441 (8.142) |

We notice that the results presented in these tables show that there is improvement for all the imputation methods and the outlier removal technique applied, with the best value for HBGR when using RF for the imputation and OC-SVM for the removal of outliers: $R^2 = 0.938$, $MAE = 77.689$, and $MAE\%$ = £7.06%. To assess the relevance of the improvement, we applied the statistical $t$-test between the models based on all data and each outlier model. The obtained $p$ values for these metrics show they are statistically significant in most cases, with values of $p < 0.05$ in half the cases (as detailed in Table 8).

Figures 7 and 8 present all these results for the combination of outlier method or no outlier method removal used (meaning all data is involved in constructing the model) and the two evaluation algorithms used thus far (XGBT and HGBR), for the metrics $R^2$ and $MAE$, respectively, in the form of box plots. From these we can see that based on the median value (in orange) and overall performance (minimum and maximum values, as well as the interquartile range—IQR), IF is the outlier removal method with the highest improvement on the models overall, followed by OC-SVM, for both the $R^2$ and $MAE$ metrics. The circles in the graph represent outlier values (at a distance greater than $Q1 - 1.5 \times IQR$ or $Q3 + 1.5 \times IQR$), providing the best $MAE$ results for LOF and OC-SVM, with the overall best performance being OC-SVM for both $R^2$ and $MAE$, while these prove to be the best approaches numerically, we are inclined to interpret them as outliers resulting form the statistical 10-fold cross-validation data split performance of five repetitions.

**Table 8.** $p$ values for each outlier removal method versus none.

| | | IF | LOF | MCD | OC-SVM |
|---|---|---|---|---|---|
| XGBT | $R^2$ | $p = 3.78$ | $p < 0.01$ | $p = 2.55$ | $p = 1.36$ |
| | $MAE$ | $p < 0.01$ | $p < 0.01$ | $p < 0.05$ | $p = 2.19$ |
| HGBR | $R^2$ | $p = 2.96$ | $p = 5.23$ | $p < 0.01$ | $p = 9.88$ |
| | $MAE$ | $p < 0.01$ | $p < 0.01$ | $p < 0.03$ | $p = 5.14$ |

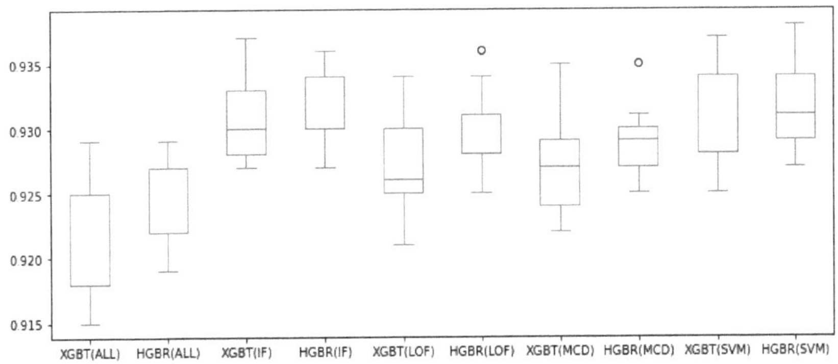


**Figure 7.** $R^2$ box plot values obtained with preprocessing techniques. The circles represent outliers.

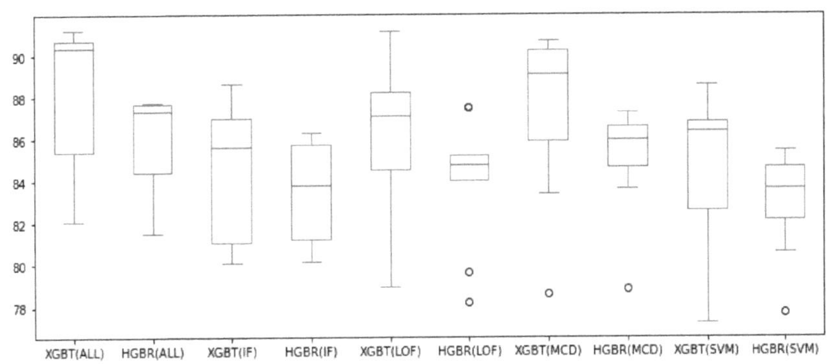


**Figure 8.** $MAE$ box plot values obtained with preprocessing techniques. The circles represent outliers.

## 5. Discussion

In terms of answering the research question regarding using imputation or not when 80% of the information for one feature is missing (considering that we have a total of 41 features as presented in Figure A1 from Appendix A), the preference would be towards the first option. Regardless of the method used for imputation, the model proved to be more accurate in all cases. On the other hand, given that we would lose 80% of the data, the risk is also to use other particularities in building the model.

To emphasise this, in Figure 9 we analysed the yield value histogram when removing instances with missing planting day, compared to using all initial instances (which contain a second peak for the histogram distribution, suggesting perhaps a separate class cluster among the initial data, which seems to be representative, and not just outliers). From this figure we notice the need for imputation to preserve relevant data, otherwise some characteristics of the model are lost. When missing data instances are removed, the values between 0 and 500 for the yield are no longer present. However, they represent relevant data for some types of crops, even if they do not represent the majority of crop types, thus losing a component. Of course, one can argue here that an extra component could be approached by building separate models. For our case, we continue to consider them as a whole, part of the same model.

To better visualise this, we rendered in Figure 10 a plot of the actual vs. predicted values, for the best result obtained, involving HGBR as the regression model, OC-SVM the unsupervised outlier removal method, and RF as the prediction imputation method. On the left, we have the plot obtained for the prediction model based on the data from which we removed instances with missing values. On the right, we have the model built using imputation, where we notice a linear trend involving two main clusters, one between 0 and 500 and one between 500 and 2500 for the yield value, in line with the histogram for the yield for the initial data. On the other hand, the left plot shows only one group, with the 0–500 yield value range missing. This shows that by removing data, we lose relevant information for the model, and the preprocessing methods involved, using imputation and outlier removal, are able to create a much more robust and reliable prediction model.

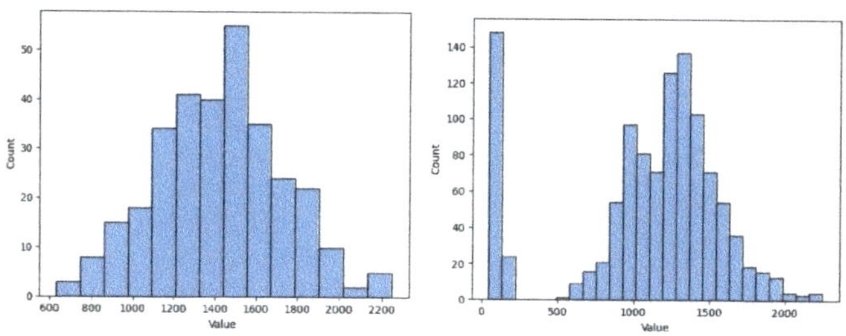


**Figure 9.** Histogram for yield values with missing data instances removed (**left**) and with all data (**right**).

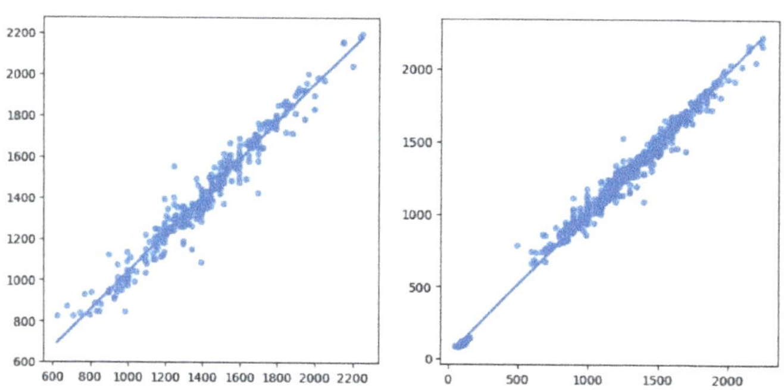

**Figure 10.** Actual vs. predicted yield for the models with missing data removed (**left**) and for the best result obtained by the HGBR model, with preprocessing OC-SVM and RF (**right**).

For the research question on which imputation method produces the best model, prediction is preferred to all others in all cases, with RF algorithms producing the highest values for $R^2$. The same trends in model improvement are present for both XGBT and HGBR, proving that the change in performance is mainly due to the preprocessing methods used, for both imputation and outliers removal.

For the latter, concerning data anomalies and unsupervised outlier removal, further experiments would be required to establish if it can be more accurately fine-tuned and if higher contamination rates, such as $c = 0.2$, could be feasible to use in a larger dataset or if it would lead to model overfitting. Looking back at the results in Figures 5 and 6, showing the variation of the model prediction for the coefficient of determination metric, the best results are obtained by OC-SVM when $c = 0.3$ ($R^2 = 0.95$ for both XBGT and HGBR), and LOF when $c = 0.2$ ($R^2 = 0.943$ for XBGT and $R^2 = 0.945$ for HGBR). For EE there is a local peak at $c = 0.1$, and a maximum value at $c = 0.5$, while IF improves as $c$ is increased (with a maximum at $c = 0.5$). More information on the initial data and the collection context could help inform the actual anomaly percentage present in the data, and what approach would indeed improve the model.

Another aspect to discuss is in relation to the regression algorithms XGBT and HGBR, which seem to be quite robust, showing little impact from unsupervised outlier removal, as opposed to the other regression algorithms which are more susceptible to data changes. However, a main finding of our study is that it is feasible and we can reliably use these algorithms for crop yield prediction even with relatively small datasets. However, we must provide a minimum amount of data to ensure performance, thus demonstrating the importance of using imputation. The most important contribution we bring is related to the problem of missing data, which can be handled effectively even if it affects 80% of the instances, resulting in an increased performance from 0.723 to 0.938 (and even up to 0.95 if we use OD with $c = 0.3$). Our findings suggest that the best method for imputation is prediction using RF. Given that historical crop data are reduced and it would take many years to collect a designated dataset (which we have started as a work in progress), we are able to address the climate change effects in agriculture now, by modelling the correlation between sowing dates and weather forecast to identify the best planting window that maximises yield production.

## 6. Conclusions

The presented paper completes the research in the field of intelligent agro-meteorological decisions to address the challenges of ensuring the sustainable provision of food crops in the context of climate change. Although there are multiple studies in the field, a new, unique approach that addresses missing data is needed.

The primary objective of our research was to improve the efficiency of sunflower cultivation by developing a yield prediction model that relies on the selection of an optimal planting day, guided by a region-specific weather forecast. In order to construct a regression model capable of accurately predicting crop yield, we aggregated several datasets encompassing information pertaining to crops, planting dates, crop varieties, geographical locations, and historical yield records. Additionally, meteorological parameters such as precipitation and temperature were incorporated into the model as predictors.

Moreover, in our experiments, we performed a comparative study of nine imputation methods, which were evaluated on two regression algorithms. We obtained an increase in the model performance for both regression algorithms. The best results were obtained using the prediction method for imputation, especially the RF. The second set of experiments involved unsupervised outlier removal algorithms, in which four methods were compared with various contamination rates. Overall, results were improved in most cases with statistical significance. The best $R^2 = 0.938$ and $MAE = 77.689$ were obtained using the Oc-SVM outlier removal and RF imputation algorithms, for the model built with HGBR. An important finding is that a very significant improvement was mainly achieved through preprocessing methods, compared to the initial results without imputation or outlier removal ($R^2 = 0.723$).

We have been able to achieve our research objective and build an accurate model based on limited data, which could support agricultural decisions to mitigate the effects of climate change and maximise production. Future research directions involve incorporating more variables as predictors, such as the use of fertilisers or pest control. There is a substantial need to collect crop datasets specific to this purpose from reliable sources to help train models for specific geographical locations and crops. As a further exploration of the impact of the planting day and weather conditions on the crop yield, we aim to also consider employing forecasting methodologies and assessing the reliability of using the same or similar preprocessing methods to improve the model performance.

**Author Contributions:** All authors have contributed equally to this research. Conceptualization, A.D.C., A.M.C. and H.B.M.; Data curation, A.D.C.; Methodology, A.D.C., A.M.C. and H.B.M.; Software, A.D.C.; Validation, A.D.C., A.M.C. and H.B.M.; Writing—original draft, A.D.C.; Writing—review & editing, A.M.C. and H.B.M. All authors have read and agreed to the published version of the manuscript.

**Funding:** The publication of this article was supported by the 2022 Development Fund of the UBB.

**Institutional Review Board Statement:** Not applicable.

**Informed Consent Statement:** Not applicable.

**Data Availability Statement:** Publicly available datasets were analysed in this study. This data can be found here: USDA for crop data https://quickstats.nass.usda.gov/ (accessed on 10 October 2022) [27] and DayMet for meteo data https://daymet.ornl.gov/ (accessed on 16 January 2023) [28].

**Conflicts of Interest:** The authors declare no conflict of interest.

## Abbreviations

The following abbreviations are used in this manuscript:

| | |
|---|---|
| CNN | Convolutional neural networks |
| EE | Elliptic envelope |
| HGBR | Histogram gradient boosting regressor |
| IF | Isolation forest |
| LOF | Local outlier factor |
| LR | Linear regression |
| MAE | Mean absolute error |
| MAPE | Mean absolute percentage error |
| MCD | Minimum covariance determinant |
| ML | Machine learning |
| OC-SVM (OneClass SVM) | One-class support vector machines |
| OD | Outlier detection |
| RF | Random forest |
| XGBT | Extreme gradient boosting tree regressor |

## Appendix A

In Figure A1, we present the correlation matrix for all data, when using the prediction method of imputation, with the RF algorithm. We observe a high correlation represented by the right bottom square with lighter yellow areas. They are between the minimum and maximum average temperatures for every month of the year. This strong correlation (value from 0.63 to 0.97) is naturally expected. Other positive correlations, represented by light orange sections in the matrix, are between the state and spring to summer monthly temperatures (highest for months 5 to 8 with a value of 0.52), and between winter–spring cumulative precipitations (months 1–3) and spring and autumn average temperatures (months 1–3 and 9–12) with values up to 0.45. The yield value is also highly correlated with the year component (0.59) and the AVGWeek (planting day) is highly correlated with the crop type (0.58), suggesting changes in the production rates each year based on the sunflower hybrid type planted. There seems to be a negative correlation between the crop type and yield, and between AVGWeek and yield (−0.74), in line with the related literature for this geographical location and crop, that earlier planting dates may lead to higher production.

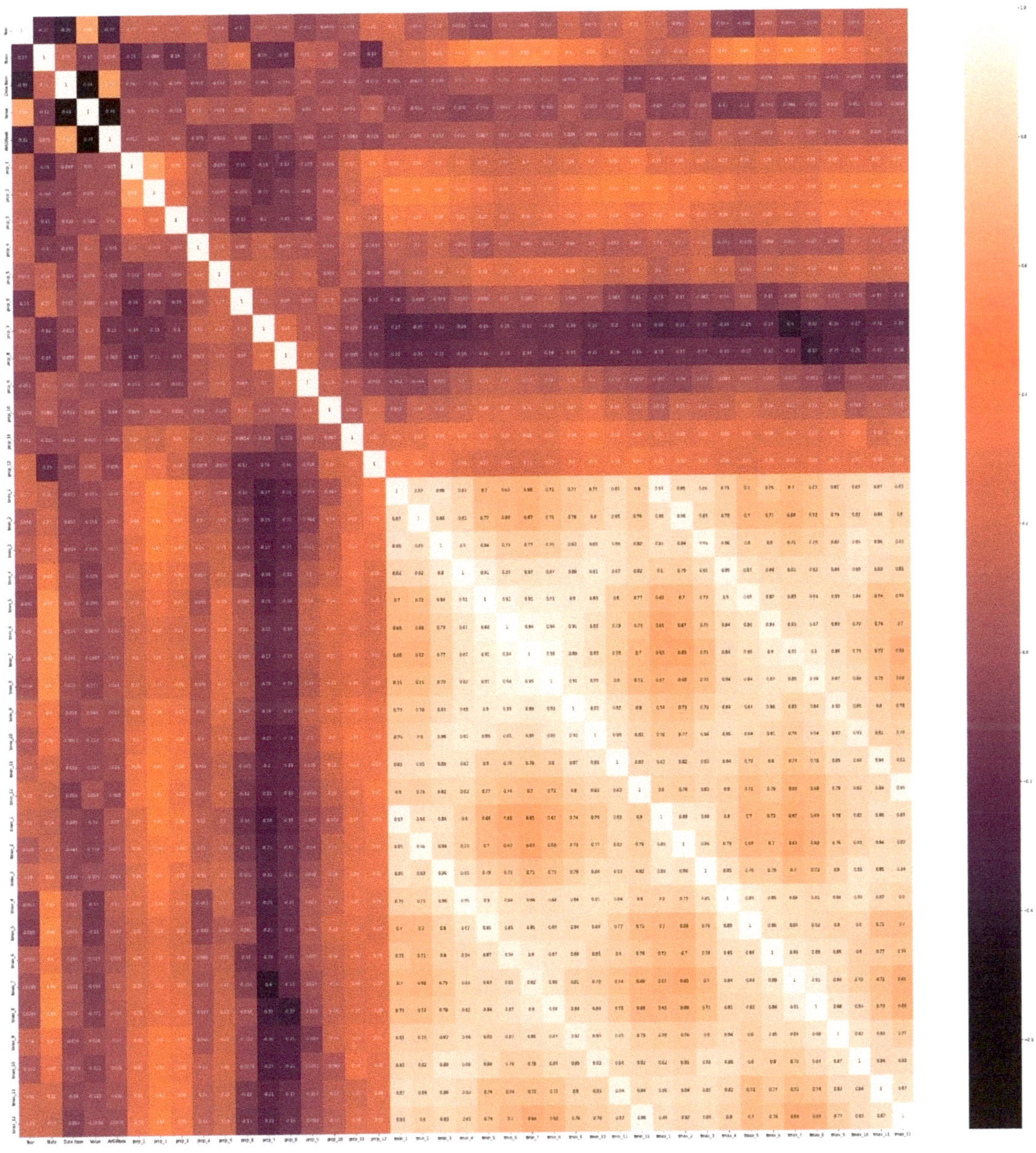

**Figure A1.** Correlation matrix for the 41 attributes, in order from top to bottom (and also from left to right): year, state ANSI, crop type, yield, planting day, then precipitations (cumulative) for each month from January to December, then minimum temperature (average) for each month from January to December, and then maximum temperature (average) for each month from January to December. Data imputation method: prediction with RF.As we can see in the image, we have different types of correlation: positive and medium correlation (0.45), strong positive correlation (0.91), but also negative and weak correlation (−0.042). Full size image source at https://www.cs.ubbcluj.ro/~alinacalin/research/corrmatr.png (accessed on 22 June 2023).

## References


1. Arora, N.K. Impact of climate change on agriculture production and its sustainable solutions. *Environ. Sustain.* **2019**, *2*, 95–96. [CrossRef]
2. Wangchen, T.; Dorji, T. Examining the Potential Impacts of Agro-Meteorology Initiatives for Climate Change Adaptation and Food Security in Bhutan. In *Climate Change Adaptations in Dryland Agriculture in Semi-Arid Areas*; Springer Nature: Singapore, 2022; pp. 19–32. [CrossRef]
3. Tui, S.H.K.; Sisito, G.; Moyo, E.N.; Dube, T.; Valdivia, R.O.; Madajewicz, M.; Descheemaeker, K.; Ruane, A.C. Developing Pathways for Sustainable Agricultural Development in Zimbabwe by 2030. In *Climate Change Adaptations in Dryland Agriculture in Semi-Arid Areas*; Springer Nature: Singapore, 2022; pp. 185–202. [CrossRef]
4. Rawal, D.S. Selection of Resilient Crop Species for Cultivation Under Projected Climate Change. In *Climate Change Adaptations in Dryland Agriculture in Semi-Arid Areas*; Springer Nature: Singapore, 2022; pp. 111–126. [CrossRef]
5. Mourtzinis, S.; Esker, P.D.; Specht, J.E.; Conley, S.P. Advancing agricultural research using machine learning algorithms. *Sci. Rep.* **2021**, *11*, 17879. [CrossRef]
6. Reed, H.K.; Karsten, H.D.; Curran, W.S.; Tooker, J.F.; Duiker, S.W. Planting green effects on corn and soybean production. *Agron. J.* **2019**, *111*, 2314–2325. [CrossRef]
7. Malhi, G.S.; Kaur, M.; Kaushik, P. Impact of climate change on agriculture and its mitigation strategies: A review. *Sustainability* **2021**, *13*, 1318. [CrossRef]
8. Patel, A.; Patel, M.; Patel, R.; Mote, B. Effect of different sowing date on phenology, growth and yield of rice—A review. *Plant Arch.* **2019**, *19*, 12–16.
9. Ma, B.; Zhao, H.; Zheng, Z.; Caldwell, C.; Mills, A.; Vanasse, A.; Earl, H.; Scott, P.; Smith, D. Optimizing seeding dates and rates for canola production in the humid eastern Canadian agroecosystems. *Agron. J.* **2016**, *108*, 1869–1879. [CrossRef]
10. Cerioli, T.; Gentimis, T.; Linscombe, S.D.; Famoso, A.N. Effect of rice planting date and optimal planting window for Southwest Louisiana. *Agron. J.* **2021**, *113*, 1248–1257. [CrossRef]
11. Partal, E. Sunflower yield and quality under the influence of sowing date, plant population and the hybrid. *Rom. Agric. Res.* **2022**, *39*, 463–470. [CrossRef]
12. Benos, L.; Tagarakis, A.C.; Dolias, G.; Berruto, R.; Kateris, D.; Bochtis, D. Machine learning in agriculture: A comprehensive updated review. *Sensors* **2021**, *21*, 3758. [CrossRef] [PubMed]
13. Lin, W.C.; Tsai, C.F. Missing value imputation: A review and analysis of the literature (2006–2017). *Artif. Intell. Rev.* **2020**, *53*, 1487–1509. [CrossRef]
14. Aparecido, L.E.d.O.; Moraes, J.R.d.S.C.d.; Rolim, G.d.S.; Martorano, L.G.; Meneses, K.C.d.; Valeriano, T.T.B. Neural networks in climate spatialization and their application in the agricultural zoning of climate risk for sunflower in different sowing dates. *Arch. Agron. Soil Sci.* **2019**, *65*, 1477–1492. [CrossRef]
15. Ansarifar, J.; Wang, L.; Archontoulis, S.V. An interaction regression model for crop yield prediction. *Sci. Rep.* **2021**, *11*, 17754. [CrossRef]
16. Cunha, R.L.; Silva, B.; Netto, M.A. A scalable machine learning system for pre-season agriculture yield forecast. In Proceedings of the 2018 IEEE 14th International Conference on e-Science (e-Science), Amsterdam, The Netherlands, 29 October–1 November 2018; pp. 423–430. [CrossRef]
17. Feng, P.; Wang, B.; Li Liu, D.; Waters, C.; Xiao, D.; Shi, L.; Yu, Q. Dynamic wheat yield forecasts are improved by a hybrid approach using a biophysical model and machine learning technique. *Agric. For. Meteorol.* **2020**, *285*, 107922. [CrossRef]
18. Gümüşçü, A.; Tenekeci, M.E.; Bilgili, A.V. Estimation of wheat planting date using machine learning algorithms based on available climate data. *Sustain. Comput. Inform. Syst.* **2020**, *28*, 100308. [CrossRef]
19. Shahhosseini, M.; Hu, G.; Huber, I.; Archontoulis, S.V. Coupling machine learning and crop modeling improves crop yield prediction in the US Corn Belt. *Sci. Rep.* **2021**, *11*, 1606. [CrossRef] [PubMed]
20. European Space Agency. Copernicus Sentinel Data, Processed by ESA. Available online: https://sentinels.copernicus.eu/web/sentinel/user-guides/sentinel-1-sar (accessed on 7 November 2022).
21. Shang, J.; Liu, J.; Poncos, V.; Geng, X.; Qian, B.; Chen, Q.; Dong, T.; Macdonald, D.; Martin, T.; Kovacs, J.; et al. Detection of crop seeding and harvest through analysis of time-series Sentinel-1 interferometric SAR data. *Remote Sens.* **2020**, *12*, 1551. [CrossRef]
22. Strike, K.; El Emam, K.; Madhavji, N. Software cost estimation with incomplete data. *IEEE Trans. Softw. Eng.* **2001**, *27*, 890–908. [CrossRef]
23. Emmanuel, T.; Maupong, T.; Mpoeleng, D.; Semong, T.; Mphago, B.; Tabona, O. A survey on missing data in machine learning. *J. Big Data* **2021**, *8*, 140. [CrossRef]
24. Langkamp, D.L.; Lehman, A.; Lemeshow, S. Techniques for handling missing data in secondary analyses of large surveys. *Acad. Pediatr.* **2010**, *10*, 205–210. [CrossRef] [PubMed]
25. Belhaouari, S.B. Unsupervised outlier detection in multidimensional data. *J. Big Data* **2021**, *8*, 80. [CrossRef]
26. Ángela, F.; Bella, J.; Dorronsoro, J.R. Supervised outlier detection for classification and regression. *Neurocomputing* **2022**, *486*, 77–92. [CrossRef]
27. United States Department of Agriculture. National Agricultural Statistics Service. 2022. Available online: https://quickstats.nass.usda.gov/ (accessed on 17 October 2022).

28. Thornton, M.; Shrestha, R.; Wei, Y.; Thornton, P.; Kao, S.C.; Wilson, B. *Daymet: Daily Surface Weather Data on a 1-km Grid for North America*, Version 4 R1; ORNL DAAC: Oak Ridge, TN, USA, 2022. [CrossRef]
29. Liu, F.T.; Ting, K.M.; Zhou, Z.H. Isolation Forest. In Proceedings of the 2008 Eighth IEEE International Conference on Data Mining, Pisa, Italy, 15–19 December 2008; pp. 413–422. [CrossRef]
30. Hubert, M.; Debruyne, M.; Rousseeuw, P.J. Minimum covariance determinant and extensions. *Wiley Interdiscip. Rev. Comput. Stat.* **2018**, *10*, e1421. [CrossRef]
31. Rousseeuw, P.J.; Driessen, K.V. A Fast Algorithm for the Minimum Covariance Determinant Estimator. *Technometrics* **1999**, *41*, 212–223. [CrossRef]
32. Schölkopf, B.; Platt, J.C.; Shawe-Taylor, J.C.; Smola, A.J.; Williamson, R.C. Estimating the Support of a High-Dimensional Distribution. *Neural Comput.* **2001**, *13*, 1443–1471. [CrossRef]
33. Călin, A.D.; Mureșan, H.B.; Coroiu, A.M. Feasibility of using machine learning algorithms for yield prediction of corn and sunflower crops based on seeding date. *Stud. Univ. Babeș-Bolyai Inform.* **2023**, *67*, 21–36. [CrossRef]
34. Geurts, P.; Wehenkel, L.; d'Alché Buc, F. Gradient boosting for kernelized output spaces. In Proceedings of the 24th International Conference on Machine Learning, Corvalis, OR, USA, 20–24 June 2007; pp. 289–296.
35. Chen, T.; Guestrin, C. XGBoost: A Scalable Tree Boosting System. In Proceedings of the 22nd ACM SIGKDD International Conference on Knowledge Discovery and Data Mining, KDD '16, San Francisco, CA, USA, 13–17 August 2016; Association for Computing Machinery: New York, NY, USA, 2016; pp. 785–794. [CrossRef]
36. Botchkarev, A. Performance metrics (error measures) in machine learning regression, forecasting and prognostics: Properties and typology. *arXiv* **2018**, arXiv:1809.03006.
37. Pan, B. Application of XGBoost algorithm in hourly PM2.5 concentration prediction. In *Proceedings of the IOP Conference Series: Earth and Environmental Science*; IOP publishing: London, UK, 2018; Volume 113, p. 012127.
38. Chicco, D.; Warrens, M.J.; Jurman, G. The coefficient of determination R-squared is more informative than SMAPE, MAE, MAPE, MSE and RMSE in regression analysis evaluation. *PeerJ Comput. Sci.* **2021**, *7*, e623. [CrossRef] [PubMed]

*applied sciences*

MDPI

*Article*

# A Novel Hybrid Spatiotemporal Missing Value Imputation Approach for Rainfall Data: An Application to the Ratnapura Area, Sri Lanka

**Shanthi Saubhagya [1,*], Chandima Tilakaratne [1,*], Pemantha Lakraj [1] and Musa Mammadov [2]**

[1] Department of Statistics, University of Colombo, Colombo P.O. Box 1490, Sri Lanka; pemantha@stat.cmb.ac.lk
[2] School of Info Technology, Faculty of Science, Engineering and Built Environment, Geelong Waurn Ponds Campus, Deakin University, Geelong, VIC 3216, Australia; musa.mammadov@deakin.edu.au
* Correspondence: shanthi@stu.cmb.ac.lk (S.S.); cdt@stat.cmb.ac.lk (C.T.)

**Abstract:** Meteorological time series, such as rainfall data, show spatiotemporal characteristics and are often faced with the problem of containing missing values. Discarding missing values or modeling data with missing values causes negative impacts on the accuracy of the final predictions. Hence, accurately estimating missing values by considering the spatiotemporal variations in data has become a crucial step in eco-hydrological modeling. The multi-layer perceptron (MLP) is a promising tool for modeling temporal variation, while spatial kriging (SK) is a promising tool for capturing spatial variations. Therefore, in this study, we propose a novel hybrid approach combining the multi-layer perceptron method and spatial kriging to impute missing values in rainfall data. The proposed approach was tested using spatiotemporal data collected from a set of nearby rainfall gauging stations in the Ratnapura area, Sri Lanka. Missing values are present in collected rainfall data consecutively for a considerably longer period. This pattern has scattered among stations discontinuously over five years. The proposed hybrid model captures the temporal variability and spatial variability of the rainfall data through MLP and SK, respectively. It integrates predictions obtained through both MLP and SK with a novel optimal weight allocation method. The performance of the model was compared with individual approaches, MLP, SK, and spatiotemporal kriging. The results indicate that the novel hybrid approach outperforms spatiotemporal kriging and the other two pure approaches.

**Keywords:** machine learning; spatial kriging; optimal weight allocation; spatiotemporal data

## 1. Introduction

### 1.1. Background

Rainfall is a natural phenomenon that shows spatiotemporally varying behavior. These characteristics with chaotic dynamic patterns make it difficult to predict its future behavior. Moreover, a common shortcoming of rainfall data is the inherent inclusion of missing values. This is because the data are collected from different gauging stations located in a widespread geographical area. The malfunctioning of equipment, relocation of gauging stations, network interruptions, natural hazards, and emergencies like pandemics may disturb the continuous measurement of this natural phenomenon [1].

Ignoring the stations with missing data leads to an information loss due to the strong spatial correlation between meteorological stations. On the other hand, modeling rainfall data with missing values negatively impacts the accuracy of rainfall models due to the discontinuity of the time sequence [2]. Hence, identification of a suitable mechanism to address this issue is a crucial step in an effective rainfall forecasting.

When the missing values occur at random, modeling them to estimate their values is not required. However, if the missing values are not random, then the missingness cannot be ignored and must be modeled and predicted [3]. This is known as missing value imputation and it is carried out as a data preprocessing step. Much research has been conducted using different types of missing value imputation methods. However, studies on imputing the missing values for spatiotemporal data (including meteorological records) are rare [4–7]. This study presents a novel and more efficient spatiotemporal methodology to impute missing values in rainfall data for a few rain gauging stations. The proposed methodology was tested using rainfall data collected from six neighbouring rain gauging stations (which are considered reference stations) of Ratnapura, which was identified as the target rain gauging station in our main study of rainfall forecasting. The reason for our choice is that Ratnapura is a flood-prone area in Sri Lanka due to its frequent exposure to heavy rainfall throughout the year [8,9]. In 2003, flash flood events in Ratnapura accounted for financial damage of LKR 50.6 million [9].

### 1.2. Related Work

Much past research has accompanied traditional statistical and/or machine learning techniques in missing value imputation of meteorological data. Some studies only captured the spatial variations (e.g., [10–13]) using spatial interpolation methods such as the inverse distance method (ID), normal ratio method (NR), geographical co-ordinates method (GC), and spatial kriging, also known as Gaussian process regression, while others only focused on their variation over time (e.g., [14–16]). The most common temporal method used is the autoregressive integrated moving average (ARIMA) models.

Some studies (e.g., [17]) pointed out that the predictions obtained from spatiotemporal methods are more accurate than those of purely spatial predictions. This is mainly because spatiotemporal interpolation can be applied to geo-referencing positions over a space–time grid. Some researchers have used the traditional spatial kriging model after some modifications to model the spatiotemporal behavior of the data [4,5].

There have been several spatiotemporal kriging-based studies conducted with weather variables. The study in [18] developed a spatiotemporal kriging model to predict wind speed and compared the results with the autoregressive moving average (ARMA) and Monte Carlo methods. Spatiotemporal kriging modeling gave a better fit for the data.

Moreover, the authors stated a few advantages of kriging models in comparison with other regression methods. Providing estimates with the mean squared error of the estimation (kriging variance), non-requirement of any distributional assumption related to the data, the ability to use a complete set of spatial and temporal information, and the ability to use a limited number of sampled data points to estimate the value of a variable over a continuous spatial field are some of them.

Due to these prominent advantages of kriging, recent studies have integrated kriging with conventional methods (e.g., regression and time series models) to gain fair and more accurate predictions for the missing observations. Nevertheless, a few research studies that use such hybrid approaches were found. The study [17] applied a spatiotemporal kriging method to model total monthly rainfall data among 269 rain gauge stations, of which nearly 80% of stations had missing data. The deterministic trend component was estimated with multiple linear regression, taking several covariates, including latitude, longitude, and quadratic effect of the corresponding longitude and latitude pairs. Since it only captured 29% of the temporal variability in rainfall, the residuals produced by the model were analyzed using a generalized product-sum spatiotemporal variogram and the interpolation was carried out with spatiotemporal kriging. The final predictor was obtained by combining trend estimate and interpolated value with kriging. In another study [5], spatial association of atmospheric temperature data was modeled with universal kriging and temporal variability was captured with autoregressive (AR) techniques. Then, they were spatiotemporally combined to predict $k$-steps (days) ahead temperature in a given spatial domain. A comparison of forecasted values with those obtained from ARIMA model indicated that the novel hybrid model performed better than the ARIMA model.

The recent advancements in machine learning (ML) and deep learning (DL) can be utilized effectively to predict missing cases in meteorological data. Both approaches have a great ability to handle large-scale problems and provide a flexible architecture in capturing spatial and temporal features [1,2]. In addition, they do not rely on hand-crafted feature engineering and prior assumptions on input data. Moreover, the aptness of deep neural networks on large volumes of spatiotemporal data compared to statistical and other classical machine learning techniques has been recognized.

A convolution bidirectional long short-term memory (LSTM) model was applied to capture spatial and temporal patterns in traffic flow data in the study [2]. This model outperformed state-of-the-art missing data imputation models. Some studies, including the study carried out in [19], demonstrated the effectiveness and efficiency of deep learning (DL) methods compared to the ARIMA model and back propagation neural network model. A convolutional neural network (CNN)-based DL model was proposed in [14] for imputing missing values in weather data of an individual weather station on a temporal basis. The performance of the model was evaluated using various stations nearest to the stations without missing values. This study used five optimizers (Rmsprop, Adam, Nadam, Stochastic Gradient Descend, (SGD), and Adagrad) and found that the SGD optimizer provides the most accurate results in predicting missing values.

Past studies reveal that the application of spatial kriging and DL methodology in missing value imputation of weather data has promising results. However, studies that impute missing values in spatiotemporal weather data using hybrid models are extremely rare, especially when there is a lower number of weather gauging stations. The existing research [5,17,20], which applies hybrid models, used more than 50 weather stations when interpolating spatiotemporal missing data. Most importantly, so far, no study has applied a spatiotemporal hybrid model to impute missing values among rainfall data at the Ratnapura gauging station. Therefore, to reduce this gap in the literature and to utilize the potential of spatial kriging, machine learning, and deep learning techniques in dealing with missing values, this study proposes a hybrid model by integrating them. Our target is to verify its appropriateness when the periods with missing values of rainfall gauging stations are different and discontinuous. Our focus is also given to the scenario where data are available only for a few rainfall stations.

The rest of this paper is organized as follows. The next section describes the adopted missing values imputation methods and the development of the new approach. The results and discussion section, followed by the conclusion are lined up last.

## 2. Materials and Methods

### 2.1. Proposed Methodology

This study introduces a hybrid method by integrating multi-layer perceptron (MLP) with spatial kriging as a tool for imputing sequential missing values of spatiotemporal data. The performance of the new model was evaluated against each of the two individual models as well as the spatiotemporal kriging model, since many past studies [17,18,20] have identified the spatiotemporal kriging model as a promising tool for estimating missing values in spatiotemporal data.

The methodology behind this study will be illustrated using the rainfall data set gathered across several neighbouring weather stations for a sufficiently longer period.

The target variable in this study represents rainfall measurements and each data point has a timestamp (day) and 2D spatial location (longitude and latitude). Our initial experiments performed for missing value imputation using machine learning methods (MLP, long short-term memory (LSTM), convolutional neural network (CNN), CNN-LSTM, ConvLSTM, random forest (RF), and nonlinear autoregressive network with exogenous inputs (NARX)) revealed that MLP can capture the temporal variation of the same set of rainfall data better than the other methods (see Table S1). Therefore, in this study, we chose MLP to capture the temporal variation of rainfall data in our hybrid model. The spatial kriging was used to model spatial variation due its promising behavior in capturing the spatial variations of the weather data and incorporation into a hybrid model [4,17,18,20–22].

### 2.1.1. Multi-Layer Perceptron Neural Network

Multi-layer perceptron (MLP) is a feed-forward neural network consisting of three types of layers: input layer, hidden layer (s), and output layer. In an MLP, the data flow in the forward direction from the input to the output layer, and the MLPs are trained with the backpropagation learning algorithm, which allows nonlinear mapping between the input and the output layer [23]. Its fast operation, ease of implementation, and requirement of a smaller training set (compared to radial basis neural networks) lead it to be popular among researchers [24].

In MLP, each neuron in a layer is connected to all neurons in the succeeding layer and connection strength is called weight. The output of each neuron of hidden layers as well as the output layer is a function of the sum of the inputs to the node modified by applying a linear or nonlinear transfer or an activation function [25,26]. The input layer passes the input vector to the network. An MLP can have one or more hidden layers.

Figure 1 illustrates an example of an MLP model with two hidden layers. Here, $X_i$ is the input to the $i^{th}$ neuron in the input layer. $w_{ij}^{(1)}$ is the weight associated with the $i^{th}$ neuron of the input layer to the $j^{th}$ neuron of the first hidden layer, $w_{ij}^{(2)}$ is the weight of the link connecting the $i^{th}$ neuron of the first hidden layer to the $j^{th}$ neuron of the second hidden layer, and $w_{ij}^{(3)}$ is the weight associated with the $i^{th}$ neuron of the second hidden layer to the $j^{th}$ neuron of the output layer. $b_i^{(1)}$ and $b_i^{(2)}$ are the bias values associated with the $i^{th}$ neuron of the first hidden layer and the $i^{th}$ neuron of the second hidden layer, respectively. $b_j$ is the bias associated with the $j^{th}$ neuron of the output layer. $\varnothing^{(1)}$, $\varnothing^{(2)}$, and $\varnothing^{(3)}$ are the activation functions associated with the first hidden layer, second hidden layer, and the output layer, respectively.

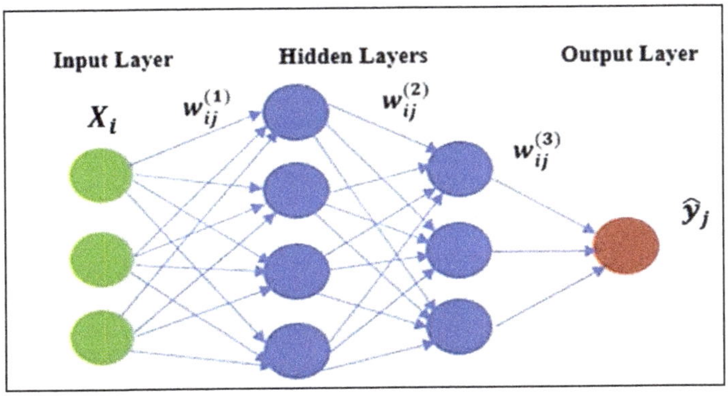


**Figure 1.** A multilayer perceptron model with two hidden layers. The nodes in Input Layer are represented in green colour. The nodes in Hidden Layer are represented in blue colour, and the node in Output Layer is coloured in red.

Then, the net output from the $i^{th}$ neuron of the first hidden layer is given by $h_i^{(1)}$ and the net output from the $j^{th}$ neuron of the second hidden layer is $h_j^{(2)}$ (see Equations (1) and (2)). The output of the $j^{th}$ neuron of the output layer will be $\hat{y}_j$ (in our study, $j = 1$). This is also noted as the imputed rainfall value at Ratnapura by MLP.

Finally, the MLP network computations can be written as follows:

$$h_i^{(1)} = \varnothing^{(1)}(\textstyle\sum_j w_{ij}^{(1)} X_i + b_j^{(1)}) \text{ where } i = 1, 2, 3 \text{ and } j = 1, 2, 3, 4 \quad (1)$$

$$h_j^{(2)} = \varnothing^{(2)}(\textstyle\sum_i w_{ij}^{(2)} h_i^{(1)} + b_i^{(2)}) \text{ where } i = 1, 2, 3, 4 \text{ and } j = 1, 2, 3 \quad (2)$$

$$\hat{y}_j = \varnothing^{(3)}\left(\sum_i w_{ij}^{(3)} h_j^{(2)} + b_j\right) \text{ where } i = 1,\ 2,\ 3 \text{ and } j = 1 \quad (3)$$

2.1.2. Spatial Kriging

Spatial kriging is an optimal interpolation technique that uses the theory of regression to predict the value at an unobserved location using values of observed neighborhood locations. Here, observed values of neighborhood locations are weighted according to the covariance values. As depicted in Figure 2, consider the location of interest, $X_0$, that is surrounded by the neighboring observed locations, $X_i$.

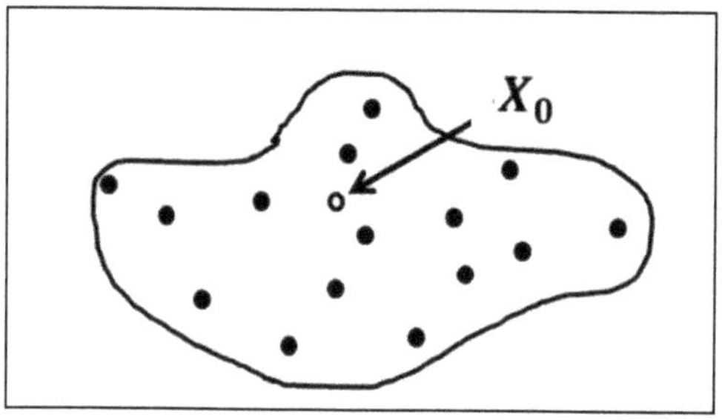


**Figure 2.** The neighboring observed locations and the location of interest, $X_0$.

The value at location $X_0$, $Z(X_0)$, is estimated through the values of $n$ neighboring sample locations taken as a linear combination of observed location values. Let the weight be associated with the observed value at location $X_i$, i.e., $Z(X_i)$ is $w_i$. Then, the spatial kriging estimate of $Z(X_0)$ can be computed as follows:

$$\hat{Z}(X_0) = k + \sum_{i=1}^{n} w_i Z(X_i) = k + w^T\mathbf{Z} \quad (4)$$

where $w \equiv (w_1,\ w_2,\ \ldots,\ w_n)^T, \mathbf{Z} \equiv (Z(X_1),\ Z(X_2),\ \ldots,\ Z(X_n))$. The values of $k$ and $w$ are calculated by minimizing the mean squared prediction error [18].

The optimal linear predictor of $Z(X_0)$, $\hat{\mathbf{Z}}(\mathbf{X}_0)$, is given by:

$$\hat{\mathbf{Z}}(\mathbf{X}_0) = \mu(X_0) + \boldsymbol{c}^T \sum\nolimits^{-1}(\mathbf{Z} - \boldsymbol{\mu}) \quad (5)$$

where $\mu$ is the Lagrange multiplier, $\boldsymbol{\mu} \equiv (\mu(X_1), \mu(X_2), \ldots, \mu(X_n))^T$, $(X_i) = E(Z(X_i))$, $i = 0, 1, 2, \ldots, n$, $\boldsymbol{c} \equiv (Cov(X_0, X_1), \ldots, Cov(X_0, X_n))^T$, and $\sum$ is the $n \times n$ matrix whose $(i,j)^{\text{th}}$ element is $Cov(X_i, X_j)$.

Then, the minimum value of $MSE(X_0,\ w,\ k)$ for a fixed location $X_0$, $\sigma^2(X_0)$ (spatial kriging variance) is given by [18]:

$$\sigma^2(X_0) = Cov(X_0,\ X_0) - \boldsymbol{c}^T \sum\nolimits^{-1} \boldsymbol{c} \quad (6)$$

The values of $\boldsymbol{c}$ and $\sum$ are calculated through the variogram or a covariance function. The different kriging models (simple, ordinary, or universal) can be obtained by changing the way of modeling $E(Z(X))$.

2.1.3. Hybrid Model for Missing Value Estimation

In the proposed hybrid model, the spatial kriging estimate and the MLP estimate are integrated with optimal weights. The optimal weights must be estimated using a sample of artificially created missing cases. Suppose the spatial kriging estimate of that sample is $\hat{y}_k$ (which was produced as $\hat{Z}(X_0)$ in Section 2.1.2) and the MLP estimate is $\hat{y}_m$ (which was produced as $\hat{y}_j$ in Section 2.1.1), weights from each estimate are $w_k$ and $w_m$, respectively, the actual value is $y_a$, and the final estimate is $\hat{y}_f$. In order to find the final prediction closer to the actual value, the optimal weights from each prediction should be found such that the prediction error is minimized. Therefore, the optimization problem can be defined as mean squared error (MSE) loss function ($f_{loss}$) between predicted and actual values:

$$f_{loss}(w_k, w_m) = \sum_{i=1}^{n}(w_k\hat{y}_{ki} + w_m\hat{y}_{mi} - y_{ai})^2 \tag{7}$$

with respect to the following constraints that provide a convex combination of two edge points $\hat{y}_{ki}$ and $\hat{y}_{mi}$:

$$w_k + w_m = 1,\ 0 \le w_k \le 1,\ 0 \le w_m \le 1 \tag{8}$$

Following the study [27], it would be logical to consider the case when the weights $w_k$ and $w_m$ are greater than 1 or less than 0. Considering this assumption and denoting $w = w_k$, Equations (7) and (8) can be formulated as an unconstrained optimization problem with respect to $w$ in the form:

$$\text{Minimize}: \ f_{loss}(w) = \sum_{i=1}^{n}(w\,\hat{y}_{ki} + (1-w)\,\hat{y}_{mi} - y_{ai})^2 \tag{9}$$

The objective function $f_{loss}(w)$ in this problem is convex and smooth; therefore, optimization Equation (9) can be easily solved. We have:

$$\frac{1}{dw} f_{loss}(w) = \sum_{i=1}^{n} 2(w\,\hat{y}_{ki} + (1-w)\,\hat{y}_{mi} - y_{ai})(\hat{y}_{ki} - \hat{y}_{mi}) = 0 \tag{10}$$

Solving Equation (10) with respect to $w$, we find optimal weight $w$ and, therefore, weights $w_k = w$ and $w_m$ in the form:

$$w_k = \left(\sum_{i=1}^{n}(\hat{y}_{mi}^2 + \hat{y}_{ki}y_{ai} - \hat{y}_{mi}y_{ai} - \hat{y}_{ki}\hat{y}_{mi})\right) / \left(\sum_{i=1}^{n}(\hat{y}_{ki}^2 + \hat{y}_{mi}^2 - 2\hat{y}_{ki}\hat{y}_{mi})\right) \tag{11}$$

$$\text{and } w_m = 1 - w_k \tag{12}$$

The found optimal weights were used to obtain the final prediction $\hat{y}_f$ at the point $i$ where the particular value is missing:

$$\hat{y}_f = w_m * \hat{y}_m + w_k * \hat{y}_k \tag{13}$$

The imputed missing values using the proposed method were compared with those obtained from spatial kriging, MLP as well as spatiotemporal kriging. The reason for considering spatiotemporal kriging is that it is a widely used spatiotemporal missing value imputation method in past studies.

#### 2.1.4. Spatiotemporal Kriging

The spatial kriging can be extended to obtain spatiotemporal predictions by incorporating an additional temporal dimension, $t$, to the spatial kriging [4,17,18,20].

The spatiotemporal set of observed data are given by $\{Z(X_1, t_1), Z(X_2, t_2), \ldots, Z(X_n, t_n)\}$, and let $Z_i = Z(X_i, t_i)$ be the value of the variable $Z$ at location $X_i$ and time $t_i$. The spatiotemporal kriging prediction at an unobserved location $X_0$ at time $t$ is defined by:

$$\hat{y}_f = \hat{Z}(X_0, t) = \sum_{i=1}^{n} w_i(X, t)(Z(X_i, t_i)) \ \text{ subject to } \sum_{i=1}^{n} w_i(X, t) = 1 \tag{14}$$

where $w_i$ are weights for $Z(X_i, t_i)$, $i = 1, 2, \ldots n$. Following the study in [18], the optimal prediction is taken by minimizing the mean squared prediction error subject to the constraint:

$$E\left[\hat{Z}(X_0, t) - Z(X_0, t)\right] = 0 \tag{15}$$

The kriging weights can be computed through the covariance function or by means of a semivariogram. Once the covariance values are calculated, the optimal weights of the kriging estimator can be computed through Lagrange multiplier application. Finally, the optimal value of $\hat{Z}(X_0, t)$ is calculated for spatiotemporal location $(X_0, t)$ [18].

The spatiotemporal covariance function has different models such as linear, exponential, spherical, Gaussian, or logistic. Capturing the spatial and temporal variability is difficult for the variogram due to their dissimilarities. Therefore, the two-dimensional kriging is modified to incorporate the time component. The type of variogram (metric, separable, SumMetric, and product sum models) varies according to the way it combines and models the temporal and spatial dependencies. The best-fitting model can be identified by comparing the mean squared errors (MSE) between the sample variogram and fitted variogram.

2.1.5. Model Evaluation

In order to evaluate the performance of the fitted MLP, spatial kriging and spatiotemporal kriging models, mean absolute error ($MAE$), root mean squared error ($RMSE$), and coefficient of determination ($R^2$) metrics were used.

The $MAE$, $RMSE$, and $R^2$ are calculated as below.

$$MAE = \frac{1}{n}\sum_{i=1}^{n}|y_{ai} - \hat{y}_{fi}| \tag{16}$$

$$RMSE = \sqrt{\frac{1}{n}\sum_{i=1}^{n}(y_{ai} - \hat{y}_{fi})^2} \tag{17}$$

$$R^2 = 1 - \frac{\sum_{i=1}^{n}(y_{ai} - \hat{y}_{fi})^2}{\sum_{i=1}^{n}(y_{ai} - \overline{y}_{ai})^2} \tag{18}$$

where $\hat{y}_{fi}$ is the predicted value, $y_{ai}$ is the actual value, and $\overline{y}_{ai}$ is the mean value of $y_{ai}$. The smaller the values of MAE and RMSE and larger the $R^2$ value, the better the forecasting is.

The hybrid model, which integrates MLP and spatial kriging, was implemented in python and the spatiotemporal kriging model was fitted using R software (version 4.3) and the related packages. In the spatiotemporal model, the data were represented as Space Time Full Data Frame (STFDF) object before fitting the variogram since data considered in this study were with complete space time grid with s substations and t time intervals of their observations.

## 2.2. Description of Data

For this study, daily rainfall readings gathered by nine rainfall neighbouring gauging stations, including the target station (Ratnapura), were considered. The other eight stations are Balangoda (St1_Bal), Detanagalla (St2_Det), Elston (St3_Els), Ilumbuluwa (St4_Ill), Keragala (St5_Ker), Moralioya (St6_Mor), Nivithigala (St7_Niv), and Ulinduwawa (St8_Uli). These eight stations are considered as reference stations.

The total number of days accounted for in this study is 1826. As mentioned earlier, these reference stations consist of various discontinuous missing patterns within the study period (1 January 2015–31 December 2019). The following heatmap (Figure 3) depicts the missing patterns in the data of eight reference stations and Table 1 summarizes percentages.

Figure 3 depicts the data availability with blue color and inconsistent missingness with white blocks along the time and space. With respect to the figure, it can be noted that, in most cases, the missingness has occurred as a block (i.e., a sequence of missing values). The percentage of missing values of the last two sub-stations, as indicated in Table 1, are 68.4% and 73.55%, respectively. Since more than half of the data values are missing, these two sub-stations were excluded from the analysis. The stations St1_Bal, St2_Det and St5_Ker had random missing cases (noncontinuous missing values). Those were interpolated using the average values of the neighbouring rainfall values of the corresponding station. Finally, there were six reference stations considered for assessing the suitability of the proposed methodology.

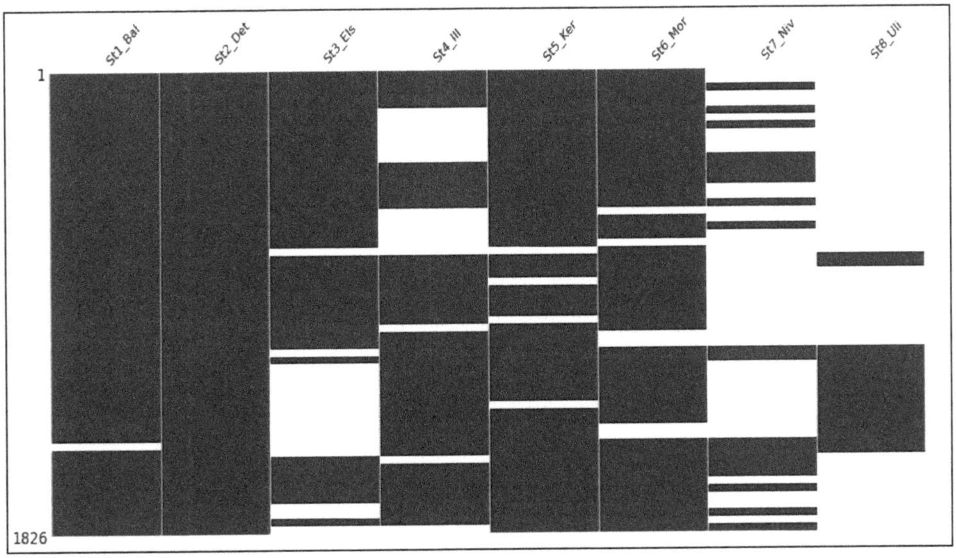


**Figure 3.** Missing patterns of sub-stations' rainfall data.

**Table 1.** Missing percentages of sub-stations' rainfall data.

| Sub Station | Missing Count | Missing Percentage |
|---|---|---|
| St1_Bal | 32 | 1.75 |
| St2_Det | 1 | 0.05 |
| St3_Els | 519 | 28.42 |
| St4_Ill | 491 | 26.89 |
| St5_Ker | 123 | 6.74 |
| St6_Mor | 183 | 10.02 |
| St7_Niv | 1249 | **68.4** |
| St8_Uli | 1343 | **73.55** |

## 3. Results and Discussion

### 3.1. Preliminary Analysis

The correlation between the rainfall values of different stations may be either linear or nonlinear. Therefore, to capture any type of correlations, the Spearman correlation coefficients were calculated (refer to Figure 4).

The correlation between all the considered sub-stations and the target station Ratnapura and among sub-stations are significant at 5% significance level (i.e., $p$ value < 0.05). A strong correlation (>0.6) can be seen between Ratnapura and sub-stations Keragala, Moralioya, and Elston. The results indicate that all six sub-stations are important in modeling rainfall at Ratnapura station. Thus, it confirms the need for imputing missing values of the reference stations.

### 3.2. The Hybrid Model Formation

The structure of the performed hybrid model with MLP and spatial kriging can be depicted as in Figure 5. In the notation, $\widehat{y}_k$ and $\widehat{y}_m$ refers to the spatial kriging and the MLP estimates corresponding to the missing rainfall value of the $i^{th}$ station, for instance, St2 (there are situations where the rainfall values of more than one station are missing on the same day).

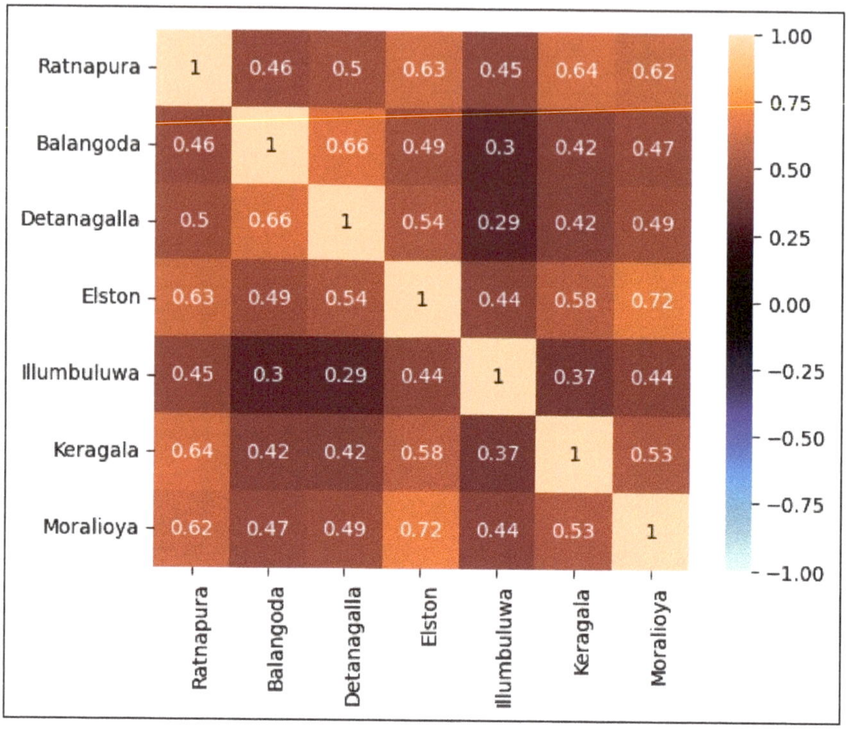


**Figure 4.** The heatmap of correlation between rainfall gauging stations.

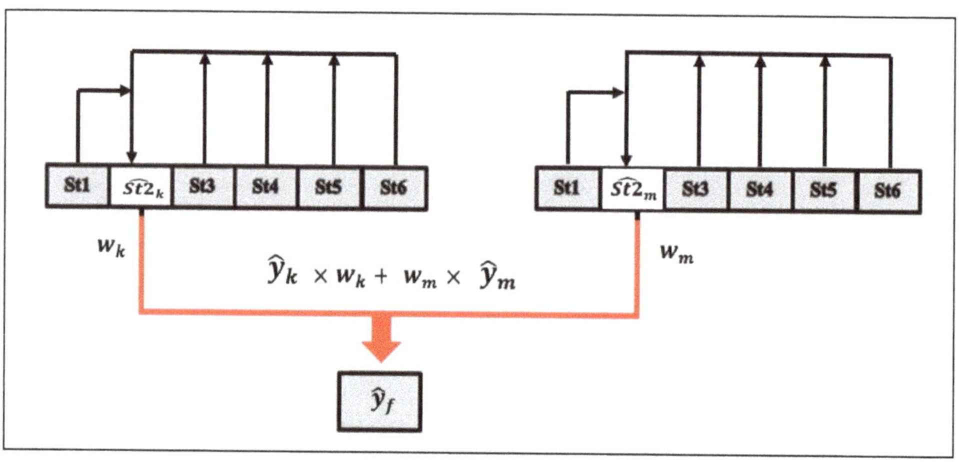


**Figure 5.** The hybrid model structure.

Note that MLP (for multivariate time series data) was trained using the parameter values tuned with grid search approach (selected from a range of values) tabularized in Table 2.

**Table 2.** Common parameter settings in MLP models.

| Parameters | Value |
|---|---|
| Activation function | ReLU |
| Epochs | 80 |
| Number of hidden layers | 1 |
| Number of neurons in hidden layer | 20 |
| Batch size | 72 |
| Learning rate | 0.01 |
| Optimizer | Adam |
| Loss Function | MAE |

The regularization parameters and number of training/testing samples were modified to obtain a convergent model in each MLP model. As depicted in Figure 5, in order to integrate the two estimates obtained from spatial kriging and MLP, the optimal weights from each estimate should be found.

For this, a data set without missing values needs to be used. Therefore, the following procedure was applied:

(a) From the original data set, three complete subsets (with no missing cases for all the stations) were selected. Consequently, subsets from the years 2015, 2016, and 2019 were selected.
(b) Consecutive missing periods were artificially created randomly within the three subsets to capture the missing pattern of the original data set.
(c) The spatial kriging and MLP were applied to estimate the missing cases.
(d) Those estimated rainfall values were combined to form a single data set of 120 estimated rainfall values.
(e) Then, from the final data set mentioned in (d), 100 simple random samples (with replacement) with a moderate sample size of 60 were drawn.
(f) For each sample, the optimal values of two weights, $w_k$ and $w_m$, were calculated by applying Equations (11) and (12) as described in Section 2.1.3. The procedure resulted in 100 optimal pairs of weights.
(g) Then, the first optimal weight pair was used to calculate the weighted estimates ($\hat{y}_f$) of the rest of the samples (99). For each sample, the RMSE values (including the first sample considered) were calculated. Using these RMSE values, the average RMSE was computed.
(h) Likewise, steps (a) to (g) were repeated using the second optimal weight pair, then third optimal weight pair, and so on.

Finally, there were 100 average RMSE values. Out of them, the pair of weights that produced the lowest average RMSE value was selected as the best optimal pair of weights for spatial kriging and MLP (Table S2). The results indicated that the 11th random sample produced the final optimal weights, $w_k = 0.50013$ and $w_m = 0.49987$. Those weights were taken to obtain optimal weighted estimates for the missing values.

### 3.3. The Spatiotemporal Kriging Model (SPTK Model)

Figure 6 summarizes the steps followed in applying the spatiotemporal kriging model.

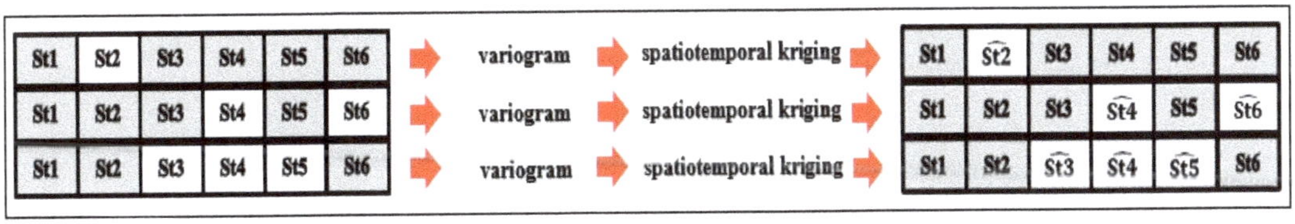


**Figure 6.** The spatiotemporal kriging method.

In this approach, a variogram for each missing sequence was fitted using the available rainfall values of stations. For example, according to Figure 6, the first gap of the above data set can be seen in station St2. Then, the data from the remaining stations were employed to fit a variogram. Similarly, the missing blocks of St4 and St6 were estimated using the available rainfall values of the other stations and so on.

Four variogram types (metric, separable, sum metric, and product sum) were compared in terms of RMSE values. Using the variogram with the lowest RMSE, the spatiotemporal kriging was applied to estimate the missing values in a substation(s) that was/were in the created grid. Table 3 provides the outputs resulting from 11 blocks of missing values.

**Table 3.** Comparison of prediction errors of variogram types.

| Gap no | Metric | Separable | SumMetric | Product Sum |
|---|---|---|---|---|
| 1 | **13.79** | 23.16 | 64.75 | 23.33 |
| 2 | 38.56 | 22.871 | 52.43 | **22.868** |
| 3 | **15.46** | 16.19 | 31.14 | 16.25 |
| 4 | **30.31** | 30.86 | 71.54 | 30.82 |
| 5 | 136.15 | 132.79 | **128.77** | 132.79 |
| 6 | 17.53 | 10.03 | 31.8 | **9.99** |
| 7 | 11.02 | 9.67 | **9.13** | 9.66 |
| 8 | **88.75** | 89.13 | 110.29 | 89.28 |
| 9 | **21.58** | 21.95 | 41.33 | 22.13 |
| 10 | **81.02** | 81.03 | 118.85 | 81.04 |
| 11 | 34.95 | **13.54** | 58.8 | 13.63 |

According to Table 3, it can be noticed that, in most of the cases, the metric variogram has become the best fit and Figure 7 depicts a sample of figures (out of 11 figures), which illustrates the comparison between variograms. In each case, the sample variogram and fitted four types of variograms are given.

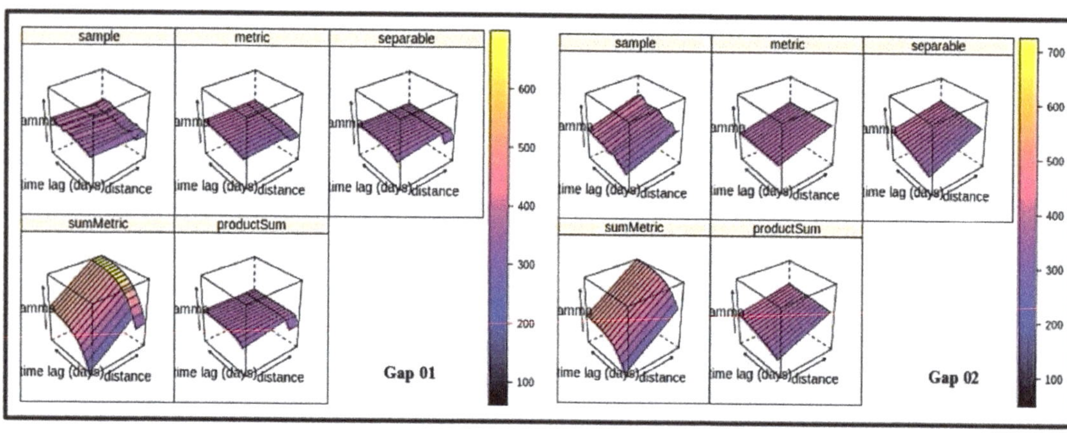


**Figure 7.** Differences between the sample and the best fitting spatiotemporal variogram of each family of the first two gaps. The half of the variogram function (γ—gamma) which gives measures of spatiotemporal correlation of the random field is plotted against each space–time co-ordinate.

In fitting the spatiotemporal model for the rainfall data, the empirical variogram surface (or sample variogram) based on space and time is computed and used as inputs for fitting different models: metric, separable, sum metric, and product sum models. Out of them, the best fitting model can be selected, comparing with the surface of the empirical variogram. When considering Missing Gap 01 in Figure 7, the metric-type variogram shows the most similar surface shape with respect to distance and time lags as that of the original sample. Nevertheless, in Missing Gap 02, the product sum variogram is more similar to the pattern of the actual sample. Likewise, in 11 gaps, the optimal variogram type deferred with the missing pattern of the data.

Through optimal variograms the covariances of the data were calculated and, thereby, the optimal weights to predict the missing value at the targeted location (see Section 2.1.4).

### 3.4. Model Evaluation

To validate the models, a two-way evaluation mechanism was carried out.

#### 3.4.1. Model Evaluation along with Actual Missing Data

Assume that the rainfall values of a station are missing from $t$ to $t + k_1$ (see Figure 8). The hybrid model was fitted, and these missing values were estimated using the available values from 1 to $t$. To check the validity of the fitted model, rainfall values from $(t + k_1)$ to $(t + k_1 + k_2)$ were estimated based on the same fitted model (refer to Section 3.2) and compared with the actual values. This validation data set was with size 55 (here, the total number of observations in all $k_2$ periods). The value $k_2$ was chosen according to the continuous availability of data within the considered time period.

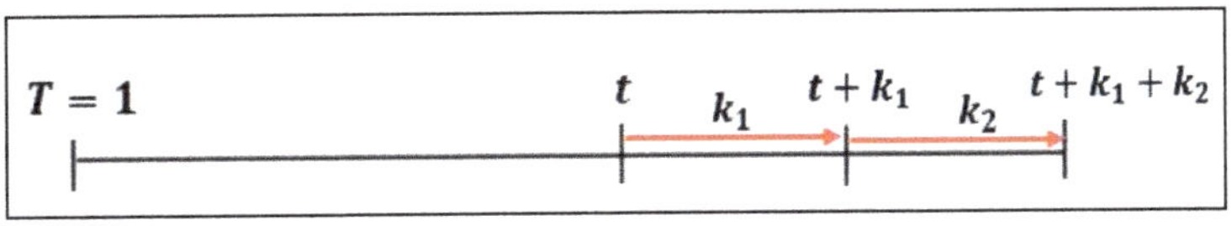


**Figure 8.** The model evaluation criterion.

Spatiotemporal kriging (SPTK) was applied to the same validation set. Finally, a comparison of RMSE, MAE, and $R^2$ (Table 4) was conducted using the results produced by individual approaches and the hybrid approach.

**Table 4.** Comparison of prediction error of all models.

| Method | Spatial Kriging | MLP | Hybrid | SPTK |
|---|---|---|---|---|
| RMSE | 12.76 | 11.68 | **10.72** | 15.97 |
| MAE | 7.12 | **4.01** | 5.12 | 10.25 |
| $R^2$ | **13%** | 3% | **13%** | 0% |

Among the considered four models, the minimum RMSE is produced by the hybrid weighted method. It also has an MAE close to its lowest value, which is produced by MLP, and the highest $R^2$ value as of the spatial kriging (although it still needs to be improved). Thus, in the first phase of model comparison, it was proved that the hybrid model outperformed the other individual models. Moreover, the hybrid model outperformed the spatiotemporal kriging model with respect to all validation measurements.

#### 3.4.2. Model Evaluation on Artificially Generated Missing Data

Since the previous evaluation could not capture all the actual missing gaps (due to the inconsistency of the data set), we thought to generalize the validation using another validation set that could capture all the missing patterns (which are and are not in the original data set) that could be found in an original data set of six rainfall gauging stations.

In year 2016, for 6 months (from January to June), there were no missing observations. Therefore, we took the data of that period to create 56 subsets with different sequential missing patterns, as shown in Table 5.

**Table 5.** Types of missing gaps within six sub-stations.

| Number Stations with Missing Observations (M) | Number of Combinations (of Stations) |
|---|---|
| 01 | ${}^6C_1 = 6$ |
| 02 | ${}^6C_2 = 15$ |
| 03 | ${}^6C_3 = 20$ |
| 04 | ${}^6C_4 = 15$ |
| Total number of data sets | **56** |

When two stations have missing observations in the same period (consider one incident out of 15 combinations in case 02), each station was modeled separately. Thus, it resulted in two trials. Finally, all combinations of two stations with missing observations (i.e., 15) generated 30 trials (15 × 2). This was the same for the rest of the cases where there were at least two stations with missing data. The case where the number of stations with missing observations, M = 5, was not considered because there should be at least two stations without missing observations in the spatiotemporal grid to model those gauging stations with missing values using spatial kriging (a model requirement). In each subset, missingness was created with the last 20 observations (without breaking the time sequence and allocating enough data points for training) of the relevant sub-station. The rest of the data were used to train and test the models and, hence, identify the best-fit model for a selected sample of data.

The estimated values from each model were compared with the actual values and tabularized in Table S3. In terms of the lowest values of RMSE and MAE and the highest values of $R^2$, the hybrid model has outperformed the other approaches. Moreover, it is important to point out that, when kriging performs better than other individual methods in terms of three validation measurements, the hybrid model has performed approximately equally in most of the cases.

The outperformance with respect to the total (where lowest RMSE and MAE values and highest $R^2$ value occur) shows the hybrid method could gain the score of 41% (see Table 6).

**Table 6.** Final comparison of model performance.

| Method | Kriging | MLP | Hybrid | SPTK |
|---|---|---|---|---|
| No. of times that each approach produced best results (as a percentage with respect to the sum of trials) | 30 | 20 | 41 | 9 |

In addition to the above outcome, all the cases (in Table S3) were taken to obtain the graphs shown in Figure 9.

Figure 9 illustrates that kriging produced most cases within the lowest value range of MAE and within the highest value range of $R^2$, whereas the MLP gained the majority of cases within the lowest value range of RMSE. In all these occurrences, the hybrid model has shown approximately the same performance as the optimal model.

This study demonstrated that the spatial and temporal variations should not be neglected in missing value imputation in spatiotemporal data. Further, considering the two-way evaluation, we could confirm that the hybrid model had the ability to outperform other pure approaches or almost equally performed compared to the best approach whenever it was selected as the second-best approach.

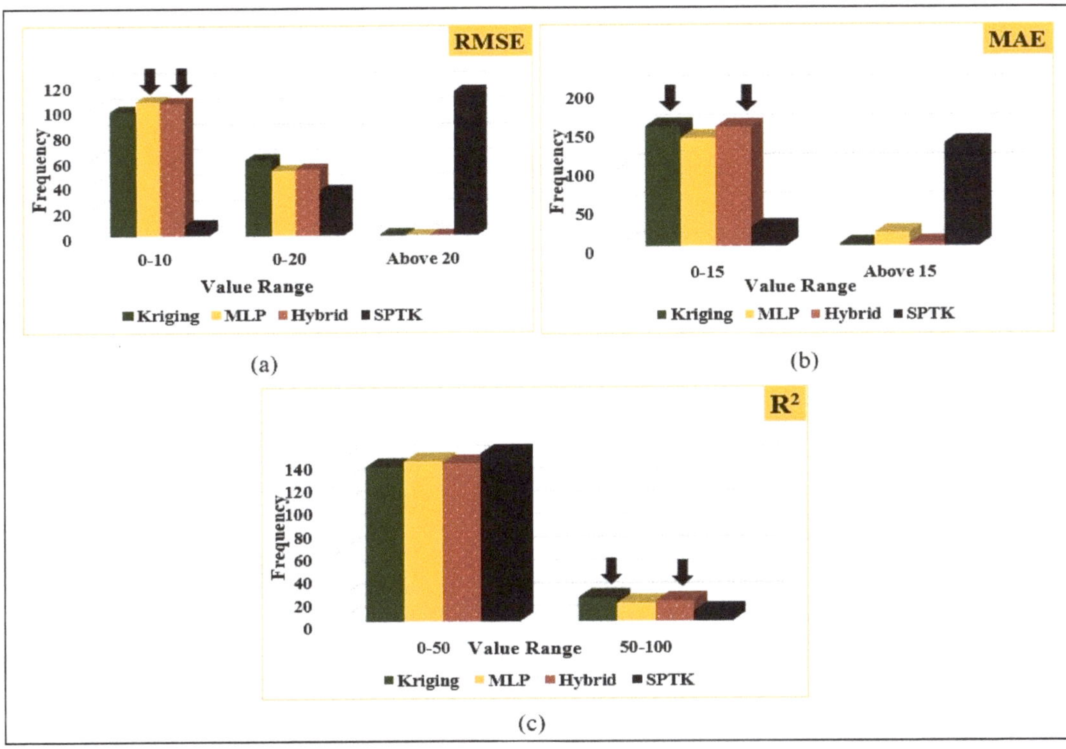


**Figure 9.** The outperformance of models with respect to RMSE (**a**), MAE (**b**), and $R^2$ (**c**) values.

## 4. Conclusions

In this paper, we proposed a novel approach for spatiotemporal missing value imputation. Furthermore, this approach was illustrated by applying it to impute rainfall data in six reference stations to compile a complete data set that could be used in building a rainfall forecasting model for a target station. The proposed approach is a hybrid approach combining MLP that captures the temporal variability and spatial interpolation (spatial kriging) that captures the spatial variations. This hybrid model was designed for imputing missing values when the missingness of reference stations was spread discontinuously and not uniformly over the given period and a few rainfall gauging stations are spatially correlated. Moreover, the results obtained by the hybrid model were compared with those resulting from spatiotemporal kriging. The study supported the claim that the proposed hybrid approach provided the lowest prediction error when estimating a sequence of missing values.

Only a single published research study that imputes the missing rainfall values of Ratnapura gauging stations is available. The accuracy measurements of the proposed method are far better than those of said study [28].

The availability of a few rain gauging stations around Ratnapura station and unavailability of data in some stations for a considerable period due to relocation or other reasons were the challenging limitations confronted during this study.

In order to verify the optimality of weight estimates and the outperformance of the hybrid method, the data for an extended period need to be gathered and tested.

While considering the aforesaid limitations, the future direction of this research will be the development of more hybrid models combining other missing value imputation methods and applying this approach to estimate missing values of spatiotemporal data obtained from other fields.

**Supplementary Materials:** The following supporting information can be downloaded at: https://www.mdpi.com/article/10.3390/app14030999/s1, Table S1: Missing value imputation of substation rainfall data using DL methods; Table S2: Final optimal weights; Table S3: Comparison of prediction error of all models in validation under Section 3.4.2.

**Author Contributions:** Conceptualization, C.T. and S.S.; methodology, S.S., C.T., P.L. and M.M.; software, S.S.; validation, S.S.; formal analysis, S.S.; investigation, C.T., M.M. and P.L.; resources, S.S.; data curation, S.S.; writing—original draft preparation, S.S.; writing—review and editing, C.T. and M.M.; visualization, S.S.; supervision, C.T., M.M. and P.L.; project administration, C.T.; funding acquisition, C.T. All authors have read and agreed to the published version of the manuscript.

**Funding:** This research was funded by Collaborative Research Grant of the University of Colombo, Sri Lanka, grant number AP/3/2019/CG/30.

**Institutional Review Board Statement:** Not applicable.

**Informed Consent Statement:** Not applicable.

**Data Availability Statement:** The data that support the findings of this study are available from the authors upon reasonable request.

**Acknowledgments:** The authors wish to acknowledge the University of Colombo, Sri Lanka, for the monetary support.

**Conflicts of Interest:** The authors declare no conflict of interest.

## References

1. Mital, U.; Dwivedi, D.; Brown, J.B.; Faybishenko, B.; Painter, S.L.; Steefel, C.I. Sequential Imputation of Missing Spatio-Temporal Precipitation Data Using Random Forests. *Front. Water* **2020**, *2*, 20. [CrossRef]
2. Asadi, R.; Regan, A. A convolution recurrent autoencoder for spatio-temporal missing data imputation. *arXiv* **2019**, arXiv:1904.12413.
3. Soley-Bori, M. *Dealing with Missing Data: Key Assumptions and Methods for Applied Analysis*; Boston University: Boston, MA, USA, 2013; Volume 4, pp. 1–19.
4. Yang, H.; Yang, J.; Han, L.; Liu, X.; Pu, L.; Chin, S.; Hwang, H. A Kriging based spatiotemporal approach for traffic volume data imputation. *PLoS ONE.* **2018**, *13*, e0195957. [CrossRef] [PubMed]
5. Agarwal, A. A New Approach to Spatio-Temporal Kriging and Its Applications. Master's Thesis, Ohio State University, OhioLINK Electronic Theses and Dissertations Center, Columbus, OH, USA, 2011. Available online: http://rave.ohiolink.edu/etdc/view?acc_num=osu1306871646 (accessed on 18 November 2023).
6. Aguilera, H.; Guardiola-Albert, C.; Hidalgo, C.S. Estimating extremely large amounts of missing precipitation data. *J. Hydroinformatics* **2020**, *22*, 578–592. [CrossRef]
7. Feng, L.; Nowak, G.; O'Neill, T.J.; Welsh, A. CUTOFF: A spatio-temporal imputation method. *J. Hydrol.* **2014**, *519*, 3591–3605. [CrossRef]
8. Hettiarachchi, P. *Inundation Maps of the Kalu Ganga Basin during the Flood in May 2003*; Department of Irrigation: Colombo, Sri Lanka, 2013.
9. Nandalal, K.D.W. Use of a hydrodynamic model to forecast floods of Kalu River in Sri Lanka. *J. Flood Risk Manag.* **2009**, *2*, 151–158. [CrossRef]
10. Rafii, F.; Kechadi, T. Collection of historical weather data: Issues with missing values. In Proceedings of the 4th International Conference on Smart City Applications (SCA'19), Casablanca, Morocco, 2–4 October 2019.
11. Burhanuddin, A.; Zahrah, S.N.; Deni, S.; Ramli, N.M. Imputation of Missing Rainfall Data Using Revised Normal Ratio Method. *Adv. Sci. Lett.* **2017**, *23*, 10981–10985. [CrossRef]
12. Jahan, F.; Sinha, N.; Rahman, M.; Rahman, M.M.; Mondal, M.S.; Islam, M. Comparison of Missing Value Estimation Techniques in Rainfall Data of Bangladesh. *Theor. Appl. Climatol.* **2019**, *136*, 1–17. [CrossRef]
13. Ahmad, R.; Noor, F.; Zakaria, R.; Azman, M.A. Estimation of missing rainfall data using spatial interpolation and imputation methods. *AIP Conf. Proc.* **2015**, *1643*, 42–48. [CrossRef]
14. Gad, I.; Doreswamy, H.; Manjunatha, B. A robust deep learning model for missing value imputation in big NCDC dataset. *Iran J. Comput. Sci.* **2021**, *4*, 67–84. [CrossRef]
15. Afrifa-Yamoah, E.; Mueller, U.; Taylor, S.; Fisher, A. Missing data imputation of high-resolution temporal climate time series data. *Meteorol. Appl.* **2020**, *27*, e1873. [CrossRef]
16. Nassir, S.; Badr, A.; Mousa, W. Estimation the Missing Data of Meteorological Variables in Different Iraqi Cities By using ARIMA Model. *Iraqi J. Sci.* **2018**, *59*, 792–801.
17. Medeiros, E.; De Lima, R.; Olinda, R.; Santos, C. Modeling Spatiotemporal Rainfall Variability in Paraíba, Brazil. *Water* **2019**, *11*, 1843. [CrossRef]

18. Cuenca, J.; Correa-Flórez, C.; Patino, D.; Vuelvas, J. Spatio-Temporal Kriging Based Economic Dispatch Problem Including Wind Uncertainty. *Energies.* **2020**, *13*, 6419. [CrossRef]
19. Duan, Y.; Lv, Y.; Liu, Y. An efficient realization of deep learning for traffic data imputation. *Transp. Res. Part C Emerg. Technol.* **2016**, *72*, 168–181. [CrossRef]
20. Zoest, V.V.; Osei, F.; Hoek, G.; Stein, A. Spatio-temporal regression Kriging for modelling urban $NO_2$ concentrations Spatio-temporal regression Kriging for modelling urban $NO_2$ concentrations. *Int. J. Geogr. Inf. Sci.* **2019**, *34*, 851–865. [CrossRef]
21. Bae, B.; Kim, H.; Lim, H.; Liu, Y.; Han, L.; Freeze, P. Missing data imputation for traffic flow speed using spatio-temporal cokriging. *Transp. Res. Part C Emerg. Technol.* **2018**, *88*, 124–139. [CrossRef]
22. Srinivasan, B.; Duraiswami, R.; Murtugudde, R. Efficient Kriging for real-time spatio-temporal interpolation. In Proceedings of the 20th Conference on Probability and Statistics in the Atmospheric Sciences, Atlanta, Georgia, 18–21 January 2010; p. 228.
23. Abirami, S.P.; Chitra, P. Chapter Fourteen-Energy-efficient edge based real-time healthcare support system. *Adv. Comput.* **2020**, *117*, 339–368.
24. Orhan, U.; Hekim, M.; Ozer, M. EEG signals classification using the K-means clustering and a multilayer perceptron neural network model. *Expert Syst. Appl.* **2011**, *38*, 13475–13481. [CrossRef]
25. Gardner, M.W.; Dorling, S.R. Artificial neural networks (the multilayer perceptron)—A review of applications in the atmospheric sciences. *Atmos. Environ.* **1998**, *32*, 2627–2636. [CrossRef]
26. Grosse, R. Lecture 5: Multilayer Perceptrons. 2018. Available online: https://www.cs.toronto.edu/~rgrosse/courses/csc321_2018/readings/L05%20Multilayer%20Perceptrons.pdf (accessed on 16 January 2022).
27. Zhou, Y.; Guan, Z.; Ji, P.; Wang, X. Drug Abuse Prediction Model Based on Relevance Analysis. In *Data Processing Techniques and Applications for Cyber-Physical Systems (DPTA 2019)–Advances in Intelligent Systems and Computing*; Huang, C., Chan, Y.W., Yen, N., Eds.; Springer: Singapore, 2020; Volume 1088. [CrossRef]
28. Jeewanthi, P.W.; Wijesuriya, W.; Liyanarachchi, L.A.T.S.; Gunatathne, L.H.P. Appropriate conventional methods forestimating missing precipitation values in Sri Lanka. *J. Agric. Value Addit.* **2023**, *5*, 45–53. [CrossRef]

applied sciences

MDPI

*Article*

# Evaluation of Machine Learning Models for Ozone Concentration Forecasting in the Metropolitan Valley of Mexico

**Rodrigo Domínguez-García [1,*,†] and Magali Arellano-Vázquez [2,*,†]**

[1] Center for Research in Advanced Materials, Av. Miguel de Cervantes Saavedra 120, Chihuahua 31136, Mexico
[2] INFOTEC Center for Research and Innovation in Information and Communication Technologies, Circuito Tecnopolo Sur No. 112, Aguascalientes 20326, Mexico
[*] Correspondence: rodrigo.dominguez@cimav.edu.mx (R.D.-G.); magali.arellano@infotec.mx (M.A.-V.); Tel.: +52-614-2535293 (R.D.-G.)
[†] These authors contributed equally to this work.

**Abstract:** In large and densely populated cities, the concentration of pollutants such as ozone and its dispersion is related to effects on people's health; therefore, its forecast is of great importance to the government and the population. Given the increased computing capacity that allows for processing massive amounts of data, the use of machine learning (ML) as a tool for air quality analysis and forecasting has gotten a significant boost. This research focuses on evaluating different models, such as Random Forest (RF), Support Vector Regression (SVR), and Gradient Boosting (GB), to forecast ozone ($O_3$) concentration 24 h in advance, using data from the Mexico City Atmospheric Monitoring System using meteorological variables that influence the phenomenon of ozone dispersion and formation.

**Keywords:** gradient boosting; machine learning; ozone forecasting; random forest; support vector regression

## 1. Introduction

The Metropolitan Area of the Valley of Mexico is 2240 m above sea level, located in a terrain of significant complexity, surrounded by mountains with an average height ranging between 600 and 800 m above the valley floor. This geographical setting makes it a region of great interest due to the substantial influence of meteorological variables on the dispersion of pollutants in the atmosphere. Furthermore, it is considered one of the largest cities in the world, characterized by a high population density, rendering it a focal point for the study of pollutant dispersion phenomena in the air. It played a pivotal role in the MILAGRO campaign (Megacity Initiative: Local And Global Research Observations) [1], in which nearly 150 institutions collaborated, supported by 450 researchers from various parts of the world. This extensive effort involved deploying diverse equipment in March 2006 to collect extensive data on pollutants and meteorological information, aiming to gain a deeper understanding of pollutant dispersion phenomena in the atmosphere of a megacity.

The air quality issue has garnered international priority, with studies conducted in Mexico City and major cities worldwide. In response to this challenge, governmental agencies have enacted regulations governing air quality levels to reduce pollutant concentrations. For instance, restrictions on the use of leaded gasoline were implemented due to the more contaminating and particularly toxic emissions from vehicles, which could reach hazardous concentrations in urban environments, posing risks to the health of residents.

Pollution poses a significant impact on public health, with the World Health Organization (WHO) estimating approximately 7 million premature deaths annually, equivalent to 800 deaths every hour or 13 per minute. Numerous studies have been conducted to assess the adverse effects resulting from prolonged exposure to various pollutants. For example, the study by Rosalba Rojas-Martinez et al. [2] on the lung development issues in children in Mexico City due to prolonged exposure to air pollutants concluded, after three years of follow-up that the children involved in the study exhibited adverse effects on lung development. This implies long-term health risks associated with an increased likelihood of developing heart-related conditions. As mentioned by Baldasano et al. [3], the established regulations have succeeded in reducing air pollutant concentrations, except ozone ($O_3$), which has shown a global upward trend, making its impact on health a priority. This is evident in studies such as Karthik L. et al. [4], which conducted a review of 55 medical articles from 1980 to 2014 on the health impacts of ozone exposure, and Niu et al. [5], where the results indicate that prolonged exposure to ozone ($O_3$) significantly affects cardiac mortality in China. Given its substantial health impact, understanding the formation and dispersion of ozone has become critically important, as well as the ability to forecast its concentrations to enable timely control measures.

Currently, this process is accomplished through conventional techniques such as mathematical models to simulate pollutant dispersion and statistical tools to comprehend and infer the behavior of this phenomenon. The advancement of technology and the capacity for massive data processing through machine learning have opened up new avenues of research to address this issue. Section 2 explores some research endeavors that apply machine learning to air quality.

## 2. Related Works

Currently, the use of machine learning as a forecasting tool in various fields is on the rise, and the field of air quality has yet to be an exception. Several related research studies have been conducted in different countries; in their research, Ahmad et al. [6] utilized machine learning techniques to predict ground-level ozone concentrations in Mexico City using hourly data from March 2015 to February 2016 and aimed to elucidate the relationship between variables and high ozone levels. The performance of three distinct models, Artificial Neural Network (ANN), Support Vector Regression (SVR), and Random Forest (RF), was evaluated based on the coefficient of determination ($R^2$) and the index of agreement (IOA); Yarragunta et al. [7] conducted a study analyzing air pollution data from various cities in India, encompassing nine attributes, including location details and pollutant levels. The study focused on daily data of pollutants, such as $SO_2$, $NO_2$, $PM_{10}$, $PM_{2.5}$, $CO$, and $O_3$, aiming to forecast air pollution levels for the subsequent days. Six supervised machine learning techniques were used to build predictive models, including logistic regression, support vector machines, random forests, K-nearest neighbors, naive Bayes classifier, and decision tree. The research emphasized learning and predicting the air quality index through adaptable machine learning algorithms, with Accuracy as a metric for model evaluation; Liang et al. [8] conducted a study based on data collected by Taiwan's Environmental Protection Administration (EPA) from 2008 to 2018, focusing on three specific regions within Taiwan. The primary objective was to develop models to efficiently forecast the Air Quality Index (AQI) for short-term durations: 1 h, 8 h, and 24 h. Five machine learning algorithms, including random forest, AdaBoost, support vector machine, artificial neural network, and stacking ensemble methods, were examined to achieve this. Model performance was evaluated using scale-dependent error indexes: MAE, RMSE, and $R^2$. In a study led by Aljanabi et al. [9], data from the Jordanian Ministry of Environment, covering the period from 1 May 2014 to 4 June 2019, were analyzed. This dataset captured daily averages of ozone readings alongside meteorological variables, such as temperature and wind patterns. The study's objective was to forecast the daily ozone concentration in Amman by leveraging a blend of meteorological and seasonal indicators from the preceding day, including distinct events like special days. The study evaluated several algorithms, namely, MLP, SVR, DTR, and XGBoost, and found MLP to be the most proficient. Additionally, the team explored the potential outcome improvement by integrating smoothing filters into the time-series data. The efficacy of the models was gauged using metrics like MAE, RMSE, and $R^2$.

In research conducted by Di et al. [10], data from various regions within the United States, spanning 1 January 2000 to 31 December 2015, were examined. The study employed three machine learning algorithms, neural network, random forest, and gradient boosting, to model $PM_{2.5}$ levels. These algorithms incorporated a broad range of predictor variables, encompassing satellite data, meteorological factors, land-use metrics, elevation, chemical transport model predictions, and several reanalysis datasets. An ensemble approach was adopted to amalgamate the outcomes of these three algorithms, yielding a consolidated $PM_{2.5}$ forecast. The models' effectiveness was gauged using metrics such as $R^2$, RMSE, MAE, and mean bias error (MBE). In their comprehensive study, Srivastava et al. [11] harnessed meteorological parameters, including vertical wind, wind speed and direction, temperature, and relative humidity, to predict concentrations of pollutants like $CO$, $NO_2$, $O_3$, $SO_2$, $PM_{10}$, and $PM_{2.5}$ across three strategic sites in New Delhi's districts. The research incorporated an array of machine learning methodologies, such as Linear Regression, Stochastic Gradient Descent Regression, Multi-layer Perceptron, and Gradient Boosting Regression. The performance of the models was evaluated using MSE, MAE, and $R^2$. In a study by Zhu et al. [12], the multi-task learning (MTL) method was proposed to predict hourly air pollution concentrations, incorporating various regularization techniques for optimal model selection. The model leverages historical meteorological and pollutant data from the Department of Meteorology at the University of Utah between 2006 and 2015 to predict pollution levels for the following day.

Model effectiveness was assessed using the root mean square error. In a study by Aditya et al. [13], two machine learning models, logistic regression and autoregression, were employed to analyze data from an Italian city between 2004 and 2005. While logistic regression classified samples as polluted or not, autoregression predicted $PM_{2.5}$ levels seven days in advance. The logistic regression model's performance was assessed using mean accuracy (MA) and standard deviation accuracy (SDA), while the autoregression model was evaluated with MAE. Contreras-Ochando et al. [14] introduced airVLC, a web application designed to predict and map air pollution levels in Valencia, Spain. This application harnesses real-time open data sources, capturing metrics like pollution readings, weather conditions, calendar events, and traffic intensities. Analyzing historical data from 2013 to 2015, the team explored multiple regression techniques to pinpoint the most effective pollution prediction method.

Additionally, the study assessed various interpolation methods, emphasizing a novel approach that factors in wind direction, enhancing traditional methods like IDW and Kriging. Several machine learning models were employed to predict the primary pollutants in Valencia in real-time, such as Linear Regression, quantile regression with the lasso method, K-nearest neighbors, decision tree regression, and Random Forest. The Root Mean Squared Error was the chosen metric to evaluate each model's efficacy.

## 3. Materials and Methods

### 3.1. Data Set

The data used for the study were obtained from two monitoring networks in the Mexico Valley area. The data on pollutants and meteorological variables were obtained from the Automatic Atmospheric Monitoring Network (RAMA) and the Meteorological Network (REDMET) of the Atmospheric Monitoring System of Mexico City (SIMAT) of the Environmental Secretariat of the Government of Mexico City [15]. Solar radiation data were obtained from the EMA stations of the CONAGUA monitoring network [16]. The study period covers from the years 2015 to 2022. The geolocation of the measurement points is shown in Figure 1.

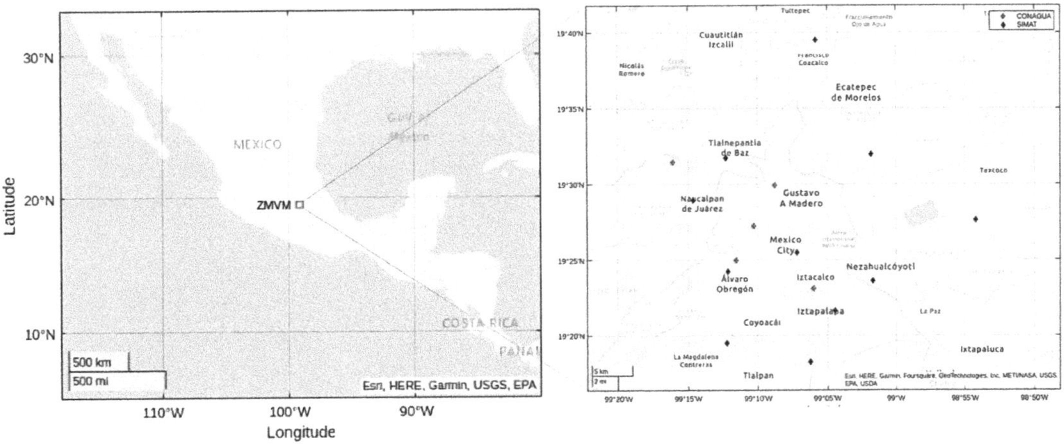


**Figure 1.** Location of measurement sites. Red diamonds belong to CONAGUA's Automatic Weather Stations, black diamonds belong to the SIMAT monitoring network of the Mexico City Environmental Secretariat.

### *3.2. Feature Vector Construction*

Feature vector construction is a critical step in the machine learning pipeline that has a profound impact on every subsequent step, from model training and evaluation to the interpretability of the results. It involves not just selecting the right features but also appropriately processing and engineering these features to best represent the problem space for the learning algorithm, hence the importance of understanding the variables within our research domain and their relationships in order to extract patterns from our data and enhance the precision of our predictions. Next, we will delve into the various factors and their influence on ozone concentrations.

The concentration of tropospheric ozone ($O_3$) is influenced by various atmospheric and meteorological factors, as mentioned in the research in Table 1, including temperature, humidity, wind direction, and wind speed. Next, we present a general overview of how each of these factors can impact ozone concentration:

1. Temperature:
    - Photochemical Reactions: Ozone formation in the troposphere is a result of photochemical reactions. Higher temperatures generally increase the rate of these reactions, leading to a faster and more efficient production of ozone.
    - Stability of the Atmosphere: On hot days, especially under high-pressure systems, the atmosphere can become more stable, trapping pollutants, including ozone and its precursors, close to the ground and increasing concentrations.
    - Volatile Organic Compound (VOC) Emissions: Higher temperatures can also lead to increased emissions of VOCs from vegetation and certain human-made sources, further promoting ozone formation.
2. Humidity:
    - $OH$ Radical Production: Water vapor can contribute to the formation of hydroxyl radicals ($OH$), which play a crucial role in oxidizing VOCs and other pollutants, leading to the production of ozone. However, the exact relationship between humidity and ozone production can be complex and might vary depending on other prevailing conditions.
    - Dilution: On the other hand, extremely high humidity levels can lead to condensation and cloud formation, which may reduce solar radiation, slowing down photochemical reactions.

3. Wind Direction:
    - Transport of Precursors: The direction of the wind can transport ozone precursors (like $NO_x$ and VOCs) from their sources to other areas. For instance, if a city has major industrial zones on its eastern side and the wind is blowing from east to west, areas downwind can experience elevated ozone levels due to the transported pollutants.
    - Clean Air Advection: Conversely, winds from rural or oceanic directions can bring cleaner air, reducing ozone concentrations.
4. Wind Speed:
    - Dispersion: Faster wind speeds can help disperse pollutants, diluting their concentration. This can decrease the buildup of ozone precursors in a particular area and reduce localized ozone formation.
    - Vertical Mixing: Strong winds, especially when accompanied by turbulence, can enhance the vertical mixing of the atmosphere, distributing ozone and its precursors over a larger vertical layer. This can lead to a decrease in ground-level ozone concentrations.

**Table 1.** Overview of research on machine learning applications for air quality forecasting models.

| Research Paper | Predicted | Predictors | Models | Metrics |
|---|---|---|---|---|
| A Machine Learning approach to investigate the build-up of surface ozone in Mexico City (2022) [6]. | $O_3$. | Temperature, Relative humidity, Wind speed and direction, $NO$, $NO_2$, UV-A and Planetary Boundary Layer Height. | Random Forest, Gradient Boosting, Deep Neural Network. | $R^2$, Index of Agreement (IOA). |
| Prediction of Air Pollutants Using Supervised Machine Learning (2021) [7]. | Air quality index for $PM_{10}$, $PM_{2.5}$, $NO_2$, $CO$, $SO_2$, $NH_3$, $O_3$. | Country, State, City, Place, Last updated, Min, Max, Average, and Pollutants($PM_{10}$, $PM_{2.5}$, $SO_2$, $CO$, $NO_2$, $O_3$). | Decision Tree, Support Vector Machine, Logistic Regression, Random Forest, Naive Bayes, K-Nearest Neighbor. | Accuracy. |
| Machine Learning-Based Prediction of Air Quality (2020) [8] | Air quality index for 1 h, 8 h, and 24 h. | $PM_{2.5}$ and $PM_{10}$ moving average, $O_3$ average of the last eight hours, $CO$ concentration for the last eight hours, Air uality index based on the maximum concentration of $PM_{10}$, $PM_{2.5}$, $NO_2$, $SO_2$, $O_3$ and $CO$. | Random Forest, AdaBoost, Support Vector Regression, Artificial Neural Network. | RMSE, MAE, $R^2$. |
| Ground-level Ozone Prediction Using Machine Learning Techniques: A Case Study in Amman, Jordan (2020) [9] | $O_3$. | Ozone, Temperature, Humidity, Wind direction, and speed, Memorable day (weekend, holiday), Day of the year. | Multi-Layer Perceptron, Support Vector Regression, Decision Tree, XGBoost. | RMSE, MAE, $R^2$. |
| An ensemble-based model of $PM_{2.5}$ concentration across the contiguous United States with high spatiotemporal resolution (2019) [10] | $PM_{2.5}$. | Satellite-derived aerosol optical depth, Satellite-based measurements, Chemical transport model predictions, Land-use variables, and Meteorological variables. | Ensemble Model (Neural Network, Random Forest, Gradient Boosting). | RMSE, $R^2$. |

**Table 1.** *Cont.*

| Research Paper | Predicted | Predictors | Models | Metrics |
|---|---|---|---|---|
| Estimation of Air Pollution in Delhi Using Machine Learning Techniques (2018) [11] | Air pollution levels for $CO$, $NO_2$, $O_3$, $SO_2$, $PM_{10}$, $PM_{2.5}$. | Vertical wind, Wind speed and direction, Temperature, and Relative humidity. | Linear Regression, Stochastic Gradient Descent, Random Forest, Decision Tree, Support Vector Regression, Multi-layer Perceptron, Gradient Boosting Adaptive Boosting. | RMSE, MAE, $R^2$. |
| A Machine Learning Approach for Air Quality Prediction: Model Regularization and Optimization (2018) [12]. | Next day concentration for $O_3$, $PM_{2.5}$, $SO_2$. | Air temperature, Relative humidity, Wind speed, and direction, Wind gust, Precipitation accumulation, Visibility, Dew point, Wind cardinal direction, Pressure, Weather conditions, Weekday/weekend, Concentration pollutant, and Bias term. | MTL with Linear Regression. | RMSE. |
| Detection and Prediction of Air Pollution Using Machine Learning Models (2018) [13]. | Classification of Samples into Polluted or Non-Polluted Categories, $PM_{2.5}$. | Temperature, Wind speed, Dew point, Pressure, $PM_{2.5}$ Concentration, Classification result. | Autoregression, Logistic Regression. | MA, SDA, MAE. |
| AirVLC: an Application for Visualizing Wind-sensitive Interpolation of Urban Air Pollution Forecasts (2016) [14]. | $NO$, $NO_2$, $SO_2$, $O_3$. | Pollution level, Meteorological conditions (Temperature, Relative humidity, Pressure, Wind speed, Rain), Calendar features (Year, Month, Day in the month, Day in the week, Hour), and Traffic intensity features. | Linear Regression, Quantile Regression, K-Nearest Neighbor, Random Forest, Decision Tree. | RMSE. |

It's essential to understand that these factors often interact in multifaceted ways. For instance, a hot, calm day might be conducive to ozone buildup due to reduced dispersion and enhanced photochemical reactions. However, if that hot day is also humid with cloud cover, the reduced sunlight might counteract some of the enhanced ozone production. For this reason, it is important to depict the relationships within the process that involves interactions between various precursor pollutants, including nitrogen oxides ($NO_x$, which includes $NO$ and $NO_2$) and volatile organic compounds (VOCs), in the presence of sunlight, as shown in the research by Lelieveld and Dentener [17], or in that by Finlayson-Pitts and Pitts [18]. Next, we provide a breakdown of this phenomenon:

1. Emission of Precursors: Primary pollutants like nitrogen oxides ($NO_x$) and volatile organic compounds (VOCs) are emitted into the atmosphere. These are typically released from automobile exhaust, industrial processes, power plants, and other combustion processes.
2. Photodissociation of Nitrogen Dioxide ($NO_2$):

$$NO_2 + hv \rightarrow NO + O \quad (1)$$

In the presence of sunlight, $NO_2$ undergoes photodissociation, breaking down into nitrogen monoxide ($NO$) and a free oxygen atom ($O$). The symbol "$hv$" represents a photon of sunlight.

3. Formation of ozone:

$$O + O_2 \rightarrow O_3 \quad (2)$$

The free oxygen atom ($O$) rapidly reacts with molecular oxygen ($O_2$) in the atmosphere to form ozone ($O_3$).

4. Reconversion:

$$NO + O_3 \rightarrow NO_2 + O_2 \quad (3)$$

Nitrogen monoxide ($NO$) can also react with the ozone ($O_3$) to form nitrogen dioxide ($NO_2$) and molecular oxygen ($O_2$). This essentially reduces the concentration of ozone.

5. VOCs Role in the Cycle: VOCs, in the presence of $NO_x$ and sunlight, can generate more reactive intermediates, which will react with $NO$ to form $NO_2$. This reaction "removes" $NO$ from the environment, allowing more ozone to form without it being quickly converted back to oxygen. In other words, the VOCs help "tie up" $NO$, preventing it from immediately destroying the ozone that's been formed.

Finally, it is important to show how the ozone concentration could be influenced by temporal factors such as the month, day of week, and hour, or by geospatial factors as longitude, latitude and altitude; you can see a brief explanation of how each of these variables might impact ozone concentration:

1. Month:
    - Sunlight Intensity and Duration: Ozone formation is a photochemical process that requires sunlight. Therefore, months with longer daylight hours and more intense sunlight, typically the spring and summer months, tend to have higher ozone concentrations.
    - Temperature: Months with warmer temperatures, typically summer months, can lead to higher ozone concentrations.
    - Vegetation Growth and Emissions: Certain months, especially spring and early summer, might see increased biogenic emissions of volatile organic compounds (VOCs) from vegetation, which can contribute to ozone formation.
2. Day of week:
    - Emissions Variability: Weekdays often have higher vehicular traffic and industrial activities compared to weekends. This can lead to higher emissions of ozone precursors like $NO_x$ on weekdays.
    - Weekend Effect: Despite reduced precursor emissions on weekends, some urban areas observe higher ozone levels during weekends, a phenomenon known as the "weekend effect." This can be due to the disproportionate reduction in $NO$ emissions compared to VOCs on weekends, altering the chemical balance and facilitating ozone production.
3. Hour:
    - Daily Cycle: Shown in the ozone concentration pattern, there are usually lower levels in the early morning because the sun has not risen or is low in the sky, reducing the intensity of UV radiation needed for ozone formation; ozone peaks during the afternoon when sunlight is most intense and temperatures are highest; in the evening, the rate of ozone production decreases, but the loss processes are slower. UV radiation needed for ozone formation changes throughout the day, affecting the intensity of UV radiation reaching the surface.
    - Emissions Patterns: Human activities, such as traffic and industrial operations, have specific hourly patterns.
    - Mixing Layer Depth: The depth of the atmospheric mixing layer changes throughout the day, affecting the dispersion of pollutants.

4. Latitude:
    - Sunlight Intensity: Near the equator (low latitudes), the sun's rays are more direct, leading to more intense UV radiation, which can enhance photochemical reactions and thus ozone formation.
    - Distribution of Emission Sources: Industrialized regions and urban centers, significant sources of ozone precursors like $NO_x$ and VOCs, may be concentrated at specific latitudes.
    - Stratospheric Intrusions: At high latitudes, stratospheric intrusions can introduce ozone-rich air from the stratosphere to the troposphere.
5. Longitude:
    - Time of Day: Due to the Earth's rotation, the position of the sun changes with longitude, affecting the daily cycle of photochemical reactions.
    - Distribution of Emission Sources: Significant emission sources might be concentrated at specific longitudes.
    - Meteorological Patterns: Weather systems vary longitudinally, especially in regions influenced by oceanic or continental effects.
6. Altitude:
    - Decreased Pressure: As altitude increases, atmospheric pressure decreases, potentially affecting ozone formation.
    - Temperature Profile: The temperature can either increase or decrease with altitude, affecting ozone concentrations.
    - Vertical Distribution of $O_3$: Ozone concentrations generally increase with altitude in the troposphere and are high in the stratosphere.
    - Transport of Ozone Precursors: Elevated regions might be exposed to ozone precursors transported from lower altitudes.

With the goal of predicting ozone concentrations in the study area with a 24-h lead time, considering the existing relationships between these variables and the influence they have on said concentrations, the feature vector was formed, as shown in Table 2.

**Table 2.** Feature vector.

| **Temporal and Geospatial Variables** | | | | | | | |
|---|---|---|---|---|---|---|---|
| longitude | latitude | | altitude | month | | weekday | hour |
| **24 h prior meteorological and pollutant variables** | | | | | | | |
| $O_3$ | $NO$ | $NO_2$ | $NO_x$ | Relative humidity (rh) | Temperature (tmp) | Wind direction (wdr) | Wind speed (wsp) |
| **Solar radiation from EMAs stations 24 h prior** | | | | | | | |
| ECOGUARDAS | TEZONTLE | | MOLINODELREY | ENCBI | | ENCBII | PRESAMADIM |
| **Meteorological variables** | | | **Pollutant variables** | | | **EMAs Stations** | |
| Mean 00to03 | | | Mean 00to03 | | | Mean 00to03 | |
| Mean 04to07 | | | Mean 04to07 | | | Mean 04to07 | |
| Mean 08to11 | | | Mean 08to11 | | | Mean 08to11 | |
| Mean 12to15 | | | Mean 12to15 | | | Mean 12to15 | |
| Mean 16to19 | | | Mean 16to19 | | | Mean 16to19 | |
| Mean 20to23 | | | Mean 20to23 | | | Mean 20to23 | |
| previous day's maximum | | | previous day's maximum | | | previous day's maximum | |
| previous day's minimum | | | previous day's minimum | | | previous day's minimum | |

The feature vector consists of 132 variables.

### 3.3. Hyperparameter Optimization

The optimization of hyperparameters in machine learning models is a process of critical importance, significantly impacting model performance and accuracy. This procedure involves fine-tuning the hyperparameters, which govern the learning algorithm's behavior and its capability to accurately interpret and learn from underlying data patterns. Optimal hyperparameter settings enhance the model's performance and improve the results obtained. One of the key roles of hyperparameter optimization is to mitigate the risks of overfitting and underfitting, striking a balance where the model is sufficiently complex to elucidate essential data patterns without being excessively tailored to the training data. This balance is crucial in ensuring the model's ability to generalize effectively from training data to new, unseen data. There are different approaches to address this issue, as mentioned by Feurer and Hutter [19]. In this research, we decided to use GridSearchCV, which has some significant advantages in its implementation but also presents some disadvantages that we need to address. The operational scheme of GridsearchCV is based on the wrapper method proposed by Kohavi and Jonh [20] and is shown in Figure 2.

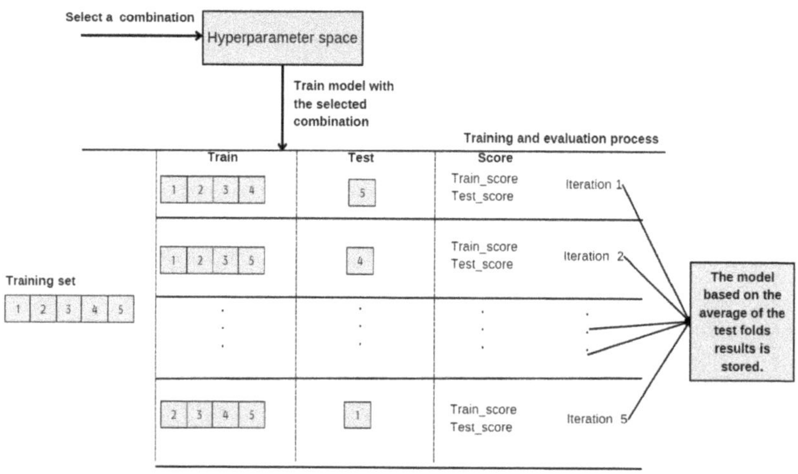


**Figure 2.** Hyperparameter optimization process: this figure shows the process of the fine-tuning of hyperparameters using the GridSearchCV tool.

GridSearchCV is a systematic approach employed in the field of machine learning for the optimization of model hyperparameters. This method is instrumental in enhancing the performance of a machine learning model by exhaustively searching through a predefined space of hyperparameter values. The fundamental premise of Grid Search is to evaluate and compare the model's performance across different combinations of hyperparameters, thereby identifying the most effective set of parameters. This process of GridSearch involves the following key steps:

1. Definition of Hyperparameter Space: The first step involves delineating the range or set of values for each hyperparameter under consideration. This set forms a grid of hyperparameter combinations, where each node represents a unique combination. The generation of this grid of options and evaluating all solutions is a task that demands too many resources and is impossible to carry out because many hyperparameters take continuous values. Therefore, it is chosen to define recommended or well-known ranges of values for these hyperparameters, creating a finite space of combinations.
2. Cross-Validation Mechanism: GridSearch is typically coupled with cross-validation to assess the performance of the model for each hyperparameter combination. Cross-validation involves dividing the training dataset into multiple smaller sets or folds. The model is trained on all but one fold (the training set) and validated on the remaining fold (the test set). This process is repeated so that each fold serves as the validation set once, ensuring comprehensive evaluation.

The utilization of cross-validation helps to improve the model's performance by reducing variance through averaging performance estimates from multiple iterations of training and testing on different data subsets. It presents a better generalization by evaluating the model on multiple subsets of the data, aiding in assessing its generalization capabilities. This is especially important for detecting overfitting, as the model's performance is evaluated on various data partitions, resulting in a more robust estimate of its accuracy on unseen data, as is mentioned in the study guided by Kohavi [21].

3. Selection of Optimal Hyperparameters: Post evaluation, the combination of hyperparameters that produces the best performance is selected based on the minimal average error of the test folds.

As mentioned before, GridSearchCV presents the advantages of increasing the model's precision and improving the generalization and potentially reduced bias in the estimation of model performance. Another advantage is that it facilitates the comparison between various model families because, although each model has its own sets of hyperparameters, the evaluation is performed based on the same metric to measure the error. On the other hand, its main disadvantage is the computational complexity that can arise for very large datasets or complex models.

The optimization process in this research was conducted utilizing the GridSearchCV tool from the Scikit-learn library [22]. The models subjected to testing included RandomForest [23], GradientBoosting [24], and Support Vector Regression (SVR) [25]. In the case of SVR, a pipeline was established to assess the impact of data scaling, involving MinMax normalization and Z-score standardization, alongside hyperparameter tuning. The comprehensive list of hyperparameters is presented in Table 3.

**Table 3.** Evaluated models.

| Model | Hyperparameters |
|---|---|
| RandomForest | Max depth : 40–50<br>Max features: 10–25 |
| SVR (kernel RBF) | Scaling: [StandardScaler, MinMaxScaler]<br>Gamma: [0.001, 0.01, 0.1, 1, 10, 100]<br>C: [0.001, 0.01, 0.1, 1, 10, 100] |
| SVR (kernel poly) | Scaling: [StandardScaler, MinMaxScaler]<br>Degree: [2, 3, 4, 5, 6, 7, 8, 9]<br>C: [0.001, 0.01, 0.1, 1, 10, 100] |
| GradientBoosting | n estimators: [1, 2, 5, 10, 20, 50, 100, 200, 300]<br>Max depth: [5, 6, 7, 8, 9, 10, 11, 12, 13, 14, 15, 16, 17, 18, 19]<br>Learning rate: [0.001, 0.01, 0.1, 0.2, 0.3, 0.4, 0.5, 0.6, 0.7, 0.8, 0.9] |

GridSearchCV is a process that can be time-consuming because it must test every combination of hyperparameters on the training sets. For this reason, Cochran's formula [26] was used for sample size selection for quantitative variables when the population size is known to train the models with a smaller sample size and reduce execution time. The formula used is shown in Equation (4).

$$n = \frac{NZ^2\sigma^2}{(N-1)E^2 + Z^2\sigma^2} \tag{4}$$

where:

$n$ = sample size.
$N$ = population size.
$Z$ = critical Z value; for a confidence level of 99%, z equals 2.58.
$\sigma^2$ = population variance.
$E$ = absolute precision level; 1% of the population's standard deviation.

The dataset, containing data from 2015 to 2022, comprises 577,031 records. The sample size selection formula determined that a sample size of 59,680 records would provide a 99% confidence level, representing 10.34% of the total records. For the validation sample, 10% of the complete dataset was chosen, resulting in 57,704 records. It is important to note that the training and validation sets are entirely exclusive.

### 3.4. Model Evaluation

As shown in the hourly profile in Figure 3, ozone concentration exhibits a clear trend with the time of day, and there is significant variation compared to the study period's mean. To effectively measure the performance of the evaluated models, their performance will be evaluated using two approaches. The first approach will involve comparing the MAE of the models with the MAE calculated for predictions based on Mean and Median strategies throughout the entire period from 2015 to 2022. The second approach will compare the MAE based on Mean and Median strategies, grouping by hour to evaluate which of the models performs better throughout the hours of the day. The reference MAE values are presented in Table 4.

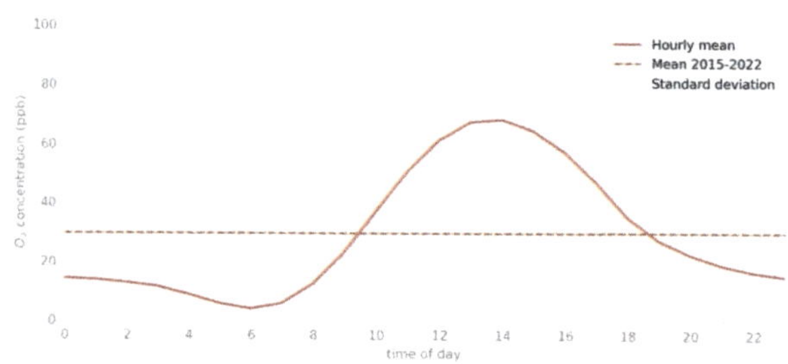


**Figure 3.** Hourly ozone concentration profile; the dashed line represents the daily average for the study period 2015–2022, and the solid line represents the hourly average, while the shaded area is the standard deviation.

**Table 4.** Baseline Mean Absolute Error.

| Timeframe | MAE from Mean | MAE from Median | Timeframe | MAE from Mean | MAE from Median |
|---|---|---|---|---|---|
| **2015–2022** | **21.53** | **20.77** | | | |
| 00:00 | 9.03 | 8.95 | 12:00 | 15.83 | 15.82 |
| 01:00 | 8.85 | 8.77 | 13:00 | 17.82 | 17.81 |
| 02:00 | 8.50 | 8.39 | 14:00 | 19.10 | 19.09 |
| 03:00 | 8.01 | 7.84 | 15:00 | 19.38 | 19.34 |
| 04:00 | 6.87 | 6.54 | 16:00 | 18.69 | 18.63 |
| 05:00 | 5.08 | 4.45 | 17:00 | 16.53 | 16.43 |
| 06:00 | 3.42 | 2.85 | 18:00 | 14.01 | 13.91 |
| 07:00 | 4.01 | 3.67 | 19:00 | 12.54 | 12.43 |
| 08:00 | 6.66 | 6.52 | 20:00 | 11.24 | 11.13 |
| 09:00 | 9.38 | 9.31 | 21:00 | 10.37 | 10.26 |
| 10:00 | 12.03 | 11.94 | 22:00 | 9.70 | 9.60 |
| 11:00 | 13.92 | 13.88 | 23:00 | 9.33 | 9.26 |

The MAE was calculated using predictions based on both the mean and median strategies applied to the complete dataset.

### 3.5. Setup for the Experiment

The programs were executed on a Beowulf cluster with Torque 3.0.3, using four computing nodes running Ubuntu 20.04.4. Each node was equipped with 2 Intel(R) Xeon(R) CPU E5-2640 v4 processors @ 2.40 GHz, featuring 20 processing cores and 128 GB of RAM. The software versions used were Anaconda 22.9.0, Python 3.9.12, and Scikit-learn 1.0.2.

## 4. Results.

### 4.1. GridSearch

The results presented in Table 5 were selected using the following criteria: the top five results were chosen for each of the models, from which the one with the lowest MAE in the test results and the one with the slightest difference between the training and test score (gap) were selected. In the case of the RandomForest model, the result with the lowest MAE in the test set also had the slightest difference between the training and test sets.

**Table 5.** Gridsearch results.

| Model | Hyperparameters | Test Score | Train Score | Gap |
|---|---|---|---|---|
| RandomForest<br>Execution time: 2600 | max depth = 45,<br>max features = 25. | 7.825020 | 2.923992 | 4.901028 |
| StandardScaler → SVR (RBF)<br>Execution time: 29,672 | C = 100,<br>gamma = 0.01. | 7.845238 | 3.350762 | 4.494476 |
| | C = 10,<br>gamma=0.001. | 8.757496 | 8.652644 | 0.104852 |
| StandardScaler → SVR (poly)<br>Execution time: 104,571 | C = 100,<br>degree = 3. | 9.062664 | 5.348223 | 3.714441 |
| | C = 10,<br>degree=2. | 11.562271 | 10.979601 | 0.582670 |
| MinMaxScaler → SVR (RBF)<br>Execution time: 22,465 | C = 100,<br>gamma = 0.1. | 7.785040 | 6.806308 | 0.978732 |
| | C = 100,<br>gamma = 0.01. | 8.700342 | 8.617988 | 0.082355 |
| MinMaxScaler → SVR (poly)<br>Execution time: 1,705,128 | C = 100,<br>degree = 3. | 7.925763 | 6.892926 | 1.032837 |
| | C = 10,<br>degree=4. | 8.060671 | 7.198237 | 0.862434 |
| GradientBoosting<br>Execution time: 42,584 | learning rate = 0.1,<br>max depth = 10,<br>max features = 12,<br>n estimators = 300. | 7.144314 | 1.735895 | 5.408419 |
| | learning rate = 0.1,<br>max depth = 9,<br>max features = 11,<br>n estimators = 300. | 7.187491 | 2.818148 | 4.369343 |

The grid search was executed using n_jobs = 20 option; the execution time unit is in seconds.

### 4.2. Optimal Model Selection

Each model listed in Table 5 underwent a comprehensive evaluation utilizing a dataset comprising 57,704 records. The derived results, systematically arranged in descending order based on their respective evaluation scores, are detailed in Table 6. Notably, every model demonstrated superior performance compared to the median of the Mean Absolute Error (MAE) observed during 2015–2022. However, selecting the optimal model requires an in-depth assessment beyond mere evaluation scores. This includes a detailed analysis of the models' hourly MAE fluctuations, as depicted in Figure 4. Additionally, a critical review of each model's computational efficiency, particularly their execution times during both the GridSearch process and subsequent training phases, is essential. This aspect of model performance is thoroughly explicated in Figure 5.

**Table 6.** Model results.

| Model | Fit Time | Evaluation Score [1] |
|---|---|---|
| GradientBoosting[0] [2] | 522 | 7.015008 |
| GradientBoosting[1] | 423 | 7.126916 |
| StandardScaler → SVR (RBF)[0] | 54,058 | 7.689650 |
| RandomForest | 392 | 7.808124 |
| MinMaxScaler → SVR (poly)[0] | 8172 | 7.901960 |
| MinMaxScaler → SVR (poly)[1] | 3250 | 8.037673 |
| MinMaxScaler → SVR (RBF)[0] | 1968 | 8.717526 |
| StandardScaler → SVR (RBF)[1] | 4191 | 8.758239 |
| StandardScaler → SVR (poly)[0] | 73,851 | 9.468176 |
| MinMaxScaler → SVR (RBF)[1] | 1959 | 10.733147 |
| StandardScaler → SVR (poly)[1] | 4242 | 11.405547 |

[1] The results are organized in descending order based on their evaluation scores. [2] The number inside the brackets represents the position within the hyperparameters column in Table 5 for each of the models.

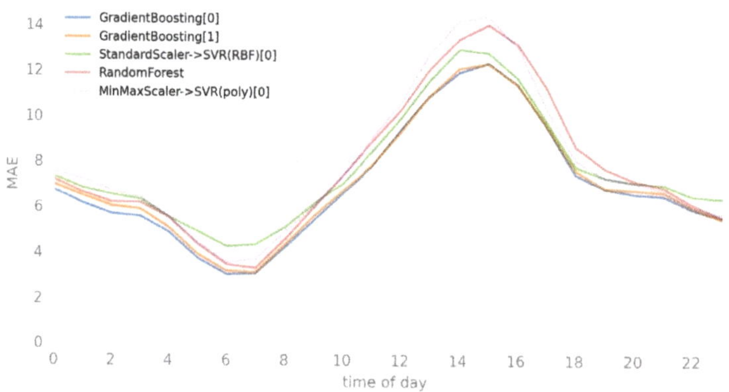


**Figure 4.** Hourly MAE Profile. This graph illustrates the variations in Mean Absolute Error (MAE) throughout the day for the top five models, as referenced in Table 6. Each model demonstrates satisfactory performance, with GradientBoosting[0] consistently exhibiting the lowest error across most periods.

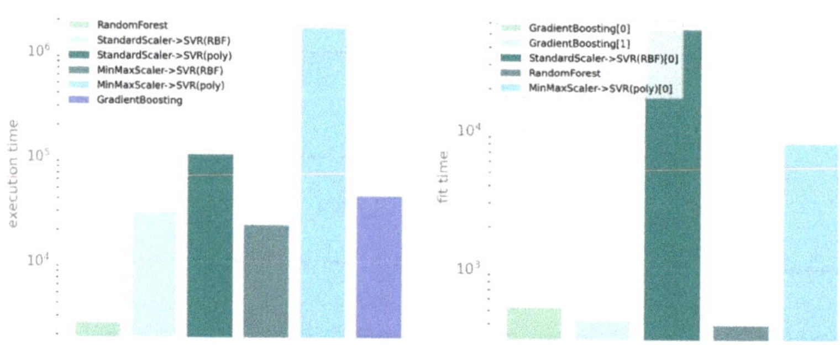


**Figure 5.** Performance Profiling. The graph on the **left** depicts the execution time for the GridSearch process as outlined in Table 5. Meanwhile, the graph on the **right** shows the specific training times of the top five models, as listed in Table 6. Notably, in both graphs, the time axis is presented on a logarithmic scale.

## 5. Discussion

This section is bifurcated into two distinct segments for a comprehensive analysis. The first segment delves into a generalized discussion centered around the performance outcomes discerned from the hyperparameter optimization processes and an evaluation of the models selected thereafter. The second segment, on the other hand, is dedicated to an in-depth analysis of the best-performing model identified through these processes.

### 5.1. General Discussion

In the GridSearch results, RandomForest showed the shortest execution time and acceptable training times with results in the Training and Testing. However, it is one of the models with the greatest difference between the Training and Test sets, indicating a slight overfitting. The SVR models that use the RBF kernel outperformed their counterparts with the polynomial kernel in terms of execution times, and they did not show significant differences in their Test scores. In general, the SVR-based models had the lowest level of overfitting, as they exhibited the smallest differences in the Training–Test gap. However, it is essential to consider the computational complexity of this model because it will consume much time when the number of records exceeds 10,000, especially when using Sklearn's SVR implementation based on libsvm. This implementation has complexities greater than quadratic $n^2$, as mentioned by Abdiansah and Wardoyo [27]. GradientBoosting achieved the best results for Train and Test scores with quite acceptable times, although it did show a higher level of overfitting due to differences in the Train–Test gap.

Concerning the evaluation results, as can be seen in Figure 4, the top five selected models show acceptable performance in terms of the MAE calculated by the time of day range, exhibiting a similar behavior. It is worth noting that the models reflect the ozone hourly profile quite well, as they capture the periods with the highest MAE during the hours when ozone concentration varies the most, from 12:00 to 18:00, as shown in Figure 3. GradientBoosting[0] exhibited lower MAE from 00:00 to 11:00, 13:00–14:00, and 17:00–22:00, while GradientBoosting[1] performed better at 12:00, 15:00–16:00, and 23:00. Therefore, the first model was selected as the one with the best performance.

An additional critical factor to consider in model selection is the execution time associated with different models, especially when dealing with a substantial volume of records. This aspect becomes increasingly significant, as large datasets can entail considerable processing durations. Consequently, the ability to conduct preliminary phases of hyperparameter optimization and model evaluation efficiently, utilizing a smaller yet adequately representative subset of the data, is imperative for effectively identifying and selecting the most suitable model.

### 5.2. Analysis of the Optimal Performing Model

Figure 6 presents an analysis of the performance exhibited by the GradientBoosting[0] model, designated as GB_99, which was trained on a subset comprising 59,680 records. This subset accounts for 10.34% of the training dataset and is statistically significant, offering a 99% confidence level, as delineated in Equation (4). In contrast, the model labeled GB_full refers to the GradientBoosting[0] variant trained on the entirety of the training dataset, encompassing 519,327 records. Additionally, the graph includes MEAN and MEDIAN, which indicate the MAE values when predictions are based on these respective statistical measures. This comparison offers insight into the efficacy and scalability of the GradientBoosting[0] model under varying training data volumes and their performance against the MEAN and MEDIAN prediction approaches.

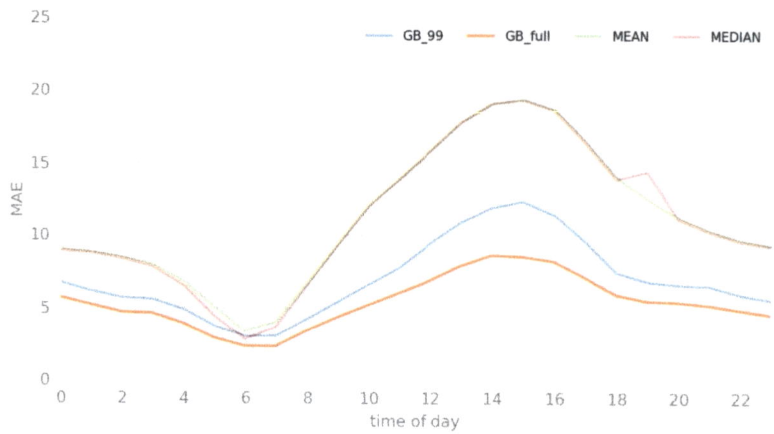


**Figure 6.** Optimal performing model hourly MAE profile. The GB_99 represents the GradientBoosting model trained on a sample size corresponding to 10.34%; GB_full denotes the GradientBoosting model trained with the entire training dataset. MEAN and MEDIAN indicate the MAE values when predictions are based on these respective statistical measures.

Table 7 compares the hourly MAE performance for the GradientBoosting[0] model. Here are some observations and opinions on these data:

- **Data Size Impact:** The GB_full model, trained on a significantly larger dataset (519,327 records) compared to GB_99 (57,704 records), consistently shows lower MAE across all timeframes. This indicates the potential benefits of training on more extensive data, likely capturing more nuances and patterns, leading to better predictive performance.
- **Performance Consistency:** Both models exhibit a similar pattern in MAE fluctuations over the 24 h, suggesting that the underlying data characteristics influencing error rates are similar for both datasets. However, the magnitude of the error is consistently lower in the GB_full model, reinforcing the value of a more extensive training set.
- **Timeframe Sensitivity:** There are periods (like early morning hours) where the MAE is relatively lower for both models and periods (like afternoon to early evening) where MAE peaks. This pattern could indicate varying model performance based on time-specific factors, suggesting that certain hours have characteristics that are either more predictable or more challenging for the model.

**Table 7.** Optimal Model's Hourly MAE Performance.

| Timeframe | GB_99 | GB_full | Timeframe | GB_99 | GB_full |
|---|---|---|---|---|---|
| 00:00 | 6.772 | 5.754 | 12:00 | 9.444 | 6.893 |
| 01:00 | 6.172 | 5.223 | 13:00 | 10.905 | 7.919 |
| 02:00 | 5.709 | 4.718 | 14:00 | 11.932 | 8.639 |
| 03:00 | 5.595 | 4.645 | 15:00 | 12.345 | 8.546 |
| 04:00 | 4.9 | 3.941 | 16:00 | 11.413 | 8.22 |
| 05:00 | 3.76 | 2.958 | 17:00 | 9.582 | 7.125 |
| 06:00 | 3.054 | 2.39 | 18:00 | 7.443 | 5.932 |
| 07:00 | 3.088 | 2.369 | 19:00 | 6.824 | 5.493 |
| 08:00 | 4.239 | 3.441 | 20:00 | 6.6 | 5.428 |
| 09:00 | 5.44 | 4.377 | 21:00 | 6.521 | 5.217 |
| 10:00 | 6.628 | 5.218 | 22:00 | 5.924 | 4.885 |
| 11:00 | 7.789 | 6.05 | 23:00 | 5.565 | 4.567 |

In total, 57,704 records were used to calculate the MAE for the GB_99 model, while in the case of GB_full, 519,327 records were used.

The comparison between the "Optimal Model's Hourly MAE Performance" (Table 7) and the "Baseline Mean Absolute Error" (Table 4) is quite revealing in terms of understanding the effectiveness of the Gradient Boosting (GB) models relative to basic baseline methods. Here are some observations and opinions on these data:

- Significant Improvement Over Baseline: Both Gradient Boosting models (GB_99 and GB_full) consistently outperform the baseline models across almost all timeframes. The MAEs for the baseline methods are significantly higher than those for the Gradient Boosting models, indicating the superior predictive capability of the latter.
- Effectiveness of Machine Learning Models: The considerable reduction in MAE when using the Gradient Boosting models compared to the baseline methods illustrates the value of machine learning in capturing complex patterns and relationships in the data that simple statistical measures cannot.

## 6. Conclusions

Based on the results obtained in the present research, the following conclusions have been reached:

- Machine learning models are a significant alternative for ozone concentration forecasting. However, it is paramount to identify the variables influencing the phenomenon in constructing the feature vector. This enables the models to discern patterns and relationships among the variables correctly.
- Computational complexity can significantly impact the best model selection, as the computational resources required for hyperparameter optimization can be time-consuming and may not be feasible.
- A substantial volume of historical records to train models can enhance their precision. However, certain models do not efficiently handle large datasets, leading to disproportionately increased evaluation times. Therefore, employing a technique that allows for selecting a sufficiently representative sample to achieve results with an acceptable level of reliability without adversely affecting the outcomes of the models is of paramount importance. This approach ensures both the effectiveness and efficiency of the model training and evaluation process.
- Establishing a baseline is a critical step in model evaluation. It helps set realistic expectations and understand the value added by complex models.
- The GB models' lower MAE scores, especially compared to the relatively high baseline MAEs, suggest that these models have successfully captured significant underlying trends and patterns in the hourly ozone concentration profile.
- Elevated errors observed during specific time intervals warrant further investigation as potential focal points for future enhancements in model performance. Delving into the underlying reasons for these heightened error rates during particular hours and exploring what additional data or modifications in feature engineering might mitigate these discrepancies could yield significant advancements in model accuracy and reliability.
- Tree-based models like Random Forests or Gradient Boosting demonstrated better generalization to unseen data, but they tend to be more prone to overfitting than SVR models. This might necessitate more frequent retraining of tree-based models compared to SVR. However, given their shorter training times, they still present a better option in terms of model maintainability.

**Author Contributions:** All authors have contributed equally to this research. Conceptualization, R.D.-G. and M.A.-V.; methodology, R.D.-G. and M.A.-V.; software, R.D.-G.; validation, R.D.-G. and M.A.-V.; formal analysis, R.D.-G.; investigation, R.D.-G.; resources, R.D.-G. and M.A.-V.; data curation, R.D.-G.; writing—original draft preparation, R.D.-G.; writing—review and editing, R.D.-G. and M.A.-V.; visualization, R.D.-G.; supervision, R.D.-G. and M.A.-V.; project administration, R.D.-G. All authors have read and agreed to the published version of the manuscript.

**Funding:** This research received no external funding.

**Institutional Review Board Statement:** Not applicable.

**Informed Consent Statement:** Not applicable.

**Data Availability Statement:** The data utilized in this study are publicly accessible via the Atmospheric Monitoring System of Mexico City, under the auspices of the Environmental Secretariat of the Mexico City Government [15] and the EMA stations of the CONAGUA monitoring network [16]. Additionally, the software and datasets employed for the assessment of the machine learning models are available in the GitHub repository at https://github.com/ruy2311/EMLMOCFMVM, accessed on 30 November 2023.

**Acknowledgments:** Thanks to the High-Performance Computing Department at the Center for Advanced Materials Research (CIMAV) for providing resources from the prometeo.cimav.edu.mx cluster.

**Conflicts of Interest:** The authors declare no conflict of interest.

## Abbreviations

The following abbreviations are used in this manuscript:

| | |
|---|---|
| ANN | Artificial Neural Network |
| AQI | Air Quality Index |
| CO | Carbon Monoxide |
| CONAGUA | Comisión Nacional del Agua |
| GB | Gradient Boosting |
| IOA | Index of Agreement |
| MAE | Mean Absolute Error |
| ML | Machine Learning |
| NO | Nitric Oxide |
| $NO_2$ | Nitrogen Dioxide |
| $NO_x$ | Nitrogen oxides |
| $O_3$ | Ozone |
| OH | Hydroxyl radicals |
| $PM_{10}$ | Particulate matter 10 μm or less in diameter |
| $PM_{2.5}$ | Particulate matter 2.5 μm or less in diameter |
| $R^2$ | Coefficient of determination |
| RAMA | Automatic Atmospheric Monitoring Network |
| REDMET | Meteorological Network |
| RF | Random Forest |
| RH | Relative humidity |
| RMSE | Root Mean Square Error |
| SIMAT | Atmospheric Monitoring System of Mexico City |
| $SO_2$ | Sulfur dioxide |
| SVR | Support Vector Regression |
| tmp | Temperature |
| VOC | Volatile Organic Compound |
| wdr | Wind direction |
| wsp | Wind speed |

## References

1. Molina, L.T.; Madronich, S.; Gaffney, J.S.; Apel, E.; de Foy, B.; Fast, J.; Ferrare, R.; Herndon, S.; Jimenez, J.L.; Lamb, B.; et al. An overview of the MILAGRO 2006 Campaign: Mexico City emissions and their transport and transformation. *Atmos. Chem. Phys.* **2010**, *10*, 8697–8760. [CrossRef]
2. Rojas-Martinez, R.; Perez-Padilla, R.; Olaiz-Fernandez, G.; Mendoza-Alvarado, L.; Moreno-Macias, H.; Fortoul, T.; McDonnell, W.; Loomis, D.; Romieu, I. Lung Function Growth in Children with Long-Term Exposure to Air Pollutants in Mexico City. *Am. J. Respir. Crit. Care Med.* **2007**, *176*, 377–384. [CrossRef] [PubMed]
3. Baldasano, J.; Valera, E.; Jimenez, P. Air quality data from large cities. *Sci. Total Environ.* **2003**, *307*, 141–165. [CrossRef] [PubMed]
4. Karthik L, B.; Sujith, B.; Rizwan A, S.; Sehgal, M. Characteristics of the Ozone Pollution and its Health Effects in India. *Int. J. Med. Public Health* **2017**, *7*, 56–60. [CrossRef]
5. Niu, Y.; Zhou, Y.; Chen, R.; Yin, P.; Meng, X.; Wang, W.; Liu, C.; Ji, J.S.; Qiu, Y.; Kan, H.; et al. Long-term exposure to ozone and cardiovascular mortality in China: A nationwide cohort study. *Lancet Planet. Health* **2022**, *6*, e496–e503. [CrossRef] [PubMed]

6. Ahmad, M.; Rappenglück, B.; Osibanjo, O.; Retama, A. A machine learning approach to investigate the build-up of surface ozone in Mexico-City. *J. Clean. Prod.* **2022**, *379*, 134638. [CrossRef]
7. Yarragunta, S.; Nabi, M.A.; Jeyanthi, P.; Revathy, S. Prediction of Air Pollutants Using Supervised Machine Learning. In Proceedings of the 2021 5th International Conference on Intelligent Computing and Control Systems (ICICCS), Madurai, India, 6–8 May 2021; pp. 1633–1640. Available online: https://ieeexplore.ieee.org/document/9432078 (accessed on 30 November 2023).
8. Liang, Y.C.; Maimury, Y.; Chen, A.H.L.; Juarez, J.R.C. Machine Learning-Based Prediction of Air Quality. *Appl. Sci.* **2020**, *10*, 9151. [CrossRef]
9. Aljanabi, M.; Shkoukani, M.; Hijjawi, M. Ground-level Ozone Prediction Using Machine Learning Techniques: A Case Study in Amman, Jordan. *Int. J. Autom. Comput.* **2020**, *17*, 667–677. [CrossRef]
10. Di, Q.; Amini, H.; Shi, L.; Kloog, I.; Silvern, R.; Kelly, J.; Sabath, M.B.; Choirat, C.; Koutrakis, P.; Lyapustin, A.; et al. An ensemble-based model of PM2.5 concentration across the contiguous United States with high spatiotemporal resolution. *Environ. Int.* **2019**, *130*, 104909. [CrossRef]
11. Srivastava, C.; Singh, S.; Singh, A.P. Estimation of Air Pollution in Delhi Using Machine Learning Techniques. In Proceedings of the 2018 International Conference on Computing, Power and Communication Technologies (GUCON), Greater Noida, India, 28–29 September 2018; pp. 304–309. [CrossRef]
12. Zhu, D.; Cai, C.; Yang, T.; Zhou, X. A Machine Learning Approach for Air Quality Prediction: Model Regularization and Optimization. *Big Data Cogn. Comput.* **2018**, *2*, 5. [CrossRef]
13. Aditya, C.R.; Deshmukh, C.R.; Nayana, D.K.; Vidyavastu, P.G. Detection and Prediction of Air Pollution using Machine Learning Models. *Int. J. Eng. Trends Technol.* **2018**, *59*, 204–207. [CrossRef]
14. Contreras-Ochando, L.; Ferri, C. airVLC: An Application for Visualizing Wind-Sensitive Interpolation of Urban Air Pollution Forecasts. In Proceedings of the 2016 IEEE 16th International Conference on Data Mining Workshops (ICDMW), Barcelona, Spain, 12–15 December 2016; pp. 1296–1299. Available online: https://ieeexplore.ieee.org/document/7836819 (accessed on 30 November 2023).
15. CDMX, G. Dirección de Monitoreo Atmosférico. 2003. Available online: http://www.aire.cdmx.gob.mx/aire/default.php (accessed on 18 January 2023).
16. México, G. Estaciones Meteorológicas Automáticas (EMAS). 2008. Available online: https://smn.conagua.gob.mx/es/observando-el-tiempo/estaciones-meteorologicas-automaticas-ema-s (accessed on 23 March 2023).
17. Lelieveld, J.; Dentener, F.J. What controls tropospheric ozone? *J. Geophys. Res. Atmos.* **2000**, *105*, 3531–3551. [CrossRef]
18. Finlayson-Pitts, B.; Pitts, J. Atmospheric Chemistry of Tropospheric Ozone Formation: Scientific and Regulatory Implications. *Air Waste* **1993**, *43*, 1091–1100. [CrossRef]
19. Feurer, M.; Hutter, F. Hyperparameter Optimization. In *Automated Machine Learning*; Hutter, F., Kotthoff, L., Vanschoren, J., Eds.; Series Title: The Springer Series on Challenges in Machine Learning; Springer: Cham, Switzerland; pp. 3–33. Available online: https://link.springer.com/chapter/10.1007/978-3-030-05318-5_12019 (accessed on 30 November 2023).
20. Kohavi, R.; John, G.H. Automatic Parameter Selection by Minimizing Estimated Error. In *Machine Learning Proceedings 1995*; Elsevier: Amsterdam, The Netherlands, 1995; pp. 304–312. Available online: https://www.sciencedirect.com/science/article/abs/pii/B9781558603776500451?via%3Dihub (accessed on 30 November 2023).
21. Kohavi, R. A Study of Cross-Validation and Bootstrap for Accuracy Estimation and Model Selection. In Proceedings of the 14th International Joint Conference on Artificial Intelligence-Volume 2, Montreal, QC, Canada, 20–25 August 1995; IJCAI'95, pp. 1137–1143.
22. Pedregosa, F.; Varoquaux, G.; Gramfort, A.; Michel, V.; Thirion, B.; Grisel, O.; Blondel, M.; Prettenhofer, P.; Weiss, R.; Dubourg, V.; et al. Scikit-learn: Machine Learning in Python. *J. Mach. Learn. Res.* **2011**, *12*, 2825–2830.
23. Liu, Y.; Wang, Y.; Zhang, J. New Machine Learning Algorithm: Random Forest. In *Information Computing and Applications*; Series Title: Lecture Notes in Computer Science; Hutchison, D., Kanade, T., Kittler, J., Kleinberg, J.M., Mattern, F., Mitchell, J.C., Naor, M., Nierstrasz, O., Pandu Rangan, C., Steffen, B., et al., Eds.; Springer: Berlin/Heidelberg, Germany, 2012; Volume 7473, pp. 246–252. [CrossRef]
24. Friedman, J.H. Greedy Function Approximation: A Gradient Boosting Machine. *Ann. Stat.* **2001**, *29*, 1189–1232. [CrossRef]
25. Smola, A.J.; Schölkopf, B. A tutorial on support vector regression. *Stat. Comput.* **2004**, *14*, 199–222. [CrossRef]
26. Cochran, W.G. *Sampling Techniques*, 3rd ed.; John Wiley: Hoboken, NJ, USA, 1977.
27. Abdiansah, A.; Wardoyo, R. Time Complexity Analysis of Support Vector Machines (SVM) in LibSVM. *Int. J. Comput. Appl.* **2015**, *128*, 28–34. [CrossRef]

*applied sciences*

MDPI

*Article*

# Deep-Learning-Based Approach for Automated Detection of Irregular Walking Surfaces for Walkability Assessment with Wearable Sensor

**Hui R. Ng [1,*], Xin Zhong [1], Yunwoo Nam [2] and Jong-Hoon Youn [1,*]**

[1] Department of Computer Science, University of Nebraska Omaha, Omaha, NE 68182, USA; xzhong@unomaha.edu

[2] Community and Regional Planning, University of Nebraska-Lincoln, Lincoln, NE 68588, USA; ynam2@unl.edu

* Correspondence: hng@unomaha.edu (H.R.N.); jyoun@unomaha.edu (J.-H.Y.)

**Abstract:** A neighborhood's walkability is associated with public health, economic and environmental benefits. The state of the walking surface on sidewalks is a key factor in assessing walkability, as it promotes pedestrian movement and exercise. Yet, conventional practices for assessing sidewalks are labor-intensive and rely on subject-matter experts, rendering them subjective, inefficient and ineffective. Wearable sensors can be utilized to address these limitations. This study proposes a novel classification method that employs a long short-term memory (LSTM) network to analyze gait data gathered from a single wearable accelerometer to automatically identify irregular walking surfaces. Three different input modalities—raw acceleration data, single-stride and multi-stride hand-crafted accelerometer-based gait features—were explored and their effects on the classification performance of the proposed method were compared and analyzed. To verify the effectiveness of the proposed approach, we compared the performance of the LSTM models to the traditional baseline support vector machine (SVM) machine learning method presented in our previous study. The results from the experiment demonstrated the effectiveness of the proposed framework, thereby validating its feasibility. Both LSTM networks trained with single-stride and multi-stride gait feature modalities outperformed the baseline SVM model. The LSTM network trained with multi-stride gait features achieved the highest average AUC of 83%. The classification performance of the LSTM model trained with single-stride gait features further improved to an AUC of 88% with post-processing, making it the most effective model. The proposed classification framework serves as an unbiased, user-oriented tool for conducting sidewalk surface condition assessments.

**Keywords:** deep learning; gait analysis; sidewalk surface assessment; walkability; wearable sensor

## 1. Introduction

Walking is one of the most common forms of physical activity that promotes individual mental and physical well-being. There are many health, environmental and economic benefits associated with high walking levels in communities [1–4], which has led to increased interest in maintaining walkable neighborhoods through walkability assessments. Walkability can be defined as the way individuals perceive the quality of the walking environment by measuring the friendliness of the built environment to walking [1,4]. Although many built environment features are used to define walkability, the presence and quality of sidewalks serve as substantial indicators influencing the perceived safety and overall satisfaction within the pedestrian environment [5,6]. Therefore, sidewalk assessments are an essential component of walkability assessment tools [7].

Pedestrian interviews or surveys are examples of commonly practiced sidewalk assessment methods that consider pedestrians' perceptions [8]. Nevertheless, these responses can be biased and lack expert insight. Government agencies also rely on trained experts to perform on-site inspections to identify violations of pre-defined regulations [9]. These conventional practices are ineffective and inefficient because they require significant financial expenditure, time and intensive labor.

Hitherto, the limitations mentioned above can be addressed with the advancement of sensing technology. The methods for automated sidewalk assessments can be divided into two categories: approaches based on infrastructure-based data collected from the surroundings and approaches based on wearable sensor data.

For approaches based on infrastructure-based data, various advanced methods have been presented for applying deep learning techniques on infrastructure-based data to automate sidewalk assessments. Some examples of these urban data include street-view images, videos or geographic information system (GIS) data. Several works have also explored using deep learning approaches on vehicle responses measured with smartphone inertial sensors mounted on vehicles to identify sidewalk and roadway anomalies. However, these approaches do not consider the involvement of pedestrians in their evaluations.

On the other hand, utilizing wearable sensors for automated sidewalk assessments considers individuals' behaviors. Wearable sensors can be placed on pedestrians to measure human physiological reactions and the signals captured can in turn be used to examine how human physiological reactions are influenced as a result of their surrounding environments. Earlier studies demonstrated that various sidewalk features or defects led to changes in human response. Yet, these studies focused on investigating the association of signal magnitude or specific gait parameters with surface conditions or built environments with statistical modeling.

Thus far, there have been limited studies involving pedestrians in sidewalk surface condition assessments using machine learning or deep learning techniques. Nevertheless, existing works were either not generalizable to individual differences due to the absence of gait features, thereby lacking the ability to capture biomechanical characteristics, or the focus was not on assessing sidewalk surface conditions for the purpose of a walkability assessment. To the best of our knowledge, none of the existing works explored incorporating gait analysis techniques with machine learning or deep learning approaches for sidewalk surface assessments. To bridge this gap, in our previous study [10], we identified the ideal body location for placing a sensor, which is at the right ankle. Then, we developed a traditional machine-learning-based classification framework for identifying irregular walking surfaces using gait features extracted from the right-ankle sensor to train machine learning models and demonstrated the effectiveness of the approach [10]. Nonetheless, the traditional machine-learning-based method requires manual feature extraction and selection, which can be time-consuming and labor-intensive. Considering one of the main advantages of deep learning is its automated feature learning capability on raw data [11], adopting a deep-learning-based approach could circumvent manual feature extraction and selection. Furthermore, when a deep-learning-based approach is fed with handcrafted features, knowledge can be distilled from those features to improve performance [12]. Therefore, in this paper, we introduced a novel deep-learning-based classification framework that analyzed the acceleration data from a single right-ankle sensor for the automated detection of irregular walking surfaces. The acceleration data collected from the right-ankle sensors of 12 subjects from our previous experiment were labelled and applied to our proposed approach. Concretely, because the acceleration data were collected in a time series manner, we proposed using a deep LSTM network. Three different input modalities—raw accelerometer data, single-stride and multi-stride hand-crafted accelerometer-based gait features—were explored, and their effects on the classification performance of the proposed framework were compared and analyzed. To verify the effectiveness and feasibility of our approach, the classification performance of our proposed approach was compared to the traditional machine-learning-based method from our previous study.

This paper provided the following contributions:

1. We presented a novel classification framework using a deep LSTM network to distinguish good and irregular walking surfaces with a single wearable sensor placed on the right ankle. To the best of our knowledge, no existing studies in the walkability assessment domain have proposed a framework that combines deep learning and gait analysis techniques to analyze wearable sensor data for the purpose of conducting sidewalk surface assessments.
2. We compared the performance of three different input modalities for the LSTM-based framework and identified the most suitable modality. It was shown that the LSTM networks that took gait feature modalities as the input were able to achieve convergence and robust performance with limited samples compared to the LSTM networks fed with raw data modalities.
3. We demonstrated that the LSTM networks with gait feature modalities could outperform conventional machine-learning-based methods in the problem domain.
4. We showed that post-processing on several consecutive per-stride predictions of LSTM networks fed with single-stride gait feature modalities to generate final predictions on a larger segment could improve classification performance.

The rest of the paper is organized in the following manner: We first discuss a review of related works. Next, we present the research methodology utilized in this work, followed by the experiments section where the experimental setup and results are presented. Lastly, a discussion on the findings and implications of this study is provided.

This paper was based on Chapter 4 of the first author's master's thesis [13].

## 2. Related Works

### 2.1. Conventional Methods for Sidewalk Assessments

Some of the prevalent methods employed to maintain sidewalk facilities have relied on conducting pedestrian surveys, interviews and self-reporting [8]. However, these methods are subjective, rely on pedestrians' voluntary participation, lack reliability and are inadequate in providing a comprehensive analysis of sidewalk defects [8]. Governmental agencies also often conduct field inspections carried out by trained inspectors to identify regulatory violations [9]. Studies have also explored new ways to enhance conventional sidewalk assessment practices. Sousa et al. presented a multi-criteria sorting methodology to evaluate sidewalk performance [14]. Meanwhile, Corazza et al. proposed an evaluation index for sidewalk conditions that was derived from the standardized pavement condition index (PCI) used for roads and airports [15]. Nonetheless, these methods require significant labor and financial resources [9]. Additionally, scaling these methods for larger cities poses considerable challenges.

### 2.2. Machine Learning Methods with Hand-Crafted Features for Automated Sidewalk Assessments

With the rapid progress in sensing technologies, multiple research studies have shown the feasibility of detecting various sidewalk features or defects by utilizing wearable sensors to measure pedestrians' physiological responses [8,16,17]. Studies have also examined the impacts of irregular and uneven surfaces on human walking patterns [18–22]. However, these studies were inference-based, aiming to uncover relationships between signal magnitude or specific gait parameters and surface conditions or the built environments.

Consequently, to stimulate advancements in automated sidewalk assessments, few studies have explored the automated assessment of road or surface conditions that integrate human bodily responses utilizing robust machine learning or deep learning techniques. One study [23] utilized features extracted from raw acceleration data gathered from pedestrians' smartphones to train a conventional machine learning model to detect barriers and obstacles in a large area. Takahashi et al. [24] proposed a step-classifying algorithm to detect steps based on features extracted from $x$-axis accelerations gathered from smartphones affixed onto cyclists. Kobayashi et al. predicted different sidewalk surface types using random forest and acceleration data from smartphones stored in pedestrians' front pockets [25]. In our previous study [10], we proposed a traditional machine learning approach that analyzes hand-crafted accelerometer-based gait features extracted from a right-ankle sensor.

### 2.3. Deep Learning Methods for Automated Sidewalk Assessments

Numerous advanced deep-learning-based approaches have been developed for the automated evaluation of roadways or sidewalks utilizing infrastructure-based data such as images, videos or GIS technologies [26–32]. In one study [33], acceleration data from smartphones mounted on vehicles were used to train deep learning models for road surface monitoring and pothole detection. However, determining the presence of poor sidewalk conditions relies on how individuals interact with sidewalks [34], and such interactions can vary in different contexts [35]. Infrastructure-based data and data collected from moving vehicles, nonetheless, fail to address how the human body reacts to external walking environments [36]. Individuals respond differently to the same surroundings based on their characteristics; therefore, their variability must be analyzed [8].

Limited studies have applied deep neural networks to analyze human responses for walking surface condition detection. Kim et al. verified the effectiveness of a cascaded LSTM-based deep recurrent neural network method to classify abnormal and normal gaits, and demonstrated that the ratio of abnormal gaits could indicate the existence of an environmental barrier to walkability, as they were highly correlated [37]. The confirmed relationship between the ratio of abnormal gaits and the presence of an environmental barrier is in line with our observation of a higher rate of disrupted gaits on irregular walking surface segments. However, the focus of their study on the environmental barrier was on surrounding facilities instead of sidewalk conditions. Hu et al. demonstrated the effectiveness of using deep learning approaches to analyze data from six wearable sensors placed on different body locations to identify irregular walking surfaces [38]. However, the surfaces that were tested in the study did not accurately reflect the usual uneven surfaces found on sidewalks in neighborhoods. Furthermore, deploying sensors at various locations for continuous monitoring in real-time is impractical due to the computational demands of processing data from multiple locations [39], as well as the discomfort caused by wearing multiple sensors. Kobayashi et al. also expanded their study to propose a deep learning approach by training a convolutional neural network (CNN) with acceleration data and window-based features extracted from smartphones [40]. The limitation of this approach is that the models trained with features extracted from smartphone data using a sliding window were unable to be generalized to individual differences.

To address the gaps in existing works and to improve the prediction performance of the traditional machine-learning-based classification framework from our previous study [10], we introduced a novel deep-LSTM-based classification framework to automatically detect irregular walking surfaces with a single wearable sensor in this paper. In our previous study [10], we identified the right ankle as the ideal location for sensor placement for detecting irregular walking surfaces. Hence, in this paper, we used the acceleration data collected from a right-ankle sensor from our previous experiment and the traditional machine learning approach as the benchmark to validate the feasibility of our proposed deep LSTM framework.

## 3. Materials and Methods

### 3.1. Proposed Framework

Figure 1 illustrates the overview of the proposed framework. The data collection and labelling process is described in Section 3.2. The measured raw acceleration data from the previous study were pre-processed in three different ways to generate three different modalities to feed distinct LSTM networks, because the workflow for implementing a recurrent deep learning method differs based on the input modality, which is discussed in Section 3.3. Next, hyper-parameters for each LSTM network had to be tuned to determine the optimal network structure for each input modality. The setup is discussed in Section 4.1.

Finally, all LSTM networks were then evaluated with the leave-one-subject-out test set procedure. All five scenarios of irregular walking surfaces were consolidated into a single class labeled as "Irregular", framing the problem as a binary classification task.

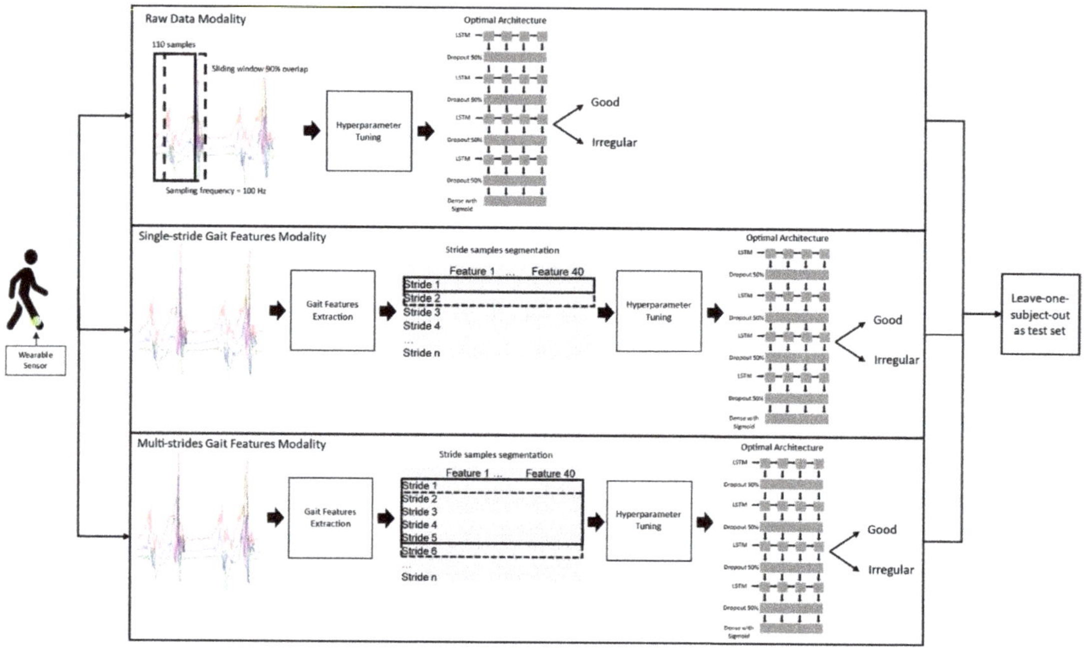


**Figure 1.** Overview of the proposed framework.

### *3.2. Data Collection*

We used the data collected from the accelerometer positioned at the right ankle of 12 subjects from our previous experiment [10] for this study, since the right ankle was determined to be the most suitable location to identify irregular walking surfaces. To collect the acceleration data, we conducted the experiment at The Peter Kiewit Institute of the University of Nebraska at Omaha. We selected a segment of a well-paved, smooth and leveled walking route in that area and denoted the starting and ending points. Then, four irregular walking surface segments were set up within that path: a segment covered in grass, an object-obstructed segment, an uneven segment and a segment covered with debris. These segments represented irregular sidewalk walking surfaces that are highly probable in less walkable neighborhoods in the real-world. The good and irregular walking segments are shown in Figure 2.

We recruited twelve healthy participants, comprising eight males and four females, for this study. A tri-axial accelerometer was affixed at the right ankle on each subject, as shown in Figure 3. It was affixed to the outer side of the shoe of each participant. We measured the linear acceleration along the X, Y and Z axes of the subject's body with Mbient sensors (MetaMotionR, Mbient Lab, San Francisco, CA, USA) that were configured to capture data at a rate of 100 Hz. The subjects were directed to walk at their usual pace along the path, starting from the initial point, proceeding towards the endpoint and then returning to the starting point along the reverse path. Video recordings were taken throughout the experiment for each subject to help facilitate data labeling.

**Figure 2.** Good and irregular walking surfaces; (**a**) well-paved (good), even; (**b**) grassed surface (irregular); (**c**) surface obstructed with objects (irregular); (**d**) uneven (irregular); and (**e**) surface covered with debris (irregular).

**Figure 3.** Placement of sensor at the right ankle of a subject.

Figure 4 displays the raw acceleration measurements captured with the right-ankle sensor of a subject. The figure visualizes an individual's gait for five seconds, which is equivalent to 500 data points. The raw acceleration data points were categorized by cross-referencing with the experiment videos.

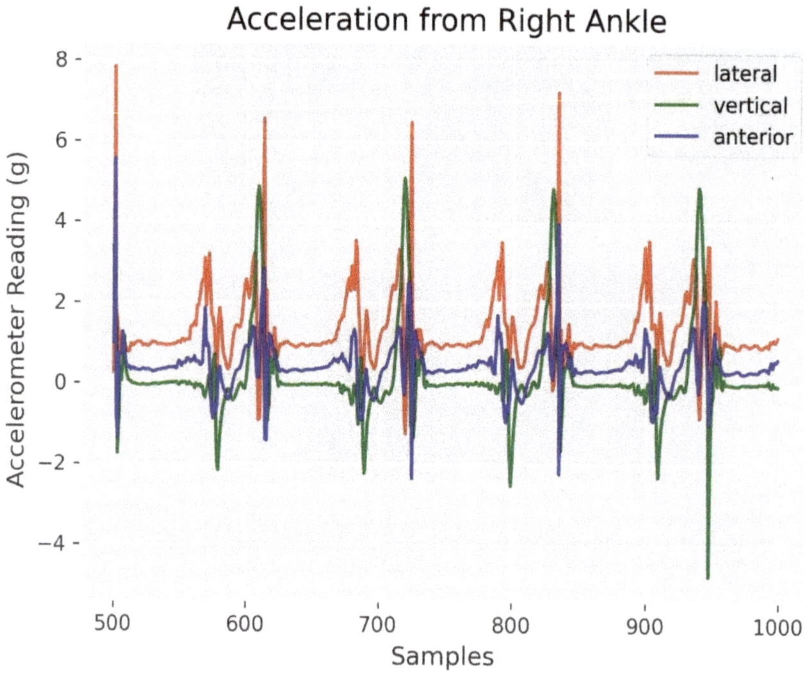


**Figure 4.** Five seconds of raw walking acceleration signal of a subject captured with a sensor positioned at the right ankle.

### 3.3. Data Pre-Processing

The acceleration data from the accelerometer positioned at the right ankle of subjects were analyzed to discriminate between good and irregular walking surfaces. As shown in Figure 5, the X, Y and Z axes of the right ankle accelerometer captured acceleration data corresponding to motion in the vertical (V), antero-posterior (AP) and medio-lateral (ML) directions, respectively.

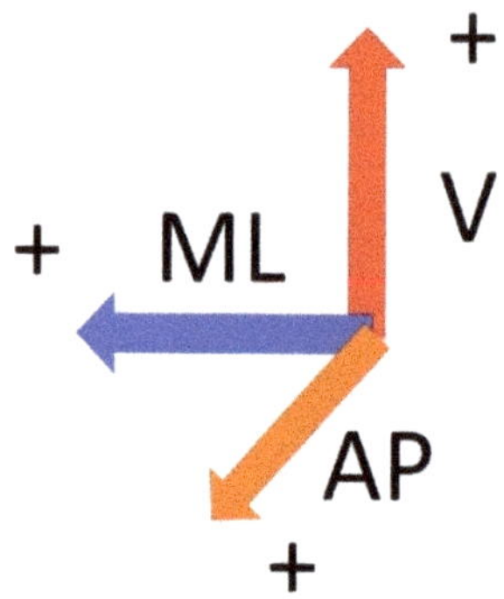


**Figure 5.** Accelerometers' directions for right ankle.

To compare how the three different modalities affected the classification performance of the proposed network, three distinct LSTM models had to be trained and fed with different data dimensions. The raw acceleration data needed to be pre-processed as described in the following section.

#### 3.3.1. Raw Data Modality

We collected a total of 646,500 samples of right-ankle raw acceleration data, with 426,500 samples falling on good walking surfaces and 220,000 samples on irregular walking surfaces, as shown in Table 1. Since taking large values directly to train a LSTM network could lead to large gradient updates that would result in a slower convergence or even divergence of the training process, we normalized our input data to have a standard deviation of 1 and a mean of 0. The input to be fed into the network had to be fixed-size sequential data, which was a short time series segmented from the raw acceleration signal. Therefore, the acceleration data were sampled into each segment with a 1.10 s fixed-width sliding window, which is equivalent to 110 data points, with a 90% overlap between them. Since the acceleration data had X, Y and Z dimensions, the sliding window would sample data points from all three dimensions into each segment, resulting in a three-dimensional input segment vector.

**Table 1.** Distribution of class labels of raw acceleration data.

| Label | Count | Percentage |
|---|---|---|
| Good | 426,500 | 66% |
| Irregular | 220,000 | 34% |
| Total | 646,500 | 100% |

This window size was chosen because each window should have included at least one complete period [41], which was one stride. The average stride time for all subjects was 1.10 s. The 90% overlap rate was chosen because it would result in more segmented data samples due to the limitation of our sample size. Additionally, an overlap between windows would carry information from the previous window.

#### 3.3.2. Single-Stride and Multi-Stride Gait Feature Modalities

For the training of the proposed network using gait features, we adopted the same gait features employed in our previous study [10]. The extracted features were shown to be useful and robust in training predictive models in previous mobility studies [42,43], since these features captured the biomechanical gait characteristics of various phases of a person's gait cycle. To extract the gait features from raw acceleration data, the first step involved segmenting the raw acceleration data into strides using the AP directional acceleration of the accelerometer [42]. Next, we computed 20 base gait features from the segmented strides before computing the variability of those gait features between strides, thereby resulting in a total of 40 gait features [10]. A complete description of the base gait features can be found in Table 2, while the distribution of stride samples for each label is shown in Table 3.

**Table 2.** Description of extracted base features.

| Gait Feature | Gait Feature Description | Gait Feature Formula |
|---|---|---|
| VM | Magnitude of the vector for the entire stride | $\sqrt{ML^2+V^2+AP^2}$ computed from the acceleration of the three axes for the entire stride |
| VM5 | Magnitude of the vector for the first 5% portion of the stride | $\sqrt{ML^2+V^2+AP^2}$ computed from the acceleration of the three axes for the first 5% portion of the stride |
| LVM | Magnitude of the vector of the ML axis for the entire stride | $\sqrt{ML^2}$ computed from the acceleration of the ML axis for the entire stride |
| VVM | Magnitude of the vector of the V axis for the entire stride | $\sqrt{V^2}$ computed from the acceleration of the V axis for the entire stride |

**Table 2.** *Cont.*

| Gait Feature | Gait Feature Description | Gait Feature Formula |
|---|---|---|
| AVM | Magnitude of the vector of the AP axis for the entire stride | $\sqrt{AP^2}$ computed from the acceleration of the AP axis for the entire stride |
| VMD | Magnitude of the vector for the double stance | $\sqrt{ML^2 + V^2 + AP^2}$ computed from the acceleration of the three axes for the ±10% portion surrounding the heel strike event |
| LVMD | Magnitude of the vector of the ML axis at the time of a double stance | $\sqrt{ML^2}$ computed from the acceleration of the ML axis for the ±10% portion surrounding the heel strike event |
| VVMD | Magnitude of the vector of the V axis at the time of a double stance | $\sqrt{V^2}$ computed from the acceleration of the V axis for the ±10% portion surrounding the heel strike event |
| AVMD | Magnitude of the vector of the AP axis at the time of a double stance | $\sqrt{AP^2}$ computed from the acceleration of the AP axis for ±10% portion surrounding the heel strike event |
| VM30 | Magnitude of the vector for the mid-stance | $\sqrt{ML^2 + V^2 + AP^2}$ computed from the acceleration of the three axes for the 30% portion of the gait cycle |
| LVM30 | Magnitude of the vector of the ML axis at the time of the mid-stance | $\sqrt{ML^2}$ computed from the acceleration of the ML axis for the 30% portion of the gait cycle |
| VVM30 | Magnitude of the vector of the V axis at the time of a mid-stance | $\sqrt{V^2}$ computed from the acceleration of the V axis for the 30% portion of the gait cycle |
| AVM30 | Magnitude of the vector of the AP axis at the time of a mid-stance | $\sqrt{AP^2}$ computed from the acceleration of the AP axis for the 30% portion of the gait cycle |
| LHM | Magnitude of heel strike of the ML axis | Max (ML) at the heel strike |
| LHSD | Standard deviation of the acceleration of the ML axis for the first 10% portion of the stride | Std (ML) computed from the acceleration of the ML axis for the first 10% portion of the stride |
| VHM | Magnitude of heel strike of the V axis | Max (V) at the heel strike event |
| VHSD | Standard deviation of the acceleration of the V axis for the first 10% portion of the stride | Std (V) computed from the acceleration of the V axis for the first 10% portion of the stride |
| AHM | Magnitude of heel strike of the AP axis | Max (AP) at the heel strike event |
| AHSD | Standard deviation of the acceleration of the AP axis for the first 10% portion of the stride | Std (AP) computed from the acceleration of the AP axis for the first 10% portion of the stride |
| ST | Stride time | Duration of two consecutive heel strike events |

**Table 3.** Distribution of class labels of stride samples.

| Label | Count | Percentage |
|---|---|---|
| Good | 3774 | 65% |
| Irregular | 1995 | 35% |
| Total | 5769 | 100% |

The stride samples were also normalized to have a standard deviation of 1 and a mean of 0. Subsequently, the stride samples were also segmented into a fixed-size data sequence. To prepare the stride samples for the training of the single-stride gait feature modality, since one sample was equivalent to one stride, a sliding window with the width of one sample with no overlap was used to segment the data, as shown in Figure 6. Since there were 40 features, the input segment vector would contain 40 dimensions.

In our previous study [10], we observed that gaits were not always disrupted when subjects traversed irregular walking surfaces. Abnormal gaits would intermittently occur alongside normal gaits. Therefore, compared to walking on a good walking surface, there was a higher rate of interrupted gaits. Based on this observation, we hypothesized that aggregating multiple consecutive strides to train an LSTM network would improve classification performance. This led to the experimentation of the multi-stride gait feature modality. For this modality, a larger sliding window width of five samples was used to segment the data, which was equivalent to five strides, with an 80% overlap, as illustrated in Figure 7. The input segment vector had the shape of 40 dimensions as well.

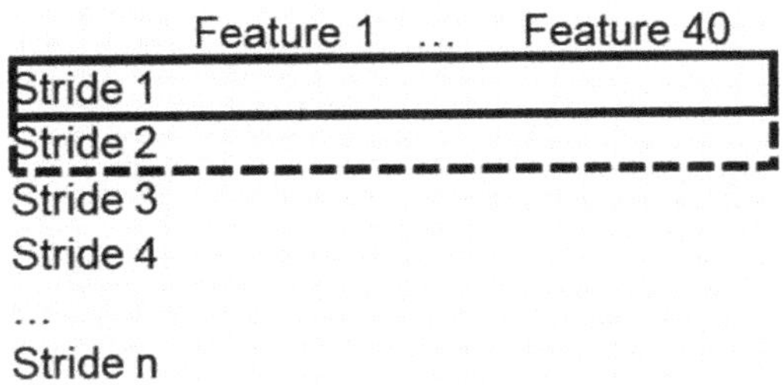


**Figure 6.** Segmentation of gait feature data into fixed-size segments of one sample with a sliding window.

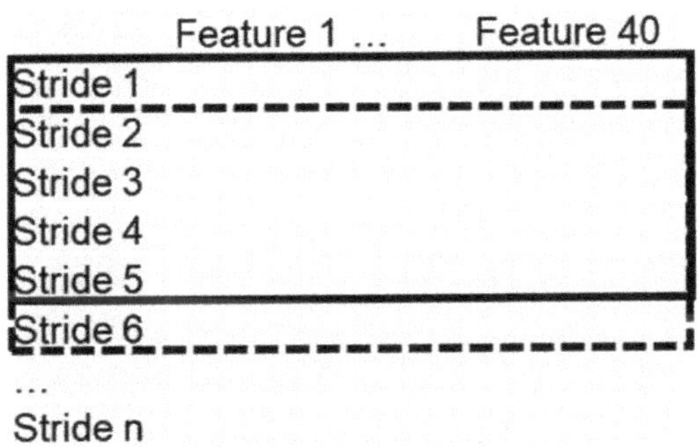


**Figure 7.** Segmentation of gait feature data into fixed-size segments of five samples with a sliding window with 80% overlap.

*3.4. Proposed Architecture*

Since the architecture of a LSTM model is input-dependent, the number of layers and the optimal network structure for each of the three modalities differed. For ease of reference, the LSTM networks trained with raw data, single-stride gait features and multi-stride gait features were referred to as LSTM-Raw, LSTM-Features-1 and LSTM-Features-5, respectively. The tuning methodology is delineated in Section 4.1.1.

The resulting optimal architectures turned out to be identical for all three networks, as illustrated in Figure 8. It consisted of four layers of a LSTM layer with dropout layers in between each LSTM layer. At the end of the architecture was a dense layer, followed by a Sigmoid activation function that yielded the probability of the pre-processed sample being an irregular class.

However, the optimal number of neurons per LSTM layer for LSTM-Raw was 224, while the optimal number of neurons for both LSTM-Features networks was 100. This meant that the dimensionality of the input vector per time-step fed into a LSTM layer in LSTM-Raw was three and the output vector, which was also the hidden state vector, of the layer had a dimensionality of 224. On the other hand, the dimensionality of the input vector per time-step fed into a LSTM layer in the LSTM-Features networks was 40 and would output a hidden state vector with a dimensionality of 100.

Stacking multiple LSTM layers could transform the raw acceleration and gait feature inputs into a more abstract representation that enabled the network to learn the complex relationships between the inputs and walking surface conditions [44]. We kept the number of neurons the same for each layer when tuning, because using the same number of neurons for all layers performed generally better than increasing or decreasing the neurons down the network [45]. As shown in Figure 8, the pre-processed data were fed into the stacked LSTM layers to extract temporal features. The temporal features were then processed with the dense layer, followed by a sigmoid function to obtain the probability of the pre-processed sample being an irregular class.

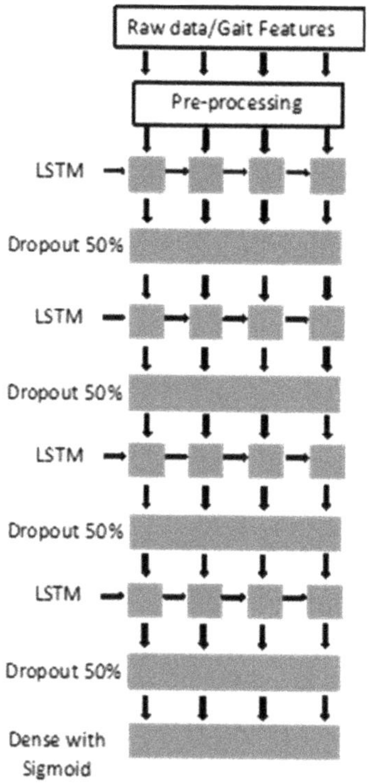


**Figure 8.** Stacked LSTM architecture.

### 3.4.1. LSTM Layer

LSTM is a specialized variant of the recurrent neural network (RNN), and it was introduced by Hochreiter et al. [46]. Unlike a traditional neural network, which is incapable of capturing temporal information as the nodes in each layer are disconnected, the RNN compensates for that limitation by mapping input sequences to output sequences. However, the RNN has the disadvantage of recognizing data for only short periods of time due to the vanishing/exploding gradient [47]. The LSTM solves the problem of the RNN with special memory cells that can solve complex, artificial, long-time-lag tasks, which resulted in it being an appropriate solution for our problem, since acceleration data are time series data [46]. The LSTM network introduced a new mechanism called a memory cell.

A memory cell is regulated with three main gates: an output gate, an input gate and a forget gate. The output gate protects other neurons from being perturbed by a currently irrelevant memory cell state, while the input gate determines what input can alter the memory cell state [46]. Lastly, the forget gate is responsible for gathering prior data and what past information to forget from the cell's previous state [46].

A LSTM memory cell would take in an input $x_t$ at time $t$, the hidden state $h_{t-1}$ and the cell state $c_{t-1}$ from the previous LSTM memory cell, and would output the current hidden state $h_t$ plus the memory cell state $c_t$. $U$, $W$ and $V$ denote the weight matrices, while $b$ represents the bias vector. The forward pass of the LSTM unit could be expressed as follows:

$$f_t = \sigma(W_f x_t + U_f h_{t-1} + b_f) \tag{1}$$

$$i_t = \sigma(W_i x_t + U_i h_{t-1} + b_i) \tag{2}$$

$$\tilde{c}_t = tanh(W_c x_t + U_c h_{t-1} + b_c) \tag{3}$$

$$c_t = i_t \circ \tilde{c}_t + f_t \circ c_{t-1} \tag{4}$$

$$o_t = \sigma(W_o x_t + U_o h_{t-1} + V_o c_t + b_o) \tag{5}$$

$$h_t = o_t \circ tanh(c_t) \tag{6}$$

where $\circ$ represents the element-wise multiplication, while $f_t$, $i_t$, $\tilde{c}_t$ and $o_t$ represent the forget, input, cell, output gates' outputs, respectively. $c_t$ and $h_t$ are passed on to the next time step.

As mentioned above, the LSTM-Raw network had 224 memory cells for each LSTM layer and would take in a three-dimensional input vector $x_t$ per time-step. Each of the LSTM layers would produce a hidden state output vector $h_t$ with 224 dimensions. As for the LSTM-Features networks, it would take in an input vector $x_t$ with 40 dimensions per time step. As each LSTM layer had 100 memory cells, each layer would generate a hidden state output vector $h_t$ with 100 dimensions.

#### 3.4.2. Dropout Layer

Dropout is a technique commonly used to prevent overfitting in a deep neural network with a vast number of parameters [44]. Limited training data in our study would lead to overfitting, since we were using multiple LSTM layers. The main idea is to randomly drop input units into the next layer during training, which prevents the units from co-adapting too much [44]. We set the dropout rate to be 50%. This meant that when the hidden state vector output by the previous LSTM layer was fed to the dropout layer, the dropout layer would randomly set 50% of the hidden state vector dimensions to 0, which would be the input vector into the next layer.

#### 3.4.3. Dense Layer

The dense layer and a Sigmoid function were necessary to process feature representations extracted with the LSTM layers to complete our classification task. The dense layer was also a fully connected layer, which meant that hidden state vectors generated by each LSTM neuron after being randomly dropped out were being fed to every node in the dense layer.

Since the output of the dense layer was not interpretable, it was fed into a Sigmoid function so that it could be converted into a probability of the given sample being an irregular class. The formula for Sigmoid is as follows:

$$S(x) = \frac{1}{1 + e^x} \tag{7}$$

where $x$ is the one-dimensional output vector of the densely connected layer.

## 4. Experiments Section

### *4.1. Experimental Setup*

#### 4.1.1. Hyper-Parameter Tuning

To determine the optimal network structure for each of the three modalities, the number of neurons and layer hyper-parameters had to be tuned independently for each modality. We first split the samples for each modality into training and test data subsets using an 80:20 split. The training data subset was further split into 80% for training and 20% for validation during the model fitting, so that the model learning behavior could be monitored through training and validation learning curves to avoid underfitting or overfitting. The test set was used to evaluate the structure.

We tuned the number of layer and number of neuron hyper-parameters with the automated tuning package in Keras Tuner [48]. The hyper-parameters were optimized using random searches to minimize validation loss in 30 maximum trials.

Neural networks are commonly trained using mini-batch processing. According to Keskar et al. [49], using a larger batch size would lead to a less generalizable model. Hence, upon determining the network structure, we also examined the effect of the batch size on the classification performance to determine the most effective batch size.

#### 4.1.2. Model Implementation

The proposed LSTM structure was implemented with Keras libraries [48], written in Python and utilizing Tensorflow [50] as the backend. All the LSTM models with different modalities were trained in a supervised manner. Each layer's weights and biases were initialized with randomly selected values. The LSTM parameters were optimized through minimizing the binary cross-entropy loss function. The binary cross-entropy loss function measures the distance between the predicted probability and the actual class. The binary cross-entropy loss for a batch of N samples was defined as:

$$L = -\sum_{i=1}^{N} y_i log(\hat{y}_i) + (1 - y_i) log(1 - \hat{y}_i) \tag{8}$$

where $y_i$ denotes the truth value, taking the value 1 or 0, and $\hat{y}_i$ is the predicted Sigmoid probability.

An optimizer used to update the network parameters to minimize the loss function needed to be selected as well. We chose the Adam optimizer, since it was shown that it had the best fitting effect for the purpose of human activity recognition [41]. A learning rate of 0.0001 was used to control the extent of the parameter updates.

#### 4.1.3. Evaluation Metrics

We had a disproportionate sample of irregular classes in our dataset, as shown in Tables 1 and 3. Hence, we used the area under the receiver operating characteristic (ROC) curve (AUC), which described the relationship between the false positive rate and true positive rate, as our performance metric because it is unaffected by skewed data [51,52].

Furthermore, once we determined the optimal network structure for all three modalities, to verify the generalizability of the models to subject differences, we employed the leave-one-subject-out test set procedure for the evaluation of each modality. During each iteration of the protocol, to avoid overfitting for each model, the best epoch to halt training was determined by utilizing the early-stopping strategy [45]. We initially set the training epoch to an arbitrary large number of 200 in Keras and configured the early-stopping criterion to halt training when there was no improvement in the validation AUC after 15 epochs. The optimal number of epochs for each respective model was then used to retrain the models, and the models were evaluated with the test set.

#### 4.1.4. Traditional Machine Learning Baseline Method

We verified the effectiveness of the proposed approach by benchmarking the approach against the shallow machine learning method that was presented in our previous study [10]. We used an SVM model as our baseline shallow machine learning model for this experiment. The workflow of training an SVM model is shown in Figure 9.

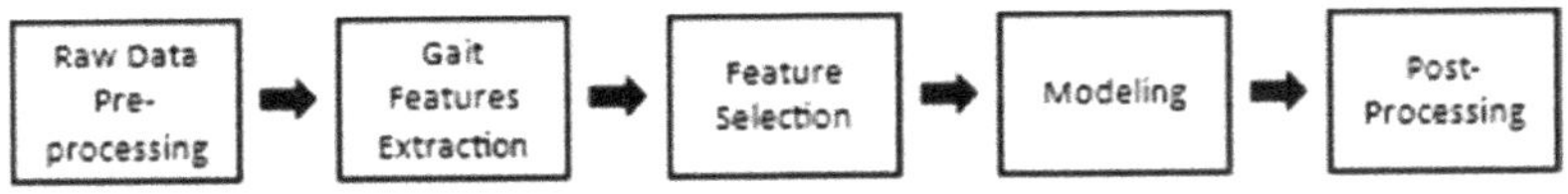


**Figure 9.** Workflow of training an SVM model with gait features.

We pre-processed the raw data and performed stride segmentation prior to extracting the 40-dimensional gait features described in Table 2, which was identical to the pre-processing steps performed for the gait feature modalities delineated in Section 3.3.2. The optimal feature subset was, subsequently, identified from the extracted gait feature set to train the SVM model. The trained SVM model would generate predictions on a stride-by-stride basis to discern whether a stride occurred on an irregular surface or not.

Our preliminary study also demonstrated that the classification performance of the SVM model could be improved with post-processing on the per-stride predictions of the SVM, since there were more frequent gait interruptions on irregular walking surfaces compared to the good walking surfaces. We segmented the per-stride predictions by sampling them into five consecutive strides for each segment using a sliding window with the step size of one stride and averaging the predicted probability to obtain the final prediction of that segment. The ground truth of the segment was based on the majority of stride labels in the segment. Furthermore, for a complete comparison, we also conducted the same pre-processing steps on LSTM-Features-1's per-stride predictions and compared the classification performance of the per-stride and post-processing predictions between our proposed approach and the shallow SVM approach.

## 4.2. Experimental Results

### 4.2.1. Selected Architectures

After hyper-parameter tuning, the resulting optimal structure for LSTM-Raw was four hidden layers with 224 neurons at each layer. For both the LSTM-Features-1 and LSTM-Features-5 modalities, the optimal architecture was identical, consisting of a configuration with four hidden layers and 100 neurons at each layer. Tables 4–6 summarize the list of the selected hyper-parameters for all three models, as well as the total number of trainable parameters for each network.

**Table 4.** List of selected hyper-parameters for LSTM-Raw.

| Stage | Hyper-Parameters | Selected Values |
|---|---|---|
| Data Pre-Processing | Window Size | 110 |
| | Step Size | 11 |
| Architecture | LSTM_1 Neurons | 224 |
| | LSTM_2 Neurons | 224 |
| | LSTM_3 Neurons | 224 |
| | LSTM_4 Neurons | 224 |
| | Dropout Rate | 0.5 |
| Training | Optimizer | Adam |
| | Batch Size | 32 |
| | Learning Rate | 0.0001 |
| Total Trainable Parameters | | 1,411,425 |

**Table 5.** List of selected hyper-parameters for LSTM-Features-1.

| Stage | Hyper-Parameters | Selected Values |
|---|---|---|
| Data Pre-Processing | Window Size | 1 |
| | Step Size | 1 |

Table 5. *Cont.*

| Stage | Hyper-Parameters | Selected Values |
| --- | --- | --- |
| Architecture | LSTM_1 Neurons | 100 |
| | LSTM_2 Neurons | 100 |
| | LSTM_3 Neurons | 100 |
| | LSTM_4 Neurons | 100 |
| | Dropout Rate | 0.5 |
| Training | Optimizer | Adam |
| | Batch Size | 32 |
| | Learning Rate | 0.0001 |
| Total Trainable Parameters | | 297,701 |

**Table 6.** List of selected hyper-parameters for LSTM-Features-5.

| Stage | Hyper-Parameters | Selected Values |
| --- | --- | --- |
| Data Pre-Processing | Window Size | 5 |
| | Step Size | 1 |
| Architecture | LSTM_1 Neurons | 100 |
| | LSTM_2 Neurons | 100 |
| | LSTM_3 Neurons | 100 |
| | LSTM_4 Neurons | 100 |
| | Dropout Rate | 0.5 |
| Training | Optimizer | Adam |
| | Batch Size | 32 |
| | Learning Rate | 0.0001 |
| Total Trainable Parameters | | 297,701 |

#### 4.2.2. Effect of Batch Size

We tuned our hyper-parameters using the default batch size of 32, which is widely considered as a practical and effective value [45]. Here, we examined the effect of batch sizes of 16, 32, 64, 128 and 256 on the classification performance for all three architectures. Table 7 shows the classification results of different batch sizes for LSTM-Raw, LSTM-Features-1 and LSTM-Features-5. It was noticeable that boosting the batch size resulted in a reduction in the prediction accuracy of each LSTM, which was in line with the conclusions drawn by Keskar et al. [49]. At a batch size of 16, the classification results were similar to those attained at the batch size of 32. Since a larger batch size yielded faster computation [45], we picked 32 as the best batch size and used it for the training of our LSTM models.

**Table 7.** Classification results of different batch sizes across all LSTM models.

| Batch Size | LSTM-Raw (AUC) | LSTM-Features-1 (AUC) | LSTM-Features-5 (AUC) |
| --- | --- | --- | --- |
| 16 | 0.92 | 0.86 | 0.93 |
| 32 | 0.92 | 0.86 | 0.93 |
| 64 | 0.91 | 0.85 | 0.92 |
| 128 | 0.91 | 0.85 | 0.91 |
| 256 | 0.90 | 0.85 | 0.90 |

#### 4.2.3. Leave-One-Subject-Out Assessment

The classification outcomes for every test subject of the leave-one-subject-out assessment for each LSTM model and the SVM baseline model are summarized in Table 8.

**Table 8.** Classification results for each test subject for all LSTM models and SVM.

| Test Subject | LSTM-Raw (AUC) | LSTM-Features-1 (AUC) | LSTM-Features-5 (AUC) | SVM (AUC) |
|---|---|---|---|---|
| A | 0.62 | 0.82 | 0.86 | 0.74 |
| B | 0.60 | 0.84 | 0.80 | 0.81 |
| C | 0.78 | 0.87 | 0.87 | 0.83 |
| D | 0.77 | 0.78 | 0.79 | 0.70 |
| E | 0.85 | 0.84 | 0.85 | 0.85 |
| F | 0.55 | 0.82 | 0.83 | 0.70 |
| G | 0.85 | 0.91 | 0.94 | 0.84 |
| H | 0.70 | 0.77 | 0.84 | 0.87 |
| I | 0.70 | 0.79 | 0.82 | 0.82 |
| J | 0.65 | 0.76 | 0.76 | 0.72 |
| K | 0.51 | 0.71 | 0.72 | 0.75 |
| L | 0.70 | 0.85 | 0.87 | 0.92 |
| Average | 0.69 | 0.81 | 0.83 | 0.80 |

LSTM-Raw was the least efficient, as it exhibited an inferior classification performance compared to the SVM baseline, and had the lowest average AUC. Both the LSTM-Features models slightly outperformed the SVM model, with LSTM-Features-5 achieving the highest average AUC of 83%. These results validated the feasibility of utilizing hand-crafted features to guide the learning of a LSTM network into convergence with the limited sample size and subject count. When comparing the individual subject outcomes between LSTM-Features-1 and LSTM-Features-5, we observed that introducing multiple strides during training in LSTM-Features-5 resulted in an AUC improvement ranging from 1% to 7%, leading to a 2% increase in the average AUC performance. This finding confirmed the hypothesis that incorporating multiple strides during training could enhance the performance of the LSTM-Features model. The LSTM-Features-5 model demonstrated the highest level of robustness, as it was able to consistently attain an AUC of over 71% regardless of the selection of subject data excluded from training. Compared to the LSTM model trained with raw acceleration data, the impact of individual differences on the performance of both the LSTM and SVM models was less noticeable when trained with gait features. For completeness, Figure 10 shows the ROC curve of LSTM-Features-5 with one of the test subject iterations that was closest to the average AUC. The area under the ROC curve was 83%.

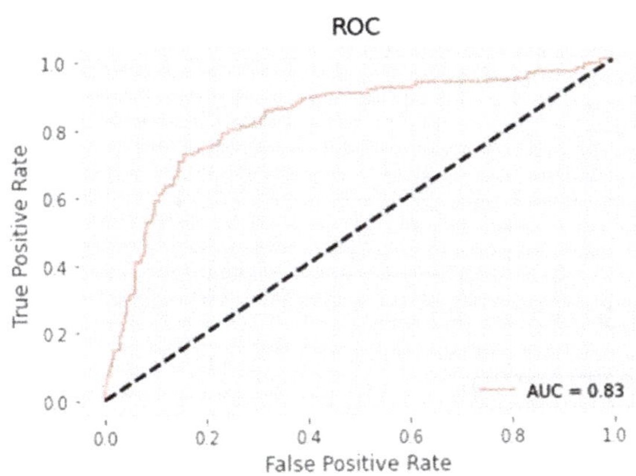


**Figure 10.** The ROC curve of one of the test subject iterations for LSTM-Features-5.

Figures 11 and 12 depict the training process of one of the leave-one-subject-out iterations for LSTM-Features-5. During the network training, the training loss decreased gradually, while the validation AUC stabilized, indicating that the model achieved convergence. With the early-stopping strategy, the training stopped at epoch 78 when the validation AUC stopped improving after 15 epochs to prevent overfitting. As shown in Figure 11, the gaps between the training and validation curves in the binary cross-entropy loss were small. Figure 12 shows that the gaps between the training and validation curves in terms of the AUC were exceedingly small. These results indicated that the dropout technique was effective in preventing overfitting. After the learning curves stabilized and the model achieved a good fit, training beyond that point could lead to overfitting. To prevent this, the early-stopping strategy was employed.

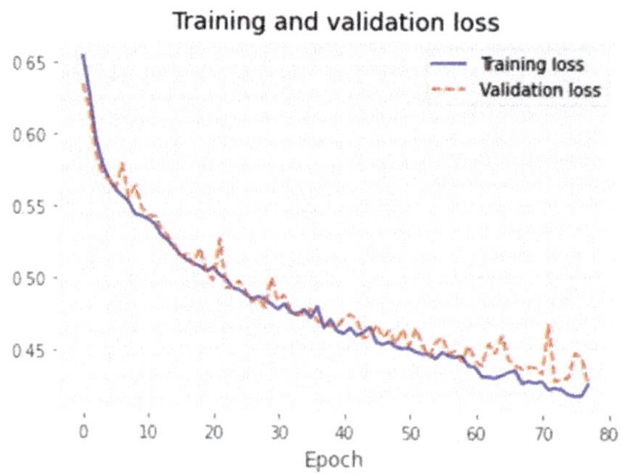


**Figure 11.** Training progress of one of the leave-one-subject-out iterations.

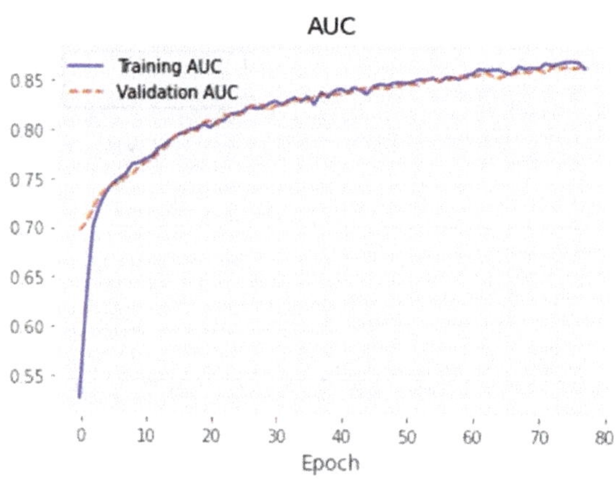


**Figure 12.** Training and validation AUC at each epoch for one of the leave-one-subject-out iterations.

4.2.4. Post-Training Stride Aggregation Post-Processing

The five-stride post-processing classification results for the SVM and LSTM-Features-1 for each test subject are shown in Table 9. The subject-wise classification results of the SVM and LSTM-Features-1 improved across the board with post-processing compared to the per-stride predictions in Table 8. The SVM's average classification performance was approximately 5% higher after post-processing, while LSTM-Features-1's average AUC improved by 7%. Post-processing on the SVM's per-stride predictions resulted in an AUC improvement for all subjects in the range of 1% to 10%, while post-processing on LSTM-Features-1's per-stride predictions led to an AUC improvement in the range of 3% to 9%. Comparing the post-processing results of the SVM and LSTM-Features-1, we could see that LSTM-Features-1 outperformed the SVM by an average of 2%. This meant that LSTM-Features-1 with post-processing was the most effective model, as it exceeded LSTM-Features-5's classification performance by 5%. This finding suggested that post-training stride aggregations could lead to better classification results, and they could be more effective than incorporating multiple strides during the training stage.

**Table 9.** Five-stride post-processing classification results for each test subject for SVM and LSTM-Features-1.

| Test Subject | SVM (AUC) | LSTM-Features-1 (AUC) |
|---|---|---|
| A | 0.77 | 0.91 |
| B | 0.91 | 0.90 |
| C | 0.88 | 0.92 |
| D | 0.79 | 0.83 |
| E | 0.91 | 0.87 |
| F | 0.73 | 0.89 |
| G | 0.94 | 0.96 |
| H | 0.94 | 0.86 |
| I | 0.89 | 0.87 |
| J | 0.77 | 0.79 |
| K | 0.76 | 0.80 |
| L | 0.95 | 0.91 |
| Average | 0.85 | 0.88 |

## 5. Discussion

In this study, we endeavored to improve upon the traditional baseline support vector machine (SVM) machine learning method from our previous study [10] by leveraging the LSTM network's automated feature learning and knowledge distillation abilities. We first examined how three input modalities impacted the performance of the LSTM network and verified their effectiveness by using the baseline model as the benchmark. The results showed that the LSTM trained with single-stride and multi-stride gait features improved the overall performance compared to the baseline model, as the model's ability was enhanced to capture relevant patterns. This also confirmed the feasibility of the proposed approach.

The leave-one-subject-out test set assessment evaluated the robustness of the models to individual differences. Our results, displayed in Section 4, showed that the LSTM models trained with gait features outperformed the LSTM model with raw data and were more generalizable to individual walking pattern differences. As presented in Table 8, the prediction results of LSTM-Raw were considerably low, with only 51% AUC for subject K and 55% AUC for subject F, which were deemed unacceptable. The LSTM-Feature models, on the other hand, could produce satisfactory outcomes for both subjects. The analysis presented here examined the causes of the inadequate performance of LSTM-Raw for Subjects F and K. Figures 13 and 14 illustrate the boxplots of two top gait features identified in our previous study, VM and VMD, and the distribution of values of each subject for those gait features. Subjects F and K were distributed towards the lower fence of the boxplots.

Figure 15 illustrates the walking patterns of all subjects by combining those two features on a scatterplot to examine if clusters were formed. Three distinct clusters could be observed in the plot. Subjects F and K's walking patterns were distinctively different from the general pattern of the other two clusters. The plausible explanation for the less than satisfactory performance of the LSTM network trained with raw data was that deep learning models are negatively affected by noise effects in a raw signal, limited sample size and subject variety [53,54]. The limited subject sample size and variety of walking patterns led to the less comprehensive learning of feature representation from raw signals. This constraint was mitigated by using hand-crafted gait features to train the LSTM network so that the LSTM model could focus on identifying discriminative features [53]. Furthermore, raw signals measured with the accelerometer were noisy, therefore, producing large intra-class variances. Acceleration data that varied significantly for the same walking surface condition led to overfitting. Utilizing gait features would reduce noise and overfitting, hence, making the model more generalizable. Additionally, the LSTM networks trained with gait features also required less training time and computational cost, as the optimal models had fewer parameters to train. This is highly desirable for the development of a real-time irregular walking surface detection application.

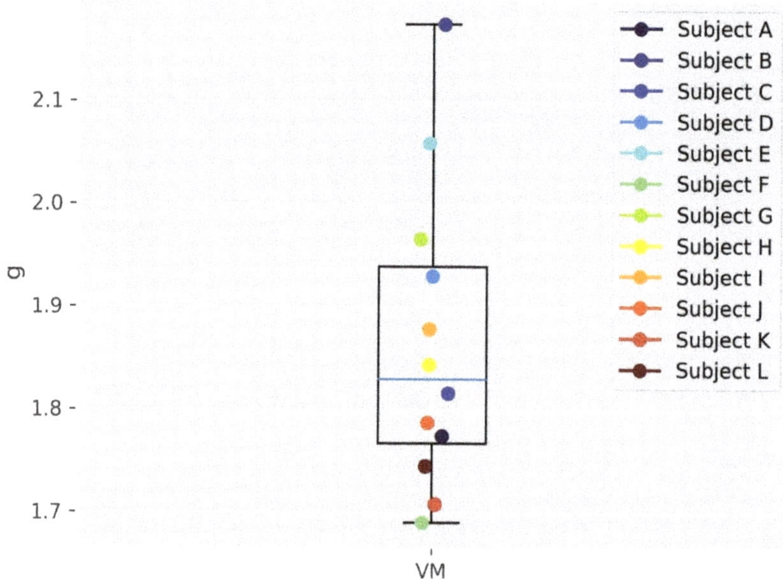


**Figure 13.** Distribution of mean vector magnitude (VM) of each subject on boxplot.

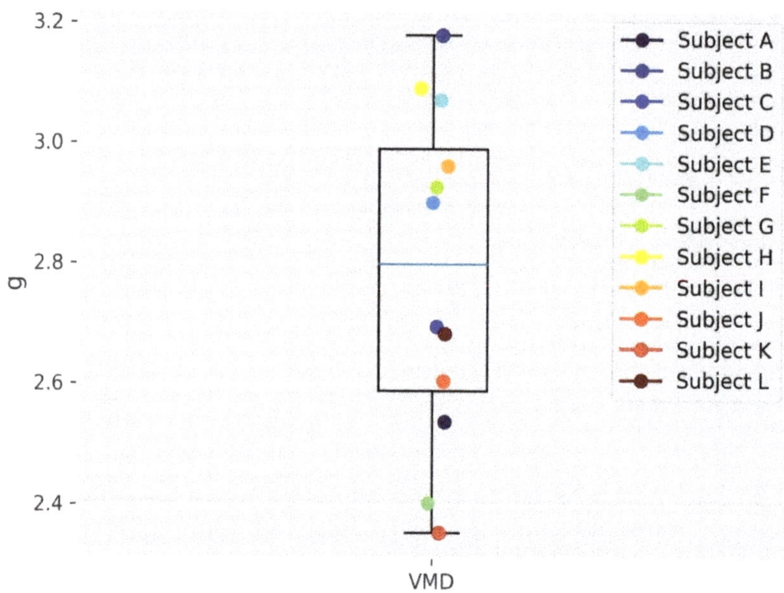


**Figure 14.** Distribution of mean vector magnitude for double-stance phase (VMD) of each subject on boxplot.

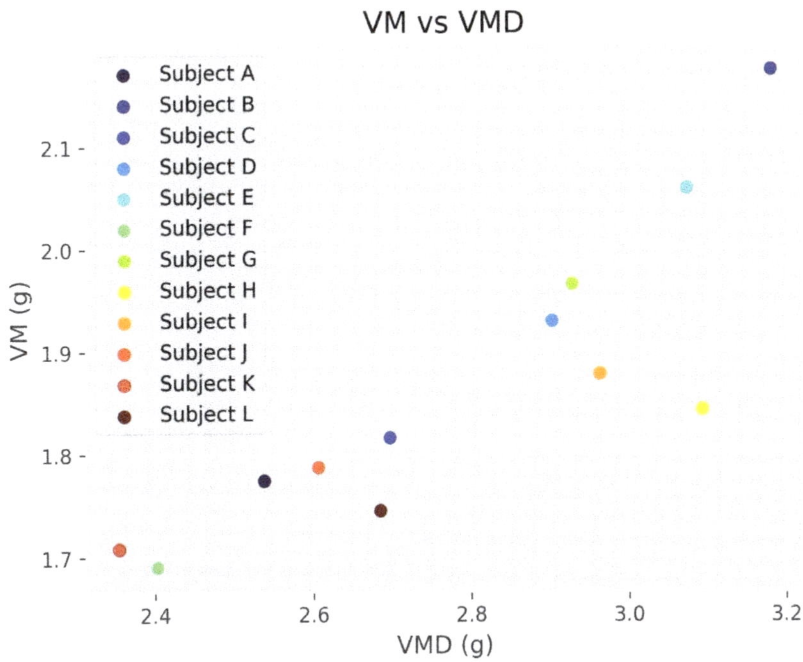


**Figure 15.** Subject distribution based on VM and VMD features in scatterplot.

The experimental results also indicated that post-processing on several consecutive per-stride predictions and incorporating multiple strides per window in the training stage to generate a final prediction for a larger segment could improve the classification performance. This observation was consistent with Kobayashi et al.'s research, which showed that accuracy improved when segmenting smartphone acceleration into a larger window size for convolutional neural network training for a sidewalk type estimation [40]. If the recommended LSTM technique was to be applied in a real-world scenario, it would be essential to capture at least five seconds of data, since a typical stride time for pedestrians is approximately 1.10 s.

Conventional practices for sidewalk condition assessments, which depend on trained experts from governmental agencies or the voluntary participation of residents or pedestrians, are subject to staffing and budget constraints. As a result, the time span between assessments becomes extended [8]. Besides being user-oriented, the practicality of the proposed deep learning approach was also evident, as it achieved a high classification performance in detecting irregular walking surfaces using just a single wearable sensor. In contrast to the shallow machine learning approach, the proposed deep learning approach had an inherent ability to automatically distill knowledge from a high dimensional feature set to extract a good representation, which is analogous to automated feature selection, while simultaneously enhancing the classification performance. This scalable deep learning method could be deployed as a tool to continuously analyze pedestrians' acceleration data to monitor the surface conditions of sidewalks. The system, by removing human biases during the evaluation, could introduce new perspectives to walkability assessments and minimize the time and expense needed for on-site inspections.

Nonetheless, this study had its limitations. One of them was that the experiment was conducted in an experimental setting instead of real-world neighborhoods that vary in walkability. The subjects could have demonstrated distinct walking patterns in a real-world environment as opposed to the experimental setting. Another limitation was the small sample size of subjects. Therefore, we evaluated the approach by iterating through each subject to draw conclusions repeatedly. Another drawback of the proposed framework was its inability to track the subjects' locations due to the lack of global positioning system (GPS) data. Finally, the LSTM is inherently a sequential model that relies on recurrence. This sequential nature impeded parallelization during training [55] and could present challenges in capturing long-term dependencies for longer data sequences in future experiments.

In the future, we plan to include more subjects to increase the number of subject samples and conduct our experiment in real-world walkable and less walkable neighborhoods. Furthermore, GPS data could be integrated in future works to locate participants and pinpoint the source of problematic sidewalk walking surfaces. To address the limitations of the LSTM and to further enhance the classification performance, we also plan to consider the use of a state-of-the-art deep network called the Transformer, which relies on a self-attention mechanism instead of recurrence.

## 6. Conclusions

In this study, we presented a novel classification approach for the automated detection of irregular walking surfaces based on a LSTM network using a single wearable accelerometer placed at the right ankle. Three input modalities for the training of the LSTM network were explored and their effectiveness was evaluated by comparing their classification performance to the traditional baseline support vector machine (SVM) machine learning method [10]. Based on the experimental results, it was found that the LSTM network trained with single-stride hand-crafted gait features with post-processing achieved the best performance. This affirmed the feasibility and effectiveness of the proposed approach. The results indicated that the proposed method could be used as an unbiased tool for detecting potentially problematic walking surfaces. Furthermore, this study unveiled new avenues for the development of real-time sidewalk assessment systems. Considering the sensitivity of our method to subtle variations in gait patterns, which is critical in clinical and therapeutic settings, the proposed method could potentially be extended to the healthcare domain as well. The application of the proposed method in monitoring gait patterns in individuals with neurological disorders or assessing the effectiveness of gait-improving interventions presents a promising direction for future research.

**Author Contributions:** Conceptualization: J.-H.Y., Y.N., X.Z. and H.R.N.; Methodology: X.Z., J.-H.Y. and H.R.N.; Formal analysis: H.R.N.; Investigation: H.R.N.; Resources: H.R.N.; Data Curation: J.-H.Y. and H.R.N.; Writing—original draft preparation: H.R.N.; Writing—review and editing: J.-H.Y., Y.N., X.Z. and H.R.N.; Supervision: J.-H.Y., X.Z. and Y.N. All authors have read and agreed to the published version of the manuscript.

**Funding:** This research received no external funding.

**Institutional Review Board Statement:** The study was conducted in accordance with the Declaration of Helsinki and approved by the institutional review board (or ethics committee) of the University of Nebraska Medical Center (protocol code 242-18-EP, approved 26 February 2020).

**Informed Consent Statement:** Informed consent was obtained from all subjects involved in the study.

**Data Availability Statement:** The data presented in this study are available on request from the corresponding author. The data are not publicly available because data has been collected for a specific research project, and the terms of data collection do not allow for public release.

**Conflicts of Interest:** The authors declare no conflict of interest.

## References

1. Ewing, R.; Handy, S. Measuring the Unmeasurable: Urban Design Qualities Related to Walkability. *J. Urban Des.* **2009**, *14*, 65–84. [CrossRef]
2. Frank, L.D.; Sallis, J.F.; Conway, T.L.; Chapman, J.E.; Saelens, B.E.; Bachman, W. Many Pathways from Land Use to Health: Associations between Neighborhood Walkability and Active Transportation, Body Mass Index, and Air Quality. *J. Am. Plan. Assoc.* **2006**, *72*, 75–87. [CrossRef]

3. Lee, R.J.; Sener, I.N.; Jones, S.N. Understanding the Role of Equity in Active Transportation Planning in the United States. *Transp. Rev.* **2017**, *37*, 211–226. [CrossRef]
4. Leslie, E.; Coffee, N.; Frank, L.; Owen, N.; Bauman, A.; Hugo, G. Walkability of Local Communities: Using Geographic Information Systems to Objectively Assess Relevant Environmental Attributes. *Health Place* **2007**, *13*, 111–122. [CrossRef]
5. Moura, F.; Cambra, P.; Gonçalves, A.B. Measuring Walkability for Distinct Pedestrian Groups with a Participatory Assessment Method: A Case Study in Lisbon. *Landsc. Urban Plan.* **2017**, *157*, 282–296. [CrossRef]
6. Landis, B.W.; Vattikuti, V.R.; Ottenberg, R.M.; McLeod, D.S.; Guttenplan, M. Modeling the Roadside Walking Environment: Pedestrian Level of Service. *Transp. Res. Rec.* **2001**, *1773*, 82–88. [CrossRef]
7. Aghaabbasi, M.; Moeinaddini, M.; Zaly Shah, M.; Asadi-Shekari, Z.; Arjomand Kermani, M. Evaluating the Capability of Walkability Audit Tools for Assessing Sidewalks. *Sustain. Cities Soc.* **2018**, *37*, 475–484. [CrossRef]
8. Kim, H.; Ahn, C.R.; Yang, K. A People-Centric Sensing Approach to Detecting Sidewalk Defects. *Adv. Eng. Inform.* **2016**, *30*, 660–671. [CrossRef]
9. Cheng, H.D.; Shi, X.J.; Glazier, C. Real-Time Image Thresholding Based on Sample Space Reduction and Interpolation Approach. *J. Comput. Civ. Eng.* **2003**, *17*, 264–272. [CrossRef]
10. Ng, H.R.; Sossa, I.; Nam, Y.; Youn, J.H. Machine Learning Approach for Automated Detection of Irregular Walking Surfaces for Walkability Assessment with Wearable Sensor. *Sensors* **2023**, *23*, 193. [CrossRef]
11. Abada, R.; Abubakar, A.M.; Bilal, M.T. An Overview on Deep Leaning Application of Big Data. *Mesopotamian J. Big Data* **2022**, *2022*, 31–35. [CrossRef]
12. Chen, Z.; Zhang, L.; Cao, Z.; Guo, J. Distilling the Knowledge From Handcrafted Features for Human Activity Recognition. *IEEE Trans. Ind. Inform.* **2018**, *14*, 4334–4342. [CrossRef]
13. Ng, H.R. Artificial Intelligence-Based Approaches for Automated Detection of Irregular Walking Surfaces with Wearable Sensor. Master's Thesis, University of Nebraska at Omaha, Omaha, NE, USA, 2022.
14. Sousa, N.; Coutinho-Rodrigues, J.; Natividade-Jesus, E. Sidewalk Infrastructure Assessment Using a Multicriteria Methodology for Maintenance Planning. *J. Infrastruct. Syst.* **2017**, *23*, 5017002. [CrossRef]
15. Corazza, M.V.; Di Mascio, P.; Moretti, L. Managing Sidewalk Pavement Maintenance: A Case Study to Increase Pedestrian Safety. *J. Traffic Transp. Eng. (Engl. Ed.)* **2016**, *3*, 203–214. [CrossRef]
16. Kim, J.; Ahn, C.R.; Nam, Y. The Influence of Built Environment Features on Crowdsourced Physiological Responses of Pedestrians in Neighborhoods. *Comput. Environ. Urban Syst.* **2019**, *75*, 161–169. [CrossRef]
17. Twardzik, E.; Duchowny, K.; Gallagher, A.; Alexander, N.; Strasburg, D.; Colabianchi, N.; Clarke, P. What Features of the Built Environment Matter Most for Mobility? Using Wearable Sensors to Capture Real-Time Outdoor Environment Demand on Gait Performance. *Gait Posture* **2018**, *68*, 437–442. [CrossRef]
18. Thies, S.B.; Richardson, J.K.; Ashton-Miller, J.A. Effects of Surface Irregularity and Lighting on Step Variability during Gait:: A Study in Healthy Young and Older Women. *Gait Posture* **2005**, *22*, 26–31. [CrossRef]
19. Dixon, P.C.; Schütte, K.H.; Vanwanseele, B.; Jacobs, J.V.; Dennerlein, J.T.; Schiffman, J.M. Gait Adaptations of Older Adults on an Uneven Brick Surface Can Be Predicted by Age-Related Physiological Changes in Strength. *Gait Posture* **2018**, *61*, 257–262. [CrossRef]
20. Zurales, K.; DeMott, T.K.; Kim, H.; Allet, L.; Ashton-Miller, J.A.; Richardson, J.K. Gait Efficiency on an Uneven Surface Is Associated with Falls and Injury in Older Subjects with a Spectrum of Lower Limb Neuromuscular Function. *Am. J. Phys. Med. Rehabil.* **2016**, *95*, 83–90. [CrossRef]
21. Merryweather, A.; Yoo, B.; Bloswick, D. Gait Characteristics Associated with Trip-Induced Falls on Level and Sloped Irregular Surfaces. *Minerals* **2011**, *1*, 109–121. [CrossRef]
22. Menz, H.B.; Lord, S.R.; Fitzpatrick, R.C. Acceleration Patterns of the Head and Pelvis When Walking on Level and Irregular Surfaces. *Gait Posture* **2003**, *18*, 35–46. [CrossRef] [PubMed]
23. Miyata, A.; Araki, I.; Wang, T. Barrier Detection Using Sensor Data from Unimpaired Pedestrians. In *Universal Access in Human-Computer Interaction. Virtual, Augmented, and Intelligent Environments, Proceedings of the 12th International Conference, UAHCI 2018, Held as Part of HCI International 2018, Las Vegas, NV, USA, 15–20 July 2018*; Antona, M., Stephanidis, C., Eds.; Springer International Publishing: Cham, Switzerland, 2018; pp. 308–319.
24. Takahashi, J.; Kobana, Y.; Tobe, Y.; Lopez, G. Classification of Steps on Road Surface Using Acceleration Signals. In Proceedings of the 12th EAI International Conference on Mobile and Ubiquitous Systems: Computing, Networking and Services, Coimbra, Portugal, 22–24 July 2015; ICST (Institute for Computer Sciences, Social-Informatics and Telecommunications Engineering): Brussels, Belgium, 2015; pp. 229–234.
25. Kobayashi, S.; Katsurada, R.; Hasegawa, T. Estimation of Sidewalk Surface Type with a Smartphone. In Proceedings of the Proceedings of the 2019 7th International Conference on Information Technology: IoT and Smart City, Shanghai, China, 20–23 December 2019; Association for Computing Machinery: New York, NY, USA, 2019; pp. 497–502.
26. Ki, D.; Lieu, S.; Chen, Z.; Lee, S. A Novel Walkability Index Using Google Street View and Deep Learning. *Sustain. Cities Soc.* **2023**, *99*, 104896. [CrossRef]

27. Blečić, I.; Cecchini, A.; Trunfio, G.A. Towards Automatic Assessment of Perceived Walkability. In *Computational Science and Its Applications—ICCSA 2018, Proceedings of the 18th International Conference, Melbourne, Australia, 2–5 July 2018*; Gervasi, O., Murgante, B., Misra, S., Stankova, E., Torre, C.M., Rocha, A.M.A.C., Taniar, D., Apduhan, B.O., Tarantino, E., Ryu, Y., Eds.; Springer International Publishing: Cham, Switzerland, 2018; pp. 351–365.
28. Koo, B.W.; Guhathakurta, S.; Botchwey, N. How Are Neighborhood and Street-Level Walkability Factors Associated with Walking Behaviors? A Big Data Approach Using Street View Images. *Environ. Behav.* **2022**, *54*, 211–241. [CrossRef]
29. Nagata, S.; Nakaya, T.; Hanibuchi, T.; Amagasa, S.; Kikuchi, H.; Inoue, S. Objective Scoring of Streetscape Walkability Related to Leisure Walking: Statistical Modeling Approach with Semantic Segmentation of Google Street View Images. *Health Place* **2020**, *66*, 102428. [CrossRef] [PubMed]
30. Weld, G.; Jang, E.; Li, A.; Zeng, A.; Heimerl, K.; Froehlich, J.E. Deep Learning for Automatically Detecting Sidewalk Accessibility Problems Using Streetscape Imagery. In Proceedings of the The 21st International ACM SIGACCESS Conference on Computers and Accessibility, Pittsburgh, PA, USA, 28–30 October 2019; Association for Computing Machinery: New York, NY, USA, 2019; pp. 196–209.
31. Yoon, H.-Y.; Kim, J.-H.; Jeong, J.-W. Classification of the Sidewalk Condition Using Self-Supervised Transfer Learning for Wheelchair Safety Driving. *Sensors* **2022**, *22*, 380. [CrossRef] [PubMed]
32. Zhou, H.; He, S.; Cai, Y.; Wang, M.; Su, S. Social Inequalities in Neighborhood Visual Walkability: Using Street View Imagery and Deep Learning Technologies to Facilitate Healthy City Planning. *Sustain. Cities Soc.* **2019**, *50*, 101605. [CrossRef]
33. Varona, B.R.; Monteserin, A.; Teyseyre, A.R. A Deep Learning Approach to Automatic Road Surface Monitoring and Pothole Detection. *Pers. Ubiquitous Comput.* **2019**, *24*, 519–534. [CrossRef]
34. Iwarsson, S.; Nygren, C.; Oswald, F.; Wahl, H.-W.; Tomsone, S. Environmental Barriers and Housing Accessibility Problems Over a One-Year Period in Later Life in Three European Countries. *J. Hous. Elder.* **2006**, *20*, 23–43. [CrossRef]
35. Lee, G.; Asce, S.M.; Choi, B.; Jebelli, H.; Asce, A.M.; Ahn, R.C.; Lee, S.; Asce, M. Wearable Biosensor and Collective Sensing-Based Approach for Detecting Older Adults' Environmental Barriers. *J. Comput. Civ. Eng.* **2020**, *34*, 04020002. [CrossRef]
36. Wan, L.; Gao, S.; Wu, C.; Jin, Y.; Mao, M.; Yang, L. Big Data and Urban System Model—Substitutes or Complements? A Case Study of Modelling Commuting Patterns in Beijing. *Comput. Environ. Urban Syst.* **2018**, *68*, 64–77. [CrossRef]
37. Kim, H. Feasibility of DRNN for Identifying Built Environment Barriers to Walkability Using Wearable Sensor Data from Pedestrians' Gait. *Appl. Sci.* **2022**, *12*, 4384. [CrossRef]
38. Hu, B.; Li, S.; Chen, Y.; Kavi, R.; Coppola, S. Applying Deep Neural Networks and Inertial Measurement Unit in Recognizing Irregular Walking Differences in the Real World. *Appl. Ergon.* **2021**, *96*, 103414. [CrossRef] [PubMed]
39. Rastegari, E.; Azizian, S.; Ali, H. Machine Learning and Similarity Network Approaches to Support Automatic Classification of Parkinson's Diseases Using Accelerometer-Based Gait Analysis. In Proceedings of the Hawaii International Conference on System Sciences, Maui, HI, USA, 8–11 January 2019.
40. Kobayashi, S.; Hasegawa, T. Smartphone-Based Estimation of Sidewalk Surface Type via Deep Learning. *Sens. Mater.* **2021**, *33*, 35–51. [CrossRef]
41. Xia, K.; Huang, J.; Wang, H. LSTM-CNN Architecture for Human Activity Recognition. *IEEE Access* **2020**, *8*, 56855–56866. [CrossRef]
42. Youn, I.-H.; Youn, J.-H.; Zeni, J.; Knarr, B. Biomechanical Gait Variable Estimation Using Wearable Sensors after Unilateral Total Knee Arthroplasty. *Sensors* **2018**, *18*, 1577. [CrossRef] [PubMed]
43. Choi, J.; Parker, S.M.; Knarr, B.A.; Gwon, Y.; Youn, J.-H. Wearable Sensor-Based Prediction Model of Timed up and Go Test in Older Adults. *Sensors* **2021**, *21*, 6831. [CrossRef]
44. Srivastava, N.; Hinton, G.; Krizhevsky, A.; Sutskever, I.; Salakhutdinov, R. Dropout: A Simple Way to Prevent Neural Networks from Overfitting. *J. Mach. Learn. Res.* **2014**, *15*, 1929–1958.
45. Bengio, Y. Practical Recommendations for Gradient-Based Training of Deep Architectures. In *Neural Networks: Tricks of the Trade*; Springer: Berlin/Heidelberg, Germany, 2012; pp. 437–478.
46. Hochreiter, S.; Schmidhuber, J. Long Short-Term Memory. *Neural Comput.* **1997**, *9*, 1735–1780. [CrossRef]
47. Bengio, Y.; Simard, P.; Frasconi, P. Learning Long-Term Dependencies with Gradient Descent Is Difficult. *IEEE Trans. Neural Netw.* **1994**, *5*, 157–166. [CrossRef]
48. Chollet, F. Keras: Deep Learning for Humans. 2015. Available online: https://keras.io/ (accessed on 13 May 2022).
49. Keskar, N.S.; Mudigere, D.; Nocedal, J.; Smelyanskiy, M.; Tang, P.T.P. On Large-Batch Training for Deep Learning: Generalization Gap and Sharp Minima. *arXiv* **2016**, arXiv:1609.04836.
50. Abadi, M.; Agarwal, A.; Barham, P.; Brevdo, E.; Chen, Z.; Citro, C.; Corrado, G.; Davis, A.; Dean, J.; Devin, M.; et al. TensorFlow: Large-Scale Machine Learning on Heterogeneous Systems. *arXiv* **2015**, arXiv:1603.04467.
51. Jeni, L.; Cohn, J.; la Torre, F. Facing Imbalanced Data—Recommendations for the Use of Performance Metrics. In Proceedings of the 2013 Humaine Association Conference on Affective Computing and Intelligent Interaction, ACII 2013, Geneva, Switzerland, 2–5 September 2013; IEEE: Piscataway, NJ, USA, 2013; Volume 2013.
52. Chawla, N.V.; Bowyer, K.W.; Hall, L.O.; Kegelmeyer, W.P. SMOTE: Synthetic Minority Over-Sampling Technique. *J. Artif. Intell. Res.* **2002**, *16*, 321–357. [CrossRef]

53. Han, Y.; Chung, S.L.; Chen, S.F.; Su, S.F. Two-Stream LSTM for Action Recognition with RGB-D-Based Hand-Crafted Features and Feature Combination. In Proceedings of the 2018 IEEE International Conference on Systems, Man, and Cybernetics (SMC), Miyazaki, Japan, 7–10 October 2018; IEEE: Piscataway, NJ, USA, 2019; pp. 3547–3552. [CrossRef]
54. Lin, W.; Hasenstab, K.; Cunha, G.M.; Schwartzman, A. Comparison of Handcrafted Features and Convolutional Neural Networks for Liver MR Image Adequacy Assessment. *Sci. Rep.* **2020**, *10*, 20336. [CrossRef] [PubMed]
55. Khan, H.; Hussain, T.; Ullah Khan, S.; Ahmad Khan, Z.; Baik, S.W. Deep Multi-Scale Pyramidal Features Network for Supervised Video Summarization. *Expert Syst. Appl.* **2024**, *237*, 121288. [CrossRef]

*applied sciences*

MDPI

*Article*

# Classification of Motor Competence in Schoolchildren Using Wearable Technology and Machine Learning with Hyperparameter Optimization

**José Sulla-Torres *, Alexander Calla Gamboa, Christopher Avendaño Llanque, Javier Angulo Osorio and Manuel Zúñiga Carnero**

Escuela Profesional de Ingeniería de Sistemas, Universidad Católica de Santa María, Arequipa 04000, Peru; christopher.avendano@ucsm.edu.pe (C.A.L.); jangulo@ucsm.edu.pe (J.A.O.)

* Correspondence: jsullato@ucsm.edu.pe; Tel.: +51-9599-50467

**Abstract:** Determining the classification of motor competence is an essential aspect of physical activity that must be carried out during school years. The objective is to evaluate motor competence in schoolchildren using smart bands, generate percentiles of the evaluation metrics, and classify motor performance through machine learning with hyperparameter optimization. A cross-sectional descriptive study was carried out on 764 schoolchildren (451 males and 313 females) aged 6 to 17 years. Five state schools in the city of Arequipa, Peru were evaluated. Weight, height, and waist circumference were assessed, and body mass index (BMI) was calculated. The tests evaluated in the schoolchildren measured walking and running for 6 minutes. These tests were carried out using smart bands, capturing cadence, number of steps, calories consumed, speed, stride, and heart rate. As a result, the percentiles were created through the LMS method [L (asymmetry: lambda), M (median: mu), and S (coefficient of variation: sigma)]. The cut-off points considered were <P25 (below average), p25 to p75 (average), and >p75 (above average). For classification, the machine-learning algorithms random forest, decision tree, support vector machine, naive Bayes, logistic regression, k-nearest neighbor, neural network, gradient boosting, XGBboost, LightGBM, and CatBoost were used, and the hyperparameters of the models were optimized using the RandomizedSearchCV technique. In conclusion, it was possible to classify motor competence with the tests carried out on schoolchildren, significantly improving the accuracy of the machine-learning algorithms through the selected hyperparameters, with the gradient boosting classifier being the best result at 0.95 accuracy and in the ROC-AUC curves with a 0.98. The reference values proposed in this study can be used to classify the walking motor competence of schoolchildren. Finally, the mobile software product built based on the proposed model was validated using the prototype of the Software Quality Systemic Model (SQSM) based on three specific categories: functionality, reliability, and usability, obtaining 77.09%. The results obtained can be used in educational centers to achieve the suggested recommendations for physical activity in schoolchildren.

**Keywords:** machine learning; classification; motor competence; schoolchildren; wearable; hyperparameters

## 1. Introduction

### 1.1. Background

Machine-learning classification is training a computer model to recognize and categorize data based on specific characteristics. It is typically classified as supervised, unsupervised, semi-supervised, or reinforced [1]. In supervised classification, the model is trained using labeled data to identify patterns and predict new data [2]. This technique has many applications, including healthcare, education, and technology. One such application is using smart bands in schoolchildren to monitor their physical activity and health status [3].

Physical activity, such as motor competence, is crucial for developing children and adolescents, as it promotes overall health and well-being. Unfortunately, sedentary lifestyles and lack of physical activity have become increasingly common among school students. Smart bands have emerged as a tool to combat this problem and measure physical activity levels in students [4].

Smart bands are wearable devices that can monitor a person's vital health statistics, including heart rate, using a combination of sensors and machine-learning algorithms [3]. In the context of schoolchildren, smart bands can be used to track their physical activity levels, sleep patterns, and overall health status. Machine-learning classification can be used to analyze the data collected with smart bands and identify patterns that can help improve the health and well-being of schoolchildren [1].

The importance of machine-learning classification for schoolchildren lies in its ability to provide personalized and adaptive learning experiences. By analyzing data collected from smart bands, machine-learning algorithms can create profiles for individual students and design learning paths tailored to their specific needs and abilities [5,6]. Additionally, machine-learning classification can identify students at risk for health issues and provide early interventions to prevent or mitigate these issues [7]. Overall, the use of machine-learning classification with smart bands in school children has the potential to improve their physical and mental health and academic performance significantly. Machine-learning algorithms can be optimized by tuning with hyperparameters, obtaining better results [8].

This research aims to explore the use of smart bands and the application of machine learning to promote physical activity and motor competence in educational centers and analyze the potential benefits of this approach. We will examine how smart bands measure levels of motor competence, how machine learning with hyperparameter optimization is used, and the benefits of using them in educational centers. In doing so, we hope to shed light on the potential of these technologies to improve levels of motor competence among students and ultimately contribute to improved health and academic outcomes.

### 1.2. Related Work

Smart bands are wearable devices that have become increasingly popular for tracking and monitoring various physical and health activities, including motor competence. The main works in this regard are presented.

The work of Kounoudes, Kapitsaki, and Katakis [1] indicates that smart bands and wearable fitness devices can measure physical activity levels through various sensors and tracking mechanisms. One of the most common ways smart bands can measure physical activity levels is by monitoring the number of steps the user takes throughout the day. Pedometer readings are commonly used to describe physical activity levels in adults, and fitness trackers like Fitbit record the number of steps the user takes each day. Additionally, VO2max measurements are often used to determine whether the user has increased or decreased fitness level, and variations in VO2max are used as an indicator of overall health. Garmin activity data include VO2max measurements, which can help determine fitness levels. Daily step counts can show people's habits and lifestyle as well as their risk of mortality that may occur to them.

Amor and James [2] suggest that activity monitoring (AM) is a well-established method for assessing an individual's physical activity. The swift emergence of smartwatch technology provides the capability to monitor activity and seamlessly engage with other healthcare systems. Al-Janabi and Hamza [3] propose an intelligent data analysis model to find optimal patterns in human activities based on biometric characteristics obtained from smartwatches and smartphones. The forward and backward rule-based pattern finder generates the optimal patterns that help humans organize their activities. The results show that good patterns are generated for human activities. In addition, Weiss, Yoneda, and Hayajneh [5] suggest that wearable devices include sensors that provide a platform to implement and deploy motion-based mobile behavioral biometrics using the smartwatch accelerometer by basically investigating the physical activity of walking. Therefore, they used different sensors to evaluate physical activity better. The results show that motion-based biometrics using smartwatches yield good results for the activities assessed.

Ali et al. [7] concentrated on introducing innovative techniques for identifying and recording physical activities using machine-learning methods and wearable sensors. Everyday physical activities tend to be unstructured or unplanned, with specific activities or actions (such as sitting or standing) occurring more frequently than others (such as walking or going up and down stairs). Existing activity classification systems have not explored the impact of such class imbalances on the effectiveness of machine-learning classifiers. Therefore, the study's primary aim was to examine the influence of class imbalance on the performance of machine-learning classifiers and to identify which classifiers are more sensitive to class imbalance than others. The research utilized motion sensor data from 30 participants recorded during the performance of various activities of daily living.

Wang, Lizardo, and Hachen [9] demonstrate that social, psychological, and environmental characteristics are related to physical activity among students by using Fitbit devices to collect data on daily movement activities, number of calories, and heart rate, among other measurements from a sample of 692 students, taking four indicators; they showed that there is a strong relationship between the growth of group and individual physical activity.

According to Sabry et al. [10], the application of machine learning to promote physical activity includes fall detection, seizure detection, vital sign monitoring and prediction, and activity recognition. Machine-learning techniques are also being explored for health monitoring, elder care, and fitness tracking. Additionally, machine-learning techniques have been used to link physical activity to obesity by examining the relationship between physical activity and weight status in a large-scale dataset. The study found that the weighted SVM algorithm with a penalized approach offered the best classification performance, followed by ADA(RF).

Zhou et al. [11] indicate that machine learning can also automate and personalize physical activity promotion programs by tracking people's activity patterns and developing therapy and exercise plans to reduce obesity. Additionally, machine-learning methods predict exercise relapse and improve physical activity interventions by identifying unlikely individuals to adhere to a physical exercise regimen.

Creaser et al. [12] note that smart bands and machine learning can promote the health, well-being, or understanding of children or adolescents in schools. However, more research is needed to explore their full impact. Wearables can also be used beyond encouraging physical activity, such as studying and teaching health concepts. However, research indicates when and how wearable devices with the most frequently used functions can be used in schools. It suggests that they are acceptable instruments in the school environment to monitor students' physical activity levels or educate them about the importance of physical activity.

Site, Nurmi, and Lohan [13] reviewed machine-learning algorithms to analyze eHealth data collected from wearable devices, emphasizing the significant potential for enhancing healthcare quality and customer satisfaction through machine learning (ML). The ML algorithms were applied to both time and frequency domain healthcare data derived from wearable devices and sensors. The authors explored how ML techniques can effectively process and analyze health sensor data, noting that accelerometers, gyroscopes, ECG (electrocardiogram), EEG (electroencephalogram) monitors, and blood glucose sensors are the primary sources of eHealth data. The study delved into various aspects, including types of features and methods for feature extraction and ML algorithms commonly used in eHealth data analysis. Notably, the authors concluded that, among the ML algorithms studied in the literature, neural network (NN) algorithms and support vector machines (SVMs) had demonstrated the most promising performance for analyzing healthcare data.

Himi et al. [14] introduce a predictive system named "MedAi", which is based on a smartwatch and employs machine-learning algorithms to predict multiple diseases. The system consists of three main components: a "Sense O'Clock" smartwatch prototype equipped with eleven sensors to gather body statistics, a machine-learning model for analyzing the collected data and making predictions, and a mobile application to display the prediction results. The researchers obtained a dataset of body statistics from patients at a local hospital. Several machine-learning algorithms were utilized in the study, including support vector machine (SVM), support vector regression (SVR), k-nearest neighbor (KNN), extreme gradient boost (XGBoost), long short-term memory (LSTM), and random forest (RF). The goal was to identify the most effective algorithm. The experimental results on the dataset revealed that the random forest (RF) algorithm outperformed the other machine-learning algorithms tested.

Machine-learning algorithms commonly rely on a set of hyperparameters, the values of which need to be chosen thoughtfully, and these choices often have a substantial impact on the algorithm's performance [15]. Hyperparameters are settings that are not directly learned from the dataset but especially impact model performance. The most used search strategies are grid search, manual search, and random search [14]. Several works are related to optimization with hyperparameters, such as the one developed by Yagin et al. [16], who used neural networks with hyperparameter optimization to predict obesity based on physical activity. Rivera, Avilés, and Castillo-Castaneda [17] classified the physical activity indicator using machine learning, and after feature, importance selection, and hyperparameter were tuned. There are also works regarding health in general with the optimization of hyperparameters [18].

## 2. Materials and Methods

### 2.1. Methodology

Machine-learning classification with smart bands in schoolchildren involves several steps, including data collection and analysis. Smart bands are equipped with sensors that collect data on physiological parameters, such as heart rate and physical activity levels. The data are then analyzed to identify patterns and trends that can be used to develop machine-learning models for classification.

Feature selection and preprocessing are crucial steps in the machine-learning classification process. Feature selection involves identifying the most relevant features from the data that will be used to train the model. Preprocessing involves cleaning and transforming the data to ensure they are suitable for analysis. These steps aim to provide the machine-learning model access to high-quality data that will enable accurate classification.

The machine-learning model is trained and tested once the data have been collected, analyzed, and preprocessed. Supervised machine-learning techniques are commonly used for classification tasks, where the model is trained on labeled data. The model's performance is evaluated using accuracy, precision, f1-score, and recall metrics. The goal is to develop a model that can accurately classify schoolchildren based on their physiological parameters, which can be used to monitor their health and well-being.

The methodology used was CRISP-DM [19]. It comprises six phases: business understanding, data understanding, data preparation, modeling, evaluation, and deployment.

#### 2.1.1. Business Understanding

This initial phase will identify the problem caused by traditional methods of evaluating motor competence in educational centers, and a solution will be projected to resolve the present issue. In this phase, there are different activities for understanding the business, each of which will be described below.

1. Determination of objectives: The main goal focuses on exploring the use of smart bands and the application of machine learning optimized to promote physical activity and motor competence in schoolchildren and analyzing the potential benefits of this approach.
2. Evaluation of the situation: A descriptive cross-sectional study was conducted on 764 schoolchildren (451 males and 313 females) aged 6 to 17. The sample selection was non-probabilistic by convenience. Five state schools in the city of Arequipa, Peru, were evaluated. The schoolchildren attended physical education classes twice a week. Permission was requested from each school's administration to conduct the study in

both schools. Then, parents were informed about the objective of the project. Parents who agreed to participate in the study signed the informed consent form to authorize their children's participation.

3. Determination of the goal of machine learning: At this stage, the determination will be made to apply a correct supervised machine-learning technique to determine the best algorithm that finds the best accuracy, precision, f1-score, and recall in students' motor competence classification. A classifier is a function f that takes as input a set of features $x \in X$, where $X$ is the feature space, and outputs a class label $y \in \{1, \ldots, C\}$, where $C$ is the class space.

2.1.2. Data Understanding

Anthropometric measurements and the utilization of the smart band followed the recommendations outlined by the local ethics committee (UCSM-096-2022) and adhered to the principles of the Declaration of Helsinki (World Medical Association) concerning ethical standards for human research.

1. Collection of initial data: Anthropometric measurements were conducted on-site at each school. The evaluation team comprised professional physical education teachers and research assistants. Weight and height were measured using Ross and Marfell Jones's standardized method. To determine body weight (kg), a BC 730 (Tanita Corporation) electronic scale was used, with a scale from 0 to 150 kg. Standing height was measured using a portable stadiometer (Seca 216, Seca Gmbh and Co., Hamburg, Germany), accurate within 0.1 mm. Waist circumference (WC) was measured using a tape measure (Seca) to the nearest 1 mm. The body mass index (BMI) was calculated by dividing the kilograms of weight by the square of the height in meters: BMI = weight (kg)/height$^2$ (m).
   According to the BMI Z-score, patients were classified as underweight/normal weight with Z-scores between −2 and +0.99, overweight from 1 to 1.99, obese from 2 to 2.99, and very obese ≥3 [20]. To categorize abdominal adiposity (WC) by age and sex, the suggestions described by Fernández et al. [21] were used. It was categorized into two groups (without risk < p75 and with risk > p75).
   The motor competence tests that were evaluated were the quantification of the number of steps during school recess, and the 6-minute walk test was performed using a smart band (Huawei band 7) with an AMOLED screen of 194 × 368 and with 1.47 inches. This smart band has been used in other similar research [22]. The smart band was placed on the wrist of each student's hand, and its use was explained.
2. Describe and explore the data: The Kolmogorov–Smirnov test verified the dataset's normality. Descriptive statistics (mean, standard deviation, min, and max) were calculated. Table 1 shows the description of the data of the schoolchildren.

**Table 1.** Description of schoolchildren's data.

| | Age | Weight | Height | Waist | BMI | Cadence | Steps | Speed | Stride |
|---|---|---|---|---|---|---|---|---|---|
| mean | 12.48 | 47.57 | 1.49 | 71.93 | 20.74 | 59.58 | 910.64 | 2.99 | 79.73 |
| std | 2.75 | 16.18 | 0.16 | 11.37 | 4.27 | 34.46 | 504.13 | 1.93 | 10.35 |
| min | 6 | 18.00 | 1.140 | 50.00 | 11.71 | 10.00 | 126.00 | 0.310 | 53.00 |
| 25% | 10 | 34.00 | 1.370 | 63.00 | 17.66 | 30.00 | 499.00 | 1.315 | 72.50 |
| 50% | 13 | 48.00 | 1.520 | 70.50 | 20.30 | 53.00 | 833.00 | 2.570 | 78.00 |
| 75% | 15 | 58.10 | 1.630 | 78.50 | 23.35 | 82.50 | 1241.50 | 4.365 | 86.00 |
| max | 17 | 107.70 | 1.810 | 114.60 | 39.95 | 163.00 | 2189.00 | 9.760 | 111.00 |

*t*-test was used to calculate differences between both sexes in independent samples. Differences between BMI and waist values were determined via one-way ANOVA and Tukey's specificity test. In all cases, $p < 0.05$ was significant.

2.1.3. Data Preparation

In this phase, the data are selected according to the most critical attributes to train and test the algorithms that will be chosen for the study.

1. Data selection: Through data selection, it became feasible to identify and emphasize those fields that would provide valuable contributions to the analysis of physical activity for motor skill tests. Each data record has the following attributes within the database:
    a. Anthropometric data: age (years), weight (kg), height (m), sitting height (cm), and waist circumference (cm).
    b. Average pace: the time the person can walk a kilometer; they are a number in minutes and seconds format.
    c. Average cadence: these are the steps per minute you can do; they are raw numbers.
    d. Steps: these are all the steps the person has taken during the activity; they are raw numbers.
    e. Calories: the calories the person has burned during the activity; they are numbers without formats.
    f. Average speed: the average speed at which the person has moved during the activity in kilometers/hour; it is in number format with decimals without arrangements.
    g. Average stride: it is the average distance taken by each step; they are numbers without formats.
    h. Heart rate: these are the beats per minute the heart has given during the activity; they are numbers without formats.
    i. Maximum heart rate: this is the maximum number of beats per minute the individual has given in the activity; they are numbers without formats.
2. Data cleaning: Data cleaning tasks allowed us to discover correct and sometimes eliminate erroneous data records or outliers and convert and standardize the data types necessary for processing in machine-learning algorithms. The Jupyter dashboard [23] was used with the Python 3 programming language, with its Pandas library; it is a rapid, robust, adaptable, and user-friendly open-source tool for data analysis and manipulation. The Seaborn library was used with its boxplot function to visualize the classes, as shown in Figure 1, where the high class has the highest proportion for both sexes. Points outside a boxplot are visual indicators of values that may be unusual or outliers compared to the rest of the data in the set.

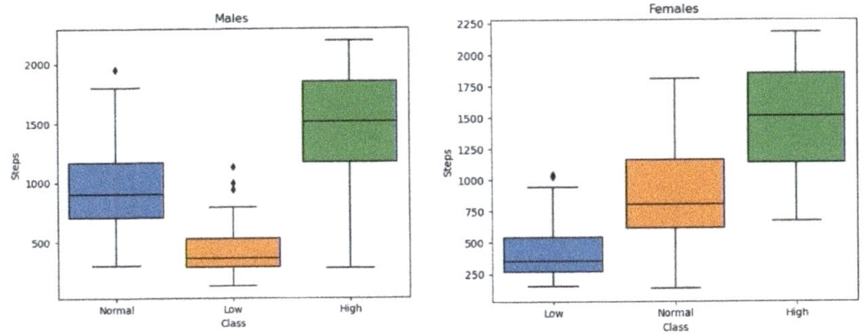


**Figure 1.** Types of motor competence according to the tests the male and female schoolchildren carried out.

#### 2.1.4. Modeling

When conducting a detailed analysis of the data source, it was determined that the classification output resulting from the motor competence tests is labeled as high, normal, and low. For this reason, the decision was made that the most appropriate type of prediction would be classification.

To do this, a comparison of popular supervised machine-learning techniques for a classification model will be conducted. According to the literature, the most used algorithms and optimizers are:

1. Decision tree: A non-parametric supervised technique that constructs a classification model as a tree structure, applicable for classification and regression tasks [24].
2. Random forest: It generates a set of decision trees by employing random resampling on the training set [25].
3. Support vector machine: Creates effective boundaries to separate datasets by solving a constrained quadratic optimization problem [26].
4. Naive Bayes: It is a probabilistic classifier based on Bayes' theorem, assuming strong independence within attributes of an instance [27].
5. Logistic regression: This type of regression analysis is used to predict the outcome of a categorical variable based on the independent or predictor variables [28]. While commonly recognized as a classifier, logistic regression can also be employed as a regressor to predict numeric values. Its adaptability allows it to address classification and regression problems, depending on the nature of the data and the analysis objectives [28].
6. Neuronal network: Most current neural network applications are concerned with pattern recognition problems. Artificial neural networks consist of assemblies of perceptrons designed for multi-layer feedforward networks [29].
7. K-nearest neighbors: It seeks to predict outputs by computing the distance between the test data and training points, subsequently selecting the K number of points closest to the test data [30].
8. Gradient boosted: This ensemble learning technique builds and combines several weak learning models to form a more robust model. The main idea is to correct the errors of the previous model by iteratively adding soft models. It focuses on fitting the residuals of the previous model using a gradient-based approach [31].
9. XGBoost: short for "eXtreme Gradient Boosting", is a specific implementation of gradient boosting. It was developed to be fast and efficient in terms of resource usage. It includes regularization, missing value handling, and a custom cost function [32].
10. LightGBM: Gradient boosting machines build sequential decision trees, with each tree constructed based on the errors of the preceding tree. In the end, predictions are made by summing the contributions of all these trees.
11. CatBoost: CatBoost stands for "Category" and "Boost"; it handles categorical, numeric, and text features. The CatBoost algorithm employs a symmetric tree or an oblivious tree structure [33].

Anaconda Navigator Software 2.5.1 was used with its Jupyter Notebook 6.5.2 with the Python 3 programming language and its Scikit-learn optimization library to compare supervised machine-learning techniques for classification.

With careful preparation of the input data, it will be imported in a specific CSV format, representing it as a table with the attributes selected in the "Data selection" section. Figure 2 shows the modeling developed to classify motor competence data, using information generated by smart bands. This encompasses data processing, modeling, comparisons with machine-learning algorithms, and achieving classification with optimization using hyperparameters in the study.

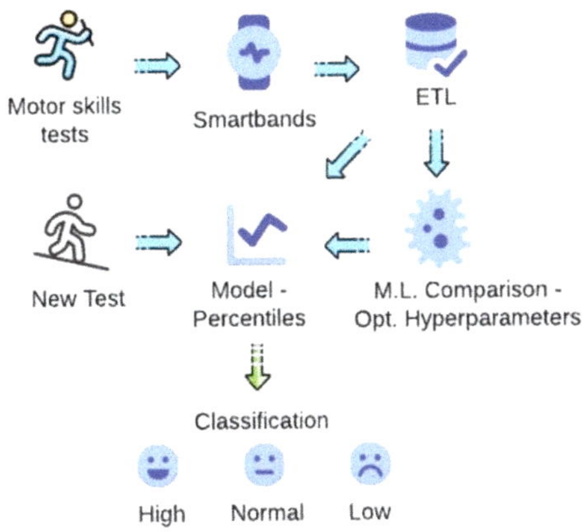


**Figure 2.** Modeling of data from the proposed study.

The percentiles were constructed using the LMS method [34]. The curves L represent skewness (lambda), M represents the median (mu), and S represents the coefficient of variation (sigma). The LMS method uses the Box–Cox transformation to fit the data distribution to a normal distribution by minimizing the effects of skewness.

For this purpose, the P25, P50, and P75 percentiles of males (Table 2) and females (Table 3) were created about the motor competence metrics: cadence (Figure 3), steps (Figure 4), speed (Figure 5), and stride (Figure 6) for schoolchildren males and females.

**Table 2.** Percentiles of motor competence metrics of schoolchildren males.

| **Metrics** | **Age** | | | | | |
|---|---|---|---|---|---|---|
| Cadence | 6–7 | 8–9 | 10–11 | 12–13 | 14–15 | 16–17 |
| L | 0.94 | −0.22 | 0.22 | 0.33 | 0.85 | 1.52 |
| M | 28 | 96 | 60 | 63 | 49 | 29 |
| S | 0.72 | 0.42 | 0.46 | 0.50 | 0.55 | 0.53 |
| P25 | 20 | 55 | 44 | 38.5 | 29 | 21 |
| P50 | 28 | 96 | 60 | 63 | 49 | 29 |
| P75 | 65.5 | 120 | 88 | 86.8 | 68 | 44 |
| Steps | | | | | | |
| L | 1.33 | −0.16 | 0.42 | 0.30 | 0.67 | 1.09 |
| M | 455 | 1437 | 884 | 1000 | 732 | 496 |
| S | 0.70 | 0.42 | 0.48 | 0.45 | 0.54 | 0.55 |
| P25 | 299 | 772 | 628 | 690 | 470 | 309 |
| P50 | 455 | 1437 | 884 | 1000 | 732 | 496 |
| P75 | 796 | 1747 | 1179 | 1299 | 1097 | 726 |
| Velocity | | | | | | |
| L | 0.85 | 0.19 | 0.80 | 0.33 | 0.93 | 1.85 |
| M | 1.62 | 4.69 | 3.08 | 3.15 | 2.28 | 1.16 |
| S | 0.70 | 0.47 | 0.53 | 0.52 | 0.63 | 0.61 |
| P25 | 1.11 | 2.73 | 2.10 | 1.84 | 1.17 | 0.90 |
| P50 | 1.62 | 4.69 | 3.08 | 3.15 | 2.28 | 1.16 |
| P75 | 3.48 | 6.00 | 4.30 | 4.51 | 3.69 | 1.92 |
| Stride | | | | | | |
| L | −0.02 | 0.65 | 0.91 | 0.41 | 0.27 | 0.66 |
| M | 88 | 82 | 80 | 82 | 76 | 71 |
| S | 0.14 | 0.12 | 0.12 | 0.12 | 0.106 | 0.12 |
| P25 | 74.5 | 76 | 74 | 76 | 71 | 66 |
| P50 | 88 | 82 | 80 | 82 | 76 | 71 |
| P75 | 97.5 | 90 | 86 | 87 | 83 | 78 |

Legend: P: percentile, L: (skewness, lambda), M: (median, mu), S: (coefficient of variation, sigma).

**Table 3.** Percentiles of motor competence metrics of schoolchildren females.

| Metrics | Age | | | | | |
|---|---|---|---|---|---|---|
| Cadence | 6–7 | 8–9 | 10–11 | 12–13 | 14–15 | 16–17 |
| L | −0.06 | −0.41 | 0.25 | 0.41 | 1.04 | 1.48 |
| M | 75 | 94 | 69 | 60 | 36 | 29 |
| S | 0.52 | 0.34 | 0.47 | 0.49 | 0.67 | 0.53 |
| P25 | 40 | 68.75 | 33 | 35 | 20 | 20 |
| P50 | 75 | 94 | 69 | 60 | 36 | 29 |
| P75 | 108 | 111.3 | 89 | 84 | 60.5 | 44 |
| Steps | | | | | | |
| L | 0.21 | −0.24 | 0.58 | 0.54 | 0.99 | 1.29 |
| M | 941 | 1391 | 802 | 784 | 613 | 529 |
| S | 0.52 | 0.37 | 0.57 | 0.49 | 0.61 | 0.52 |
| P25 | 615 | 989 | 462 | 578 | 426 | 359 |
| P50 | 941 | 1391 | 802 | 784 | 613 | 529 |
| P75 | 1584 | 1608 | 1233 | 1226 | 937 | 762 |
| Velocity | | | | | | |
| L | −0.06 | −0.29 | 0.79 | 7.97 | 1.11 | 1.84 |
| M | 3.91 | 4.75 | 2.91 | 3.04 | 1.58 | 1.27 |
| S | 0.52 | 0.36 | 0.62 | 5.50 | 0.74 | 0.62 |
| P25 | 2.15 | 3.33 | 1.52 | 1.77 | 0.94 | 0.92 |
| P50 | 3.91 | 4.75 | 2.91 | 3.04 | 1.58 | 1.27 |
| P75 | 5.41 | 5.69 | 4.16 | 4.26 | 3.09 | 1.78 |
| Stride | | | | | | |
| L | −2.97 | 1.47 | 1.11 | 0.79 | 0.27 | 0.57 |
| M | 84 | 82 | 78 | 77 | 76 | 71 |
| S | 0.24 | 0.10 | 0.11 | 0.11 | 0.09 | 0.12 |
| P25 | 81 | 79 | 75 | 73 | 72 | 65.5 |
| P50 | 84 | 82 | 78 | 77 | 76 | 71 |
| P75 | 89.5 | 86.3 | 86.5 | 86 | 81.5 | 77.5 |

Legend: P: percentile, L: (skewness, lambda), M: (median, mu), S: (coefficient of variation, sigma).

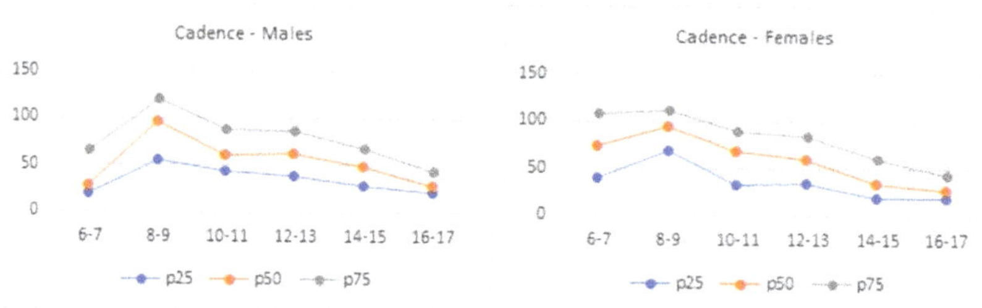


**Figure 3.** Distribution of percentiles for the cadence in schoolchildren in both sexes.

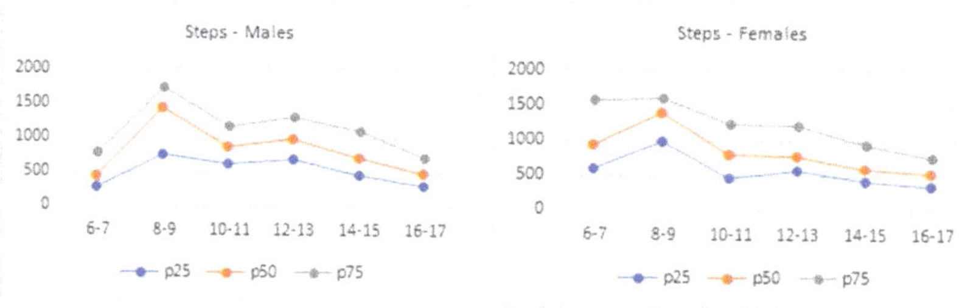


**Figure 4.** Distribution of percentiles for the number of steps in schoolchildren in both sexes.

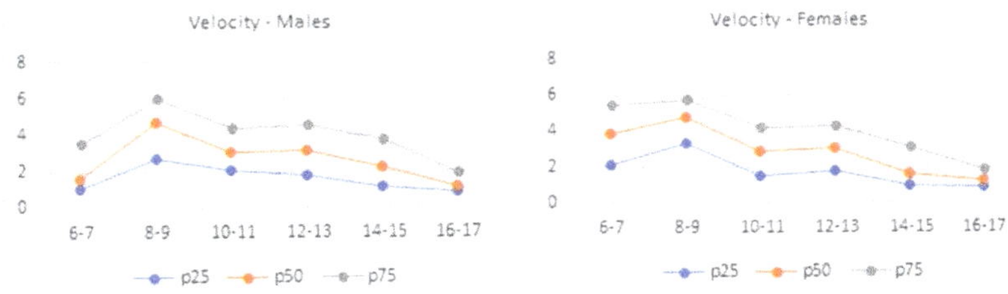


**Figure 5.** Distribution of percentiles for the velocity in schoolchildren in both sexes.

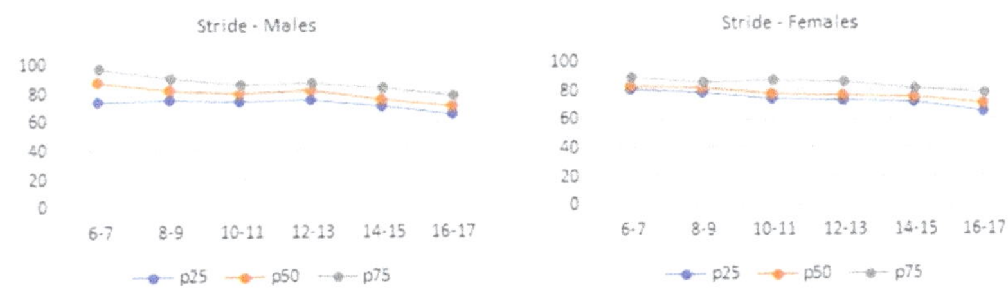


**Figure 6.** Distribution of percentiles for the stride in schoolchildren in both sexes.

## 3. Evaluation and Results

For the Anaconda Navigator platform with Jupyter Notebook, different machine-learning techniques used in further research were modeled [35], which were decision tree, support vector machine, random forest, naive Bayes, logistic regression, k-nearest neighbors, neuronal network, gradient boosted, and smart bands. Of the data to model, 80% was used for training and 20% for testing.

Jupyter Notebook is a widely used tool in the machine-learning community, where you can import a set of libraries, train a dataset classification classifier, and evaluate the model by just using a few lines of code in Python with its library Scikit-learn.

Likewise, the optimization of hyperparameters with the Scikit-learn optimization library was used. Hyperparameters are parameters that are not directly learned by the learning algorithm. The basic hyperparameter tuning models are manual search, grid search, and random search. Random search was used for training since it allows us to find equal or better models in computing time.

The configuration used for the hyperparameters in the case of gradient boosted was the loss function to optimize with the "log_loss" option, the criterion with the process to measure the quality of a division with the "friedman_mse" option, the "learning_rate" with 0.1, "max_depth": 3, "min_samples_leaf": 1, "min_samples_split": 2, "n_estimators": 100, "random_state": none, "subsample": 1.0, "tol": 0.0001, "validation_fraction": 0.1, and with the other default parameters.

Next, the tests were carried out, and the results of the modeling that was executed for the different techniques that were previously chosen were obtained using the CSV file as input data and made up of the motor competence variables.

To evaluate the model [36], accuracy in Equation (1), recall in Equation (2), precision in Equation (3), and the f1-score in Equation (4) were used. For many classes $C_i$, $fp_i$ represents false positive, $tp_i$ true positive, $fn_i$ false negative, and $tn_i$ true negative.

$$Accuracy = \frac{tp_i + tn_i}{tp_i + tn_i + fp_i + fn_i} \quad (1)$$

$$Recall = \frac{\sum_{i=1}^{l} \frac{tp_i}{tp_i + fn_i}}{l} \quad (2)$$

$$Precision = \frac{\sum_{i=1}^{l} \frac{tp_i}{tp_i + fp_i}}{l} \quad (3)$$

$$F1 - score = 2 \times \frac{(Precision) \times (Recall)}{(Precision) + (Recall)} \quad (4)$$

Tables 4 and 5 compare the classical and optimized machine-learning techniques results with selected hyperparameters and the accuracy, f1-score, recall, and precision metrics for both schoolchildren males and females.

**Table 4.** Comparison of results of supervised machine-learning techniques in males.

| Algorithm | DT | SVM | RF | NB | LR | KNN | MLP | GB | XGB | LGBM | CB |
|---|---|---|---|---|---|---|---|---|---|---|---|
| Accuracy | 0.88 | 0.69 | 0.92 | 0.74 | 0.78 | 0.81 | 0.68 | 0.93 | 0.92 | 0.94 | 0.93 |
| Accuracy optimized hyperparameter | 0.87 | 0.82 | 0.92 | 0.75 | 0.79 | 0.85 | 0.70 | 0.95 | 0.91 | 0.94 | 0.93 |
| f1-score | 0.87 | 0.74 | 0.93 | 0.77 | 0.82 | 0.88 | 0.72 | 0.92 | 0.91 | 0.93 | 0.92 |
| Recall | 0.86 | 0.67 | 0.94 | 0.73 | 0.84 | 0.88 | 0.67 | 0.92 | 0.90 | 0.94 | 0.92 |
| Precision | 0.88 | 0.82 | 0.92 | 0.82 | 0.80 | 0.88 | 0.77 | 0.92 | 0.92 | 0.92 | 0.92 |

Legend: DT: decision tree, SVM: support vector machine, RF: random forest, NB: naïve Bayes, LR: Logistic Regression; KNN: k-nearest neighbors, MLP: multilayer perceptron, GB: gradientboosted, XGB: extreme gradient boosting, LGBM: light gradient boosting machine, CB: CatBoost.

**Table 5.** Comparison of results of supervised machine-learning techniques in females.

| Algorithm | DT | SVM | RF | NB | LR | KNN | MLP | GB | XGB | LGBM | CB |
|---|---|---|---|---|---|---|---|---|---|---|---|
| Accuracy | 0.86 | 0.68 | 0.88 | 0.71 | 0.78 | 0.72 | 0.72 | 0.84 | 0.87 | 0.88 | 0.90 |
| Accuracy optimized hyperparameter | 0.86 | 0.80 | 0.87 | 0.72 | 0.83 | 0.81 | 0.74 | 0.89 | 0.84 | 0.88 | 0.88 |
| f1-score | 0.91 | 0.68 | 0.92 | 0.76 | 0.89 | 0.88 | 0.82 | 0.93 | 0.92 | 0.90 | 0.93 |
| Recall | 0.97 | 0.61 | 0.94 | 0.69 | 0.94 | 0.92 | 0.86 | 0.92 | 0.86 | 0.91 | 0.94 |
| Precision | 0.86 | 0.76 | 0.89 | 0.83 | 0.85 | 0.82 | 0.78 | 0.94 | 0.94 | 0.89 | 0.92 |

Legend: DT: decision tree, SVM: support vector machine, RF: random forest, NB: naïve Bayes, LR: Logistic Regression; KNN: k-nearest neighbors, MLP: multilayer perceptron, GB: gradient boosted, XGB: extreme gradient boosting, LGBM: light gradient boosting machine, CB: CatBoost.

In the results of the previous tables, it can be identified that, for the classification techniques, those that gave the best results concerning accuracy for the case of males and females were gradient boosting, whose values were the highest, indicating a better adjustment to the estimated prediction with a value of 0.95. For the f1-score metrics, the algorithms gave similar values of 0.92 between males and females. In the case of *recall*, it was 0.92. The confusion matrix of the gradient boosting machine-learning algorithm with the highest score found is shown in Figure 7.

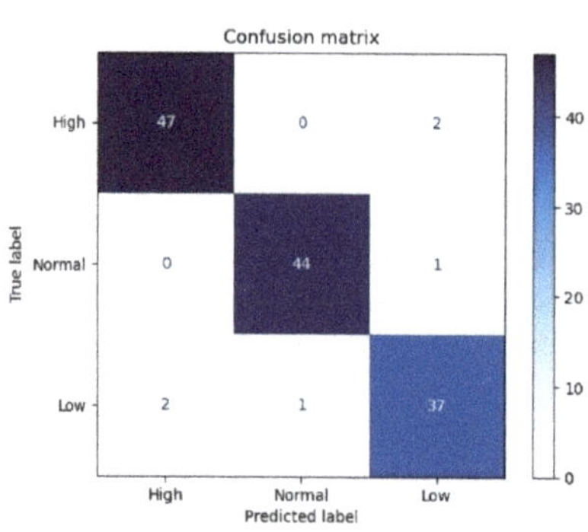


**Figure 7.** The confusion matrix of the gradient boosting machine-learning algorithm.

Figures 8 and 9 show a graph of the ROC-AUC curves of gradient boosting for males and females.

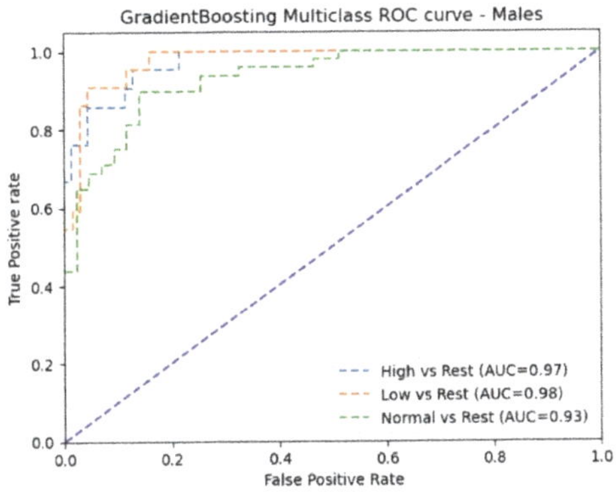


**Figure 8.** ROC-AUC curves of gradient boosting in males.

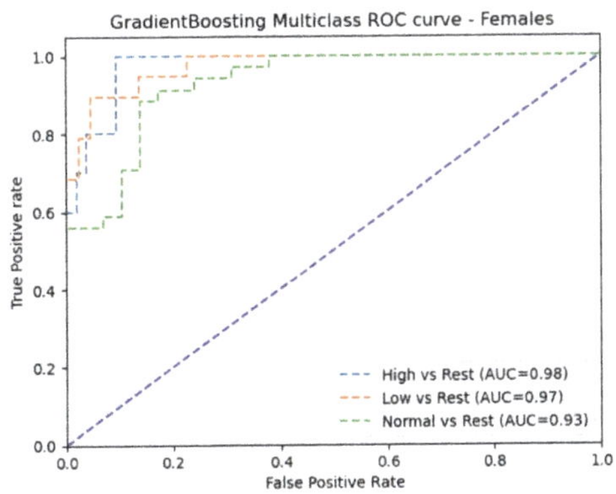


**Figure 9.** ROC-AUC curves of gradient boosting in females.

Observing the results of the ROC curves, in the case of male schoolchildren, the "Low" class shows an intense elevation towards the upper left corner of the graph and has a high area under the curve (AUC) of 0.98; this indicates that the model has a high sensitivity to detect the "Low" classification of motor competence. The false positive rate is low, suggesting the model does not misidentify many schoolchildren with the "Low" motor competence classification.

In the case of the female schoolchildren, the "High" class shows an intense elevation towards the upper left corner of the graph and has a high area under the curve (AUC) of 0.98; this indicates that the model has a high sensitivity to detect the classification "High" motor competence. The false positive rate is low, suggesting the model does not misidentify many schoolchildren with the "High" motor competence classification. On the other hand, the dark blue dotted line refers to the fact that the test has been bad, which is not the case of the study.

*Deployment*

A mobile app was developed in Android Studio using the Flutter framework. The code structure was organized by the best mobile application development practices and following the design pattern recommended by Flutter, which is the model–view–controller (MVC) design pattern. Firebase real-time database was used for storage.

The primary interfaces are shown in Figure 10, where you have the login screen and the options menu.

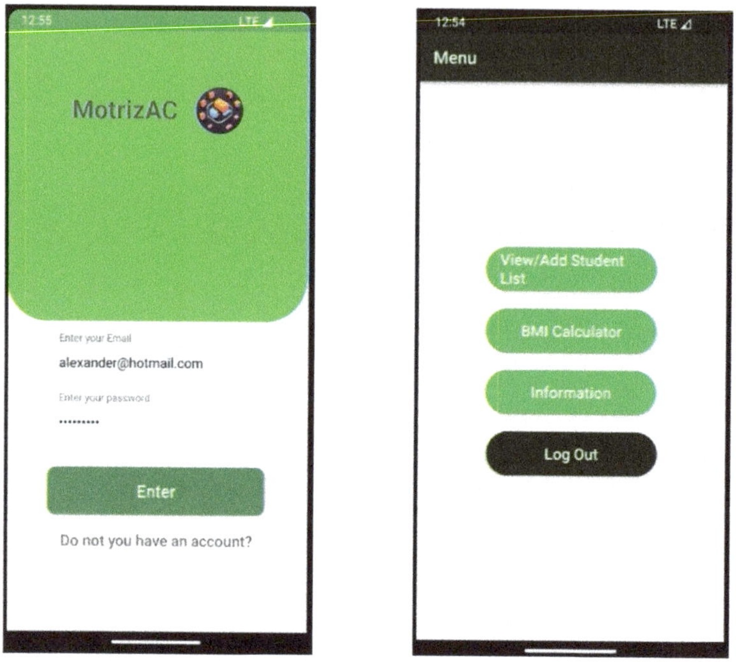


**Figure 10.** Initial interfaces of the mobile app.

Figure 11 shows the interface that allows entering the data corresponding to the student; the body mass index (BMI) will be able to be calculated automatically. Additionally, table is provided to identify the student's BMI classification. Likewise, the interface that allows entering the data captured with the smart band, such as speed, cadence, stride, and steps of the schoolchildren, is shown. It contains an Artificial Intelligence function that allows you to locate your position within the percentiles generated from the sample of schoolchildren.

The process was evaluated through the prototype of the Software Quality Systemic Model (SQSM). This model is planned based on six standardized international quality characteristics through a set of characteristic categories and metrics, which measure and evaluate the software quality of a product; this model is made into an instrument for measuring great value covering essential aspects of software quality.

It was carried out in the selected educational centers to evaluate the application's functionalities. The information collected meets expectations as it explains the population's needs.

Once the various interviewees were integrated, we proceeded with the evaluation method based on the Systemic Quality Model, which includes 11 categories. We have selected three specific classes related to the software: functionality, reliability, and usability because these apply to the case study. Table 6 shows a detailed description of each category with the interviews.

Considering the levels of satisfaction achieved in the categories of functionality, reliability, and usability, by calculating the arithmetic mean, it is observed that the degree of satisfaction of the application for the specialists of the educational centers is 77.09%. By contrasting this result with the quality level, it is evident that the application meets significant standards.

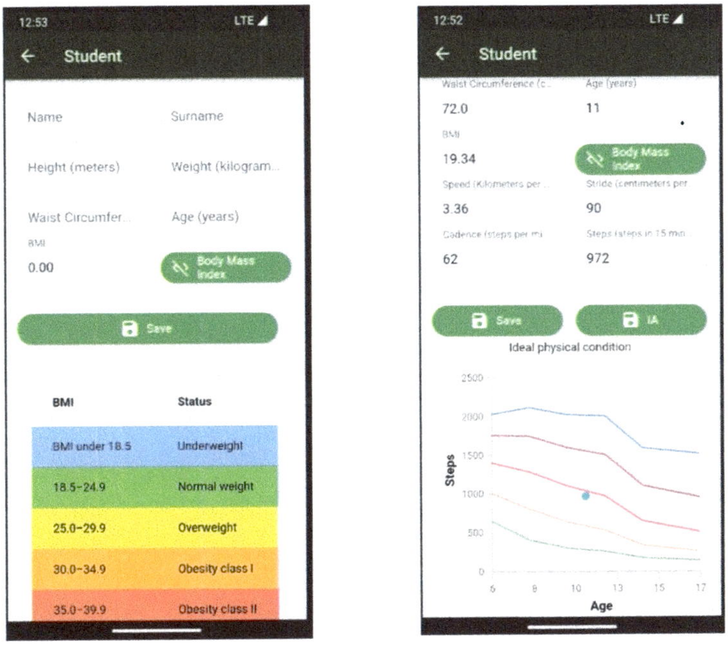


**Figure 11.** Calculation interfaces and use of AI to generate the value of your motor competence within the percentiles.

**Table 6.** Categories and characteristics according to the prototype of Software Quality Systemic Model (SQSM).

| Characteristics | Subcharacteristics | Metrics | Percentage of Compliance | Quality Level |
|---|---|---|---|---|
| Functionality (FUN) | FUN. 1 Fit for purpose | 20 | 84.00% | Satisfied |
| | FUN. 2 Accuracy | 6 | 86.67% | Satisfied |
| | FUN. 3 Interoperability | 4 | 86.67% | Satisfied |
| | FUN. 4 Security | 3 | 53.33% | Does not satisfy |
| | Subtotal | 33 | 81.88% | Satisfied |
| Usability (USA) | USA.1 Ease of Compression | 5 | 90.00% | Satisfied |
| | USA. 2 Learning Capacity | 8 | 92.00% | Satisfied |
| | USA. 3 Graphical Interface | 4 | 95.00% | Satisfied |
| | USA. 4 Operability | 3 | 52.00% | Does not satisfy |
| | Subtotal | 20 | 82.73% | Satisfied |
| Reliability (RIA) | RIA. 1 Maturity | 5 | 60.00% | Does not satisfy |
| | RIA. 2 Fault tolerance | 4 | 90.00% | Satisfied |
| | RIA. 3 Recovery | 2 | 50.00% | Does not satisfy |
| | Subtotal | 11 | 69.09% | Does not satisfy |
| | Total | 64 | 77.09% | Satisfied |

## 4. Discussion

The study's objective was to classify the motor competence of schoolchildren performed in a school using smart bands according to age range and sex, using machine-learning techniques optimized with hyperparameters acceptably for the classification indicated through the passing results in the tests carried out.

The results of the study have shown that according to the motor competence tests carried out, step cadence values obtained range from 96 to 29 steps in both sexes and the number of steps ranges from 1437 to 455, with speed from 4.75 to 1.16 and the stride from

88 to 71. Furthermore, it was verified that the measurements obtained decreased rapidly with age, being more pronounced in females than in males.

In this context, the cut-off points suggested in other recent research [37] were taken as a basis, where the study proposed percentiles of the number of steps in a day. The percentiles indicate <p25 below average, p25 to p75 average, and >p75 above average. In essence, percentiles, regardless of the method used, can be applied to establish improvement goals, especially for schoolchildren below the 25th percentile [38]. For example, the schoolchildren in this study classified below the p25th percentile in the tests performed showed higher BMI values.

Precisely, these results coincide with those found in [4], when it states that the measurements obtained decrease rapidly with age. This information could help promote strategies for developing physical activity in schoolchildren in educational centers to improve their performance. However, a limitation found in the study was the need for a broader set of tests to be performed.

Furthermore, the results of the study have shown that using machine-learning techniques such as those evaluated by Himi et al. [14,39], then optimized with hyperparameters like work carried out by Yadav et al. [38] and Yang et al. [40], they achieve reasonable classifications for schoolchildren according to their motor competence. It can also be seen that the naïve Bayes algorithm obtains the lowest results [41,42].

It was determined that the most suitable supervised machine-learning technique would be the gradient-boosted model, which has obtained the best accuracy of 0.95 with an f-score of 0.93, recall of 0.92, and precision of 0.94, which was used in works such as [43,44]. This has been corroborated by the ROC-AUC curves, where the "Low" classes for males and "High" for females show a substantial elevation towards the upper left corner of the graph and have a high area under the curve of 0.98; this indicates that the model has a high sensitivity to detect motor competence classification.

This study represents a significant contribution with the use of wearable devices for data capture and classification using machine-learning algorithms optimized with hyperparameters for motor competence in schoolchildren that can support people interested in finding more precise ways to evaluate motor competence with the support of technology.

## 5. Conclusions

In conclusion, smart bands have shown great potential to improve the motor competence of schoolchildren through machine learning and hyperparameters. The gradient-boosted algorithm is a good model for classifying schoolchildren. Motor competence is a crucial aspect of the development of children and adolescents, and smart bands can facilitate this process by providing personalized feedback. By harnessing the power of technology, smart bands can help children develop essential motor skills, leading to better physical health and overall well-being. As more research is conducted in this field, we expect to see more advancements in smart band technology, which will undoubtedly positively impact child development.

Finally, the mobile software product built based on the proposed model was validated using the prototype of the Software Quality Systemic Model (SQSM) based on three specific categories: functionality, reliability, and usability, obtaining 77.09%

Expanding the determining attributes for classifying motor competence in schoolchildren is recommended in future work. Additionally, constructing the application of other classification algorithms is essential to compare results and assess efficiency, as well as deep learning. Different approaches, such as transfer learning, can be used to adapt domain data to train at high fidelity.

**Author Contributions:** Methodology, J.A.O.; Software, A.C.G. and C.A.L.; Validation, A.C.G. and C.A.L.; Formal analysis, J.S.-T.; Investigation, J.S.-T.; Writing—original draft, J.S.-T.; Writing—review & editing, M.Z.C. All authors have read and agreed to the published version of the manuscript.

**Funding:** This research was funded by Catholic University of Santa María grant number 7995-CU-2022.

**Institutional Review Board Statement:** Anthropometric measurements and the utilization of the smart band followed the recommendations outlined by the local ethics committee (UCSM-096-2022) and adhered to the principles of the Declaration of Helsinki (World Medical Association) concerning ethical standards for human research (Universidad Católica de Santa Maria (096-07/10/2022)).

**Informed Consent Statement:** Informed consent was obtained from all subjects involved in the study.

**Data Availability Statement:** The data presented in this study are available on request from the corresponding author. The data is not publicly available due to the privacy of handling schoolchildren's data.

**Conflicts of Interest:** The authors declare no conflict of interest.

## References


1. Dini Kounoudes, A.; Kapitsaki, G.M.; Katakis, I. Enhancing user awareness on inferences obtained from fitness trackers data. *User Model. User Adapt. Interact.* **2023**, *33*, 967–1014. [CrossRef] [PubMed]
2. Amor, J.D.; James, C.J. Validation of a Commercial Android Smartwatch as an Activity Monitoring Platform. *IEEE J. Biomed. Health Inform.* **2018**, *22*, 968–978. [CrossRef] [PubMed]
3. Al-Janabi, S.; Salman, A.H. Sensitive integration of multilevel optimization model in human activity recognition for smartphone and smartwatch applications. *Big Data Min. Anal.* **2021**, *4*, 124–138. [CrossRef]
4. Sulla-Torres, J.; Vidal-Espinoza, R.; Avendaño Llanque, C.; Calla Gamboa, A.; Zúñiga Carnero, M.; Cossio-Bolaños, M.; Gomez-Campos, R. Quantification of the Number of Steps in a School Recess by Means of Smart Bands: Proposal of Referential Values for Children and Adolescents. *Children* **2023**, *10*, 915. [CrossRef] [PubMed]
5. Weiss, G.M.; Yoneda, K.; Hayajneh, T. Smartphone and Smartwatch-Based Biometrics Using Activities of Daily Living. *IEEE Access* **2019**, *7*, 133190–133202. [CrossRef]
6. Cosoli, G.; Antognoli, L.; Scalise, L. Wearable Electrocardiography for Physical Activity Monitoring: Definition of Validation Protocol and Automatic Classification. *Biosensors* **2023**, *13*, 154. [CrossRef] [PubMed]
7. Alsareii, S.A.; Awais, M.; Alamri, A.M.; AlAsmari, M.Y.; Irfan, M.; Aslam, N.; Raza, M. Physical Activity Monitoring and Classification Using Machine Learning Techniques. *Life* **2022**, *12*, 1103. [CrossRef]
8. Ali, Y.A.; Awwad, E.M.; Al-Razgan, M.; Maarouf, A. Hyperparameter Search for Machine Learning Algorithms for Optimizing the Computational Complexity. *Processes* **2023**, *11*, 349. [CrossRef]
9. Wang, C.; Lizardo, O.; Hachen, D.S. Using Fitbit data to examine factors that affect daily activity levels of college students. *PLoS ONE* **2021**, *16*, e0244747. [CrossRef]
10. Sabry, F.; Eltaras, T.; Labda, W.; Alzoubi, K.; Malluhi, Q. Machine Learning for Healthcare Wearable Devices: The Big Picture. *J. Healthc. Eng.* **2022**, *2022*, 4653923. [CrossRef]
11. Zhou, M.; Fukuoka, Y.; Goldberg, K.; Vittinghoff, E.; Aswani, A. Applying machine learning to predict future adherence to physical activity programs. *BMC Med. Inform. Decis. Mak.* **2019**, *19*, 169. [CrossRef] [PubMed]
12. Creaser, A.V.; Frazer, M.T.; Costa, S.; Bingham, D.D.; Clemes, S.A. The Use of Wearable Activity Trackers in Schools to Promote Child and Adolescent Physical Activity: A Descriptive Content Analysis of School Staff's Perspectives. *Int. J. Environ. Res. Public Health* **2022**, *19*, 14067. [CrossRef] [PubMed]
13. Site, A.; Nurmi, J.; Lohan, E.S. Systematic Review on Machine-Learning Algorithms Used in Wearable-Based eHealth Data Analysis. *IEEE Access* **2021**, *9*, 112221–112235. [CrossRef]
14. Himi, S.T.; Monalisa, N.T.; Whaiduzzaman, M.; Barros, A.; Uddin, M.S. MedAi: A Smartwatch-Based Application Framework for the Prediction of Common Diseases Using Machine Learning. *IEEE Access* **2023**, *11*, 12342–12359. [CrossRef]
15. Bischl, B.; Binder, M.; Lang, M.; Pielok, T.; Richter, J.; Coors, S.; Thomas, J.; Ullmann, T.; Becker, M.; Boulesteix, A.; et al. Hyperparameter optimization: Foundations, algorithms, best practices, and open challenges. *WIREs Data Min. Knowl. Discov.* **2023**, *13*, e1484. [CrossRef]
16. Yagin, F.H.; Gülü, M.; Gormez, Y.; Castañeda-Babarro, A.; Colak, C.; Greco, G.; Fischetti, F.; Cataldi, S. Estimation of Obesity Levels with a Trained Neural Network Approach optimized by the Bayesian Technique. *Appl. Sci.* **2023**, *13*, 3875. [CrossRef]
17. Rivera, O.; Avilés, O.F.; Castillo-Castaneda, E. Classifying the physical activity indicator using machine learning and direct measurements: A feasibility study. *Acta Sci. Technol.* **2023**, *45*, e61317. [CrossRef]
18. Triwiyanto, T.; Pawana, I.P.A.; Purnomo, M.H. An Improved Performance of Deep Learning Based on Convolution Neural Network to Classify the Hand Motion by Evaluating Hyper Parameter. *IEEE Trans. Neural Syst. Rehabil. Eng.* **2020**, *28*, 1678–1688. [CrossRef]
19. Chapman, P.; Clinton, J.; Kerber, R.; Khabaza, T.; Reinartz, T.P.; Shearer, C.; Wirth, R. CRISP-DM 1.0: Step-by-step data mining guide. *PSS Inc.* **2000**, *9*, 1–73.
20. Freedman, D.S.; Berenson, G.S. Tracking of BMI z Scores for Severe Obesity. *Pediatrics* **2017**, *140*, e20171072. [CrossRef]
21. Fernández, J.R.; Redden, D.T.; Pietrobelli, A.; Allison, D.B. Waist circumference percentiles in nationally representative samples of African-American, European-American, and Mexican-American children and adolescents. *J. Pediatr.* **2004**, *145*, 439–444. [CrossRef] [PubMed]

22. Bayoumy, K.; Gaber, M.; Elshafeey, A.; Mhaimeed, O.; Dineen, E.H.; Marvel, F.A.; Martin, S.S.; Muse, E.D.; Turakhia, M.P.; Tarakji, K.G.; et al. Smart wearable devices in cardiovascular care: Where we are and how to move forward. *Nat. Rev. Cardiol.* **2021**, *18*, 581–599. [CrossRef] [PubMed]
23. Piazentin Ono, J.; Freire, J.; Silva, C.T. Interactive data visualization in Jupyter notebooks. *Comput. Sci. Eng.* **2021**, *23*, 99–106. [CrossRef]
24. Safavian, S.R.; Landgrebe, D. A Survey of Decision Tree Classifier Methodology. *Electr. Eng.* **1991**, *21*, 660–674. [CrossRef]
25. Qi, Y. Random Forest for Bioinformatics. In *Ensemble Machine Learning: Methods and Applications*; Springer: Berlin/Heidelberg, Germany, 2012.
26. Cristianini, N.; Shawe-Taylor, J. *An Introduction to Support Vector Machines and Other Kernel-Based Learning Methods*; Cambridge University Press: Cambridge, UK, 2000. [CrossRef]
27. Zhang, H.; Su, J. Naive Bayes for optimal ranking. *J. Exp. Theor. Artif. Intell.* **2008**, *20*, 79–93. [CrossRef]
28. Cheng, X.; Lin, S.Y.; Liu, J.; Liu, S.; Zhang, J.; Nie, P.; Fuemmeler, B.F.; Wang, Y.; Xue, H. Does physical activity predict obesity—A machine learning and statistical method-based analysis. *Int. J. Environ. Res. Public Health* **2021**, *18*, 3966. [CrossRef] [PubMed]
29. Bishop, C.M. *Neural Networks: A Pattern Recognition Perspective. Neural Networks*; Oxford University Press: Oxford, UK, 1996.
30. Cunningham, P.; Delany, S.J. k-Nearest Neighbour Classifiers—A Tutorial. *ACM Comput. Surv.* **2022**, *54*, 1–25. [CrossRef]
31. Friedman, J.H. Greedy function approximation: A gradient boosting machine. *Ann. Stat.* **2001**, *29*, 1189–1232. [CrossRef]
32. Liu, M.; Guo, C.; Guo, S. An explainable knowledge distillation method with XGBoost for ICU mortality prediction. *Comput. Biol. Med.* **2023**, *152*, 106466. [CrossRef]
33. Prokhorenkova, L.; Gusev, G.; Vorobev, A.; Dorogush, A.V.; Gulin, A. Catboost: Unbiased boosting with categorical features. In Proceedings of the 32nd Conference on Neural Information Processing Systems (NeurIPS 2018), Montréal, QC, Canada, 3–8 December 2018.
34. Cole, T.J. Establishing a standard definition for child overweight and obesity worldwide: International survey. *BMJ* **2000**, *320*, 1240–1243. [CrossRef]
35. Dai, R.; Lu, C.; Yun, L.; Lenze, E.; Avidan, M.; Kannampallil, T. Comparing stress prediction models using smartwatch physiological signals and participant self-reports. *Comput. Methods Programs Biomed.* **2021**, *208*, 106207. [CrossRef] [PubMed]
36. Sokolova, M.; Lapalme, G. A systematic analysis of performance measures for classification tasks. *Inf. Process. Manag.* **2009**, *45*, 427–437. [CrossRef]
37. Lammers, A.E.; Romanowski, A.L.; Baumgartner, H.; Diller, G.P.; Uebing, A. Reference Values for Wristband Accelerometry Data in Children Aged 6–11 Years of Age. *Front. Pediatr.* **2022**, *10*, 808372. [CrossRef] [PubMed]
38. Yadav, P.; Sharma, S.C.; Mahadeva, R.; Patole, S.P. Exploring Hyper-Parameters and Feature Selection for Predicting Non-Communicable Chronic Disease Using Stacking Classifier. *IEEE Access* **2023**, *11*, 80030–80055. [CrossRef]
39. Wang, J.; Xie, Z.; Li, Y.; Song, Y.; Yan, J.; Bai, W.; Zhou, T.; Qin, J. Relationship between Health Status and Physical Fitness of College Students from South China: An Empirical Study by Data Mining Approach. *IEEE Access* **2020**, *8*, 67466–67473. [CrossRef]
40. Yang, H.; Chen, Z.; Yang, H.; Tian, M. Predicting Coronary Heart Disease Using an Improved LightGBM Model: Performance Analysis and Comparison. *IEEE Access* **2023**, *11*, 23366–23380. [CrossRef]
41. Mannini, A.; Sabatini, A.M. Machine Learning Methods for Classifying Human Physical Activity from On-Body Accelerometers. *Sensors* **2010**, *10*, 1154–1175. [CrossRef]
42. Saez, Y.; Baldominos, A.; Isasi, P. A Comparison Study of Classifier Algorithms for Cross-Person Physical Activity Recognition. *Sensors* **2016**, *17*, 66. [CrossRef]
43. Zhang, B.; Ren, J.; Cheng, Y.; Wang, B.; Wei, Z. Health data driven on continuous blood pressure prediction based on gradient boosting decision tree algorithm. *IEEE Access* **2019**, *7*, 32423. [CrossRef]
44. Zhao, L.; Zhang, F.; Zhang, H.; Liang, Y.; Zhou, A.; Ma, H. Robust Respiratory Rate Monitoring Using Smartwatch Photoplethysmography. *IEEE Internet Things J.* **2023**, *10*, 4830–4844. [CrossRef]

applied sciences

MDPI

Systematic Review

# Machine Learning Models for Predicting Mortality in Hemodialysis Patients: A Systematic Review

Alexandru Catalin Motofelea [1,2], Adelina Mihaescu [2,3,*], Nicu Olariu [2,3], Luciana Marc [2,3], Lazar Chisavu [2,3], Gheorghe Nicusor Pop [4], Andreea Crintea [5], Ana Maria Cristina Jura [6], Viviana Mihaela Ivan [2,7], Adrian Apostol [7] and Adalbert Schiller [2,3]

1 Doctoral School, "Victor Babeș" University of Medicine and Pharmacy Timișoara, Eftimie Murgu Square No. 2, 300041 Timisoara, Romania; alexandru.motofelea@umft.ro
2 Center for Molecular Research in Nephrology and Vascular Disease, Faculty of Medicine, "Victor Babeș" University of Medicine and Pharmacy Timișoara, Eftimie Murgu Square No. 2, 300041 Timisoara, Romania; nicu.olariu@umft.ro (N.O.); marc.luciana@umft.ro (L.M.); chisavu.lazar@umft.ro (L.C.); viviana.ivan@umft.ro (V.M.I.); schiller.adalbert@umft.ro (A.S.)
3 Department of Internal Medicine II—Division of Nephrology, "Victor Babeș" University of Medicine and Pharmacy Timișoara, Eftimie Murgu Square No. 2, 300041 Timisoara, Romania
4 Center for Modeling Biological Systems and Data Analysis (CMSBAD), "Victor Babeș" University of Medicine and Pharmacy Timișoara, Eftimie Murgu Square No. 2, 300041 Timisoara, Romania; pop.nicusor@umft.ro
5 Department of Molecular Sciences, University of Medicine and Pharmacy "Iuliu Hațieganu", 400349 Cluj-Napoca, Romania; crintea.andreea@umfcluj.ro
6 Department of Obstetrics and Gynecology, "Victor Babeş" University of Medicine and Pharmacy Timișoara, Eftimie Murgu Square No. 2, 300041 Timisoara, Romania; cristina.jura@umft.ro
7 Department VII, Internal Medicine II, Discipline of Cardiology, "Victor Babeș" University of Medicine and Pharmacy Timișoara, Eftimie Murgu Square No. 2, 300041 Timisoara, Romania; apostol.adrian@umft.ro
* Correspondence: mihaescu.adelina@umft.ro

**Abstract: Background:** Hemodialysis (HD) patients have significantly higher mortality rates compared to the general population, primarily due to complex comorbidities. This systematic review and meta-analysis aimed to evaluate and compare the performance of various machine learning (ML) models in predicting mortality among HD patients. **Methods:** The analysis followed PRISMA guidelines, including studies that assessed the predictive capabilities of ML models for mortality in HD patients. Review Manager software version 5.4.1. was used for meta-analysis, and the performance of ML models was compared, including logistic regression, XGBoost, and Random Forest models. **Results:** The meta-analysis indicated that the logistic regression model predicted a true positive mortality rate of 8.23%, close to the actual rate of 10.53%. In contrast, the XGBoost and Random Forest models predicted rates of 9.93% and 8.94%, respectively, compared to the actual mortality rate of 13.73%. The highest area under the curve (AUC) was reported for the Random Forest model at a 3-year follow-up (AUC = 0.89). No significant difference was found between the performance of logistic regression and Random Forest models ($p = 0.82$). **Conclusions:** ML models, particularly Random Forest and logistic regression, demonstrated effective predictive capabilities for mortality in HD patients. These models can help identify high-risk patients early, facilitating personalized treatment strategies and potentially improving long-term outcomes. However, the observed heterogeneity among studies indicates a need for further research to refine model performance and standardize predictive features.

**Keywords:** machine learning; Random Forest; logistic regression; ESKD; mortality

## 1. Introduction

Hemodialysis (HD) remains a critical and life-sustaining treatment for patients with End-Stage Renal Disease (ESRD), a severe condition characterized by the irreversible loss of kidney function. Patients with ESRD represent approximately 89% of individuals requiring dialysis therapy, underscoring the high prevalence of this population within the dialysis setting [1,2]. Despite advances in treatment, hemodialysis patients experience significantly higher mortality rates than the general population, with cardiovascular diseases being a major contributing factor [3,4].

The elevated risk of mortality in HD patients results from a complex interplay of factors. Advanced age, high estimated glomerular filtration rate (eGFR) at dialysis initiation, the use of vascular catheters, low serum albumin, and reduced hemoglobin levels have all been identified as critical predictors of poor outcomes [5–9]. Early risk stratification using these clinical indicators is essential for improving patient management and enhancing survival rates [10].

Traditional risk prediction models, such as Cox proportional hazards regression and logistic regression, have been widely used to identify mortality risk factors in HD patients [8,11–19]. While they possess the flexibility to incorporate non-linear relationships and interaction effects through explicit inclusion of transformed variables (e.g., polynomial terms, splines) or interaction terms, identifying and specifying all relevant complex relationships in advance can be challenging. In practice, simpler model structures are often initially employed, which may not fully capture and predict unknown patterns inherent in complex biological data. This may potentially limit predictive performance compared to methods designed to automatically detect such patterns, especially when applied to large, heterogeneous patient populations [20].

The rise of big data and advanced computational techniques has paved the way for machine learning (ML) approaches, which have shown promise in addressing the limitations of traditional statistical models. Unlike conventional methods, ML algorithms such as Random Forest and XGBoost can handle complex, non-linear relationships between variables and can adapt to evolving clinical datasets [21]. These models excel in identifying novel predictive features and have demonstrated superior accuracy in mortality risk prediction compared to traditional models [22–25]. Additionally, ML models offer the capability to estimate individualized treatment effects, providing a more personalized approach to patient care.

Since traditional risk prediction models often struggle with the complex, non-linear interactions present in hemodialysis patient data, ML may offer additional advantages in addressing these complexities. Therefore, the primary objectives of this systematic review and meta-analysis are to systematically identify and summarize studies that have developed and evaluated ML models for predicting all-cause mortality in hemodialysis patients. In addition, we aim to compare the reported predictive performance of various ML models, focusing on metrics such as Area Under the Receiver Operating Characteristic curve (AUC), sensitivity, and specificity, with particular attention to commonly employed algorithms like Random Forest and Logistic Regression. These findings will help to evaluate the current state of ML application in this area and assess the potential clinical utility of these models for enhancing risk stratification and informing personalized patient management strategies in the hemodialysis setting.

## 2. Materials and Methods

### 2.1. Study Design and Protocol Registration

This meta-analysis was performed in accordance with the Preferred Reporting Items for Systematic Reviews and Meta-Analyses (PRISMA) guidelines and the Cochrane Handbook for Systematic Reviews of Interventions [26,27]. The study protocol has been registered in the PROSPERO database under the registration number CRD42024517408.

### 2.2. Literature Review

Four databases were searched: PubMed, Web of Science, Scopus, and Cochrane, without restrictions. The Mesh database was used to construct the search strategy. The search consisted of a combination of the following keywords: ("Mortality" [Mesh] OR "Mortality" OR "Mortalities" OR "Death Rate" OR "Case Fatality Rate" OR "Case Fatality Rates" OR "Case Fatality Rate") AND ("Kidney Failure, Chronic" [Mesh] OR "Chronic Renal Failure" OR "End Stage Kidney Disease" OR "End Stage Renal Disease" OR "End-Stage Renal Failure" OR "Chronic Kidney Failure" OR "Renal Dialysis" [Mesh] OR "Renal Dialyses" OR Hemodialysis OR Hemodialysis) AND (prediction OR predictors OR prognostic) AND (Machine learning OR model OR validation).

### 2.3. Eligibility Requirements and Study Selection

The inclusion criteria encompassed studies addressing the ability of ML models to predict mortality among HD patients. Articles of any study design, written in English, and with full text available were included. No limitations concerning the publication date were applied. We omitted studies with inadequate data for extraction. Reviews, book chapters, theses, editorials, letters, conference papers, non-English studies, and animal or in vitro research were excluded.

Two independent reviewers evaluated the articles obtained from the four electronic databases for eligibility by reviewing the title, abstract, and full text in an Excel spreadsheet. A third impartial reviewer resolved any disagreements.

### 2.4. Assessment of Study Quality

The Cochrane risk-of-bias instrument, the QUADAS-2 tool, assesses the risk of bias in each study across four domains: participant selection, index test, reference standard, flow and timing, as well as an overall assessment of bias risk [28]. This tool is specifically designed for systematic reviews of diagnostic or prognostic accuracy studies and evaluates potential bias across four key domains: (1) Participant Selection: Assessing whether the patient sample was representative of the target population and whether selection could introduce bias. (2) Index Test: Evaluating the conduct and interpretation of the ML model development and validation (the "index test" in this context), including whether thresholds were pre-specified. (3) Reference Standard: Assessing the method used to establish the true outcome (mortality) and whether it was likely to classify the outcome correctly. (4) Flow and Timing: Evaluating patient flow, dropouts, and the appropriateness of the time interval between the index test and reference standard ascertainment.

### 2.5. Data Extraction

Data extraction was conducted independently by two reviewers and recorded in a pre-defined Excel spreadsheet. Extracted data included study characteristics such as design, country, period, and sample size; patient demographics and clinical parameters; and the outcomes of machine learning model performance. The variables included in the datasets were demographic (age, gender, body mass index), clinical (vascular access type, comorbidities, duration of hemodialysis), and laboratory parameters (e.g., levels of hemoglobin, albumin, calcium, phosphorus, potassium, sodium, and creatinine). Mortality status during the follow-up period was the primary outcome variable. Any disagreements were resolved through discussion among the reviewers.

### 2.6. Statistical Analysis

We performed the statistical analysis using the Review Manager (Revman) software version 5.4.1. To pool the results of the meta-analysis, we used mean difference (MD) with a 95% confidence interval (CI). Significance was detected at a $p$ value less than 0.05. A random-effects model was chosen due to the anticipated clinical and methodological diversity across studies, including variations in patient populations, ML models used, features included, and study designs. Statistical heterogeneity was assessed using the Chi-square test at $p < 0.1$. Subgroup analysis based on the machine learning model tested, along with leave-one-out sensitivity analysis, was planned to explore potential sources of heterogeneity.

### 2.7. Outcomes Measures

Mortality prediction was the primary outcome of this meta-analysis. It was reported in the studies as an Area Under the Curve (AUC) and 95% CI. The sensitivity and specificity of the models were qualitatively compared. In addition, the number of true positive, true negative, false positive, and false negative cases were also qualitatively compared among the included studies.

## 3. Results

### 3.1. Study Selection

The study selection process is illustrated in Figure 1. The initial search across relevant databases yielded 6276 studies. After removing duplicates, 6114 studies were screened based on title and abstract. Subsequently, 6089 studies were excluded due to irrelevance to the research question. A full-text assessment was conducted for the remaining 84 reports. A further 64 reports were excluded for various reasons: unavailability of full text ($n = 6$), duplicate publication ($n = 7$), mismatched intervention ($n = 11$), irrelevant outcome ($n = 14$), or inappropriate population ($n = 15$). Ultimately, 11 studies met the inclusion criteria and were included in the systematic review and meta-analysis. All included studies were retrospective cohorts (Table 1).

**Table 1.** Summary of the included studies.

| Study | Design | Country | Period | Sample Size | ML Models | Summary |
|---|---|---|---|---|---|---|
| Garcia-Montemayor (2020) [10] | Retrospective Cohort | Spain | 1995–2015 | 1571 | Random Forest, Logistic Regression | Random Forest showed superior performance over logistic regression for mortality prediction in hemodialysis (HD) patients. |
| Chaudhuri (2023) [29] | Retrospective Cohort | Multicenter | Not Specified | 95,142 | XGBoost, Logistic Regression | Developed ML and traditional models for 3-year mortality risk classification in prevalent HD patients, demonstrating good accuracy. |
| Sheng (2020) [30] | Retrospective Cohort | China | 2007–2019 | 5828 | Various ML Models (e.g., Adaptive Boosting, XGBoost) | Developed and validated ML models to stratify first-year mortality risk in HD patients, aiding early risk identification. |
| Akbilgic (2019) [31] | Retrospective Cohort | US | 2007–2014 | 27,615 | Random Forest | Accurately predicted short-term mortality in incident ESRD patients, supporting clinical decision-making. |
| Lee (2023) [32] | Retrospective Cohort | Taiwan | 2006–2012 | 800 | Logistic Regression, Decision Tree, XGBoost | Provided insights for nephrologists on short-term mortality risks, enhancing patient-centered decision-making. |
| Mauri (2008) [33] | Retrospective Cohort | Spain | 1997–2003 | 946 | Logistic Regression | Developed a prognostic model for 1-year mortality, highlighting modifiable risk factors for targeted interventions. |

**Table 1.** *Cont.*

| Study | Design | Country | Period | Sample Size | ML Models | Summary |
|---|---|---|---|---|---|---|
| Thijssen (2012) [34] | Retrospective Cohort | US | 2000–2009 | 2326 | Logistic Regression | Suggested potential for prediction models to evolve into alert systems for timely intervention in high-risk patients. |
| Rankin (2022) [35] | Retrospective Cohort | US | 2008–2017 | 345,305 | XGBoost | Developed an XGBoost model with excellent calibration for early mortality prediction post-dialysis initiation. |
| Wang (2021) [36] | Retrospective Cohort | China | 2007–2016 | 1200 | Multiple ML Models (e.g., SVM, LSTM) | Employed anomaly detection with LSTM autoencoder, effectively identifying high-risk patients using longitudinal HD data. |
| Khazaei (2021) [37] | Retrospective Cohort | Iran | 2007–2017 | 758 | Decision Tree, SVM, Logistic Regression | Logistic Regression outperformed other models; key predictors included gender, age, iron levels, CRP status, and URR. |
| Gotta (2020) [38] | Retrospective Cohort | US | 2004–2016 | 363 | Random Forest | Identified key predictors (e.g., LDH, RDW) in pediatric HD patients, emphasizing the need for tailored management strategies. |

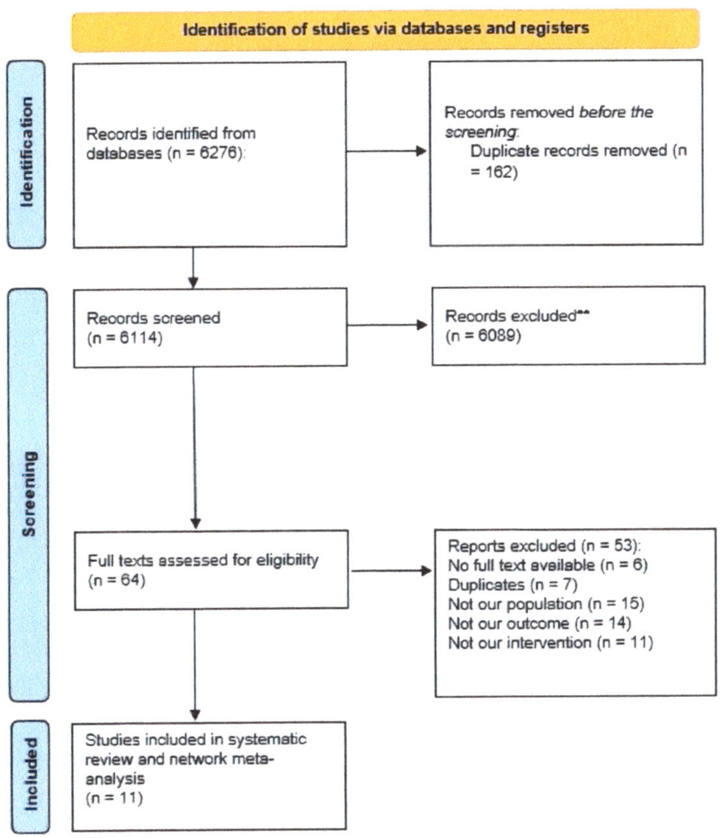


**Figure 1.** Flowchart of the study selection process. ** Records excluded** (n = 6089) due to irrelevance at title and abstract screening.

The included studies were conducted over a broad period, from 2012 to 2023, with data collection spanning from 1995 to 2019. A variety of ML models were investigated across these studies, including Logistic Regression, Adaptive Boosting, Decision Tree, Gradient Boosting, K-Nearest Neighbor, Random Forest, XGBoost, and Support Vector Machine.

### 3.2. Baseline Characteristics of the Included Patients

The age range of the included patients varied between $50.29 \pm 15.73$ and $68.7 \pm 11.2$ (Table 2). The majority of patients were male. Body mass index (BMI) ranged from $21.73 \pm 21.83$ to $30 \pm 68$. Albumin levels ranged from $3.2 \pm 0.6$ to $4 \pm 0.45$ g/dL. Sodium levels ranged from $138.5 \pm 2.6$ to $139.28 \pm 3.7$ mEq/L, while potassium levels ranged from $4.7 \pm 0.69$ to $4.91 \pm 0.89$ mEq/L. Calcium levels fluctuated between $8.86 \pm 0.64$ and $9.04 \pm 3.88$ mg/dL, while phosphorus levels ranged from $4.27 \pm 1.59$ to $5.2 \pm 1.48$ mg/dL. Creatinine levels varied widely across studies, ranging from $6.46 \pm 3.52$ to $12.9 \pm 6.1$ mg/dL. Similarly, hemoglobin levels ranged from $9.66 \pm 1.64$ to $11.7 \pm 1.1$ g/dL.

**Table 2.** Baseline characteristics of the patients within the included studies.

| Study ID | Age | Males | BMI | Albumin (g/dL) | Sodium (mEq/L) | Potassium (mEq/L) | Calcium (mg/dL) | Phosphorus (mg/dL) | Creatinine (mg/dL) | Hemoglobin (g/dL) |
|---|---|---|---|---|---|---|---|---|---|---|
| Garcia-Montemayor 2020 [10] | 62.33 ± 15.89 * | 953 (61%) | 27.1± 5.41 | 3.54± 0.55 | NR | 4.91 ± 0.89 | 9.04 ± 3.88 | 5.04 ± 1.66 | 7.3 ± 4.4 | 10.08 ± 2.79 |
| Chaudhuri 2023 [29] | 61.73 ± 15.08 * | 54.611 (57.4%) | 25.13 ± 5.53 | 3.78± 0.42 | NR | 4.87 ± 0.62 | 8.86 ± 0.64 | 4.27 ± 1.59 | 7.40 ± 2.48 | NR |
| Sheng 2020 [30] | 62.53 ± 62.45 * | 3524 (60.47%) | 21.73 ± 21.83 | 3.6 ± 0.68 | NR | NR | NR | NR | 12.9 ± 6.1 | NR |
| Akbilgic 2019 [31] | 68.7 ± 11.2 * | 27,101 (98.1%) | 29.9 ± 6.7 | 3.4 ± 0.7 | 138.9 ± 3.8 | NR | NR | NR | NR | NR |
| Lee 2023 [32] | 63.30 ± 13.26 * | 405 (50.63%) | NR | NR | 139.28 ± 3.70 | 4.70 ± 0.69 | NR | 5.20 ± 1.48 | 9.41 ± 2.3 | 10.31 ± 1.49 |
| Mauri 2008 [33] | 64.6 ± 14.4 * | 3567 (62.2%) | NR | NR | NR | NR | NR | NR | NR | NR |
| Thijssen 2012 [34] | 61.7 ± 15.5 * | 1314 (56.5%) | NR | 3.7 ± 0.4 | 138.5 ± 2.6 | NR | NR | 5.2 ± 1.2 | 7.3 ± 2.7 | 11.7 ± 1.1 |
| Rankin 2022 [35] | 63± 15 * | 198,347 (57.4%) | 30 ± 68 | 3.2 ± 0.7 | NR | NR | NR | NR | 6.46 ± 3.52 | 9.66 ±1.64 |
| Wang 2021 [36] | 52.69 ±16.94 * | 665 (63.03%) | NR | NR | NR | NR | NR | NR | NR | NR |
| Khazaei 2021[37] | 50.29 ± 15.73 * | 464 (54.2%) | 23.09 ± 4.21 | 3.74 ± 0.73 | 138.78 ± 6.8 | 4.9 ± 0.94 | 8.9 ± 0.90 | 5.11 ± 1.55 | NR | 10.48 ± 2.06 |
| Gotta 2020 [38] | 12.7(9–28.7) ** | 1473 (55%) | NR | 4 ± 0.45 | NR | NR | NR | NR | 9.9 ± 4.38 | 11.43 ± 1.79 |

NR: not reported, Values are provided as * means ± SD, median (25th–75th percentile) **, and number (%).

### 3.3. Quality Assessment Results

The risk of bias graph and summary are illustrated in Figures 2 and 3. Regarding participant selection, all studies exhibit a low risk of bias, except for five studies, which showed an unclear risk of bias: Garcia-Montemayor 2020, Gotta 2020, Khazaei 2021, Chaudhuri 2023, and Wang 2021 [10,29,36–38].

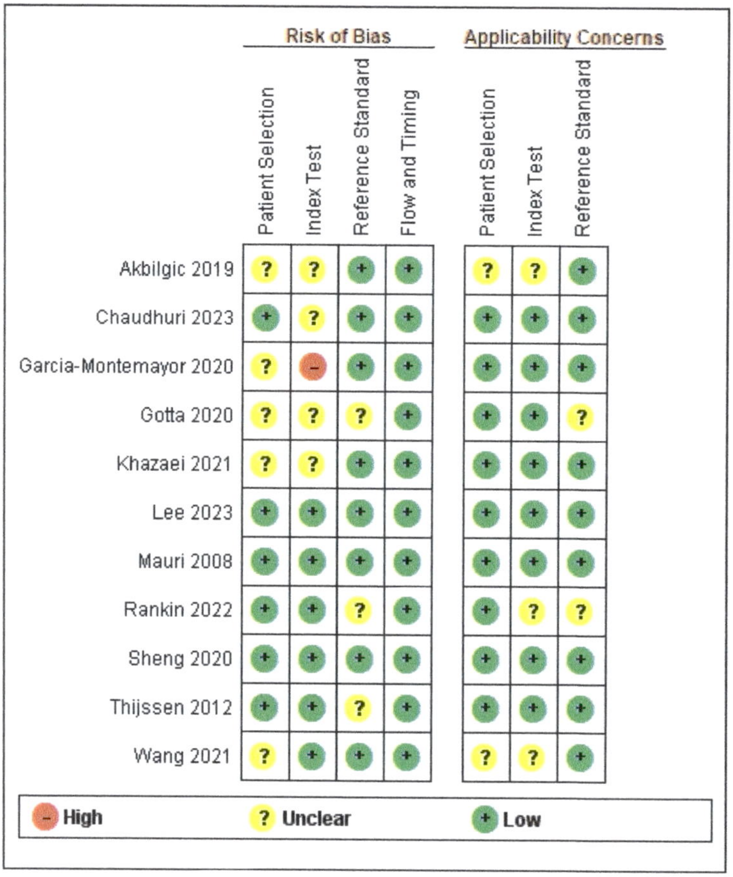


**Figure 2.** Risk of bias summary of the included studies [10,29–38].

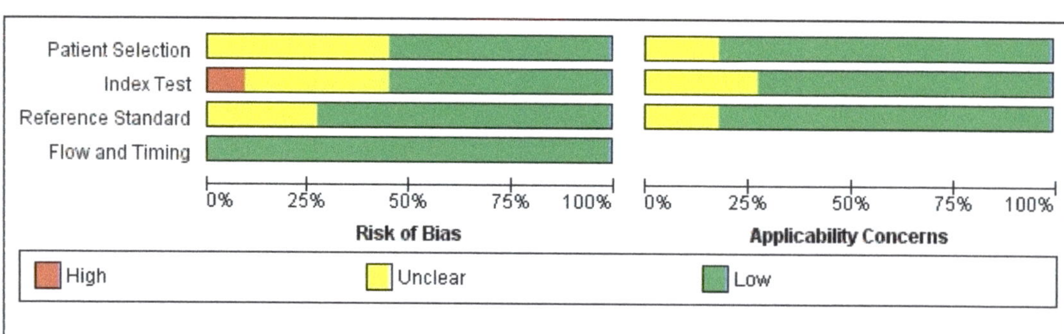


**Figure 3.** Risk of bias graph of the included studies.

Regarding the index test, all studies exhibited a low risk of bias, except for Akbilgic 2019, Chaudhuri 2023, Gotta 2020, and Khazaei 2021 [29,31,37,38], which showed unclear risk of bias; Garcia-Montemayor 2020 showed high risk of bias [10].

Concerning reference standard, all studies exhibited a low risk of bias except for Gotta 2020, Rankin 2022, and Thijssen 2012 which show unclear risk of bias [34,35,38]. Regarding flow and timing, all studies exhibit a low risk of bias.

Three studies—Sheng 2020, Mauri 2008, and Lee 2023 [30,32,33]—scored a low risk of bias across all assessed domains (Figure 2).

### 3.4. Outcomes Measure Results

Performance Characteristics of ML Models

Table 3 presents a summary of the performance characteristics of ML models for predicting mortality among HD patients in the included studies. Performance characteristics were reported in five studies [30,32,34,35,37] at various follow-up times. For instance, at one-year follow-up Sheng et al., 2020 [30], Lee et al., 2023 [32], and Thijssen et al., 2012 [34] reported the performance of logistic regression, where they found a predicted true positive mortality rate of 8.23% as compared to an actual mortality rate of 10.53%. In addition, Sheng et al., 2020 [30] and Lee et al., 2023 [32] reported the performance of XGBoost and Random Forest, where they found a predicted true positive mortality rate of 9.93% and 8.94%, respectively, as compared to an actual rate of 13.73%. This might reflect a better accuracy for the logistic regression models; however, further examination is required, particularly by comparing the models after training with the same datasets.

Since Logistic Regression, XGBoost, and Forest Plot were the most frequently assessed models within the included studies, we generated a Forest Plot for the sensitivity and specificity of the models, as shown in Figure 4. In addition, an SROC plot was generated for the three models, along with their 95% CI, as shown in Figure 5.

**Logistic regression**

| Study | TP | FP | FN | TN | Sensitivity (95% CI) | Specificity (95% CI) |
|---|---|---|---|---|---|---|
| Khazaei 2021 | 283 | 129 | 128 | 317 | 0.69 [0.64, 0.73] | 0.71 [0.67, 0.75] |
| Lee 2023 | 33 | 47 | 113 | 473 | 0.23 [0.16, 0.30] | 0.91 [0.88, 0.93] |
| Sheng 2020 | 641 | 3147 | 117 | 1923 | 0.85 [0.82, 0.87] | 0.38 [0.37, 0.39] |
| Thijssen 2012 | 46 | 335 | 1113 | 30 | 0.04 [0.03, 0.05] | 0.08 [0.06, 0.12] |

**Random forest**

| Study | TP | FP | FN | TN | Sensitivity (95% CI) | Specificity (95% CI) |
|---|---|---|---|---|---|---|
| Lee 2023 | 13 | 7 | 133 | 513 | 0.09 [0.05, 0.15] | 0.99 [0.97, 0.99] |
| Sheng 2020 | 525 | 233 | 233 | 4837 | 0.69 [0.66, 0.73] | 0.95 [0.95, 0.96] |

**XGboost**

| Study | TP | FP | FN | TN | Sensitivity (95% CI) | Specificity (95% CI) |
|---|---|---|---|---|---|---|
| Lee 2023 | 27 | 13 | 120 | 506 | 0.18 [0.12, 0.26] | 0.97 [0.96, 0.99] |
| Rankin 2022 | 6024 | 22134 | 2541 | 84124 | 0.70 [0.69, 0.71] | 0.79 [0.79, 0.79] |
| Sheng 2020 | 583 | 175 | 175 | 4895 | 0.77 [0.74, 0.80] | 0.97 [0.96, 0.97] |

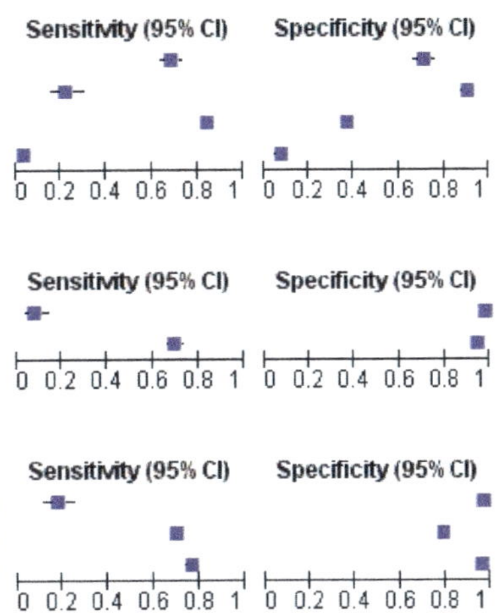


**Figure 4.** Summary Receiver Operating Characteristic (SROC) curve for logistic regression [30,32,34,37], XGBoost [30,32] and Random Forest [30,32,34] in predicting mortality at 1-year follow-up. Each data point corresponds to an individual study's sensitivity and specificity. The curve represents the trade-off between sensitivity and specificity across various decision thresholds. A curve closer to the top-left corner indicates better overall diagnostic performance.

**Table 3.** Prediction of positive and negative cases.

| Study | Follow-Up | ML Model | True Positive | False Positive | True Negative | False Negative | Total | Patients Died |
|---|---|---|---|---|---|---|---|---|
| Sheng 2020 [30] | 1 year | Adaptive Boosting | 525 | 350 | 4720 | 233 | 5828 | 764 |
| | | Decision Tree | 466 | 117 | 4954 | 291 | 5828 | 764 |
| | | Gradient Boosting | 525 | 116 | 4954 | 233 | 5828 | 764 |
| | | K-Nearest Neighbor | 408 | 58 | 5012 | 350 | 5828 | 764 |
| | | Light Gradient Boosting | 583 | 175 | 4895 | 175 | 5828 | 764 |
| | | Logistic Regression | 641 | 3147 | 1923 | 117 | 5828 | 764 |
| | | Random Forest | 525 | 233 | 4837 | 233 | 5828 | 764 |
| | | XGBoost | 583 | 175 | 4895 | 175 | 5828 | 764 |
| Lee 2023 [32] | 1 year | Logistic Regression | 0 | 23 | 691 | 46 | 760 | 42 |
| | | Decision Tree | 8 | 15 | 699 | 38 | 760 | 42 |
| | | Random Forest | 0 | 0 | 714 | 46 | 760 | 42 |
| | | Gradient Boosting | 0 | 0 | 714 | 46 | 760 | 42 |
| | | XGBoost | 0 | 23 | 692 | 45 | 760 | 42 |
| | 3 years | Logistic Regression | 33 | 47 | 473 | 113 | 666 | 147 |
| | | Random Forest | 13 | 7 | 513 | 133 | 666 | 147 |
| | | Gradient Boosting | 27 | 13 | 506 | 120 | 666 | 147 |
| | | XGBoost | 27 | 13 | 506 | 120 | 666 | 147 |
| Thijssen 2012 [34] | 7–12 months | Logistic Regression | 93 | 535 | 1651 | 47 | 2326 | 133 |
| | 13–18 months | Logistic Regression | 75 | 448 | 37 | 1306 | 1866 | 121 |
| | 19–24 months | Logistic Regression | 46 | 335 | 30 | 1113 | 1524 | 80 |
| Rankin 2022 [35] | 3 months | XGBoost | 6024 | 22,134 | 84,124 | 2541 | 114,823 | 86,083 |
| Khazaei 2021 [37] | 2.29 years | Decision Tree | 267 | 145 | 300 | 145 | 857 | 408 |
| | | Neural Network | 241 | 128 | 317 | 171 | 857 | 408 |
| | | Support Vector Machine | 274 | 137 | 309 | 137 | 857 | 408 |
| | | Logistic Regression | 283 | 129 | 317 | 128 | 857 | 408 |

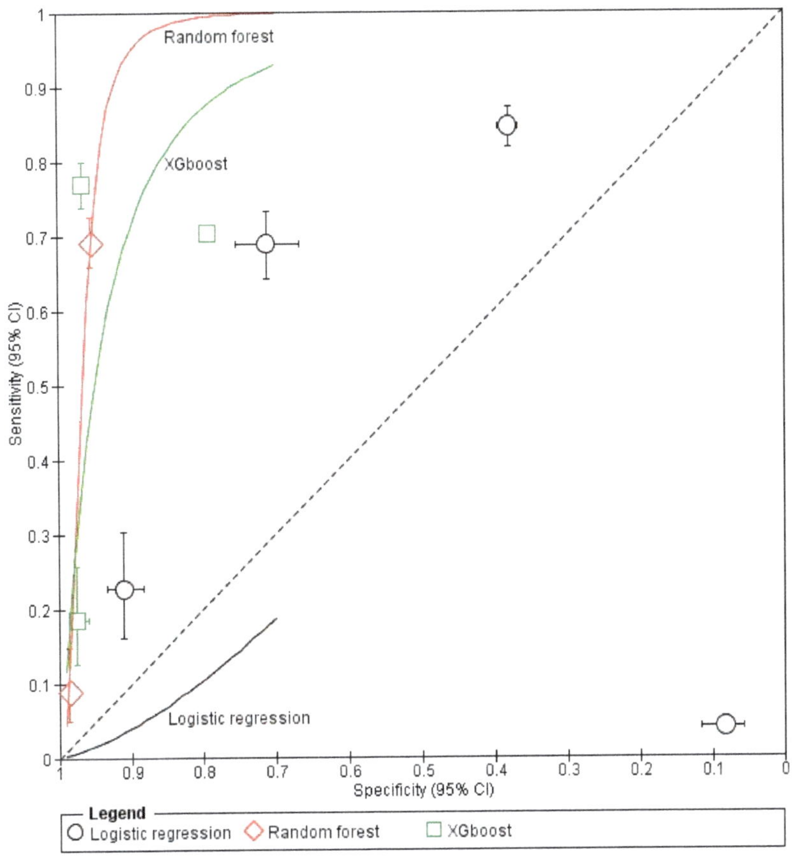


**Figure 5.** Summary Receiver Operating Characteristic (SROC) curves for logistic regression (black), Random Forest (red), and XGBoost (green) in predicting mortality among hemodialysis patients. Each symbol (circle, square, or diamond) represents the sensitivity and specificity reported by an individual study, with horizontal and vertical bars indicating 95% confidence intervals. The diagonal line from the lower-left to the upper-right corner marks chance-level performance (AUC = 0.5). Curves that track closer to the top-left corner reflect higher overall discriminative power (i.e., better sensitivity and specificity). In this analysis, Random Forest shows the highest AUC, followed by XGBoost, while Logistic Regression demonstrates slightly lower—but still clinically meaningful—performance.

### *3.5. Sensitivity and Specificity of ML Models*

The sensitivity and specificity of different ML models were reported in four studies [30,32,34,35] and are summarized in Table 4. The highest sensitivity was reported for the linear discriminant analysis model at one-year follow-up. It achieved a sensitivity of 82.81%. However, it demonstrated a very low specificity (37.76%). The lowest sensitivity was reported for the Random Forest model (0%) at one-year follow-up despite its high specificity (100%). The sensitivity of the Random Forest model was improved at two-year follow-up, reaching 9.6% with a specificity of 99.2%.

**Table 4.** Sensitivity and specificity of ML models.

| Study | Follow Up | ML Model | Sensitivity | Specificity |
|---|---|---|---|---|
| Sheng 2020 [30] | 1 year | Adaptive Boosting | 72.33 | 93.45 |
| | | Decision Tree | 63.52 | 97.45 |
| | | Gradient Boosting | 67.92 | 97.97 |
| | | k-Nearest Neighbor | 52.2 | 98.89 |
| | | Linear Discriminant Analysis | 82.81 | 37.76 |
| | | Light Gradient Boosting | 75.68 | 96.86 |
| | | Logistic Regression | 81.76 | 37.58 |
| | | Random Forest | 70.02 | 94.86 |
| | | XGBoost | 78.62 | 96.92 |
| Lee 2023 [32] | 1 year | Logistic Regression | 4.4 | 96.7 |
| | | Decision Tree | 15.6 | 98.3 |
| | | Random Forest | 0 | 100 |
| | | Gradient Boosting | 2.2 | 99.9 |
| | | XGBoost | 4.4 | 96.7 |
| | 3 years | Logistic Regression | 24.3 | 91.6 |
| | | Decision Tree | 28.6 | 86.5 |
| | | Random Forest | 9.6 | 99.2 |
| | | Gradient Boosting | 17.1 | 97 |
| | | XGBoost | 17.5 | 97 |
| Thijssen 2012 [34] | 7–12 months | Logistic Regression | 65 | 75 |
| | 13–18 months | Logistic Regression | 69 | 74 |
| | 19–24 months | Logistic Regression | 58 | 77 |
| Rankin 2022 [35] | 3 months | XGBoost | 70.3 | 79.1 |
| | | Support Vector Machine | 66 | 70 |
| | | Logistic Regression | 69 | 72 |

### 3.6. Predictive Performance of the Models Based on Area Under the Curve (AUC)

The AUC represents the predictive performance of ML models, which are summarized in Table 5. The highest AUC was reported for the Random Forest model at three-years follow-up (0.89). The lowest AUC was reported for the Decision Tree model at one-year follow-up (0.59).

**Table 5.** Summary of the predictive performance of ML levels based on the AUC and 95% CI.

| Study | Follow Up | ML Model | AUC | 95% CI | |
|---|---|---|---|---|---|
| | | | | LL | UL |
| Garcia-Montemayor 2020 [10] | 6 months | Random Forest | 0.7 | 0.68 | 0.72 |
| | 1 year | | 0.73 | 0.72 | 0.75 |
| | 2 years | | 0.73 | 0.71 | 0.74 |
| | 6 months | Logistic Regression | 0.69 | 0.67 | 0.71 |
| | 1 year | | 0.71 | 0.7 | 0.73 |
| | 2 years | | 0.69 | 0.67 | 0.7 |
| Chaudhuri 2023 [29] | 3 years | XGBoost | 0.8 | NR | NR |
| | 3 years | Logistic Regression | 0.75 | NR | NR |

**Table 5.** *Cont.*

| Study | Follow Up | ML Model | AUC | 95% CI | |
|---|---|---|---|---|---|
| | | | | LL | UL |
| Sheng 2020 [30] | 1 year | Adaptive Boosting | 0.83 | 0.8 | 0.84 |
| | | Gradient Boosting | 0.84 | 0.82 | 0.85 |
| | | K-Nearest Neighbor | 0.82 | 0.81 | 0.86 |
| | | Light Gradient Boosting | 0.85 | 0.8 | 0.85 |
| | | Logistic Regression | 0.73 | 0.73 | 0.86 |
| | | Random Forest | 0.82 | 0.8 | 0.85 |
| | | XGBoost | 0.85 | 0.81 | 0.86 |
| Akbilgic 2019 [31] | 1 month | Random Forest | 0.719 | 0.699 | 0.738 |
| | 3 months | | 0.745 | 0.735 | 0.755 |
| | 6 months | | 0.750 | 0.743 | 0.758 |
| | 1 year | | 0.749 | 0.742 | 0.755 |
| Lee 2023 [32] | 1 year | Logistic Regression | 0.734 | NR | NR |
| | | Decision Tree | 0.59 | NR | NR |
| | | Random Forest | 0.806 | NR | NR |
| | | Gradient Boosting | 0.793 | NR | NR |
| | | XGBoost | 0.734 | NR | NR |
| | 3 years | Logistic Regression | 0.756 | NR | NR |
| | | Decision Tree | 0.66 | NR | NR |
| | | Random Forest | 0.763 | NR | NR |
| | | Gradient Boosting | 0.773 | NR | NR |
| | | XGBoost | 0.788 | NR | NR |
| Mauri 2008 [33] | 1 year | Logistic Regression | 0.78 | NR | NR |
| Thijssen 2012 [34] | 7–12 months | Logistic Regression | 0.698 | 0.679 | 0.717 |
| | 13–18 months | Logistic Regression | 0.717 | 0.696 | 0.737 |
| | 19–24 months | Logistic Regression | 0.67 | 0.646 | 0.694 |
| Wang 2021 [36] | 3 months | Logistic Regression | 0.8 | 0.797 | 0.802 |
| | 6 months | | 0.77 | 0.768 | 0.772 |
| | 1 year | | 0.86 | 0.8577 | 0.8623 |
| | 3 months | Support Vector Machine | 0.77 | 0.7667 | 0.7733 |
| | 6 months | | 0.75 | 0.7484 | 0.7516 |
| | 1 year | | 0.8 | 0.7982 | 0.8018 |
| | 3 months | Random Forest | 0.84 | 0.8365 | 0.8435 |
| | 6 months | | 0.81 | 0.8084 | 0.8116 |
| | 1 year | | 0.81 | 0.8034 | 0.8166 |
| Gotta 2020 [38] | 3 years | Random Forest | 0.89 | NR | NR |
| | 5 years | | 0.82 | NR | NR |
| | 8 years | | 0.77 | NR | NR |

NR: not reported.

### 3.7. Meta-Analysis

The meta-analysis was conducted to evaluate the predictive performance of ML models, represented by the Area Under the Curve (AUC), for Random Forest and Logistic Regression models at a one-year follow-up. Four studies assessed the Random Forest model, demonstrating significant results, with a pooled mean difference (MD) of 0.78 (95% CI: 0.74–0.82, $p < 0.00001$) (Figure 6). Similarly, the Logistic Regression model was evaluated in four studies, yielding a pooled MD of 0.77 (95% CI: 0.66–0.87, $p < 0.00001$).

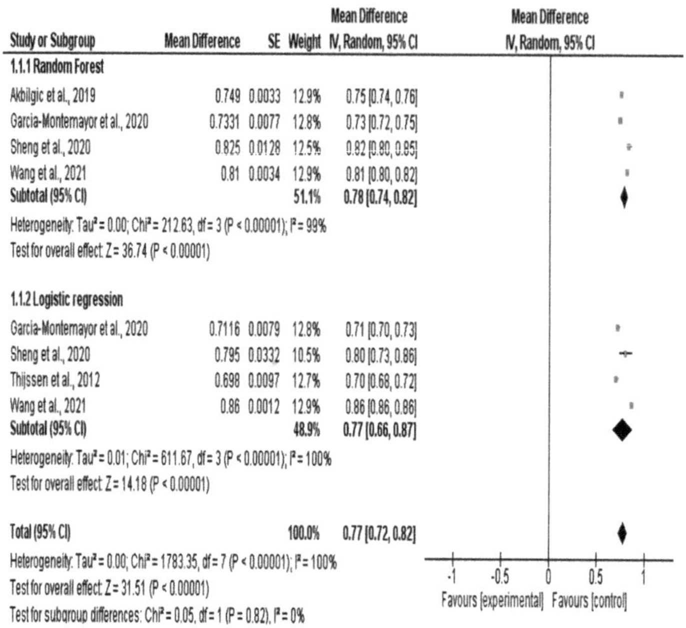


**Figure 6.** Forest plot of mortality prediction at 1-year follow-up. Random forrest [10,30,31,36] and Logistic regression [10,30,34,36].

No significant difference was found between the subgroups of the two models ($p = 0.82$). However, considerable heterogeneity was observed among the pooled studies ($p < 0.0001$), which was not resolved through the leave-one-out sensitivity analysis or subgroup analysis.

Detailed estimates for each study assessing Random Forest and Logistic Regression, along with their 95% CI, are presented in Figure 7.

**Logistic regression**

| Study | Point Estimate | Standard Error | Variance | Lower Limit | Upper Limit | Z-Value | p-Value | Relative Weight |
|---|---|---|---|---|---|---|---|---|
| Gracia-Montemayor 2020 | 0.712 | 0.008 | 0.000 | 0.696 | 0.727 | 90.076 | 0.000 | 2.22 |
| Thijssen 2012 | 0.688 | 0.010 | 0.000 | 0.679 | 0.717 | 71.969 | 0.000 | 1.47 |
| Wang 2021 | 0.860 | 0.001 | 0.000 | 0.858 | 0.862 | 716.667 | 0.000 | 96.18 |
| Sheng 2020 | 0.795 | 0.033 | 0.001 | 0.730 | 0.860 | 23.946 | 0.000 | 0.13 |
| **Overall** | **0.854** | **0.001** | **0.000** | **0.852** | **0.857** | **725.854** | **0.000** | – |

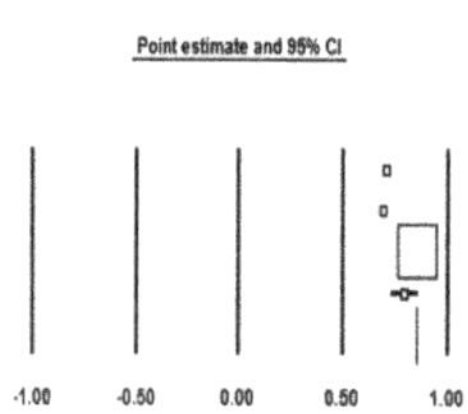


**Random forest**

| Study Name | Point Estimate | Standard Error | Variance | Lower Limit | Upper Limit | Z-Value | p-Value | Relative Weight |
|---|---|---|---|---|---|---|---|---|
| Gracia-Montemayor 2020 | 0.733 | 0.008 | 0.000 | 0.718 | 0.748 | 95.208 | 0.000 | 8.38 |
| Akbijojo 2019 | 0.749 | 0.003 | 0.000 | 0.743 | 0.755 | 226.970 | 0.000 | 45.62 |
| Wang 2021 | 0.810 | 0.003 | 0.000 | 0.803 | 0.817 | 238.235 | 0.000 | 42.97 |
| Sheng 2020 | 0.825 | 0.013 | 0.000 | 0.800 | 0.850 | 64.453 | 0.000 | 3.03 |
| **Overall** | **0.776** | **0.002** | **0.000** | **0.772** | **0.781** | **348.249** | **0.000** | – |

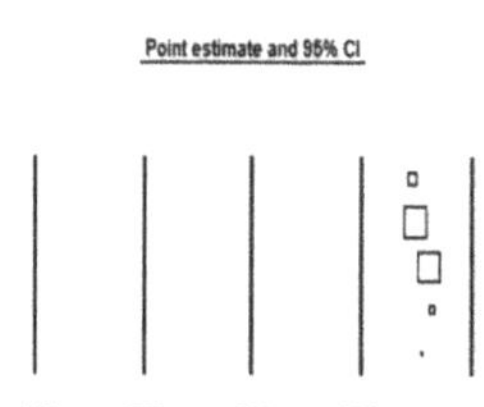


**Figure 7.** Detailed estimates and 95% confidence intervals for each study investigating the Random Forest [10,30,31,36] and Logistic Regression [10,30,31,36] models at 1 year of follow-up.

Clinical Significance of the Present Study

This study provides valuable insights into the application of machine learning (ML) models for predicting mortality in hemodialysis (HD) patients, a population with high morbidity and mortality rates. By systematically reviewing and analyzing the predictive performance of various ML models, this study highlights their potential to supplement traditional risk prediction tools, particularly in identifying high-risk patients. Accurate early mortality prediction in HD patients is crucial for several reasons, including optimizing resource allocation, tailoring individualized treatment strategies, and potentially improving patient outcomes.

The findings of this study underscore the capability of models such as Random Forest and Logistic Regression to achieve clinically relevant predictive accuracy. For instance, the Random Forest model demonstrated superior performance in long-term follow-up scenarios, achieving an area under the curve (AUC) as high as 0.89. This level of accuracy suggests that ML models can serve as reliable tools in stratifying risk, enabling clinicians to intervene earlier in high-risk cases. Logistic Regression, a more traditional approach, remains a robust and interpretable model for clinicians, reinforcing its utility in settings where simplicity and ease of implementation are prioritized.

Moreover, this review highlights the potential of ML models to incorporate diverse variables, including non-linear relationships, that may not be fully accounted for in traditional models. By doing so, these models can identify previously underappreciated risk factors, offering novel insights into the pathophysiology of mortality in HD patients. For example, factors such as albumin, hemoglobin, and body mass index, which were recurrently identified as key predictors, can inform clinical decision-making and enhance patient monitoring protocols.

This study also emphasizes the importance of advancing personalized medicine in nephrology. ML models can provide individualized risk assessments, tailoring interventions to the specific needs of each patient. This aligns with the broader shift toward precision medicine, where treatments are customized based on unique patient characteristics rather than generalized protocols.

## 4. Discussion

Artificial intelligence (AI) has expanded across many industries, including healthcare. Advanced algorithms have emerged to address intricate medical scenarios where traditional approaches have encountered limitations [39]. Notably, ML, a subfield of AI, has been integrated into medical registries to enhance the prediction of clinical events, demonstrating superior accuracy compared to human judgment [40]. This underscores the growing potential of AI-driven solutions to revolutionize healthcare by augmenting decision-making and improving patient outcomes.

In this study, we reviewed the predictive performance and characteristics of the ML models investigated in the literature for predicting mortality risk in HD patients at various follow-up points.

Logistic regression showed a predicted true positive mortality rate of 8.23% compared to an actual mortality rate of 10.53%, whereas XGBoost and Random Forest showed predicted true positive mortality rates of 9.93% and 8.94%, respectively, compared to an actual rate of 13.73%. Logistic Regression appears to demonstrate potential for accurately predicting mortality. Nevertheless, it is essential to compare this model with other models trained on the same dataset to ascertain its superiority.

Regarding model sensitivity and specificity, the highest sensitivity was reported for the linear discriminant analysis model at one-year follow-up despite having a very low specificity, while the lowest sensitivity was reported for the Random Forest model at one-year follow-up, despite its high specificity. The sensitivity of the Random Forest model was improved at two-year follow-up.

The highest AUC was reported for the Random Forest model at three-year follow-up (0.89) and the lowest AUC was reported for the Decision Tree model at one-year follow-up (0.59), despite the fact that meta-analysis at one-year follow-up showed no significant sub-group difference between Random Forest and Logistic Regression models.

Khazaei et al., 2021 demonstrated that Logistic Regression achieved the best predictive performance over Decision Tree, Neural Network, and Support Vector Machine [37]. Conversely, other reports contradicted these findings [10,29,32]. For instance, Garcia-Montemayor et al., 2020 reported that mortality prediction models developed using Random Forest demonstrated promising levels of accuracy, with reported area under the curve (AUC) values ranging from 0.68 to 0.73. Furthermore, these models exhibited superior performance as compared to traditional Logistic Regression models at two-year follow-up [10]. Moreover, Lee et al., 2023 and Chaudhuri et al., 2023 reported that Decision Tree, Random Forest, Gradient Boosting, and XGBoost models showed better predictive capabilities in comparison to Logistic Regression [29,32].

The predictive performance of different models depends on various clinical, laboratory, and demographic factors. In particular, Logistic Regression predictions depend primarily on age, type of vascular access, and albumin levels [36,41,42], whereas Random Forest models detected variables as levels of albumin, urea, and hemoglobin, as well as age and BMI as the major predictors of mortality [10]. Therefore, the predictive ability of the models differs according to the variables supplied. In addition, a small sample size may reduce the predictive ability of the model; thus, studies that trained their models with a large dataset may reflect greater accuracy.

The primary strength of this study is that it is the first to review the ML predictors of mortality in HD patients by comparing the AUC, sensitivity, and specificity of the models. In addition, our findings underscore the potential of ML models as valuable tools in the clinical management of hemodialysis patients, a population facing exceedingly high mortality risk. Models like Random Forest, which demonstrated high AUC values (up to 0.89) in certain long-term follow-up scenarios, and Logistic Regression, which remains a robust and interpretable option, show promise for enhancing risk stratification beyond traditional methods. Clinically, the higher AUC of ML models suggests that these models can offer good discriminatory power, potentially aiding clinicians in identifying patients at heightened risk who might benefit from more intensive monitoring, tailored counseling regarding prognosis, or earlier consideration of advanced care planning or specialized interventions.

The ability of ML models to integrate diverse variables and capture non-linear relationships, as highlighted by the recurrent importance of predictors like albumin, hemoglobin, age, and BMI across different studies, can provide clinicians with a more holistic patient assessment. Identifying these key predictors reinforces their clinical relevance and can guide monitoring protocols.

## 5. Limitations

A major limitation of this study is the significant heterogeneity among the included studies, arising from several sources. First, the studies utilized different machine learning (ML) models, each trained on varying sets of clinical, demographic, and laboratory variables. This variability in feature selection and model design complicates direct comparisons and limits the generalizability of findings. Additionally, the datasets span a wide timeframe, from 1995 to recent years, during which significant advancements in laboratory techniques, data collection practices, and clinical management protocols have occurred. These temporal variations introduce inconsistencies that may affect the predictive performance of the models.

Another limitation is the scarcity of studies evaluating the same ML model at specific follow-up intervals. This scarcity hindered the ability to perform comprehensive subgroup analyses or meta-analyses for all the included models, which could have provided a more robust assessment of their comparative effectiveness. Furthermore, variations in study design, sample sizes, and regional differences in patient populations further contribute to the heterogeneity, making it challenging to draw definitive conclusions.

To address these challenges, we recommend future research prioritize standardizing datasets through collaborative multicenter studies. This involves establishing common data elements and uniform variable definitions, specifying consistent data collection timepoints relative to dialysis initiation, harmonizing laboratory techniques (e.g., using central laboratories or standardized assay protocols and units), employing prospective data collection with standardized electronic tools, and ensuring uniform outcome ascertainment. Such efforts, particularly leveraging prospective designs with modern, standardized laboratory techniques, could mitigate the temporal and methodological biases observed in this review and provide a stronger foundation for evaluating and refining the predictive capabilities of ML models in hemodialysis populations.

Furthermore, our review primarily identified studies using "classic" machine learning algorithms. The absence of studies employing deep learning methods meeting our inclusion criteria suggests this may be an emerging area within hemodialysis mortality prediction that warrants future investigation as more relevant studies become available.

## 6. Conclusions

This systematic review and meta-analysis indicate that machine learning models, particularly Random Forest and Logistic Regression, hold considerable potential for predicting mortality risk in hemodialysis patients. While some studies reported high discriminatory power, notably Random Forest achieving AUCs up to 0.89 in long-term follow-up, our meta-analysis focused on one-year mortality found no statistically significant difference in pooled AUC between Random Forest and Logistic Regression.

Clinically, these findings suggest that ML tools can supplement existing methods for risk stratification, potentially enabling earlier identification of high-risk individuals who may benefit from tailored interventions and enhanced monitoring. However, the significant heterogeneity observed across studies—stemming from diverse populations, time periods, included features, ML methodologies, and reporting standards—currently limits definitive conclusions about the superiority of any single model and hinders the generalizability of findings.

To advance the field and facilitate reliable clinical implementation, future research should prioritize conducting large-scale, multi-center prospective studies using standardized data collection protocols, including common data elements, harmonized laboratory techniques, and consistent follow-up schedules, to minimize temporal and methodological biases. In addition, performing rigorous head-to-head comparisons of different ML models trained and validated on these shared, standardized datasets.

**Author Contributions:** Conceptualization, A.C.M. and A.M.; methodology, A.C.M. and N.O.; software, A.C.; validation, A.C.M., N.O. and L.M.; formal analysis, N.O.; investigation, L.M. and L.C.; resources, G.N.P.; data curation, V.M.I.; writing—original draft preparation, A.C.M.; writing—review and editing, A.M., A.M.C.J. and A.A.; visualization, A.C.; supervision, A.S.; project administration, A.M.; funding acquisition, G.N.P. All authors have read and agreed to the published version of the manuscript.

**Funding:** We would like to acknowledge "Victor Babeș" University of Medicine and Pharmacy Timișoara for their support in covering the costs of publication for this research paper.

**Institutional Review Board Statement:** Not applicable.

**Informed Consent Statement:** Not applicable.

**Data Availability Statement:** The data are available from the corresponding author upon reasonable request.

**Conflicts of Interest:** The authors declare no conflicts of interest.

## References

1. Himmelfarb, J.; Vanholder, R.; Mehrotra, R.; Tonelli, M. The current and future landscape of dialysis. *Nat. Rev. Nephrol.* **2020**, *16*, 573–585. [CrossRef]
2. Yang, Q.Z.C. Timing of dialysis initiation and end-stage kidney disease incidence. *JAMA Intern. Med.* **2021**, *181*, 724–725. [CrossRef] [PubMed]
3. Venuta, F.; Rendina, E.A. Combined pulmonary artery and bronchial sleeve resection. *Oper. Tech. Thorac. Cardiovasc. Surg.* **2008**, *13*, 260–273. [CrossRef]
4. Lai, A.C.; Bienstock, S.W.; Sharma, R.; Skorecki, K.; Beerkens, F.; Samtani, R.; Coyle, A.; Kim, T.; Baber, U.; Camaj, A.; et al. A Personalized Approach to Chronic Kidney Disease and Cardiovascular Disease: JACC Review Topic of the Week. *J. Am. Coll. Cardiol.* **2021**, *77*, 1470–1479. [CrossRef]
5. Karaboyas, A.; Morgenstern, H.; Waechter, S.; Fleischer, N.L.; Vanholder, R.; Jacobson, S.H.; Sood, M.M.; Schaubel, D.E.; Inaba, M.; Pisoni, R.L.; et al. Low hemoglobin at hemodialysis initiation: An international study of anemia management and mortality in the early dialysis period. *Clin. Kidney J.* **2019**, *13*, 425–433. [CrossRef] [PubMed]
6. Karaboyas, A.; Morgenstern, H.; Li, Y.; Bieber, B.A.; Hakim, R.; Hasegawa, T.; Jadoul, M.; Schaeffner, E.; Vanholder, R.; Pisoni, R.L.; et al. Estimating the Fraction of First-Year Hemodialysis Deaths Attributable to Potentially Modifiable Risk Factors: Results from the DOPPS. *Clin. Epidemiol.* **2020**, *12*, 51. [CrossRef]
7. Saleh, T.; Sumida, K.; Molnar, M.Z.; Potukuchi, P.K.; Thomas, F.; Lu, J.L.; Gyamlani, G.G.; Streja, E.; Kalantar-Zadeh, K.; Kovesdy, C.P. Effect of Age on the Association of Vascular Access Type with Mortality in a Cohort of Incident End-Stage Renal Disease Patients. *Nephron* **2017**, *137*, 57–63. [CrossRef]
8. Wick, J.P.; Turin, T.C.; Faris, P.D.; MacRae, J.M.; Weaver, R.G.; Tonelli, M.; Manns, B.J.; Hemmelgarn, B.R. A Clinical Risk Prediction Tool for 6-Month Mortality After Dialysis Initiation Among Older Adults. *Am. J. Kidney Dis.* **2017**, *69*, 568–575. [CrossRef] [PubMed]
9. Jassal, S.V.; Karaboyas, A.; Comment, L.A.; Bieber, B.A.; Morgenstern, H.; Sen, A.; Gillespie, B.W.; De Sequera, P.; Marshall, M.R.; Fukuhara, S.; et al. Functional Dependence and Mortality in the International Dialysis Outcomes and Practice Patterns Study (DOPPS). *Am. J. Kidney Dis.* **2016**, *67*, 283–292. [CrossRef]
10. Garcia-Montemayor, V.; Martin-Malo, A.; Barbieri, C.; Bellocchio, F.; Soriano, S.; de Mier, V.P.R.; Molina, I.R.; Aljama, P.; Rodriguez, M. Predicting mortality in hemodialysis patients using machine learning analysis. *Clin. Kidney J.* **2021**, *14*, 1388. [CrossRef]
11. Kasza, J.; Wolfe, R.; McDonald, S.P.; Marshall, M.R.; Polkinghorne, K.R. Dialysis modality, vascular access and mortality in end-stage kidney disease: A bi-national registry-based cohort study. *Nephrology* **2016**, *21*, 878–886. [CrossRef] [PubMed]
12. Chen, Y.M.; Wang, Y.C.; Hwang, S.J.; Lin, S.H.; Wu, K.D. Patterns of Dialysis Initiation Affect Outcomes of Incident Hemodialysis Patients. *Nephron* **2015**, *132*, 33–42. [CrossRef] [PubMed]
13. Bradbury, B.D.; Fissell, R.B.; Albert, J.M.; Anthony, M.S.; Critchlow, C.W.; Pisoni, R.L.; Port, F.K.; Gillespie, B.W. Predictors of Early Mortality among Incident US Hemodialysis Patients in the Dialysis Outcomes and Practice Patterns Study (DOPPS). *Clin. J. Am. Soc. Nephrol.* **2007**, *2*, 89–99. [CrossRef]
14. Canaud, B.; Tong, L.; Tentori, F.; Akiba, T.; Karaboyas, A.; Gillespie, B.; Akizawa, T.; Pisoni, R.L.; Bommer, J.; Port, F.K. Clinical practices and outcomes in elderly hemodialysis patients: Results from the Dialysis Outcomes and Practice Patterns Study (DOPPS). *Clin. J. Am. Soc. Nephrol.* **2011**, *6*, 1651–1662. [CrossRef] [PubMed]
15. Foley, R.N.; Parfrey, P.S.; Hefferton, D.; Singh, I.; Simms, A.; Barrett, B.J. Advance Prediction of Early Death in Patients Starting Maintenance Dialysis. *Am. J. Kidney Dis.* **1994**, *23*, 836–845. [CrossRef]
16. Wagner, M.; Ansell, D.; Kent, D.M.; Griffith, J.L.; Naimark, D.; Wanner, C.; Tangri, N. Predicting mortality in incident dialysis patients: An analysis of the United Kingdom Renal Registry. *Am. J. Kidney Dis.* **2011**, *57*, 894–902. [CrossRef]
17. Chen, J.Y.; Tsai, S.H.; Chuang, P.H.; Chang, C.H.; Chuang, C.L.; Chen, H.L.; Chen, P.L. A comorbidity index for mortality prediction in Chinese patients with ESRD receiving hemodialysis. *Clin. J. Am. Soc. Nephrol.* **2014**, *9*, 513–519. [CrossRef]

18. Couchoud, C.G.; Beuscart, J.B.R.; Aldigier, J.C.; Brunet, P.J.; Moranne, O.P. Development of a risk stratification algorithm to improve patient-centered care and decision making for incident elderly patients with end-stage renal disease. *Kidney Int.* **2015**, *88*, 1178–1186. [CrossRef]
19. Couchoud, C.; Labeeuw, M.; Moranne, O.; Allot, V.; Esnault, V.; Frimat, L.; Stengel, B.; French Renal Epidemiology and Information Network (REIN) registry. A clinical score to predict 6-month prognosis in elderly patients starting dialysis for end-stage renal disease. *Nephrol. Dial. Transplant.* **2009**, *24*, 1553–1561. [CrossRef]
20. Hsu, J.Y.; Roy, J.A.; Xie, D.; Yang, W.; Shou, H.; Anderson, A.H.; Landis, J.R.; Jepson, C.; Wolf, M.; Isakova, T.; et al. Statistical Methods for Cohort Studies of CKD: Survival Analysis in the Setting of Competing Risks. *Clin. J. Am. Soc. Nephrol.* **2017**, *12*, 1181–1189. [CrossRef]
21. Lancet, T. Artificial intelligence in health care: Within touching distance. *Lancet* **2017**, *390*, 2739. [CrossRef]
22. Genuer, R.; Poggi, J.M.; Tuleau-Malot, C. Variable selection using random forests. *Pattern Recognit. Lett.* **2010**, *31*, 2225–2236. [CrossRef]
23. Matsuki, K.; Kuperman, V.; Van Dyke, J.A. The Random Forests statistical technique: An examination of its value for the study of reading. *Sci. Stud. Read.* **2016**, *20*, 20–33. [CrossRef]
24. Dankowski, T.; Ziegler, A. Calibrating random forests for probability estimation. *Stat. Med.* **2016**, *35*, 3949–3960. [CrossRef] [PubMed]
25. Su, X.; Peña, A.T.; Liu, L.; Levine, R.A. Random forests of interaction trees for estimating individualized treatment effects in randomized trials. *Stat. Med.* **2018**, *37*, 2547–2560. [CrossRef] [PubMed]
26. Moher, D.; Liberati, A.; Tetzlaff, J.; Altman, D.G.; Group, P. Preferred reporting items for systematic reviews and meta-analyses: The PRISMA statement. *PLoS Med.* **2009**, *6*, e1000097. [CrossRef]
27. Brooker, J.; Synnot, A.; McDonald, S.; Elliott, J.; Turner, T.; Hodder, R.; Weeks, L.; Ried, J.; MacLehose, H.; Akl, E.; et al. Guidance for the Production and Publication of Cochrane Living Systematic Reviews: Cochrane Reviews in Living Mode; Cochrane Community: London, UK, December 2019: 60. Available online: https://community.cochrane.org/sites/default/files/uploads/inline-files/Transform/201912_LSR_Revised_Guidance.pdf (accessed on 9 May 2025).
28. Whiting, P.F.; Rutjes, A.W.S.; Westwood, M.E.; Mallett, S.; Deeks, J.J.; Reitsma, J.B.; Leeflang, M.M.; Sterne, J.A.; Bossuyt, P.M.; QUADAS-2 Group. Quadas-2: A revised tool for the quality assessment of diagnostic accuracy studies. *Ann. Intern. Med.* **2011**, *155*, 529–536. [CrossRef] [PubMed]
29. Chaudhuri, S.; Larkin, J.; Guedes, M.; Jiao, Y.; Kotanko, P.; Wang, Y.; Usvyat, L.; Kooman, J.P. Predicting mortality risk in dialysis: Assessment of risk factors using traditional and advanced modeling techniques within the Monitoring Dialysis Outcomes initiative. *Hemodial. Int.* **2023**, *27*, 62–73. [CrossRef]
30. Sheng, K.; Zhang, P.; Yao, X.; Li, J.; He, Y.; Chen, J. Prognostic machine learning models for first-year mortality in incident hemodialysis patients: Development and validation study. *JMIR Med. Inform.* **2020**, *8*, e20578. [CrossRef]
31. Akbilgic, O.; Obi, Y.; Potukuchi, P.K.; Karabayir, I.; Nguyen, D.V.; Soohoo, M.; Streja, E.; Molnar, M.Z.; Rhee, C.M.; Kalantar-Zadeh, K.; et al. Machine learning to identify dialysis patients at high death risk. *Kidney Int. Rep.* **2019**, *4*, 1219–1229. [CrossRef]
32. Lee, W.T.; Fang, Y.W.; Chang, W.S.; Hsiao, K.Y.; Shia, B.C.; Chen, M.; Tsai, M.H. Data-driven, two-stage machine learning algorithm-based prediction scheme for assessing 1-year and 3-year mortality risk in chronic hemodialysis patients. *Sci. Rep.* **2023**, *13*, 21453. [CrossRef]
33. Mauri, J.M.; Cleries, M.; Vela, E.; Registry, C.R. Design and validation of a model to predict early mortality in haemodialysis patients. *Nephrol. Dial. Transplant.* **2008**, *23*, 1690–1696. [CrossRef] [PubMed]
34. Thijssen, S.; Usvyat, L.; Kotanko, P. Prediction of mortality in the first two years of hemodialysis: Results from a validation study. *Blood Purif.* **2012**, *33*, 165–170. [CrossRef]
35. Rankin, S.; Han, L.; Scherzer, R.; Tenney, S.; Keating, M.; Genberg, K.; Rahn, M.; Wilkins, K.; Shlipak, M.; Estrella, M. A machine learning model for predicting mortality within 90 days of dialysis initiation. *Kidney360* **2022**, *3*, 1556–1565. [CrossRef] [PubMed]
36. Wang, Y.; Zhu, Y.; Lou, G.; Zhang, P.; Chen, J.; Li, J. A maintenance hemodialysis mortality prediction model based on anomaly detection using longitudinal hemodialysis data. *J. Biomed. Inform.* **2021**, *123*, 103930. [CrossRef]
37. Khazaei, S.; Najafi-GhOBADI, S.; Ramezani-Doroh, V. Construction data mining methods in the prediction of death in hemodialysis patients using support vector machine, neural network, logistic regression and decision tree. *J. Prev. Med. Hyg.* **2021**, *62*, E222.
38. Gotta, V.; Tancev, G.; Marsenic, O.; Vogt, J.E.; Pfister, M. Identifying key predictors of mortality in young patients on chronic haemodialysis—A machine learning approach. *Nephrol. Dial. Transplant.* **2021**, *36*, 519–528. [CrossRef]
39. Hueso, M.; Vellido, A.; Montero, N.; Barbieri, C.; Ramos, R.; Angoso, M.; Cruzado, J.M.; Jonsson, A. Artificial intelligence for the artificial kidney: Pointers to the future of a personalized hemodialysis therapy. *Kidney Dis.* **2018**, *4*, 1–9. [CrossRef] [PubMed]
40. Krumholz, H.M. Big data and new knowledge in medicine: The thinking, training, and tools needed for a learning health system. *Health Aff.* **2014**, *33*, 1163–1170. [CrossRef]

41. Pisoni, R.L.; Gillespie, B.W.; Dickinson, D.M.; Chen, K.; Kutner, M.H.; Wolfe, R.A. The Dialysis Outcomes and Practice Patterns Study (DOPPS): Design, data elements, and methodology. *Am. J. Kidney Dis.* **2004**, *44*, 7–15. [CrossRef]
42. Chan, K.E.; Maddux, F.W.; Tolkoff-Rubin, N.; Karumanchi, S.A.; Thadhani, R.; Hakim, R.M. Early outcomes among those initiating chronic dialysis in the United States. *Clin. J. Am. Soc. Nephrol.* **2011**, *6*, 2642–2649. [CrossRef] [PubMed]

applied sciences

MDPI

Article

# A Knowledge-Guided Competitive Co-Evolutionary Algorithm for Feature Selection

Junyi Zhou [1], Haowen Zheng [1], Shaole Li [1], Qiancheng Hao [2], Haoyang Zhang [1], Wenze Gao [3] and Xianpeng Wang [4,*]

1 School of Computer Science and Engineering, Northeastern University, Shenyang 110169, China; 20216003@stu.neu.edu.cn (J.Z.); 20225833@stu.neu.edu.cn (H.Z.); 20216074@stu.neu.edu.cn (S.L.); 20226513@stu.neu.edu.cn (H.Z.)
2 School of Information Science and Engineering, Northeastern University, Shenyang 110004, China; 20224769@stu.neu.edu.cn
3 School of Mechanical Engineering and Automation, Northeastern University, Shenyang 110819, China; 20225040@stu.neu.edu.cn
4 Key Laboratory of Data Analytics and Optimization for Smart Industry, Ministry of Education, National Frontiers Science Center for Industrial Intelligence and Systems Optimization, Northeastern University, Shenyang 110819, China
* Correspondence: wangxianpeng@ise.neu.edu.cn

**Abstract:** In real-world applications, feature selection is crucial for enhancing the performance of data science and machine learning models. Typically, feature selection is a complex combinatorial optimization problem and a multi-objective optimization problem. Its primary goals are to reduce the dimensionality of the dataset and enhance the performance of machine learning algorithms. The selection of features in high-dimensional datasets is challenging due to the intricate relationships between features, which pose significant challenges to the performance and computational efficiency of algorithms. This paper introduces a Knowledge-Guided Competitive Co-Evolutionary Algorithm (KCCEA) for feature selection, especially for high-dimensional features. In the proposed algorithm, we make improvements to the foundational dominance-based multi-objective evolutionary algorithm in two aspects. First, the use of feature correlation as knowledge to guide evolution enhances the search speed and quality of traditional multi-objective evolutionary algorithm solutions. Second, a dynamically allocated competitive–cooperative evolutionary mechanism is proposed, integrating the improved knowledge-guided evolution with traditional evolutionary algorithms, further enhancing the search efficiency and diversity of solutions. Through rigorous empirical testing on various datasets, the KCCEA demonstrates superior performance compared to basic multi-objective evolutionary algorithms, providing effective solutions to multi-objective feature selection problems while enhancing the interpretability and effectiveness of prediction models.

**Keywords:** evolutionary algorithm; feature selection; multi-objective optimization; co-evolution; competitive; classification

## 1. Introduction

In today's machine learning landscape, the widespread presence of high-dimensional data in real-world scenarios presents substantial challenges [1,2]. As datasets burgeon with features, from image characteristics in computer vision to genetic markers in bioinformatics, the demand for robust feature selection has become more pressing than ever [3,4]. These complex datasets frequently include irrelevant, noisy, or redundant features that not only hinder the learning process but also impair the effectiveness of algorithms [5,6]. Effective feature selection techniques boost model accuracy by isolating and preserving only the most impactful features for predictive modeling [7]. Additionally, by reducing the number of features, these techniques cut down on storage needs and computational expenses, thus enhancing the interpretability and efficiency of models [8].

Feature selection is inherently a challenging combinatorial optimization problem aimed at reducing the feature space while simultaneously enhancing the classifier's performance [9]. These objectives typically conflict; a minimal set of features might omit critical information, adversely impacting the model's performance. This problem's complexity escalates with the exponential growth in the number of potential feature subsets as the initial feature count increases, making a robust search strategy essential for effective feature selection [10].

In response to these challenges, the past few decades have seen the emergence of many effective algorithms, including filter-based methods, embedded methods, and wrapper methods. Filter-based methods, such as chi-square tests [11] and mutual information, evaluate the relevance of features independent of any learning algorithm. Embedded methods, like LASSO regression [12], perform feature selection during the model training process. Wrapper methods, such as Recursive Feature Elimination (RFE) [13], use a predictive model to evaluate feature subsets. Among all methods, metaheuristic algorithms stand out, particularly multi-objective evolutionary algorithms (MOEAs) [14,15], which excel in balancing conflicting objectives without requiring gradient information. These algorithms, such as the NSGA-II [16], utilize principles of natural evolution—such as selection, crossover, and mutation—to explore and exploit the search space effectively. By mimicking natural selection processes, MOEAs can efficiently navigate the large and complex search spaces found in high-dimensional feature selection tasks.

Despite their advantages, the computational complexity of MOEAs scales significantly with the increase in the number of features [17]. This complexity can be attributed to the need to evaluate a vast number of potential solutions, each representing a different subset of features. The performance of these algorithms often deteriorates as the dimensionality of the data increases, necessitating innovative approaches to reduce computational overhead and enhance the search process's efficiency [18].

The evolving landscape of feature selection has prompted the development of more sophisticated approaches. Using a single algorithm to balance convergence and diversity in multi-objective optimization problems (MOPs) [19] is challenging. Thus, the current trend is to combine multiple algorithms [20,21]. This approach can be categorized into two main types: multi-algorithm methods (using various algorithms within the same population) [22,23] and multi-population methods (using multiple populations, each targeting a specific objective) [24,25]. In multi-algorithm methods, by integrating various algorithmic strategies, it is possible to effectively balance the exploration speed and the diversity of population development. It can synergize different evolutionary strategies to optimize performance across various feature selection scenarios. This method not only leverages the strengths of individual algorithms but also fosters a more dynamic and adaptive search process.

Evolutionary algorithms (EAs) are known for their high computational complexity, which often limits their practical application despite their potential for performance improvement [26]. In this study, we propose a Knowledge-Guided Competitive Co-Evolutionary Algorithm (KCCEA) to address this issue. By leveraging feature correlation knowledge and a dynamically allocated competitive–cooperative mechanism, the KCCEA significantly reduces computational complexity while enhancing performance. This approach balances the trade-off between computational efficiency and performance gain, making it a valuable contribution to real-world applications where high-dimensional data and limited computational resources are common. The main contributions of this work can be summarized as follows:

- We propose a feature grouping method based on correlation and, based on this, introduce a Knowledge-Guided Evolutionary Algorithm (KGEA). Initially, the correlations between features are assessed using Spearman's correlation coefficient. Then, using a predefined optimal threshold, features are grouped based on their correlations. Finally, the obtained grouping information serves as knowledge to guide the evolutionary process. In this way, the speed and quality of evolutionary feature selection can be significantly enhanced.

- We design a Knowledge-Guided Competitive–Cooperative Evolutionary Algorithm (KCCEA) framework. Initially, a method based on allocation ratios allows the two algorithms to cooperate. Then, during the evolutionary process, the algorithms continually update the allocation ratio dynamically by assessing the success rates of producing superior offspring, allowing the two algorithms to compete. This method achieves an improvement in search speed and solution quality;
- To verify the performance of the proposed methods, we conduct a series of experiments. The experimental results demonstrate that the proposed methods effectively enhance the performance of evolutionary algorithms in feature selection tasks.

The structure of this paper is as follows: Section 2 introduces the background. Section 3 describes the Knowledge-Guided Evolutionary Algorithm (KGEA). Section 4 presents the competitive–cooperative evolutionary mechanism (KCCEA). Sections 5 and 6 describe the experimental setup and results, respectively. Section 7 concludes the paper and outlines several themes for future research.

## 2. Background

### 2.1. Related Work

#### 2.1.1. Multi-Objective Optimization Problem

An MOP involves finding the minimum or maximum values of multiple objective functions under certain constraints [27,28]. It is generally formulated as follows:

$$\begin{aligned} \min / \max f(X) &= (f_1(X), f_2(X), \ldots, f_r(X)) \\ \text{s.t. } g_i(X) &\geq 0 (i = 1, 2, \ldots, k) \\ h_i(X) &= 0 (i = 1, 2, \ldots, l) \end{aligned} \tag{1}$$

In the above equation, the decision vector $X = (x_1, x_2, \ldots, x_n)$ and the objective vector $f(X)$ have multiple optimization combinations, which can be summarized into the following three scenarios:

- Maximize all sub-objective functions;
- Minimize all sub-objective functions;
- Maximize some sub-objective functions while minimizing others.

It is possible to transform all optimization objectives into a unified form, either all maximizing or all minimizing, to facilitate the algorithm finding the optimal solution $X^* = (x_1^*, x_2^*, \ldots, x_n^*)$ such that $f(X^*)$ is optimally achieved while satisfying constraints.

In this work, for the feature selection problem, we need to optimize two objectives: (1) the number of selected features and (2) the performance of the machine learning tasks using the selected features. Assuming a solution selects k features, then $f1(x)$ is equal to $k/D$, representing the ratio of selected features, while $f2(x)$ represents classification performance. To achieve the minimization of all sub-objective functions, we consider the classification performance as $1 - f1\_score$, where, for a multi-class problem, $f1\_score$ is the weighted average.

#### 2.1.2. Non-Dominated Sorting Genetic Algorithm II

The Non-Dominated Sorting Genetic Algorithm II (NSGA-II) is a refined version of the original NSGA [29] and is prominently used within the field of Pareto-Based Evolutionary Multi-Objective Optimization (EMO) algorithms [30]. Specifically crafted to address multi-objective optimization challenges, the NSGA-II excels in efficiently identifying a broad spectrum of Pareto optimal solutions. The core mechanism of the NSGA-II hinges on a swift non-dominated sorting procedure which organizes solutions into several tiers or 'fronts'. These fronts are formed based on how solutions dominate or are dominated by one another.

- Solutions on a lower-numbered front have no dominators from other fronts;
- Each subsequent front is progressively dominated by those in prior fronts.

In terms of operational dynamics, the NSGA-II follows a structured process:

1. Population Generation: The NSGA-II begins with the generation of a random initial population;
2. Evaluation and Sorting: Each solution is evaluated and ranked based on objective function performance and then sorted into fronts;
3. Selection: Selection favors solutions on better-ranked fronts. Within these fronts, a further selection criterion based on crowding distance determines choice, emphasizing less crowded areas to enhance diversity among the chosen solutions;
4. Genetic Operations: Following selection, genetic mechanisms like crossover and mutation are employed to generate new solutions, aiding in the exploration and expansion of the solution space;
5. Elitism and Generational Transition: To ensure robustness across generations, the NSGA-II integrates elitism, preserving top-performing solutions and carrying them forward. The blended population of parents and offspring undergoes another round of sorting and selection, emphasizing the superior solutions for the next generation.

Through this structured approach and emphasis on maintaining a diverse set of high-quality solutions, the NSGA-II not only adeptly explores the Pareto front but also ensures rapid convergence to optimal solutions, effectively addressing the complexities associated with multiple objectives.

### 2.2. *Major Motivations*

Evolutionary algorithms (EAs) have been widely applied to multi-objective feature selection [18,31,32], but most studies merely apply EAs without considering the relationships among features. We recognize that, with the increasing complexity of real-world data, especially the rise of big data, features in high-dimensional datasets are likely to encompass various complex relationships [33] which might not be merely linearly positive or negative correlations. These potential high-dimensional relationships could significantly impact the exploration process of feature selection. We can attempt to capture such relationships and examine their contributions to evolutionary optimization. The motivation to integrate knowledge-guided strategies stems from the observation that not all features contribute equally to the outcomes of predictive models. Some features are more interdependent than others and can be utilized to enhance the search process. By incorporating knowledge of feature correlations directly into the evolutionary process, this method can more effectively guide the search, reduce computational overhead, accelerate the search speed, and improve the quality of the selected feature subsets.

Furthermore, in multi-objective optimization, particularly when applied to feature selection, balancing exploration of the search space and exploitation of promising areas are crucial. This balance is difficult to achieve with a single algorithm because of the high risk of convergence to local optima [34,35]. Traditional static cooperative algorithms cannot adapt to changes in the problem landscape that might occur during the search process. A dynamic, adaptive approach can better respond to such changes, optimizing resource allocation based on the performance of competing methods, thereby ensuring that the most effective strategies are employed as conditions evolve. These motivations guide the development of the KCCEA, focusing on creating a versatile, efficient, and effective tool for feature selection that addresses the unique challenges posed by modern, high-dimensional datasets in various domains. The ultimate goal is to provide a method that not only performs well in academic benchmarks but also offers practical, real-world applicability and scalability.

## 3. Knowledge-Guided Evolutionary Algorithm

In the evolutionary optimization problem for feature selection, high-dimensional features often lead to a large number of decision variables. With the increase in decision variables, the search space for the problem expands dramatically. To effectively enhance the efficiency of solving the problem, this paper designs and improves a knowledge-guided evolutionary method, the KGEA, based on the NSGA-II [16]. Firstly, a method of grouping features based on correlation is proposed. In this method, we fully utilize the correlation among different features to achieve balanced grouping results (considered as knowledge in subsequent evolution). Then, during the evolutionary process, the algorithm uses the acquired knowledge to guide crossover and mutation, reduce the search space, and enhance the efficiency of the search while maximizing the diversity of the population.

### 3.1. Feature Grouping Based on Correlation

Datasets in real applications include various features. The correlation among different features is diverse. Some are related, and some are not. Some have positive correlation, while others have negative. Additionally, there might be numerous high-dimensional relationships between features that are difficult to identify, which could significantly impact the outcome. For instance, in finance, stock prices and market indices might show positive correlations, but interest rates and stock prices might have a negative correlation. Therefore, we aim to use correlation to group features. This strategy aims to improve the efficiency of subsequent evolutionary searches while maximizing the diversity of the population. Ideally, our expected feature grouping outcome should achieve balance among feature groups, i.e., avoid overly large feature groups and a multitude of isolated features. Through experimentation, we propose a significantly effective and simple threshold-based grouping method.

The pseudo-code of the described algorithm is shown in Algorithm 1. Initially, the algorithm conducts a detailed analysis of the correlation among features. By calculating the Pearson correlation coefficient between features, we obtain a correlation matrix where each element of the matrix represents the correlation strength between a pair of features. After obtaining the correlation matrix, we traverse each feature and check its correlation with the features in the existing groups based on a preset threshold determined through experimentation. If a feature's absolute correlation with all features in a certain group exceeds the threshold, then the feature is added to the corresponding group. If a feature cannot be placed into any existing group, a new feature group is created. This grouping mechanism ensures high correlation within groups while maintaining relative independence between groups.

**Algorithm 1** Feature _Grouping(correlation_matrix, threshold)

**Input:** correlation_matrix of size $n \times n$, threshold
**Output:** List of feature groups

```
Initialize feature_groups to an empty list
num_features ← number of columns in correlation_matrix
for i = 0 to num_features − 1 do
    added ← False
    for each group in feature_groups do
        if all |correlation_matrix[i, j]| > threshold for j in group then
            Append i to group
            added ← True
            Break
        end if
    end for
    if not added then
        Append [i] to feature_groups
    end if
end for
return [list(group) for group in feature_groups]
```

This feature grouping mechanism based on correlation analysis acts as knowledge and provides guidance for the subsequent knowledge-guided evolutionary process. Its main objective is to reduce the dimensions of the search space by focusing on combinations of features with high correlation, capturing possible higher-dimensional feature relationships and thereby improving the search efficiency of the evolutionary algorithm. In this manner, the KGEA can effectively balance exploration and exploitation in evolutionary searches, promoting the diversity and quality of solutions.

### 3.2. Knowledge-Guided Crossover and Mutation

The unique aspect of the KGEA lies in its utilization of predetermined groupings of features to direct the genetic operators of crossover and mutation. This approach contrasts sharply with traditional methods where each gene (or feature) is considered independently. In the realm of evolutionary optimization, particularly for feature selection in high-dimensional datasets, the techniques of knowledge-guided crossover and mutation play a pivotal role. By intelligently grouping features based on their correlations—as delineated in prior sections—this method not only simplifies the search space but also ensures a focused exploration that significantly enhances efficiency.

In the KGEA, features are encoded using a binary system. As shown in Figure 1, when the encoding position $x_1$ for Feature1 is 1, it indicates that we have selected this feature. This encoding is crucial as it directly influences the genetic operations that follow.

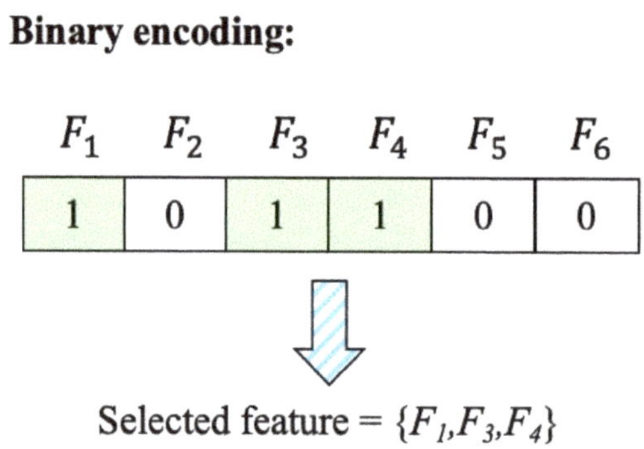


**Figure 1.** Binary encoding for feature selection.

Figure 2 provides an example of knowledge-guided crossover and mutation assuming we have six features $\{F_1, F_2, F_3, F_4, F_5, F_6\}$ with corresponding chromosome encoding $\{x_1, x_2, x_3, x_4, x_5, x_6\}$. Also, assume that we have obtained feature grouping information $\{[x_1], [x_2, x_3], [x_4], [x_5, x_6]\}$ through the method mentioned in the previous subsection. In this setup, when performing mutations or crossovers, the algorithm does not randomly pick single genes but rather entire groups, thereby preserving the intrinsic correlation structure within the data.

During a mutation event, instead of a single gene mutation, entire groups such as $\{x_1\}$ and $\{x_5, x_6\}$ are mutated. This enhances the mutation's effectiveness by ensuring that changes are made to related features together, thus maintaining the logical structure of the data. Similarly, during crossover events, entire groups like $\{x_2, x_3\}$ and $\{x_5, x_6\}$ might be swapped between two chromosomes. This group-based approach not only maintains the integrity of feature relationships but also introduces a new dimension of diversity to the gene pool.

This enhanced method of guiding the genetic operators using prior knowledge effectively reduces the dimensionality of the problem space. By focusing mutations and crossovers on groups of features that are likely to interact, the KGEA significantly boosts the algorithm's efficiency. It balances the exploration of the search space with the exploitation of known, valuable regions, thereby improving both the speed and quality of the search for optimal feature sets.

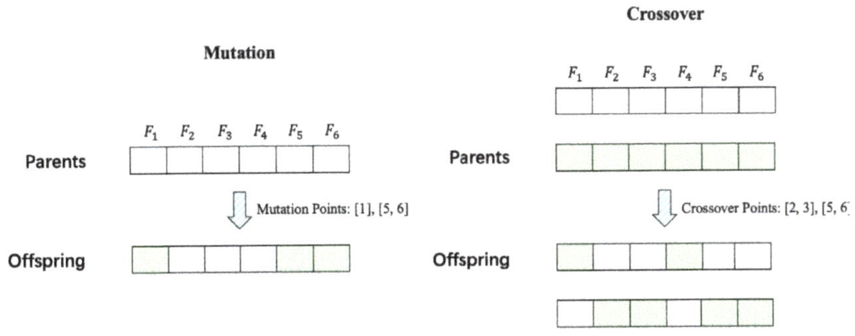


**Figure 2.** An example of knowledge-guided crossover and mutation.

## 4. Competition–Cooperation Evolution

In the KGEA, by introducing data parsing techniques and utilizing knowledge to guide the evolutionary process, the quality and search efficiency of the solutions are significantly enhanced. However, during the evolutionary process, due to the combinatorial features leading to a reduction in the solution space, the solutions obtained by the algorithm may fall into local optima. To further improve the quality of solutions and increase their convergence and diversity, we propose a competition–cooperation evolutionary mechanism called the KCCEA that combines the KGEA with the traditional NSGA-II. This method initializes an allocation ratio, allowing both models to evolve simultaneously, and, by mixing the offspring generated by the two models and randomly assigning them as parents for the next generation, it facilitates the exchange and cooperation of information between the two models. Furthermore, the allocation ratio of resources is adjusted generation by generation based on the success rates of the two evolutionary approaches, achieving dynamic allocation of computational resources and thus enabling the two algorithms to compete effectively. The overall framework of the algorithm is shown in Figure 3.

### 4.1. Competition–Cooperation Evolutionary Mechanism

The dynamic interaction between the KGEA and NSGA-II within our proposed KCCEA model is fundamentally rooted in the principles of competition and cooperation. This interaction not only enhances the diversity of the solutions but also improves their quality by preventing premature convergence to suboptimal solutions.

Initial Setup and Population Division: At the beginning of the evolutionary process, we assume the total number of individuals in the parent population $P_t$ is denoted by $N_{ind}$, and the initial allocation ratio $n$ is predetermined based on prior experimental tuning. The parent population is then randomly divided into two sub-populations, $S_1$ and $S_2$. The size of each sub-population, $n_1$ for $S_1$ and $n_2$ for $S_2$, is determined by the allocation ratio as follows:

$$n_1 = allocation\_ratio \times N_{ind} \tag{2}$$

$$n_2 = (1 - allocation\_ratio) \times N_{ind} \tag{3}$$

Evolutionary Operations: Each sub-population undergoes evolutionary operations independently. Sub-population $S_1$ is processed using the KGEA, which emphasizes knowledge-guided mutations and selections, whereas $S_2$ undergoes a more traditional evolutionary path via the NSGA-II, focusing on Pareto optimality. This dual approach ensures that, while one algorithm might explore more deeply into a certain region of the solution space, the other may explore more broadly, thereby enhancing the overall explorative capabilities of the combined algorithm.

Crossover and Mutation: After the initial evolutionary operations, both sub-populations undergo crossover and mutation processes. Mutation and crossover are applied differently in the two sub-populations to maintain their distinctive characteristics. For $S_1$, mutation is knowledge guided, whereas for $S_2$ it is more random and exploratory.

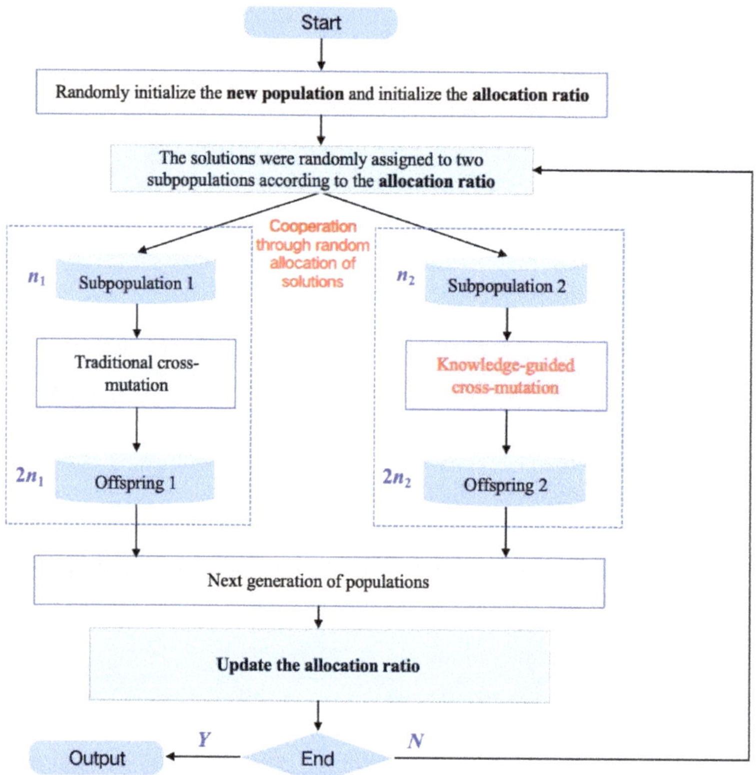


**Figure 3.** Framework of competition–cooperation evolutionary mechanism.

Integration and Selection: The offspring from both $S_1$ and $S_2$, denoted as $Q_1$ and $Q_2$, respectively, are then integrated to form a unified offspring population. This integration is crucial as it brings together the diverse traits developed independently in each sub-population. The unified population undergoes a non-dominated sorting followed by crowding distance selection to ensure that the next generation, $Q_t$, maintains a balanced representation of both exploration and exploitation traits. The size of $Q_t$ is set to be equal to $N_{ind}$, maintaining a consistent population size through the generations.

Feedback and Adjustment: The performance of each sub-population in producing high-quality offspring is monitored. Based on their performance, the allocation ratio is dynamically adjusted for the next generation, ensuring that more resources are allocated to the more successful approach in the current generation. This adaptive mechanism allows the KCCEA model to respond to the evolving landscape of the problem space effectively.

By fostering a balance between competition and cooperation, the KCCEA not only mitigates the risk of converging prematurely to local optima but also leverages the strengths of both evolutionary algorithms, leading to a robust mechanism for finding optimal solutions.

### 4.2. Dynamic Resource Allocation Based on Success Rate

Assuming the population size $N_{ind}$ is 100, initially, the allocation ratio is set to 0.5, meaning that, during the allocation, individuals are equally distributed between the two algorithms, forming their respective parent populations with 50 individuals each. Individuals generated by the KGEA are marked as 0, and those generated by the traditional NSGA-II are marked as 1.

By merging the parent and offspring populations of the two algorithms, and selecting 100 individuals to form a new generation, the elite retention mechanism ensures that excellent parent individuals will also appear in the new generation. We count the number of individuals marked as 0 and 1 to calculate the success rates of the two search methods.

Suppose that, in the new generation, there are 40 individuals marked as 0 and 30 individuals marked as 1. Then, the success rate of the KGEA is 0.8, and the success rate of the NSGA-II is 0.6. Normalize 0.8 and 0.6 so their sum equals 1, yielding new search ratios of 0.57 and 0.43. Update the allocation ratio to 0.57, and set the mark of all individuals to 2. According to the new search ratio, randomly select the corresponding number of individuals from the solutions generated by the two search methods to form the offspring. The dynamic resource allocation mechanism based on success rate is shown in Figure 4.

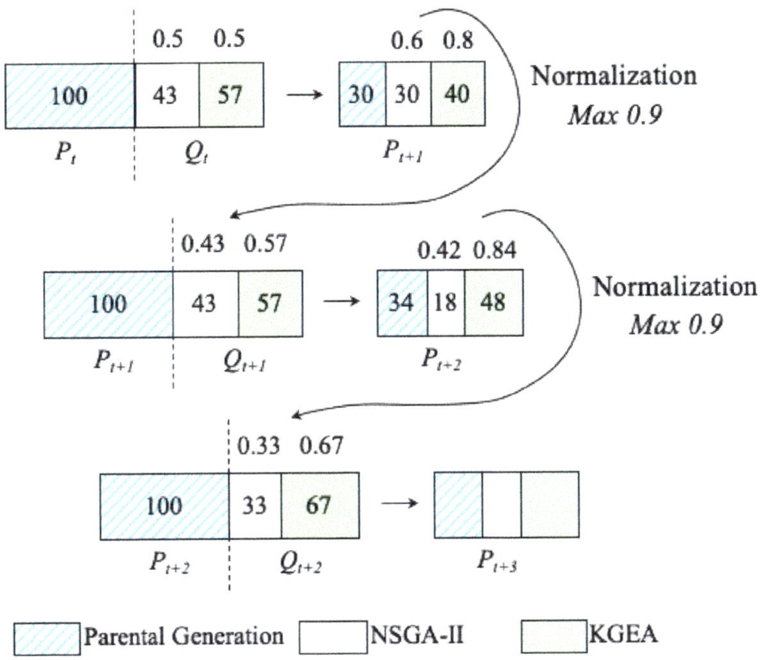


**Figure 4.** Resource allocation mechanism based on success rate.

In the process of population evolution, it may occur that, due to the strong optimization capability, one method's success rate is extremely high. Without restriction, this could lead to one model monopolizing all evolutionary resources, causing the loss of the other search method. In the later stages of iterative evolution, when the quality of individuals in the population is high, it may occur that the success rate of a certain search method is 0, which also requires manual intervention in the search ratio. The treatment for special cases is as shown in Table 1.

**Table 1.** Special case handling.

| Special Cases | Allocation _Rate |
|---|---|
| allocation_rate > 0.9 | 0.9 |
| allocation_rate < 0.1 | 0.1 |
| success_rate1 = 0 AND success_rate2 ≠ 0 | 0.1 |
| success_rate1 ≠ 0 AND success_rate2 = 0 | 0.9 |
| success_rate1 = 0 AND success_rate2 = 0 | 0.5 |

An additional simple method is to adopt a nonlinear approach for resource allocation instead of directly distributing resources based on performance proportions. For instance, a sigmoid function based on success rates can be used for resource allocation, ensuring that, even with significant performance differences, resource distribution does not become too extreme. The general form of the function used is as follows:

$$\text{sigmoid}(x) = \frac{1}{1 + e^{-\beta(x-\alpha)}} \tag{4}$$

Here, $\alpha$ and $\beta$ are adjustable parameters controlling the center point and the slope of the function, respectively. We set $\alpha$ to 0.5 (assuming an ideal state where both populations equally share resources), and $\beta$ can be adjusted based on actual needs to control the smoothness of resource distribution. A higher $\beta$ value makes the resource allocation more sensitive to performance differences, while a lower value results in more even distribution.

## 5. Experimental Setup

### *5.1. Classification Datasets*

This study utilizes five diverse datasets for classification tasks, all sourced from online website like the UCI Machine Learning Repository [36]. Each dataset is meticulously selected to encapsulate a wide spectrum of challenges commonly encountered in the machine learning domain. These challenges range from managing datasets with low to high dimensionality to addressing problems with varying numbers of classes, from simple binary classifications to more complex multi-class scenarios. This variety is crucial for testing the robustness and adaptability of proposed algorithms under varied conditions. Moreover, the datasets are not only diverse in their characteristics but also relevant to real-world applications. They include data from health, chemistry, voice recognition, and consumer preferences, which are critical areas where machine learning models are extensively applied.

Table 2 provides a concise overview of these datasets, detailing the number of instances, features, and classes for each. This diverse collection not only tests the adaptability and efficiency of the algorithms but also enhances the robustness of our experimental findings by covering a broad spectrum of data characteristics.

**Table 2.** Classification datasets.

| No. | Dataset Name | Instance | Feature | Class |
|---|---|---|---|---|
| 1 | Wine | 178 | 13 | 3 |
| 2 | MUSK1 | 476 | 166 | 2 |
| 3 | LSVT_Voice | 126 | 310 | 2 |
| 4 | ISOLET5 | 1559 | 617 | 26 |
| 5 | Toxic | 171 | 1203 | 2 |

### *5.2. Performance Metrics*

This article utilizes two principal performance indicators to assess the quality of solutions obtained by multi-objective evolutionary algorithms (MOEAs): Hypervolume

(HV) [37] and Inverted Generational Distance (IGD) [38]. These indicators are critical for evaluating an algorithm's efficacy in terms of both convergence to the Pareto front and distribution of the solutions across it.

For HV, normalization of all objective values obtained by each algorithm is performed initially against the ideal and nadir points, scaling them to the [0, 1] range in each objective direction. The ideal and nadir points are set at (0, 0) and (1.1, 1.1), respectively, with the HV's reference point subsequently established at (1, 1) [32]. This process ensures a standardized basis for comparing the extent of the objective space covered by the solutions from different algorithms.

In contrast, the calculation of IGD faces unique challenges in feature selection problems, which are discrete and complex, rendering the exact Pareto front nearly impossible to ascertain. Unlike in traditional benchmark test problems such as DTLZ [39] or WFG [40], this study adopts a novel approach for fairness. We aggregate the Pareto fronts collected from multiple runs of different algorithms into a unified population. This collective set is then subjected to non-dominated sorting, retaining only the foremost non-dominated front as the reference point set for IGD. The IGD metric, therefore, provides a comprehensive assessment by reflecting both the proximity of solutions to the Pareto front and their distribution. Lower IGD values signify superior algorithm performance, an inverse relationship compared to HV values.

### 5.2.1. Hypervolume

The Hypervolume indicator measures the volume covered by the members of a solution set in the objective space [37]. It quantifies both the convergence and diversity of the solutions by calculating the volume enclosed between the solutions and a reference point. Formally, the HV of a solution set $S$ with respect to a reference point $r = (r_1, r_2, ..., r_m)$ in an $m$-dimensional objective space is defined as the volume of the union of the hypercubes formed by each solution in $S$ and $r$. The reference point is typically chosen to be worse than the nadir point of the Pareto front. For normalization purposes, all objective values are scaled to the interval [0, 1], with ideal and nadir points set to (0, 0) and (1.1, 1.1), respectively. The HV calculation can be represented as follows:

$$\begin{aligned}\mathrm{HV}(S) &= \lambda\left(\bigcup_{x\in S}[f_1(x), r_1] \times \cdots \times [f_m(x), r_m]\right) \\ &= \lambda\left(\bigcup_{x\in S}\prod_{k=1}^{m}[f_k(x), r_k]\right)\end{aligned} \tag{5}$$

where $\lambda$ denotes the Lebesgue measure, and $f_i(x)$ is the $i$-th objective function value of solution $x$. The larger the HV, the better, indicating that the solution set covers a larger portion of the objective space up to the reference point.

### 5.2.2. Inverted Generational Distance

The Inverted Generational Distance (IGD) measures both the convergence and the diversity of the solutions [38]. For each point on the true Pareto front, the IGD finds the minimum distance to a point on the Pareto front obtained by the algorithm and then averages these minimum distances. A lower IGD value indicates that the algorithm's solutions are both closer to the true Pareto front and more evenly distributed. The specific formula for calculating IGD is as follows:

$$IGD = \frac{\sum_{j=1}^{|P^*|} d_{\min}(x_j^*, P)}{|P^*|}, \quad (6)$$

$$d_{\min}(x_j^*, P) = \min\left\{ \sqrt{\sum_{k=1}^{m} (f_k(x_i) - f_k(x_j^*))^2} \right\},$$

$$i = 1, 2, \ldots, |P|.$$

where $P$ is the set of Pareto optimal solutions obtained by the multi-objective evolutionary algorithm, $P^*$ is the set of true Pareto optimal solutions, $|P|$ is the number of obtained optimal solutions, $|P^*|$ is the number of true optimal solutions, $x_i$ represents the $i$-th solution in $P$, $x_j^*$ is the $j$-th solution in $P^*$, $m$ is the number of objectives, and $f_k(x)$ is the function value of individual $x$ on the $k$-th objective. For instance, in a two-dimensional objective space, as shown in Figure 5, the algorithm obtains three Pareto optimal solutions, H, I, and J, while the true Pareto front is formed by solutions A, B, C, D, E, F, and G. The minimum distances from the points on the true Pareto front to the points H, I, and J are $d(A,H), d(B,H), d(C,I), d(D,I), d(E,J), d(F,J)$, and $d(G,J)$, respectively. Hence, the IGD value is calculated as follows:

$$IGD = \frac{1}{7}(d(A,H) + d(B,H) + d(C,I) + d(D,I) + \cdots + d(G,J)) \quad (7)$$

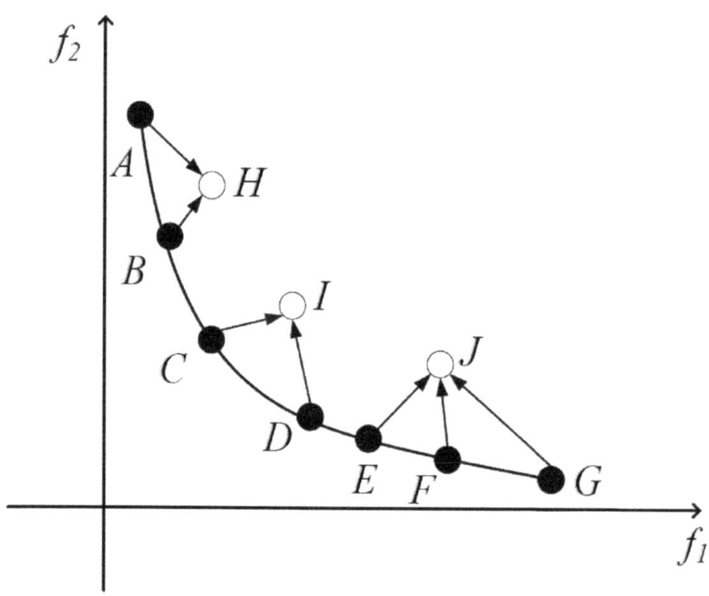


**Figure 5.** The calculation method of IGD.

When solving problems using multi-objective evolutionary algorithms, the diversity of the solutions is also an important consideration. Compared to GD, the IGD can identify uneven distribution of solutions, making the evaluation more objective. Therefore, the IGD is chosen as the final evaluation metric.

### 5.3. Parameter Settings

In this study, each algorithm undergoes 30 distinct trials on every dataset to ensure robust statistical analysis. Consistency across these trials is maintained by using a fixed initial random seed for all algorithms. As outlined in [32], we adapt the population size based on the number of features present in each dataset. Specifically, the population size $N$ is dynamically adjusted to match the number of features up to a maximum of 200. This cap is imposed to strike an optimal balance between algorithmic diversity and computational efficiency. Consequently, even for datasets with more than 200 features, the population size remains limited to 200. For the sigmoid function that equilibrates the resource allocation, $\alpha$ is set to 0.5 (assuming that, ideally, the two populations distribute the resources equally), and $\beta$ is set to 2 to control the degree of smoothing of the resource allocation. The algorithms are set to run for 100 generations, providing a deep exploration of the solution space. For the purpose of evaluating classification performance, we partition each dataset into training and testing subsets. The training set comprises roughly 70% of the data, with the remaining 30% allocated to the testing set. This split is consistently applied across all 30 executions of each algorithm on a given dataset, ensuring comparability of results. However, the specific partition varies from one dataset to another, maintaining rigorous evaluation standards across different data contexts.

## 6. Experimental Results and Analysis

### 6.1. Grouping Threshold Sensitivity Analysis

This work conducted an analysis on the sensitivity to grouping thresholds. We varied the threshold from 0.5 to 0.95 and observed how the number of groups and the balance within the groups (standard deviation of group sizes) changed. As illustrated in Figure 6, we found that, as the threshold increased, the number of groups decreased while the balance improved. By normalizing the number of groups and balance to the same scale, and identifying the threshold where the difference between them was minimal, we determined the optimal grouping threshold, as shown in Table 3. This threshold provides the best compromise between the number of groups and balance during the grouping process. Subsequently, we applied the optimal threshold for each dataset within the KCCEA and compared it with a default threshold of 0.5. The results of these comparative experiments are presented in Table 4.

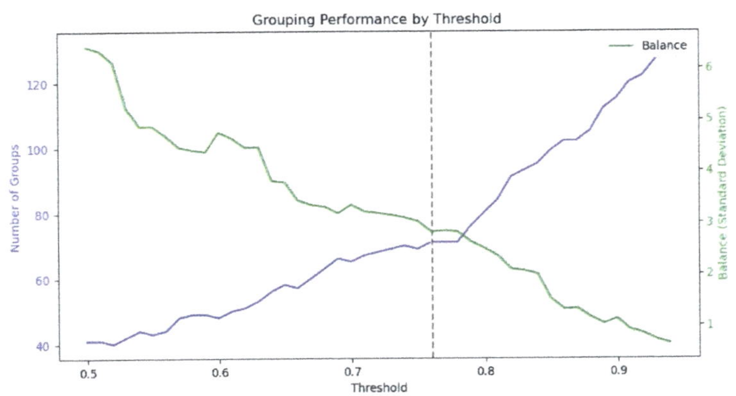


**Figure 6.** Groupingperformance by threshold.

**Table 3.** The optimal threshold for datasets.

| Dataset | Optimal Threshold | Feature | Groups |
|---|---|---|---|
| 1 | 0.65 | 13 | 11 |
| 2 | 0.76 | 166 | 71 |
| 3 | 0.77 | 310 | 96 |
| 4 | 0.72 | 617 | 260 |
| 5 | 0.75 | 1203 | 350 |

**Table 4.** Mean IGD performance on test data. The best performance is highlighted in gray.

| Dataset | KCCEA (Optimal) | | KCCEA (0.5) | |
|---|---|---|---|---|
| | Mean | Variance | Mean | Variance |
| 1 | $2.55 \times 10^{-2}$ | $2.63 \times 10^{-4}$ | $2.74 \times 10^{-2}$ | $2.91 \times 10^{-4}$ |
| 2 | $2.55 \times 10^{-2}$ | $1.11 \times 10^{-5}$ | $2.01 \times 10^{-2}$ | $1.93 \times 10^{-5}$ |
| 3 | $2.54 \times 10^{-2}$ | $3.55 \times 10^{-5}$ | $2.23 \times 10^{-2}$ | $1.39 \times 10^{-5}$ |
| 4 | $2.10 \times 10^{-2}$ | $4.12 \times 10^{-4}$ | $1.87 \times 10^{-2}$ | $5.13 \times 10^{-4}$ |
| 5 | $3.63 \times 10^{-2}$ | $1.05 \times 10^{-4}$ | $3.29 \times 10^{-2}$ | $2.70 \times 10^{-4}$ |

As can be seen from the results, the algorithm performs best when using the optimal thresholds we obtained, outperforming other takes on several test problems, especially on problems with high feature dimensions.

### 6.2. *Effectiveness of Knowledge-Guided Evolution*

The improved algorithm KGEA is compared with the traditional multi-objective evolutionary algorithm to verify the effectiveness of the knowledge-guided evolution method. The experimental method is the same as above; the NSGA-II is set according to the parameters in the paper [16], the KGEA mutation and crossover probability are both set to 0.5, and the grouping threshold is the optimal threshold calculated in the previous section.

The empirical results shown in Tables 5 and 6 indicate that the Knowledge-Guided Evolutionary Algorithm (KGEA) outperforms the traditional NSGA-II in four out of five experiments within a set number of evolutionary generations. The effectiveness of the KGEA is demonstrated through comparison with the baseline NSGA-II, which does not utilize knowledge-based feature grouping. The key differentiator is the use of correlation-based feature grouping in the KGEA, which guides the crossover and mutation processes and significantly narrows the search space. This strategy leads to more informed genetic operations and enhances the efficiency of the algorithm.

These comparisons underline the benefits of integrating domain knowledge into the evolutionary process, particularly in scenarios where the relationships among decision variables significantly impact the outcome. It supports the premise that a knowledge-guided approach in evolutionary algorithms can significantly enhance performance, especially in complex problem domains such as feature selection in high-dimensional datasets.

**Table 5.** Mean IGD performance on test data. The best performance is highlighted in gray.

| Dataset | NSGA-II | | KGEA | | KCCEA | |
|---|---|---|---|---|---|---|
| | Mean | Variance | Mean | Variance | Mean | Variance |
| 1 | $2.05 \times 10^{-2}$ | $1.43 \times 10^{-4}$ | $2.85 \times 10^{-2}$ | $2.71 \times 10^{-4}$ | $2.55 \times 10^{-2}$ | $2.63 \times 10^{-4}$ |
| 2 | $1.66 \times 10^{-1}$ | $1.09 \times 10^{-4}$ | $5.60 \times 10^{-2}$ | $1.93 \times 10^{-4}$ | $2.55 \times 10^{-2}$ | $1.11 \times 10^{-5}$ |
| 3 | $2.55 \times 10^{-1}$ | $1.19 \times 10^{-5}$ | $6.73 \times 10^{-2}$ | $8.62 \times 10^{-5}$ | $2.54 \times 10^{-2}$ | $3.55 \times 10^{-5}$ |
| 4 | $1.03 \times 10^{-1}$ | $2.70 \times 10^{-5}$ | $3.08 \times 10^{-2}$ | $3.20 \times 10^{-4}$ | $2.10 \times 10^{-2}$ | $4.12 \times 10^{-4}$ |
| 5 | $8.63 \times 10^{-2}$ | $1.05 \times 10^{-5}$ | $4.60 \times 10^{-2}$ | $4.94 \times 10^{-4}$ | $3.63 \times 10^{-2}$ | $1.05 \times 10^{-4}$ |

**Table 6.** Mean HV performance on test data. The best performance is highlighted in gray.

| Dataset | NSGA-II | | KGEA | | KCCEA | |
|---|---|---|---|---|---|---|
| | **Mean** | **Variance** | **Mean** | **Variance** | **Mean** | **Variance** |
| 1 | $8.98 \times 10^{-1}$ | $3.36 \times 10^{-5}$ | $8.95 \times 10^{-1}$ | $1.80 \times 10^{-4}$ | $8.94 \times 10^{-1}$ | $2.77 \times 10^{-4}$ |
| 2 | $1.66 \times 10^{-1}$ | $1.09 \times 10^{-4}$ | $4.67 \times 10^{-3}$ | $1.93 \times 10^{-4}$ | $8.42 \times 10^{-1}$ | $1.32 \times 10^{-4}$ |
| 3 | $6.24 \times 10^{-1}$ | $5.71 \times 10^{-5}$ | $8.34 \times 10^{-1}$ | $1.29 \times 10^{-4}$ | $8.93 \times 10^{-1}$ | $3.55 \times 10^{-5}$ |
| 4 | $2.41 \times 10^{-1}$ | $6.70 \times 10^{-4}$ | $5.16 \times 10^{-1}$ | $3.20 \times 10^{-4}$ | $5.44 \times 10^{-1}$ | $3.77 \times 10^{-4}$ |
| 5 | $3.36 \times 10^{-1}$ | $1.57 \times 10^{-4}$ | $3.84 \times 10^{-1}$ | $1.13 \times 10^{-4}$ | $3.96 \times 10^{-1}$ | $2.23 \times 10^{-4}$ |

### 6.3. *Effectiveness of Dynamic Resource Allocation*

The dynamic resource allocation mechanism in the KCCEA significantly improves performance over the KGEA by adjusting the allocation ratio based on the success rates of the two algorithms. This adaptive approach enhances the exploration and exploitation balance, leading to better overall results. As shown in Tables 5 and 6, the KCCEA achieves lower IGD values and higher HV values across multiple datasets, particularly in high-dimensional feature spaces. For instance, in the ISOLET5 dataset, the KCCEA achieves an IGD of 0.021 and an HV of 0.544, outperforming the KGEA.

This mechanism ensures that computational resources are allocated optimally, leveraging the strengths of both the KGEA and NSGA-II. By maintaining a balance between competition and cooperation, the KCCEA prevents the dominance of a single algorithm, resulting in a more robust and efficient evolutionary process. The dynamic resource allocation effectively adapts the search strategy based on real-time performance, improving the quality of solutions and providing a competitive edge in tackling complex feature selection tasks in high-dimensional datasets.

### 6.4. *Knowledge-Guided Competitive–Cooperative Evolutionary Algorithm against Baseline Algorithm*

The Knowledge-Guided Competitive–Cooperative Evolutionary Algorithm (KCCEA) effectively integrates the Knowledge-Guided Evolutionary Algorithm (KGEA) with the traditional NSGA-II, showcasing significant performance enhancements in complex feature selection tasks across high-dimensional datasets. This integration facilitates a robust comparative analysis that highlights the benefits of incorporating domain-specific knowledge into evolutionary strategies. As evidenced by the results presented in Tables 5 and 6, the KCCEA surpasses the NSGA-II in four out of five experiments. The advantage is particularly notable in datasets with complex feature interactions, such as ISOLET5 and Toxic, where the knowledge-guided approach of the KCCEA significantly improves solution quality by effectively navigating the expansive search space.

This performance enhancement stems from the structured crossover and mutation processes of the KCCEA, which utilize feature correlations to maintain relevant interactions and reduce computational overhead, enabling faster convergence towards optimal solutions. Additionally, the KCCEA framework adjusts allocation ratios dynamically based on real-time performance metrics, which helps the algorithm adapt to the most promising solution paths and prevents premature convergence to suboptimal solutions. This strategic integration of knowledge within evolutionary cycles substantiates the effectiveness of the KCCEA approach, marking it as a substantial improvement over traditional methods in tackling the complexities of advanced feature selection.

### 6.5. *Analysis of Pareto Front Distributions*

To gain a deeper and more intuitive understanding of the algorithmic performance across various setups, Figures 7 and 8 illustrate the distribution of Pareto fronts for algorithms exhibiting median IGD performance. We focus on two datasets, MUSK1 and Toxic, due to their distinct differences in the spread and quality of non-dominated solutions as produced by different algorithms. It is observed that the KCCEA consistently achieves a broader and more diverse set of Pareto optimal solutions compared to other methods. This indicates not only a wider exploration of the solution space but also superior convergence properties, managing to maintain lower classification errors with a reduced set of selected features.

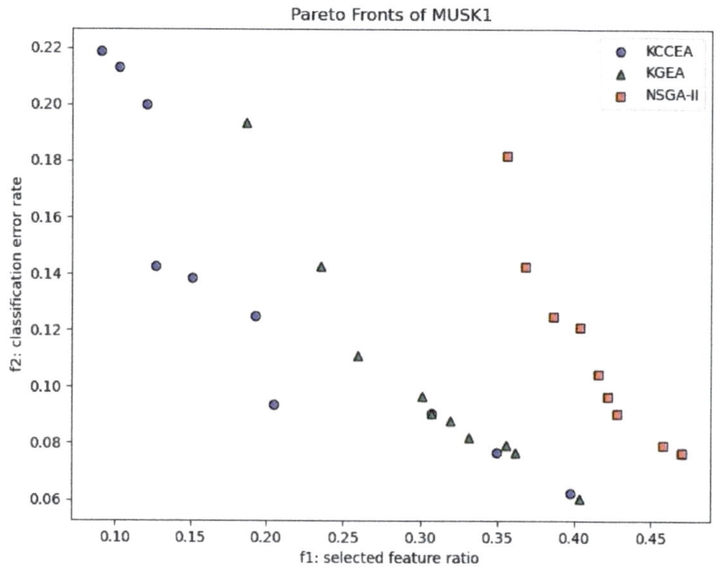


**Figure 7.** Pareto fronts obtained by each algorithm in the objective space: MUSK1.

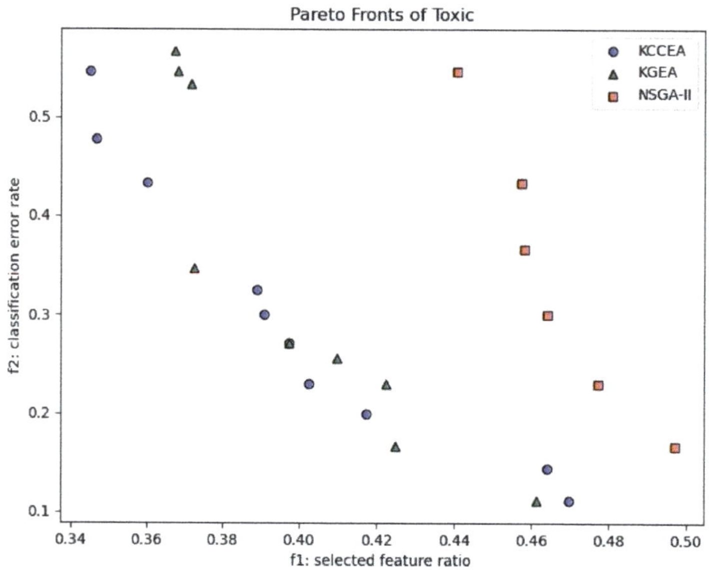


**Figure 8.** Pareto fronts obtained by each algorithm in the objective space: Toxic.

### 6.6. Discussion

The experimental results demonstrate the efficacy of the proposed KCCEA for high-dimensional feature selection. The KCCEA's superior performance, indicated by lower IGD values and higher HV values across various datasets, underscores the advantages of integrating domain knowledge and competitive–cooperative mechanisms into evolutionary algorithms. Furthermore, the design of the KCCEA considers the scalability to handle large-scale datasets. Our proposed feature correlation knowledge grouping only requires a one-time calculation using the given algorithm before the evolution starts to acquire the knowledge. This grouping method demonstrates excellent efficiency and scalability, making it easily applicable to large-scale datasets.

While the KCCEA shows significant improvements in search efficiency and solution quality, there are still some limitations in this work. For instance, noisy and imbalanced data can significantly impact the effectiveness of feature selection [41]. It would be valuable to analyze the robustness of the algorithm under different conditions, such as in the presence of noise or data imbalance. Additionally, exploring the applicability of the KCCEA to other domains, such as regression and unsupervised learning tasks, could be interesting future work. Considering the scope of this work, data complexity and imbalance will be addressed in future studies. Furthermore, traditional machine learning methods often require prior feature selection, whereas neural networks [42] might perform better with selected features. Therefore, it is valuable to evaluate the proposed method's performance before and after feature selection using neural networks. Exploring the performance of various classifiers with the KCCEA could also be considered in future work. Despite these challenges, the KCCEA represents a significant advancement in the field of high-dimensional feature selection.

## 7. Conclusions

This article proposes and examines the Knowledge-Guided Competitive–Cooperative Evolutionary Algorithm (KCCEA), demonstrating its significant advancements in the field of complex feature selection within high-dimensional datasets. Our paper not only provides an analysis but also proposes the integration of the Knowledge-Guided Evolutionary Algorithm (KGEA) with the traditional NSGA-II under a competitive–cooperative framework, which enhances the evolutionary strategy and efficiently navigates the expanded search space. The theoretical contribution of this research is the novel method of embedding domain-specific knowledge within the evolutionary processes, optimizing genetic operations and significantly boosting the algorithm's performance.

On a practical level, the KCCEA's dynamic resource allocation strategy, which adjusts based on real-time performance metrics, ensures the algorithm continuously adapts to the most promising solution paths, thus preventing premature convergence to suboptimal solutions. This adaptability underscores the practical utility of the KCCEA in real-world applications where decision variables are complexly interrelated. Nevertheless, the approach is heavily reliant on the initial accuracy of the domain knowledge used to guide the feature grouping, which is a limitation. Future work could address this by exploring autonomous methods for knowledge acquisition and integration. Further research might also consider applying the competitive–cooperative framework to other optimization domains, potentially broadening the scope and impact of this advanced evolutionary approach.

**Author Contributions:** Conceptualization, J.Z. and H.Z. (Haowen Zheng); Methodology, J.Z.; Software, J.Z.; Validation, J.Z., H.Z. (Haoyang Zhang), and X.W.; Formal Analysis, J.Z.; Investigation, S.L. and Q.H.; Resources, W.G.; Data Curation, H.Z. (Haoyang Zhang); Writing—Original Draft Preparation, J.Z.; Writing—Review and Editing, X.W.; Visualization, J.Z.; Supervision, X.W.; Project Administration, X.W.; Funding Acquisition, W.G. and X.W. All authors have read and agreed to the published version of the manuscript.

**Funding:** This research was funded by the National Training Program of Innovation and Entrepreneurship for Undergraduates, Project 241221.

**Institutional Review Board Statement:** Not applicable.

**Informed Consent Statement:** Not applicable.

**Data Availability Statement:** The data presented in this study are available on request from the corresponding author. The data are not publicly available due to privacy.

**Conflicts of Interest:** The authors declare no conflicts of interest.

## References


1. Qiu, J.; Wu, Q.; Ding, G.; Xu, Y.; Feng, S. A survey of machine learning for big data processing. *EURASIP J. Adv. Signal Process.* **2016**, *2016*, 67. [CrossRef]
2. Feng, S.; Zhao, L.; Shi, H.; Wang, M.; Shen, S.; Wang, W. One-dimensional VGGNet for high-dimensional data. *Appl. Soft Comput.* **2023**, *135*, 110035. [CrossRef]
3. Peng, H.; Long, F.; Ding, C. Feature selection based on mutual information criteria of max-dependency, max-relevance, and min-redundancy. *IEEE Trans. Pattern Anal. Mach. Intell.* **2005**, *27*, 1226–1238. [CrossRef] [PubMed]
4. Khan, M.A.; Alqahtani, A.; Khan, A.; Alsubai, S.; Binbusayyis, A.; Ch, M.M.I.; Yong, H.S.; Cha, J. Cucumber leaf diseases recognition using multi level deep entropy-ELM feature selection. *Appl. Sci.* **2022**, *12*, 593. [CrossRef]
5. Karlupia, N.; Abrol, P. Wrapper-based optimized feature selection using nature-inspired algorithms. *Neural Comput. Appl.* **2023**, *35*, 12675–12689. [CrossRef]
6. Khan, W.A.; Chung, S.H.; Awan, M.U.; Wen, X. Machine learning facilitated business intelligence (Part I) Neural networks learning algorithms and applications. *Ind. Manag. Data Syst.* **2020**, *120*, 164–195. [CrossRef]
7. Ahadzadeh, B.; Abdar, M.; Safara, F.; Khosravi, A.; Menhaj, M.B.; Suganthan, P.N. SFE: A simple, fast and efficient feature selection algorithm for high-dimensional data. *IEEE Trans. Evol. Comput.* **2023**, *27*, 1896–1911. [CrossRef]
8. Li, J.; Cheng, K.; Wang, S.; Morstatter, F.; Trevino, R.P.; Tang, J.; Liu, H. Feature selection: A data perspective. *ACM Comput. Surv. (CSUR)* **2017**, *50*, 1–45. [CrossRef]
9. Jiao, R.; Nguyen, B.H.; Xue, B.; Zhang, M. A Survey on Evolutionary Multiobjective Feature Selection in Classification: Approaches, Applications, and Challenges. *IEEE Trans. Evol. Comput.* **2023** , 1. [CrossRef]
10. Pan, H.; Chen, S.; Xiong, H. A high-dimensional feature selection method based on modified Gray Wolf Optimization. *Appl. Soft Comput.* **2023**, *135*, 110031. [CrossRef]
11. Alabrah, A. A novel study: GAN-based minority class balancing and machine-learning-based network intruder detection using chi-square feature selection. *Appl. Sci.* **2022**, *12*, 11662. [CrossRef]
12. Patil, A.R.; Kim, S. Combination of ensembles of regularized regression models with resampling-based lasso feature selection in high dimensional data. *Mathematics* **2020**, *8*, 110. [CrossRef]
13. Jeon, H.; Oh, S. Hybrid-recursive feature elimination for efficient feature selection. *Appl. Sci.* **2020**, *10*, 3211. [CrossRef]
14. Zhou, A.; Qu, B.Y.; Li, H.; Zhao, S.Z.; Suganthan, P.N.; Zhang, Q. Multiobjective evolutionary algorithms: A survey of the state of the art. *Swarm Evol. Comput.* **2011**, *1*, 32–49. [CrossRef]
15. Almutairi, M.S. Evolutionary Multi-Objective Feature Selection Algorithms on Multiple Smart Sustainable Community Indicator Datasets. *Sustainability* **2024**, *16*, 1511. [CrossRef]
16. Deb, K.; Pratap, A.; Agarwal, S.; Meyarivan, T. A fast and elitist multiobjective genetic algorithm: NSGA-II. *IEEE Trans. Evol. Comput.* **2002**, *6*, 182–197. [CrossRef]
17. Xu, Q.; Xu, Z.; Ma, T. A survey of multiobjective evolutionary algorithms based on decomposition: Variants, challenges and future directions. *IEEE Access* **2020**, *8*, 41588–41614. [CrossRef]
18. Li, L.; Xuan, M.; Lin, Q.; Jiang, M.; Ming, Z.; Tan, K.C. An evolutionary multitasking algorithm with multiple filtering for high-dimensional feature selection. *IEEE Trans. Evol. Comput.* **2023**, *27*, 802–816. [CrossRef]
19. Deb, K. *Multi-Objective Optimization Using Evolutionary Algorithms*; John Wiley & Sons: Hoboken, NJ, USA, 2001; Volume 16.
20. Goh, C.K.; Tan, K.C.; Liu, D.; Chiam, S.C. A competitive and cooperative co-evolutionary approach to multi-objective particle swarm optimization algorithm design. *Eur. J. Oper. Res.* **2010**, *202*, 42–54. [CrossRef]
21. Zhou, X.; Cai, X.; Zhang, H.; Zhang, Z.; Jin, T.; Chen, H.; Deng, W. Multi-strategy competitive-cooperative co-evolutionary algorithm and its application. *Inf. Sci.* **2023**, *635*, 328–344. [CrossRef]
22. Xie, D.; Ding, L.; Hu, Y.; Wang, S.; Xie, C.; Jiang, L. A Multi-Algorithm Balancing Convergence and Diversity for Multi-Objective Optimization. *J. Inf. Sci. Eng.* **2013**, *29*, 811–834.
23. Xiang, Y.; Lu, X.; Cai, D.; Chen, J.; Bao, C. Multi-algorithm fusion–based intelligent decision-making method for robotic belt grinding process parameters. *Int. J. Adv. Manuf. Technol.* **2024** , 1–16. [CrossRef]
24. Zhan, Z.H.; Li, J.; Cao, J.; Zhang, J.; Chung, H.S.H.; Shi, Y.H. Multiple populations for multiple objectives: A coevolutionary technique for solving multiobjective optimization problems. *IEEE Trans. Cybern.* **2013**, *43*, 445–463. [CrossRef]
25. Zou, J.; Sun, R.; Liu, Y.; Hu, Y.; Yang, S.; Zheng, J.; Li, K. A multi-population evolutionary algorithm using new cooperative mechanism for solving multi-objective problems with multi-constraint. *IEEE Trans. Evol. Comput.* **2023**, *28*, 267–280. [CrossRef]
26. Katoch, S.; Chauhan, S.S.; Kumar, V. A review on genetic algorithm: Past, present, and future. *Multimed. Tools Appl.* **2021**, *80*, 8091–8126. [CrossRef] [PubMed]

27. Gunantara, N. A review of multi-objective optimization: Methods and its applications. *Cogent Eng.* **2018**, *5*, 1502242. [CrossRef]
28. Wang, Z.; Pei, Y.; Li, J. A survey on search strategy of evolutionary multi-objective optimization algorithms. *Appl. Sci.* **2023**, *13*, 4643. [CrossRef]
29. Srinivas, N.; Deb, K. Muiltiobjective optimization using nondominated sorting in genetic algorithms. *Evol. Comput.* **1994**, *2*, 221–248. [CrossRef]
30. Dutta, S.; Das, K.N. A survey on pareto-based eas to solve multi-objective optimization problems. In *Soft Computing for Problem Solving: SocProS 2017, Volume 2*; Springer: Singapore, 2019; pp. 807–820.
31. Espinosa, R.; Jiménez, F.; Palma, J. Surrogate-assisted and filter-based multiobjective evolutionary feature selection for deep learning. *IEEE Trans. Neural Netw. Learn. Syst.* **2023.** [CrossRef] [PubMed]
32. Xu, H.; Xue, B.; Zhang, M. A duplication analysis-based evolutionary algorithm for biobjective feature selection. *IEEE Trans. Evol. Comput.* **2020**, *25*, 205–218. [CrossRef]
33. Strehl, A. *Relationship-Based Clustering and Cluster Ensembles for High-Dimensional Data Mining*; The University of Texas at Austin: Austin, TX, USA, 2002.
34. Yang, J.M.; Kao, C.Y. A combined evolutionary algorithm for real parameters optimization. In Proceedings of the IEEE International Conference on Evolutionary Computation, Nagoya, Japan, 20–22 May 1996; IEEE: New York, NY, USA, 1996; pp. 732–737.
35. Feng, Z.k.; Niu, W.j.; Liu, S. Cooperation search algorithm: A novel metaheuristic evolutionary intelligence algorithm for numerical optimization and engineering optimization problems. *Appl. Soft Comput.* **2021**, *98*, 106734. [CrossRef]
36. Dua, D.; Graff, C. UCI Machine Learning Repository. 2017. Available online: https://archive.ics.uci.edu/ml/index.php (accessed on 21 May 2024).
37. While, L.; Hingston, P.; Barone, L.; Huband, S. A faster algorithm for calculating hypervolume. *IEEE Trans. Evol. Comput.* **2006**, *10*, 29–38. [CrossRef]
38. Zitzler, E.; Thiele, L.; Laumanns, M.; Fonseca, C.M.; Da Fonseca, V.G. Performance assessment of multiobjective optimizers: An analysis and review. *IEEE Trans. Evol. Comput.* **2003**, *7*, 117–132. [CrossRef]
39. Deb, K.; Thiele, L.; Laumanns, M.; Zitzler, E. Scalable test problems for evolutionary multiobjective optimization. In *Evolutionary Multiobjective Optimization: Theoretical Advances and Applications*; Springer: London, UK, 2005; pp. 105–145.
40. Huband, S.; Barone, L.; While, L.; Hingston, P. A scalable multi-objective test problem toolkit. In *Proceedings of the Evolutionary Multi-Criterion Optimization: Third International Conference, EMO 2005, Guanajuato, Mexico, 9–11 March 2005. Proceedings 3*; Springer: Berlin/Heidelberg, Germany, 2005; pp. 280–295.
41. Khan, W.A. Balanced weighted extreme learning machine for imbalance learning of credit default risk and manufacturing productivity. *Ann. Oper. Res.* **2023**, 1–29. [CrossRef]
42. Khan, W.A.; Masoud, M.; Eltoukhy, A.E.; Ullah, M. Stacked encoded cascade error feedback deep extreme learning machine network for manufacturing order completion time. *J. Intell. Manuf.* **2024** , 1–27. [CrossRef]

*applied sciences*

MDPI

*Article*

# An Innovative Deep Learning Futures Price Prediction Method with Fast and Strong Generalization and High-Accuracy Research

**Lin Huo [1,*], Yanyan Xie [2] and Jianbo Li [2]**

1 International College, Guangxi University, Nanning 530004, China
2 School of Computer and Electronic Information, Guangxi University, Nanning 530004, China; 2213393055@st.gxu.edu.cn (Y.X.); 2313301023@st.gxu.edu.cn (J.L.)
* Correspondence: lhuo@gxu.edu.cn

**Abstract:** Futures commodity prices are affected by many factors, and traditional forecasting methods require close attention from professionals and suffer from high subjectivity, slowness, and low forecasting accuracy. In this paper, we propose a new method for predicting the fluctuation in futures commodity prices accurately. We solve the problem of the slow convergence of ordinary artificial bee colony algorithms by introducing a population chaotic mapping initialization operator and use the resulting chaotic mapping artificial bee colony algorithm as a trainer to learn long short-term memory neural network hyperparameters. With the combination of gate structures learned by the algorithm, the long short-term memory network can accurately characterize the basic rules of futures market prices. Finally, we conduct a series of backtesting experiments on gold and natural gas futures commodity prices to demonstrate the effectiveness of the proposed model. The experimental results show that, compared with various existing optimization models, our proposed model is able to obtain the lowest mean absolute error, mean square error, and root mean square error in the least number of iterations. In summary, the model can be used to predict the prices of a wide range of futures commodities.

**Keywords:** chaotic mapping; artificial bee colony algorithm; long short-term memory; futures price prediction

## 1. Introduction

Predicting commodities prices in the futures market has always been a classic and challenging problem that has an impact on many countries and even the whole world [1]. Economists and computer scientists are interested in predicting futures commodity prices in economic market research [2,3]. Known for its extensive hedging capabilities and stable value, gold holds a prominent place in the investment and financial markets. The development and export of the natural gas industry play a key role in the economic growth of many countries, and natural gas exports can generate significant foreign exchange earnings for the country. Forecasts suggest that natural gas is poised to supersede coal and oil as the predominant fossil fuel post-2030 in terms of its share of the world's primary energy consumption [4,5]. The world economy, geopolitics, inflation, and other factors all have an impact on commodities futures. Therefore, when predicting the value of these futures commodities, traditional methods require careful attention to market dynamics and relevant macroeconomic data. At the same time, researchers also face the challenge of improving the accuracy of futures commodity price volatility prediction models, as improving predictive performance is crucial for related companies and stakeholders [6]. For the investor to grasp futures commodity prices in advance of the day before the opening of the market so that they can decide whether to continue to buy or sell, thereby affecting the return on the capital, it is crucial to design an accurate forecasting model to predict commodity price trends.

During exploration and exploitation, the ABC optimization algorithm can easily slip into local optima due to its poor convergence speed [7,8]. Simultaneously, optimizing neural network hyperparameters for the faster training of high-precision prediction models is another complicated issue. Hyperparameter adjustments take a large amount of time in traditional methods, and even minor alterations can exert a huge impact on the outcome of the prediction [9,10]. In this paper, we propose a novel approach for enhancing the ABC technique by introducing a chaotic bee colony initialization operator. This operator can speed up the optimization process and be used as a hyperparameter selection for LSTM neural networks. The overarching objective is to automatically adjust the LSTM neural network's numerous combinations of hyperparameters when forecasting various futures commodities, allowing the model to withstand market fluctuations better and adjust to changing market trends. The significance of hyperparameters in neural network training is emphasized in much research. For instance, Chen et al. [11] claim that choosing the right hyperparameters is primarily responsible for the LSTM's performance. Similarly, Qi et al. [12] contend that hyperparameters wield substantial influence over machine learning algorithms, and that optimizing them can be computationally costly. They suggest using a Q-learning approach to find optimal neural network hyperparameter setups. Moreover, the hyperparameter exploration LSTM predictor (HELP), a superior stochastic exploration technique introduced by Li et al. [13], further corroborates the profound impact of LSTM hyperparameters on neural network performance. Furthermore, Albahli et al. [14] employ advanced techniques for hyperparameter adjustment to evaluate model efficacy, demonstrating how neural network hyperparameters affect the recognition of handwritten digits.

The originality of this study lies in its innovative use of a tent chaotic mapping artificial bee colony (TCM-ABC) technique to optimize the hyperparameters of LSTM neural networks, including critical parameters such as window size and neuron count. By harnessing the capabilities of the ABC algorithm, this study endeavors to find robust LSTM hyperparameters within vast decision spaces, thus enabling the effective training of neural networks for the precise prediction of futures commodity prices. Overall, the salient characteristics of this pioneering approach can be summarized as follows:

- Employing the globally optimized chaotic mapping artificial bee colony algorithm, this study endeavors to tune essential LSTM layer hyperparameters such as window size and neuron count.
- TCM-ABC-LSTM is a new combination of meta-heuristic algorithm and neural network, deployed for the precise prediction of daily closing prices in gold and natural gas futures commodities markets.
- By contrasting the anticipated closing price with actual values and forecasts based on statistical error measurements (such as MSE, MAE, and RMSE), the proposed TCM-ABC-LSTM model is assessed.
- To our best knowledge, this is the first time that machine learning technology has been used to predict commodity price fluctuations in the futures market.

This paper is organized as follows: Section 2 reviews past research related to our work. Section 3 describes the deep learning algorithms used in our study and our proposed TCM-ABC-LSTM architecture. Section 4 describes the experiment and discussion, including an introduction to the equipment used, data description and preprocessing, model parameter settings, results, and discussion. Section 5 concludes.

## 2. Related Works

Financial forecasting involves a diverse array of methodologies because the futures market, and indeed the entire financial market, are dynamic systems rife with noise and non-parameters [15]. A variety of models have been used by researchers to forecast price volatility. Four key types of price prediction methods currently in use include statistical methods, artificial intelligence methods, hybrid models, and Bayesian methods. As a result, the applications of numerous methods in the field of financial forecasting are briefly reviewed in this section.

### 2.1. Using Statistical Methods to Predict

Over the preceding decades, the autoregressive integrated moving average (ARIMA) model has emerged as a cornerstone within the domain of time series forecasting, garnering widespread acclaim across diverse disciplines. Predicting issues in the fields of medicine, engineering, social sciences, stocks, and futures are among its uses [16–20]. One of the most popular classical econometric methods for time series prediction is multiple linear regression. Multiple linear regression was employed by Jyothi Manoj et al. [21] to forecast gold prices. Ruslan et al. [22] used a series of univariate GARCH models to examine oil prices and shipping stock prices in 2021, and the study provides a realistic view for regulators and investors to predict market sentiment in the shipping market in response to global oil prices. Wahyuny et al. [23] analyzed the comparison of the accuracy of the asset pricing model (CAPM) and the arbitrage pricing theory (APT) in predicting the stock returns of manufacturing companies listed on the Indonesian stock exchange, where the outcomes of the data analysis demonstrated that the CAPM model outperforms the APT model in predicting stock returns.

### 2.2. Using Artificial Intelligence Methods to Predict

Artificial intelligence methods, including machine learning and deep learning methods, have been introduced and used to predict time series [24]. In 2020, Wang and Zhao [25] developed, tested, and validated suitable support vector regression (SVR) models for ship price prediction based on the advantages of support vector machine frameworks. They pointed out that this model provides satisfactory, robust, and promising results. Yu and Yan [26] used a deep neural network for predicting stock prices, which uses the time series phase space reconstruction (PSR) method to reconstruct the price series, and they claimed that the proposed prediction model has high prediction accuracy. In order to predict the opening price, the minimum price, and the maximum price of a stock at the same time, Guangyu Ding and Liangxi Qin designed a multiple-input–output model based on LSTM and experimentally demonstrated that the model outperforms other models in predicting multiple values at the same time [27]. To extract and forecast future properties of these markets, Ehsan et al. [28] suggested a CNN-based framework that can be applied to datasets from many sources (including different marketplaces). Wang et al. [29] used the most recent deep learning framework, the Transformer model, in 2022 to predict stock market indices. They showed that the Transformer model outperforms other neural network methods in multiple stock indices and better characterizes the fundamental rules of the stock market thanks to its encoder–decoder architecture and multi-head attention mechanism.

### 2.3. Using Hybrid Models to Predict

To predict the Bitcoin price, Kazeminia et al. proposed a hybrid model that mixes a 2D-CNN and LSTM in 2023, using a 2D-CNN for feature extraction and giving it to LSTM for prediction [30]. The results show that the hybrid model can outperform any single deep learning model. Lu et al. [31] suggested a convolutional neural network (CNN)- and LSTM-based stock price prediction technique in 2020. Effective information was extracted from the data using the CNN, and the extracted features were predicted using LSTM. According to the results, the model has the best prediction accuracy on the Shanghai Stock Exchange composite index. In 2021, Farah et al. [32] proposed a new genetic long short-term memory framework consisting of long short-term memory and a genetic algorithm to predict short-term wind power generation. The LSTM layer's window size and neuron count were optimized using the genetic algorithm's global optimization technique. The model is 30% more accurate than the current technology. In 2022, Gourav et al. [33] proposed a hybrid deep learning model based on an LSTM network and adaptive particle swarm optimization (PSO), which uses PSO to evolve the weights and biases of LSTM and a fully connected layer (FCL) for predicting the short-term and long-term stock prices of Sensex, S&P 500, and Nifty 50 stock indices. Compared with the Elman neural network and standard LSTM neural network, it achieved better prediction accuracy.

### 2.4. Using Bayesian Methods to Predict

In 2020, Massari [34] examined the impact of the market choice hypothesis on the accuracy of the probabilities implied by equilibrium prices and on the market's "learning" mechanism, using the standard machinery of dynamic general equilibrium models to generate a rich class of price probabilities, and showed that Bayes' rule is the only rational way to learn. A major limitation of traditional deep learning is the quantification of uncertainty in predictions, which can affect investor confidence. To this end, Chandra et al. [35] used a new Bayesian neural network to forecast multi-stage stock prices before and during the New Crown Pneumonia in 2021. The results show that the Bayesian neural network can provide reasonable forecasts with uncertainty quantification, despite the high market volatility during the first peak of the new crown pneumonia pandemic. Chuang and Lee [36] empirically analyzed historical block data using a Gaussian process model and compare its performance with GasStation-Express and the Geth gas price oracles. The results show that the Gaussian process model provides better estimates when trading volumes are volatile.

## 3. Methodology

In our study, we enhance the conventional artificial swarm meta-heuristic algorithm by introducing a novel swarm initialization operator, which uses a chaotic mapping algorithm to generate the initial population, and by applying this algorithm to generate optimal hyperparameters for long short-term memory neural networks. Our primary objective is to employ this optimized model to forecast the prices of gold and natural gas futures. This section provides a comprehensive exposition of our model architecture and the methodological approaches employed therein. Figure 1 shows the created TCM-ABC-LSTM model.

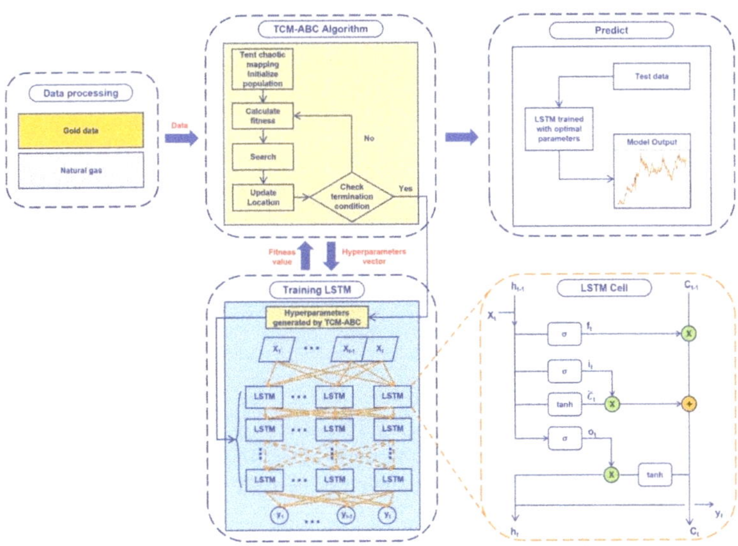


**Figure 1.** TCM-ABC-LSTM model structure. The data are first preprocessed and divided into training and testing sets. The training set is input into TCM-ABC for training. TCM-ABC continuously generates LSTM hyperparameter vectors to train the LSTM model, and the prediction accuracy of the LSTM model is returned as fitness to TCM-ABC. Finally, the LSTM model is trained using the optimal hyperparameter vector obtained after meeting the termination conditions, and predictions are made.

### 3.1. Tent Chaotic Mapping Artificial Bee Colony Algorithm

The artificial bee colony (ABC) algorithm is an effective optimization algorithm that is a natural heuristic algorithm proposed by Karaboga D et al. in 2005 [37]. Functioning akin to the organic processes observed within bee colonies, the ABC categorizes bees into three distinct groups: worker bees, onlooker bees, and scout bees.

However, despite its efficacy, the algorithm for the ABC remains subject to continual refinement. The conventional approach for the ABC is to create worker bee placements in the solution space at random to start the bee population. We found that the traditional ABC algorithm's randomly initialized bee colonies may be too concentrated, leading to poor performance. Therefore, in our research, we use tent chaotic mapping as the bee colony initialization operator, which effectively solves the inherent inefficiency problem of this traditional method [38].

Our proposed initialization operator markedly reduces exploration time by systematically distributing worker bees across the solution space. This strategy results in shorter distances for worker bee exploration, consequently enhancing search speed and efficiency. Equation (1) provides the representation of tent chaotic mapping, where $\mu$ is typically 2. We iteratively generate a series of chaotic numbers through Equation (2) and map the generated chaotic sequence $x_0, x_1, \ldots, x_n$ to the search space of the problem in Equation (3), where $x_{ij}$ represents the jth component of the current solution vector for worker bee i and $[a,b]$ is the solution space. The symbol $\lfloor \rfloor$ denotes downward rounding.

$$T(x) = \begin{cases} \mu x & ,0 \le x < \mu \\ \mu(1-x) & ,\mu \le x \le 1. \end{cases} \tag{1}$$

$$x_{n+1} = T(x_n) \tag{2}$$

$$x_{ij} = a_j + \lfloor x_i * (b_j - a_j) \rfloor \tag{3}$$

We use the mapping results obtained from the above steps as the initial population for the artificial bee colony algorithm. The fitness value of the objective function $fit$ is calculated by Equation (4), where $f_i$ is the objective function value and $fit_i$ is the fitness of bee $i$.

$$fit_i = \frac{1}{1+f_i} \tag{4}$$

We use the roulette method to calculate the probability $p_i$ that a worker bee is selected by an onlooker bee, which is obtained from Equation (5):

$$p_i = \frac{f_i}{\sum_{i=1}^{n} fit_i} \tag{5}$$

Onlooker bees searching for new solutions are calculated using Equation (6), where $x_{kj}$ is the solution vector of a randomly selected other worker bee $k$.

$$x'_{ij} = x_{ij} + rand[-1,1](x_{ij} - x_{kj}) \tag{6}$$

Scouter bees use Equation (7) to randomly generate new solutions to avoid falling into local optima, where $x''_{ij}$ is the position of the scouter bee and $x_j^{min}$ and $x_j^{max}$ represent the minimum and maximum of the $j$th component, respectively.

$$x''_{ij} = x_j^{min} + rand[-1,1](x_j^{max} - x_j^{min}) \tag{7}$$

### 3.2. Long Short-Term Memory

The long short-term memory network stands as a seminal and highly effective model for time series prediction [39]. The memory cell of the LSTM model is shown in Figure 2. The LSTM model incorporates a sophisticated gate structure to mitigate the challenges of gradient vanishing and explosion. This gate structure comprises forget gates, input gates, and output gates, and each structure has its unique role. Three gate structures are represented mathematically by Equations (8)–(11):

$$f_t = \sigma(W_f x_t + W_{hf} h_{t-1} + b_f) \tag{8}$$

$$i_t = \sigma(W_i x_t + W_{hi} h_{t-1} + b_i) \tag{9}$$

$$o_t = \sigma(W_o x_t + W_{ho} h_{t-1} + b_o) \tag{10}$$

$$h_t = tanh(C_{t-1}) \otimes o_t \tag{11}$$

$$C_t = C_{t-1} \otimes f_t + tanh(W_C x_t + W_{hC} h_{t-1} + b_C) \otimes i_t \tag{12}$$

In Equations (8)–(12), matrices $w_{xf}, w_{xi}, w_{xo}, w_{xc}$ denote the appropriate input weight matrices, $w_{hf}, w_{hi}, w_{ho}, w_{hc}$ are the recursive weight matrices, and $b_f, b_i, b_o, b_c$ denote the corresponding bias vectors. The hidden state, denoted by the $h_t$ in Equation (11), passes through the activation function tanh to produce a new hidden state after combining the input and the previous hidden state into a vector. Long-term memory is represented by $C_t$, which is the outcome of the input gate, forget gate, and memory $C_{t-1}$ from the previous moment combined. The symbol ⊗ represents the multiplication of elements by elements between units. The tanh and sigmoid kernel functions are represented as tanh and $\sigma$, respectively, and are defined mathematically as follows:

$$tanh(x) = \frac{e^x - e^{-x}}{e^x + e^{-x}} \tag{13}$$

$$\sigma(x) = \frac{1}{1 + e^{-x}} \tag{14}$$

The output $y_t$ of the LSTM is computed using Equation (15), where $w_{hy}$ is the recursive weight matrix and $b_y$ is the corresponding bias vector:

$$y_t = \sigma(w_{hy} h_t + b_y) \tag{15}$$

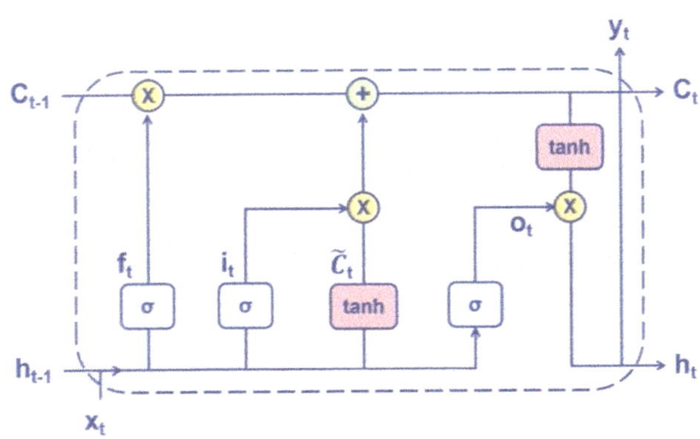


**Figure 2.** LSTM memory cell structure.

### 3.3. TCM-ABC-LSTM

To better address the difficulties associated with hyperparameter tuning in LSTM networks, this section describes an improved artificial bee colony optimization algorithm as a hyperparameter selector for LSTM networks, which is called TCM-ABC-LSTM. Leveraging the inherent strengths of the ABC algorithm as a hyperparameter selector, our proposed methodology ensures expedited convergence, heightened prediction accuracy, and enhanced robustness of the resultant LSTM network models. Notably, the ABC algorithm's aptitude for tackling NP-hard problems and swiftly identifying global optimal solutions or approximate global optima highlights its effectiveness in the complex environment of hyperparametric optimization. Tent chaotic mapping group initialization further improves the efficiency of the algorithm, allowing it to quickly traverse the solution space and find the global optimal or near-global-optimal solution faster than other meta-heuristic algorithms. The pseudo-code of the TCM-ABC algorithm is shown in Algorithm 1.

**Algorithm 1** Pseudocode of TCM-ABC-LSTM

```
Initialize population using Tent chaotic mapping
Evaluate the fitness of the population
Set Iteration = 1
while Iteration < Maximum number of Iteration do
    Employee Bee Phase
    Probability Calculation Phase
    Onlooker Bee Phase
    Scout Bee Phase
    Enroll the best solution obtained so far
    Iteration = Iteration + 1
end while
Training LSTM with Optimal Population
```

First, the ABC initializes the worker bee population by tent chaotic mapping (TCM), which serves to distribute the population uniformly in the solution space, to accelerate the bee's search process and to avoid falling into local optima. The pseudo-code of the TCM initialization operator is shown in Algorithm 2.

**Algorithm 2** Pseudocode of TCM initialization operator

```
while i = 1, 2,...,n do
    while j = 1, 2,...,m do
        Initialize population of worker bees W by Equations (1)–(3)
    end while
end while
```

In the worker bee phase following the initialization process, the worker bee evaluates the fitness value of the newly generated nectar source. Under the support of the TCM initialization operator, the searchability of the solution is enhanced. The described bee phase is demonstrated in Algorithm 3.

**Algorithm 3** Worker Bee Phase

```
for all worker bee w in W do
    Evaluate the fitness of w
end for
```

In the onlooker bee phase, worker bees share information about the location of the nectar source with onlooker bees in the beehive. The onlooker bee selects the worker bee to continue exploring the new solution based on the roulette probability. The pseudo-code for this process is represented in Algorithm 4:

**Algorithm 4** Onlooker Bee Phase

**for all** worker bee $w$ in W **do**
  Execute roulette selection based on Equation (5)
  **if** $w$ selected **then**
    Add $w$ to $O$
  **end if**
**end for**
**for all** onlooker bee $o$ in O **do**
  Generate $o_{new}$ by fine-tuning the value of $o$
  Evaluate the fitness of $o_{new}$
  **if** $f(o) < f(o_{new})$ **then**
    Replace $o$ with $o_{new}$
  **end if**
**end for**

Finally, the ABC enters the Scout Bee Phase if the adaptation does not improve after n iterations, replacing the current solution with a randomly generated one to avoid falling into a local optimum. We argue that the behavior of bees in the ABC algorithm has some similarities with LSTM neural network parameter tuning and that the behavior of worker bees exploiting a nectar source corresponds to finding a solution within the hyperparametric feasible solution space of the neural network. Onlooker bees can decide whether to exploit or not and are capable of small-scale fine-tuning. The scout bees randomly search for nectar sources and are able to prevent falling into a local optimum. Therefore, we choose to combine the ABC algorithm with LSTM in an attempt to achieve excellent prediction results.

TCM-ABC is used to train LSTM networks to solve nonlinear regression (predicting price fluctuations). The main difficulty in developing accurate neural network models lies in finding the most appropriate hyperparameters to train the neural network. The main drawbacks of traditional training algorithms include local optimum stagnation, slow convergence, and poor accuracy, thus motivating researchers to look for reliable alternatives to address these drawbacks. From this point of view, TCM-ABC intelligently chooses the hyperparameters of LSTM. The proposed model uses LSTM as the objective function of TCM-ABC and evaluates its solution in the training phase. This evaluation uses the current solution as hyperparameters, passes it to the LSTM, and subsequently calculates the fitness based on the predictive performance of the LSTM. This scenario is repeated until the maximum number of iterations is reached. The best solution is finally passed to the LSTM as a hyperparameter vector for the testing phase.

Using an improved artificial bee colony technique, we were able to determine the hidden layer size, number of hidden layers, time step, batch size, and epoch of LSTM in our work. Determining these ideal settings is crucial since, for instance, if the time step size is set to 1, hardly any information is transmitted. If we consider a large time step, then this means that early-sequence terms will act as noise. Thus, the appropriate optimization of these hyperparameters is indispensable for ensuring the efficacy and reliability of LSTM network models. Figure 3 displays the TCM-ABC-LSTM model's concrete flowchart.

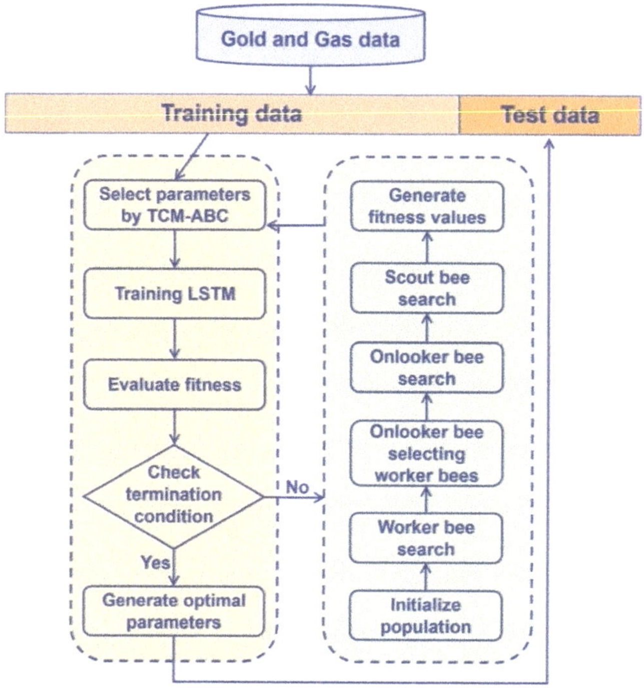


**Figure 3.** The flow chart of TCM-ABC-LSTM.

## 4. Experiment and Discussion

Gold and natural gas stand as pivotal commodities that command significant attention within the global futures market landscape. Often regarded as barometers of the world economy, fluctuations in the prices of gold and natural gas are closely scrutinized by investors and analysts alike. Changes in monetary policy, geopolitical threats, and inflation predictions are typically reflected in the direction of gold prices. Weather variations, geopolitical events, and supply–demand relationships all have an impact on natural gas prices. Recognizing the importance of comprehending market trends and making informed investment decisions, investors and stakeholders seek predictive models that can effectively anticipate price movements in these key commodities. To this end, our study opted to evaluate the predictive performance of the TCM-ABC-LSTM algorithm by focusing on futures prices for gold and natural gas commodities. By conducting a series of rigorous back-testing experiments on the next-day closing price indices of gold and natural gas futures, we aimed to elucidate the algorithm's efficacy in forecasting commodity prices within the futures market domain. Table 1 provides a comprehensive overview of the hardware and software configurations utilized in our experimental setup, ensuring transparency and reproducibility in our methodology.

**Table 1.** The main hardware and software configurations.

| Hardware/Software | Configuration |
| --- | --- |
| CPU | Kaggle CPU |
| GPU | NVIDIA Tesla P100 |
| DISK | Max 73.1 GB |
| RAM | Max 29 GB |
| GPU memory | Max 16 GB |
| Python version | Python 3.7 |
| Pytorch version | Pytorch 1.7.0 |

### 4.1. Data Description and Preprocessing

The opening, closing, highest, and lowest trade prices for natural gas from 4 April 1990–26 October 2023, and for gold from 2 January 1990–26 October 2023, are among the data analyzed in this study. Investing Financial Information provides the data instance for each index. Renowned as one of the premier financial websites globally, Investing Financial Information offers real-time updates and comprehensive market data on a diverse array of financial instruments, including stocks, funds, foreign currencies, futures, bonds, and digital currencies. One can download all of the experiment's data at https://www.investing.com/commodities/real-time-futures, accessed on 11 June 2024. To facilitate effective model training and evaluation, the closing price data were partitioned into training and test sets. Specifically, the training set comprises the initial 80% of the data, employed to train the LSTM model parameters. Then, the remaining 20% of the data are reserved as a test set, serving as a robust validation mechanism for assessing the performance and accuracy of the proposed predictive model. It is worth noting that, in order to reduce the volatility of the dataset and enhance the predictive performance and stability of the proposed model, we normalize the raw data (both training and test sets) using Equation (16). This normalization process ensures that the raw data, both in the training and test sets, are standardized to a common scale, thereby facilitating more robust and reliable model training and evaluation, where $x_{min}$ and $x_{max}$ are the minimum and maximum values of the original sequence, respectively.

$$x_{i(norm)} = \frac{x_i - x_{min}}{x_{max} - x_{min}} \tag{16}$$

To facilitate this predictive process, we adopt the moving window method, a widely employed technique for feature extraction from observed time series data. The closing prices of the previous t trading days are used in each prediction to forecast the closing price of the following trading day t + 1. This method systematically constructs features and labels by sliding a window over the time series data, as depicted in Figure 4.

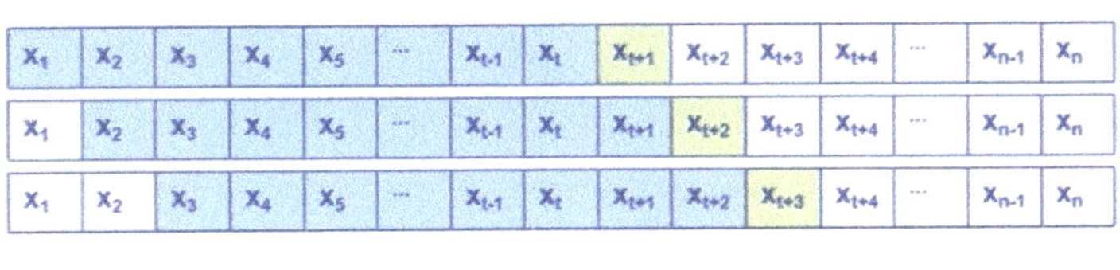


**Figure 4.** Moving window method.

### 4.2. Model Parameter Settings

We carried out a great deal of testing on the training set, and the pertinent parameters of the improved artificial bee colony algorithm were established as follows in light of many tests and related studies [40–42]: 50 honey sources, 500 iterations, 25 worker bees, and 15 onlooker bees. The number of LSTM's hidden layer cells is given in [30, 200], the number of hidden layers is given in [1, 8], the time step is given in [20, 80], the batch size is given in [30, 80], and the epoch is given in [10, 500].

We use the root mean square error to evaluate the prediction accuracy. Taking the prediction of gold prices as an example, each algorithm's loss function over time is displayed in Figure 5. The graph shows that our suggested algorithm has the fastest convergence speed and can reach the final result within approximately 10 iterations; second, the ABC-LSTM model can reach the final result after about 50 iterations, showing that the effect of our proposed swarm initialization operator on the speed of model training is effectual; and, finally, the Transformer model has the worst prediction performance, suggesting that it has limitations in capturing the intricate volatility patterns inherent in commodities traded on futures markets.

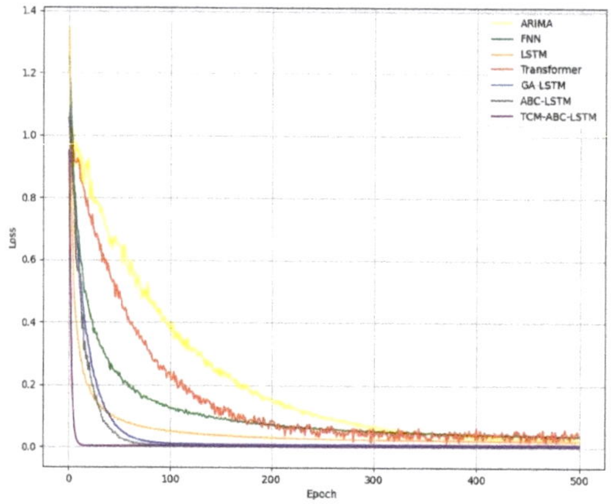


**Figure 5.** RMSE changes over time.

## 4.3. Evaluating Indicator

In this study, the model performance is evaluated by prediction accuracy, and we compare the predicted values to the real data in the test set and calculate the prediction error. The three prediction error evaluation metrics used in this study are as follows:

Mean Absolute Error (MAE):

$$MAE = \frac{1}{n}\sum_{i=1}^{n}|p - \hat{p}| \tag{17}$$

Mean Square Error (MSE):

$$MSE = \frac{1}{n}\sum_{i=1}^{n}(p - \hat{p})^2 \tag{18}$$

Root Mean Square Error (RMSE):

$$RMSE = \sqrt{\frac{1}{n}\sum_{i=1}^{n}(p - \hat{p})^2} \tag{19}$$

where $p$ is the true value, $\hat{p}$ is the predicted value, and n is the sample size. MAE is the mean absolute deviation between the predicted value and the true value, which ignores the direction of the error and focuses only on the magnitude of the error [43]. MSE is a common measure of time series forecasting performance. Similar to MAE, it also measures the absolute error in the forecast, which is squared, making MSE more sensitive to outliers but also more expressive of the distribution of the error [44]. RMSE is identical to the raw data in terms of magnitude and is therefore easier to visualize and understand. Similar to MSE, RMSE gives higher weight to large errors [45]. This study uses RMSE as the loss function for model training.

## 4.4. Results and Discussion

The empirical results of this study confirm the utility and effectiveness of the TCM-ABC-LSTM model. The same dataset is used to evaluate the prediction performance of the designed models relative to traditional neural networks and various meta-heuristic trainers, including ARIMA, LSTM, and GA-LSTM. Many researchers have demonstrated the high accuracy of the compared models before and used these models to improve many problems. Moreover, these models are among the most widely used and effective techniques in the field of prediction [29,46–49]. The performance and precision of our proposed model are evaluated in comparison to other prediction models, employing well-established metrics such as MAE, MSE, and RMSE. Among the diverse array of models compared in this study, our proposed model stands out, gaining the lowest mean absolute error, mean square error, and root mean square error, as shown in Tables 2 and 3, bold indicates the best result for each indicator. Slight differences in these evaluation indicators have a big influence on forecast accuracy because of data standardization. To provide a comprehensive insight into the performance gains facilitated by our proposed model, using the MAE prediction results as an example, Table 4 elucidates the marked enhancements in prediction accuracy following inverse normalization. From the table, it can be seen that our model has a significantly improved prediction accuracy, with improvements ranging from 26.79% to 82.16% compared to other models. This indicates that the data volatility has been well captured in the fitted model, thereby affirming its robustness and efficacy as a futures prediction model.

Figures 6 and 7 illustrate how well the ARIMA, FNN, LSTM, Transformer, GA-LSTM, and TCM-ABC-LSTM models predict the prices of gold and natural gas, respectively. It is evident from the graph that the TCM-ABC-LSTM-predicted futures commodity prices closely match the actual data.

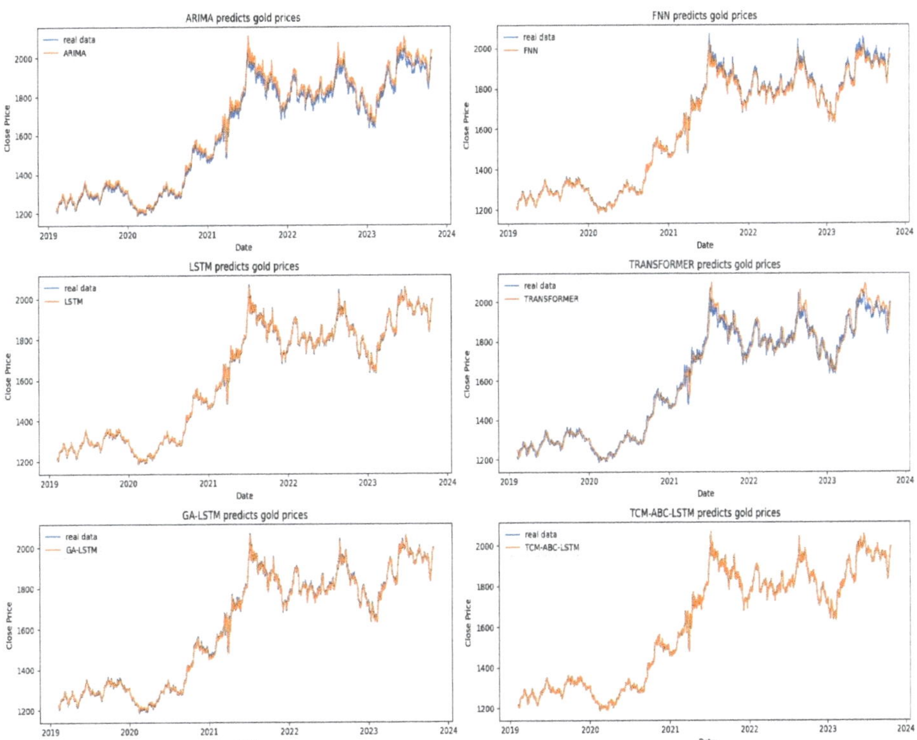


**Figure 6.** Prediction results of gold prices for various models.

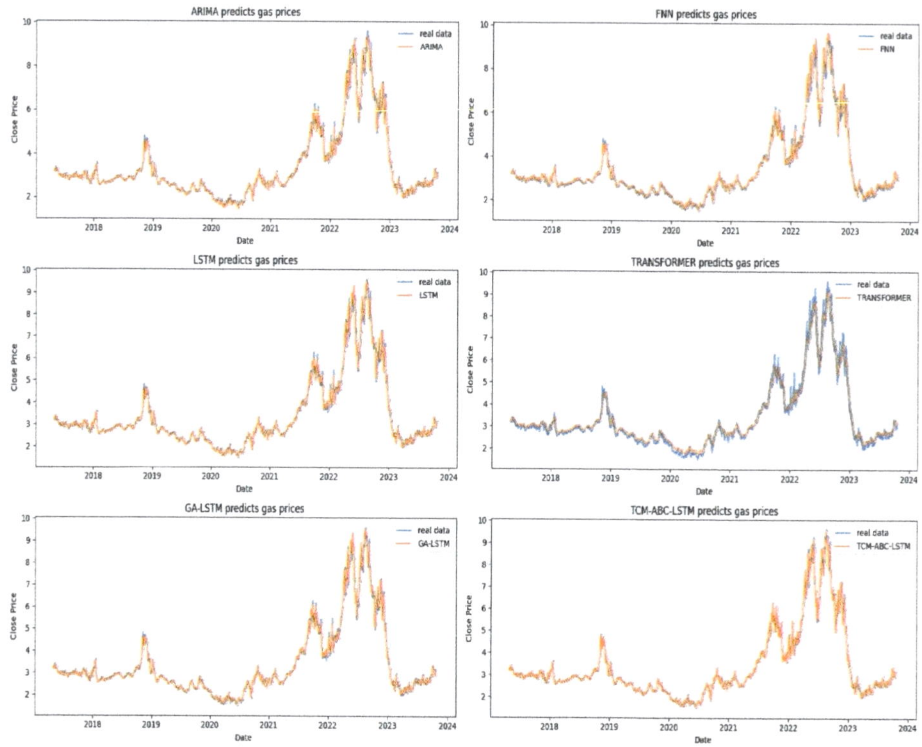


**Figure 7.** Prediction results of natural gas prices for various models.

**Table 2.** Performance comparison of gold price prediction models.

| | MAE | MSE | RMSE |
|---|---|---|---|
| ARIMA | 0.01188 | $3.0 \times 10^{-4}$ | 0.0174 |
| FNN | 0.01902 | $4.0 \times 10^{-4}$ | 0.0216 |
| LSTM | 0.00906 | $1.2 \times 10^{-4}$ | 0.0110 |
| Transformer | 0.03253 | $4.2 \times 10^{-3}$ | 0.6531 |
| GA-LSTM | 0.00755 | $9.2 \times 10^{-5}$ | 0.0095 |
| TCM-ABC-LSTM | **0.00619** | $\mathbf{6.7 \times 10^{-5}}$ | **0.0077** |

**Table 3.** Performance comparison of natural gas price prediction models.

| | MAE | MSE | RMSE |
|---|---|---|---|
| ARIMA | 0.01148 | $2.2 \times 10^{-4}$ | 0.0149 |
| FNN | 0.00621 | $1.1 \times 10^{-4}$ | 0.0109 |
| LSTM | 0.00630 | $1.2 \times 10^{-4}$ | 0.0110 |
| Transformer | 0.02451 | $1.3 \times 10^{-3}$ | 0.0368 |
| GA-LSTM | 0.00620 | $7.8 \times 10^{-5}$ | 0.0088 |
| TCM-ABC-LSTM | **0.00250** | $\mathbf{1.2 \times 10^{-5}}$ | **0.0035** |

**Table 4.** Model MAE performance improvement.

| | ARIMA | FNN | LSTM | Transformer | GA-LSTM |
|---|---|---|---|---|---|
| MAE (decline) | 57.18% | 81.24% | 56.59% | 82.16% | 26.79% |

## 5. Conclusions

In this paper, we present a new model for predicting price fluctuations of futures commodities using an improved meta-heuristic algorithm TCM-ABC to train LSTM neural networks and apply it to predict the daily closing prices of gold and natural gas, comparing the obtained prediction results with those of classical neural networks and other meta-heuristic trainers such as ARIMA, Transformer, GA- LSTM, etc. The results show that the TCM-ABC-LSTM model outperforms the other models. The evaluation metrics reveal that the TCM-ABC-LSTM network model achieved the lowest MAE, MSE, and RMSE errors of $6.19 \times 10^{-3}$, $6.7 \times 10^{-5}$, and $7.7 \times 10^{-3}$, respectively. So far, the TCM-ABC-LSTM model is considered as a promising technique for high-precision commodity price prediction. We will explore more theoretical results in the future and expect that, in practice, investors can obtain higher excess returns through predictions of TCM-ABC-LSTM.

The gold and natural gas data used in this study are classical data from futures markets, and our proposed model performs very well on these datasets; we believe that the superior performance of TCM-ABC-LSTM is mainly attributed to the innovative improvement of the artificial bee colony algorithm and its application to LSTM networks. Compared with the traditional LSTM model, the proposed TCM-ABC-LSTM model has better generalization ability because it can adaptively find the optimal hyperparameters. However, there are some limitations in this study, such as that this paper only predicts the closing price of the commodity on the following day alone, but, in fact, the longer the prediction time, the more insight into the future trend of the commodity for further analysis. These will be discussed in our future research. In the future, additional research will be carried out on the following points:

1. Extending the application of the TCM-ABC-LSTM model to diverse time series prediction tasks encompassing domains such as electricity consumption, wind power generation, and stock market dynamics.
2. Exploring alternative optimization algorithms to serve as hyperparameter selectors for LSTM models in the quest for better hybrid models.
3. Applying long-term sequence prediction using the proposed model.

**Author Contributions:** Conceptualization, L.H. and Y.X.; methodology, L.H. and Y.X.; software, Y.X.; validation, L.H., Y.X. and J.L.; formal analysis, L.H. and Y.X.; investigation, L.H. and Y.X.; resources, L.H. and Y.X.; data curation, L.H. and Y.X.; writing—original draft preparation, Y.X.; writing—review and editing, L.H. and Y.X.; visualization, L.H. and Y.X.; supervision, L.H.; project administration, L.H. and Y.X.; funding acquisition, L.H. All authors have read and agreed to the published version of the manuscript.

**Funding:** This research received no external funding.

**Institutional Review Board Statement:** Not applicable.

**Informed Consent Statement:** Not applicable.

**Data Availability Statement:** Publicly available datasets were analyzed in this study. This data can be found here: https://www.investing.com/commodities/real-time-futures, accessed on 11 June 2024.

**Acknowledgments:** We thank all of the authors of the primary studies included in this article.

**Conflicts of Interest:** The authors declare no conflicts of interest.

## Abbreviations

The following abbreviations are used in this manuscript:

| | |
|---|---|
| ABC | Artificial bee colony |
| ARIMA | Autoregressive integrated moving average |
| FNN | Feed-forward neural network |
| GA-LSTM | Genetic algorithm long short-term memory |
| LSTM | Long short-term memory |

| | |
|---|---|
| MAE | Mean absolute error |
| MSE | Mean square error |
| TCM-ABC-LSTM | Tent chaotic mapping artificial bee colony long short-term memory |
| RMSE | Root mean square error |

## References


1. Suman, S.; Kaushik, P.; Challapalli, S.S.N.; Lohani, B.P.; Kushwaha, P.; Gupta, A.D. Commodity Price Prediction for making informed Decisions while trading using Long Short-Term Memory (LSTM) Algorithm. In Proceedings of the 2022 5th International Conference on Contemporary Computing and Informatics (IC3I), Uttar Pradesh, India, 14–16 December 2022; pp. 406–411.
2. Yilanci, V.; Kilci, E.N. The role of economic policy uncertainty and geopolitical risk in predicting prices of precious metals: Evidence from a time-varying bootstrap causality test. *Resour. Policy* **2021**, *72*, 102039. [CrossRef]
3. Liu, W.; Wang, C.; Li, Y.; Liu, Y.; Huang, K. Ensemble forecasting for product futures prices using variational mode decomposition and artificial neural networks. *Chaos Solitons Fractals* **2021**, *146*, 110822. [CrossRef]
4. Caineng, Z.; Zhi, Y.; Dongbo, H.; Yunsheng, W.; Jian, L.; Ailin, J.; Jianjun, C.; Qun, Z.; Yilong, L.; Jun, L.; et al. Theory, technology and prospects of conventional and unconventional natural gas. *Pet. Explor. Dev.* **2018**, *45*, 604–618.
5. Kemfert, C.; Präger, F.; Braunger, I.; Hoffart, F.M.; Brauers, H. The expansion of natural gas infrastructure puts energy transitions at risk. *Nat. Energy* **2022**, *7*, 582–587. [CrossRef]
6. Bouri, E.; Lucey, B.; Saeed, T.; Vo, X.V. The realized volatility of commodity futures: Interconnectedness and determinants. *Int. Rev. Econ. Financ.* **2021**, *73*, 139–151. [CrossRef]
7. Thirugnanasambandam, K.; Rajeswari, M.; Bhattacharyya, D.; Kim, J.y. Directed Artificial Bee Colony algorithm with revamped search strategy to solve global numerical optimization problems. *Autom. Softw. Eng.* **2022**, *29*, 13. [CrossRef]
8. Bing, X.; Youwei, Z.; Xueyan, Z.; Xuekai, S. An improved artificial bee colony algorithm based on faster convergence. In Proceedings of the 2021 IEEE International Conference on Artificial Intelligence and Computer Applications (ICAICA), Dalian, China, 28–30 June 2021; pp. 776–779.
9. Li, Y.; Zhang, Y.; Cai, Y. A new hyper-parameter optimization method for power load forecast based on recurrent neural networks. *Algorithms* **2021**, *14*, 163. [CrossRef]
10. Bischl, B.; Binder, M.; Lang, M.; Pielok, T.; Richter, J.; Coors, S.; Thomas, J.; Ullmann, T.; Becker, M.; Boulesteix, A.L.; et al. Hyperparameter optimization: Foundations, algorithms, best practices, and open challenges. *Wiley Interdiscip. Rev. Data Min. Knowl. Discov.* **2023**, *13*, e1484. [CrossRef]
11. Chen, Y.; Rao, M.; Feng, K.; Zuo, M.J. Physics-Informed LSTM hyperparameters selection for gearbox fault detection. *Mech. Syst. Signal Process.* **2022**, *171*, 108907. [CrossRef]
12. Qi, X.; Xu, B. Hyperparameter optimization of neural networks based on Q-learning. *Signal Image Video Process.* **2023**, *17*, 1669–1676. [CrossRef]
13. Li, W.; Ng, W.W.; Wang, T.; Pelillo, M.; Kwong, S. HELP: An LSTM-based approach to hyperparameter exploration in neural network learning. *Neurocomputing* **2021**, *442*, 161–172. [CrossRef]
14. Albahli, S.; Alhassan, F.; Albattah, W.; Khan, R.U. Handwritten digit recognition: Hyperparameters-based analysis. *Appl. Sci.* **2020**, *10*, 5988. [CrossRef]
15. Gong, X.; Lin, B. Effects of structural changes on the prediction of downside volatility in futures markets. *J. Futur. Mark.* **2021**, *41*, 1124–1153. [CrossRef]
16. Benvenuto, D.; Giovanetti, M.; Vassallo, L.; Angeletti, S.; Ciccozzi, M. Application of the ARIMA model on the COVID-2019 epidemic dataset. *Data Brief* **2020**, *29*, 105340. [CrossRef]
17. Lai, Y.; Dzombak, D.A. Use of the autoregressive integrated moving average (ARIMA) model to forecast near-term regional temperature and precipitation. *Weather Forecast.* **2020**, *35*, 959–976. [CrossRef]
18. Sardar, I.; Akbar, M.A.; Leiva, V.; Alsanad, A.; Mishra, P. Machine learning and automatic ARIMA/Prophet models-based forecasting of COVID-19: Methodology, evaluation, and case study in SAARC countries. *Stoch. Environ. Res. Risk Assess.* **2023**, *37*, 345–359. [CrossRef] [PubMed]
19. Pandey, A.; Singh, G.; Hadiyuono, H.; Mourya, K.; Rasool, M.J. Using ARIMA and LSTM to Implement Stock Market Analysis. In Proceedings of the 2023 International Conference on Artificial Intelligence and Smart Communication (AISC), Greater Noida, India, 27–29 January 2023; pp. 935–940.
20. Zhang, J.; Liu, H.; Bai, W.; Li, X. A hybrid approach of wavelet transform, ARIMA and LSTM model for the share price index futures forecasting. *N. Am. J. Econ. Financ.* **2024**, *69*, 102022. [CrossRef]
21. Manoj, J.; Suresh, K. Forecast model for price of gold: Multiple linear regression with principal component analysis. *Thail. Stat.* **2019**, *17*, 125–131.
22. Ruslan, S.M.M.; Mokhtar, K. Stock market volatility on shipping stock prices: GARCH models approach. *J. Econ. Asymmetries* **2021**, *24*, e00232. [CrossRef]
23. Wahyuny, T.; Gunarsih, T. Comparative analysis of accuracy between capital asset pricing model (CAPM) and arbitrage pricing theory (APT) in predicting stock return (case study: Manufacturing companies listed on the Indonesia stock exchange for the 2015–2018 period). *J. Appl. Econ. Dev. Ctries.* **2020**, *5*, 23–30.

24. Jay, P.; Kalariya, V.; Parmar, P.; Tanwar, S.; Kumar, N.; Alazab, M. Stochastic neural networks for cryptocurrency price prediction. *IEEE Access* **2020**, *8*, 82804–82818. [CrossRef]
25. Wang, D.; Zhao, Y. Using news to predict investor sentiment: Based on svm model. *Procedia Comput. Sci.* **2020**, *174*, 191–199. [CrossRef]
26. Yu, P.; Yan, X. Stock price prediction based on deep neural networks. *Neural Comput. Appl.* **2020**, *32*, 1609–1628. [CrossRef]
27. Ding, G.; Qin, L. Study on the prediction of stock price based on the associated network model of LSTM. *Int. J. Mach. Learn. Cybern.* **2020**, *11*, 1307–1317. [CrossRef]
28. Hoseinzade, E.; Haratizadeh, S. CNNpred: CNN-based stock market prediction using a diverse set of variables. *Expert Syst. Appl.* **2019**, *129*, 273–285. [CrossRef]
29. Wang, C.; Chen, Y.; Zhang, S.; Zhang, Q. Stock market index prediction using deep Transformer model. *Expert Syst. Appl.* **2022**, *208*, 118128. [CrossRef]
30. Kazeminia, S.; Sajedi, H.; Arjmand, M. Real-Time Bitcoin Price Prediction Using Hybrid 2D-CNN LSTM Model. In Proceedings of the 2023 9th International Conference on Web Research (ICWR), Tehran, Iran, 3–4 May 2023; pp. 173–178.
31. Lu, W.; Li, J.; Li, Y.; Sun, A.; Wang, J. A CNN-LSTM-based model to forecast stock prices. *Complexity* **2020**, *2020*, 6622927. [CrossRef]
32. Shahid, F.; Zameer, A.; Muneeb, M. A novel genetic LSTM model for wind power forecast. *Energy* **2021**, *223*, 120069. [CrossRef]
33. Kumar, G.; Singh, U.P.; Jain, S. An adaptive particle swarm optimization-based hybrid long short-term memory model for stock price time series forecasting. *Soft Comput.* **2022**, *26*, 12115–12135. [CrossRef]
34. Massari, F. Price probabilities: A class of bayesian and non-bayesian prediction rules. *Econ. Theory* **2021**, *72*, 133–166. [CrossRef]
35. Chandra, R.; He, Y. Bayesian neural networks for stock price forecasting before and during COVID-19 pandemic. *PLoS ONE* **2021**, *16*, e0253217. [CrossRef] [PubMed]
36. Chuang, C.; Lee, T. A practical and economical bayesian approach to gas price prediction. In *The International Conference on Deep Learning, Big Data and Blockchain (Deep-BDB 2021)*; Springer: Cham, Switzerland, 2022; pp. 160–174.
37. Karaboga, D. *An Idea Based on Honey Bee Swarm for Numerical Optimization*; Technical Report; Erciyes University: Kayseri, Turkey, 2005.
38. Shan, L.; Qiang, H.; Li, J.; Wang, Z. Chaotic optimization algorithm based on Tent map. *Control Decis.* **2005**, *20*, 179–182.
39. Hochreiter, S.; Schmidhuber, J. Long short-term memory. *Neural Comput.* **1997**, *9*, 1735–1780. [CrossRef] [PubMed]
40. Karaboga, D.; Gorkemli, B. A quick artificial bee colony (qABC) algorithm and its performance on optimization problems. *Appl. Soft Comput.* **2014**, *23*, 227–238. [CrossRef]
41. Karaboga, D.; Gorkemli, B.; Ozturk, C.; Karaboga, N. A comprehensive survey: Artificial bee colony (ABC) algorithm and applications. *Artif. Intell. Rev.* **2014**, *42*, 21–57. [CrossRef]
42. Khataei Maragheh, H.; Gharehchopogh, F.S.; Majidzadeh, K.; Sangar, A.B. A new hybrid based on long short-term memory network with spotted hyena optimization algorithm for multi-label text classification. *Mathematics* **2022**, *10*, 488. [CrossRef]
43. Karunasingha, D.S.K. Root mean square error or mean absolute error? Use their ratio as well. *Inf. Sci.* **2022**, *585*, 609–629. [CrossRef]
44. Lehmann, E.L.; Casella, G. *Theory of Point Estimation*; Springer Science & Business Media: Berlin/Heidelberg, Germany, 2006.
45. Chai, T.; Draxler, R.R. Root mean square error (RMSE) or mean absolute error (MAE)?—Arguments against avoiding RMSE in the literature. *Geosci. Model Dev.* **2014**, *7*, 1247–1250. [CrossRef]
46. Alabdulrazzaq, H.; Alenezi, M.N.; Rawajfih, Y.; Alghannam, B.A.; Al-Hassan, A.A.; Al-Anzi, F.S. On the accuracy of ARIMA based prediction of COVID-19 spread. *Results Phys.* **2021**, *27*, 104509. [CrossRef]
47. Zhang, H.; Zhou, T.; Xu, T.; Wang, Y.; Hu, H. FNN-based prediction of wireless channel with atmospheric duct. In Proceedings of the ICC 2021-IEEE International Conference on Communications, Montreal, QC, Canada, 14–23 June 2021; pp. 1–6.
48. Huang, R.; Wei, C.; Wang, B.; Yang, J.; Xu, X.; Wu, S.; Huang, S. Well performance prediction based on Long Short-Term Memory (LSTM) neural network. *J. Pet. Sci. Eng.* **2022**, *208*, 109686. [CrossRef]
49. Wang, K.; Hua, Y.; Huang, L.; Guo, X.; Liu, X.; Ma, Z.; Ma, R.; Jiang, X. A novel GA-LSTM-based prediction method of ship energy usage based on the characteristics analysis of operational data. *Energy* **2023**, *282*, 128910. [CrossRef]

applied sciences

MDPI

*Article*

# Integrating Machine Learning and Material Feeding Systems for Competitive Advantage in Manufacturing

**Müge Sinem Çağlayan [1] and Aslı Aksoy [2,*]**

[1] Jaguar Land Rover-Solihull, Lode Lane, Solihull B92 8NW, UK
[2] Industrial Engineering Department, Bursa Uludag University, Gorukle Campus, 16059 Bursa, Turkey
* Correspondence: asliaksoy@uludag.edu.tr

**Abstract:** In contemporary business environments, manufacturing companies must continuously enhance their performance to ensure competitiveness. Material feeding systems are of pivotal importance in the optimization of productivity, with attendant improvements in quality, reduction of costs, and minimization of delivery times. This study investigates the selection of material feeding methods, including Kanban, line-storage, call-out, and kitting systems, within a manufacturing company. The research employs six machine learning (ML) algorithms—logistic regression (LR), decision trees (DT), random forest (RF), support vector machines (SVM), K-nearest neighbors (K-NN), and artificial neural networks (ANN)—to develop a multi-class classification model for material feeding system selection. Utilizing a dataset comprising 2221 materials and an 8-fold cross-validation technique, the ANN model exhibits superior performance across all evaluation metrics. Shapley values analysis is employed to elucidate the influence of pivotal input parameters within the selection process for material feeding systems. This research provides a comprehensive framework for material feeding system selection, integrating advanced ML models with practical manufacturing insights. This study makes a significant contribution to the field by enhancing decision-making processes, optimizing resource utilization, and establishing the foundation for future studies on adaptive and scalable material feeding strategies in dynamic industrial environments.

**Keywords:** material feeding systems; machine learning; multi-class classification; manufacturing systems

## 1. Introduction

In the context of the contemporary era, manufacturing companies are engaged in efforts to enhance their competitiveness in the global market. This is pursued through the pursuit of two key objectives: the maximization of quality and the minimization of costs and delivery times. Material feeding systems represent a significant factor influencing productivity. Manufacturing companies must select the optimal material feeding method by considering variables such as material variety, size and weight, product demand volume, space requirements, and labor force. Material feeding systems can be classified into three categories: stocking of materials, transportation of materials, and material feeding policy. In the literature, material feeding policies are analyzed under four distinct categorizations, as follows: continuous feeding (line storage), material feeding with Kanban, kitting, and hybrid approaches.

The objective of the line-storage strategy is to ensure the storage and distribution of materials in a separate container or on a dedicated shelf located in close proximity to the assembly line. The quantity of materials stored in the container is determined by the specific product type and is replenished when the container is empty. The operator responsible for assembly or material preparation retrieves the requisite materials from the designated storage location and prepares them in accordance with the specifications outlined in the production plan. In the event of a material shortage on the assembly line, production can continue uninterrupted by procuring new products directly from the adjacent container, as a consistent supply of materials is maintained in close proximity to the line. In manufacturing companies with a high degree of product variety, the time spent searching for the requisite parts and the space required for their placement next to the assembly line are considerable [1].

Kanban is a tool that facilitates the communication of information in accordance with the principles of lean production pull. Kanban facilitates the transfer of materials by enabling the circulation of information from the final production stage to the initial production stage. Upon withdrawal of the product from the designated area, a signal is generated to indicate the transition to the preceding stage of the process. The Kanban method is a material feeding technique that is employed to prevent overproduction and to reduce the number and cost of components in the production process that are not yet complete. The subsequent process stage transmits a signal to the preceding process stage, indicating whether production should continue or cease, utilizing a Kanban card. As the production decision is based on information from the subsequent process, there is no requirement for external planning, and the process is straightforward to manage.

The term "kit" is used generically to describe a box containing parts used in one or more assembly steps [2]. A kit is defined as a specialized collection of parts [3] and a collection of materials that are required to produce a product or complete a production step [4]. The term 'kitting' is defined as the process of supplying the requisite components by placing predetermined quantities of parts together in specially designed containers and the process of handling only those parts that have been defined as necessary for a specific period and dispatching them to designated stations [5]. The use of kits represents an advantageous material feeding method in manufacturing companies characterized by high product variety, low product demand, and a low number of standard components [6]. Limere et al. [7] identified several advantages associated with kitting. These include a reduction in stock levels, a reduction in the time operators spend locating and retrieving materials, a reduction in the time required to search for materials, an improvement in ergonomic conditions, and easier access for operators to ergonomically designed kits.

Hybrid approaches are those in which two or more material feeding methods are used together. A hybrid approach may be defined as one in which two or more material feeding methods are employed in conjunction with one another. Moreover, this approach may entail the feeding of a defined subset of materials from line storage or the utilization of Kanban management while another subset is fed from the warehouse or kitting.

This study considers the problem of material feeding method decision-making to assembly lines in a hydraulic motor manufacturing company in Turkey. This study presents a number of issues encountered by a manufacturing company engaged in the production of hydraulic motors, as follows:

- The system exhibits a high order of volume yet displays a low production capacity;
- The assembly lines are subject to lengthy lead times;
- A substantial number of tasks are performed by the assembly operator that does not enhance the value of their work;
- The space requirements for the purchase of new machinery with the objective of increasing production capacity;

- A review of customer complaints revealed a recurring issue with incorrect material assembly on the assembly line;
- Given the extensive range of available materials, identifying the most appropriate ones is a time-consuming task;
- The operational procedures of the assembly line and the activities of the operators are not optimally efficient;
- The lack of sufficient space for materials next to the line has been identified as a potential issue;
- The demand for each material varies considerably depending on customer requirements.

To address the issues that have been identified, it was decided that a standardized and systematic material feeding method should be selected for use on assembly lines. The objective of this study is to identify the most efficient material feeding method for existing materials in assembly lines with varying value streams in the factory and to determine an effective material feeding method for new materials. The remainder of this paper is organized as follows. Section 2 presents a literature review. Section 3 explains the proposed approaches. Developed models and results are provided in Section 4. Finally, conclusions are presented in Section 5.

## 2. Literature Review

This study investigates assembly line feeding methods and material feeding method selection problems in the literature. In many studies in the literature, material feeding methods are compared with each other, and various methods are used to solve the material selection problem. In this section, different material feeding methods in the literature are explained. Just-in-time production, line-side stocking, kitting, Kanban, sequencing, and hybrid material feeding methods are mentioned in the literature. In the articles, line-side storage, kitting, and just-in-time production material feeding methods are mostly mentioned [8].

There is an urgent demand to improve the material feeding performance in automobile mixed-model assembly lines [9]. For automotive mixed-model assembly lines, the excessive work-in-process inventory will cause confusion in the assembly line, which will damage the product quality and reduce the enterprise's reputation [9]. Zhou and Zhao [9] proposed a fuzzy-neural model-based model for the material feeding problem for the Kanban strategy. The fundamental principle of the material feeding strategy is the determination of whether the supply of materials is continuous or discontinuous [10]. As an alternative to kitting, the Kanban method is a continuous supply strategy that allows a stock of each needed part type to be continuously held at the workstation with small-sized containers. Conversely, when substantial quantities of parts are stored in larger containers along the production line, and these containers are replenished at regular intervals, this is referred to as line storage [10]. Kitting is the feeding of multiple specific parts required at a specific workstation for the production of a specific product [11].

Tardif and Maaseidvaag [12] established the definition of "Kanban" as a material flow-control mechanism. This mechanism is employed to regulate the appropriate quantity and temporal allocation of products, ensuring that only the necessary quantity is produced. In a Kanban material feeding system, each bin is associated with a card containing information about the product. Kanban cards always move through the processes together with the products. The Kanban card refills stations with relevant parts based on consumption [13,14]. The Kanban material feeding method reduces inventory costs, increases flexibility as production occurs in line with customer demand, and does not require an additional management system [15]. The Kanban system has been demonstrated to exhibit a high degree of adaptability in responding rapidly to fluctuations in demand [9].

Line-storage feeding is considered to be the process of moving parts from a central warehouse to an area in which they will be utilized. Parts are stocked in the relevant area, and when the operator on the assembly line requires material, it is obtained from the stock areas adjacent to the line. Conversely, when a specific component is no longer required, or the designated parts bin is depleted, it is returned to the central warehouse, thereby freeing up space in the line-side stock area [16]. This systematic approach ensures the continuous availability of materials in the stock area adjacent to the assembly line. In the automotive industry, line-storage feeding is the most common parts feeding strategy due to its simplicity and the low material handling efforts it entails [17]. However, this approach is associated with higher space utilization and no time savings during the assembly worker's picking process [18]. Kitting is collecting the parts required to produce a specific product in the required quantity and bringing them to the assembly line in a designated box [16]. The time needed to prepare the kit is non-value added time; additional space is needed to prepare the kit, the list of materials needed must be shared with the kitting operators in advance, and additional planning is required. Handling is high and risky for parts that may suffer quality damage or be stolen. It can be challenging to place extensive and heavy or tiny parts into the kit [2]. It has been demonstrated that each material feeding strategy has its own advantages and disadvantages. This poses a significant challenge to the effective allocation of each part to a feeding strategy [7,19].

The assembly line feeding problem was first formulated and investigated by Bozer and McGinnis [2]. This pioneering research paper explores the impact of various feeding policies through cost-based comparisons. A notable constraint of the study is its utilization of a binary approach, presupposing that a single feeding policy is implemented for the feeding of all components. Descriptive models and optimization-based models are widely used for material feeding strategy selection in the literature. In the existing literature, there is a wide prevalence of both descriptive [5,20,21] and optimization-based models [11,22–25] in the context of the material feeding strategy selection problem. Bozer and McGinnis [2] presented the differences between line-storage feeding and kitting and developed a decision-making model to determine the material feeding strategy by using a linear programming model. Bozer and McGinnis [2] compared two material feeding systems based on the amount of inventory between processes, the space requirements for a central warehouse and a line-storage warehouse, and the material handling quantity criterion. Caputo and Pelagagge [20] evaluated kitting and line-storage feeding with an optimization model that aims to minimize the cost of labor, space requirement, and in-process stock quantity parameters. Wänström and Medbo [26] compared line-storage and sequential feeding systems by examining how they affect labor, production flexibility, material planning parameters, and assembly process performance. Battini et al. [27] conducted a study for a pallet to workstation, trolley to workstation, and locking as a part of the feeding methods. They evaluated the most important factors affecting the material feeding strategy as follows: the distance between the line and the warehouse, the average number of components of each finished product, the average lot size, and the number of stations on the line. Hua and Johnson [28] explained the factors for choosing the right line feeding method as follows: the effect of the product and components on production volume, the effect of the variety and size, the effect of component stocking and material handling, the effect of production control, and the effect of system selection on operational performance. Caputo and Pelagagge [21] demonstrated a model to support decision-making for kitting, just-in-time Kanban-based continuous feeding, and line-storage feeding methods. Hanson et al. [29] compared the time taken to bring materials from kitting and line-storage stocking to the assembly line in the automobile industry. It was interpreted that kitting increases material picking and counting, line-side stocking increases in-process material stock and increases the holding cost, and if the same component is to be used in different assembly stations, it will require multiple space requirements in the line. Limere et al. [30] developed a labor-based mathematical cost method to select a material feeding strategy comparing kitting and line-storage methods. Hanson and Brolin [31] defined line storage and kitting regarding product quality, assembly support, flexibility, finished product inventory level, and required stock space. Caputo et al. [22] developed a mathematical model to select the optimal material feeding method for parts fed to the assembly line to minimize the total cost. Labor costs, investment costs, in-process inventory holding costs, and factory floor space costs were considered as parameters. Limere et al. [7] developed a mixed-integer programming model to minimize logistics costs to choose between line-storage feeding and kitting. Sali et al. [23] examined the kit, line-side, and sequencing methods with a total cost formulation that evaluates material preparation costs before assembly, picking, transportation from the central warehouse to the assembly line, and stocking. Caputo et al. [10] developed a cost model for supplying materials to assembly lines according to the kit, line-storage, and just-in-time production methods that depend on the part characteristics and performed sensitivity and parametric analyses to determine the best method for each material. Baller et al. [18] extended the mixed-integer programming formulations in the literature by allowing flexible line-edge spacing by modeling different line feeding methods per material family for different material feeding methods. Zennaro et al. [32] developed a mathematical model that aims to reduce the cost of a material feeding system. Kang et al. [33], Bertolini et al. [34], Moretti et al. [35], and Zangaro et al. [36] investigated the potential of machine learning (ML) methodologies in addressing the material feeding problem. Moretti et al. [35] presented a DT model for the material feeding problem. Faccio et al. [37] presented a simulation-based model and statistical analysis for the material feeding strategy problem. As asserted by Kang et al. [33], artificial neural network (ANN), decision tree (DT), random forest (RF), support vector machine (SVM), and K-nearest neighbor (K-NN) are the most frequently applied ML models, and binary classification is the major dependent variable for production line problems.

A literature review reveals significant advancements in understanding and modeling the problems associated with feeding materials during the assembly process. Many extant studies, beginning with Bozer and McGinnis [2], adopt a binary or uniform approach, presuming a uniform feeding policy for all components. This simplification does not reflect the complexity of real-world assembly lines, where different components may require different material feeding strategies. In practice, many assembly lines are characterized by the deployment of multiple material feeding systems, which are utilized concurrently to accommodate various product types, production volumes, part characteristics, and supply chain constraints. This necessitates exploring hybrid material feeding systems capable of integrating and dynamically adjusting between different feeding methods. The implementation of such systems would enable manufacturers to optimize material handling processes in a flexible and adaptive manner, allowing for real-time adjustments based on shifting production needs and environmental conditions. Research on hybrid feeding systems, where multiple feeding strategies coexist and incorporate dynamic decision-making frameworks, ensuring that material feeding systems can be switched or combined in response to specific operational requirements, remains limited. Integrating traditional material feeding strategies with data, predictive analytics, and ML models can potentially optimize manufacturing systems' performance and cost efficiency. Recent research (e.g., Kang et al. [33]; Moretti et al. [35]) introduces ML-based methodologies for material feeding problems, but applications remain exploratory and limited to specific ML models. Most models primarily aim to minimize costs, neglecting other crucial performance metrics that influence assembly lines' overall performance and effectiveness. In environments with high variability or frequent product changes, a system optimized only for the cost may lack flexibility and efficiency. Material feeding strategies prioritizing cost minimization can lead to quality issues or delays. The rapid pace of technological advancements in manufacturing, driven by Industry 4.0, increases the importance of system adaptability. Therefore, there is a need for multi-criteria decision-making models that address broader operational and strategic objectives beyond cost reduction. The lack of empirical evidence and case studies on the implementation and effectiveness of proposed models in diverse industrial settings also needs to be addressed. ML models have demonstrated considerable potential in predicting the optimal material feeding strategy. Nevertheless, a pivotal element of their implementation, namely the interpretability of the models, is frequently disregarded. For manufacturing companies to confidently adopt ML-based decision-making systems, providing clear insights into how various input features influence the model's predictions is essential. One promising method to enhance interpretability is the application of Shapley values, a concept from cooperative game theory that can quantify the contribution of each input feature to the final prediction of a model. Despite the potential of combining Shapley values with ML models, this approach remains underexplored in the material feeding strategy literature. The incorporation of Shapley values into ML models has the potential to generate actionable insights that elucidate the rationale behind the selection of a specific feeding strategy in a given context. However, there is a lack of research exploring the potential of Shapley values to enhance the interpretability of ML models, particularly in the context of multi-class classification problems such as material feeding strategy selection.

## 3. Materials and Methods

ML algorithms can be classified into four subclasses as follows: (1) supervised learning, where the algorithm uses a set of labeled training data to derive a function between the input(s) and the output(s); (2) unsupervised learning, where the algorithm does not require labeled data; (3) semi-supervised learning, where the training dataset includes both labeled and unlabeled data, and (4) reinforcement learning, where the algorithm rewards positive actions and penalizes negative actions using a feedback mechanism [33]. Although the availability and quality of data are critical to the performance of ML algorithms, supervised learning usually achieves better results than semi-supervised and unsupervised learning approaches [33].

A DT is a supervised ML model that supports decision-making processes. It is represented as a logical tree, with a range of conditions and conclusions as nodes and branches [38,39]. At each stage of the decision-making process, a decision tree takes a decision and considers alternative choices of action, selecting the most relevant alternatives [40]. It employs estimates and probabilities to calculate probable outcomes and assist in determining the net gain from a decision. Various techniques are employed to accomplish classification, including information gain, chi-square, Gini, entropy, and others [41]. The DT method is characterized by its simplicity, ease of understanding and visualization, rapid execution, minimal data preprocessing requirements, and capacity to effectively handle both categorical and numerical data; however, it should be noted that this algorithm can occasionally result in a complex tree structure that lacks sufficient generalization, and it is a relatively unstable model [42].

The RF model can be considered an ensemble learning method for regression and classification [43]. The RF model builds an ensemble of DTs using a training sample, which, in turn, results in the appropriate classification of data or the provision of suitable predictors for one or more characteristics of the individual trees. The RF method is employed in the construction of a bagging ensemble, with the process being informed by DTs and introducing random attribute selection during the training process [44]. The RF algorithm divides the training set into multiple subsets, and each subset is then assigned an independent DT [45]. The model's output is determined by a voting system that integrates the outputs from all the DTs [46]. In contradistinction to alternative conventional methods, which necessitate a substantial computational load, the RF model entails a reduced computational demand for the DT and enhances prediction accuracy [47]. Zhai et al. [48] demonstrated that a single DT is sensitive to the noise present within the training dataset. However, the RF classifier has been shown to be capable of reducing the correlation between the trained multiple DTs, thereby effectively reducing the overfitting problem.

The logistic regression (LR) model aims to construct a linear model of the output, which can be interpreted as an estimate of the posteriori probability of class membership [49]. LR is a widely used classification algorithm in industry and because of its simplicity and efficiency, LR still attracts wide attention from researchers [50]. LR is a statistical model with an assumption that the variables are independently and identically distributed. LR is one of the wrapper methods known for its decent predictability performance but is computationally expensive [51]. LR does not require the optimization of any hyperparameter and is thus easier to implement [52]. Based on the observation of input variables, LR describes the probability of realization of the output variable(s). LR applies the Newton–Raphson algorithm to determine the coefficients of the regression equation [53].

The SVM is an algorithm that is capable of handling both regression and classification tasks, although they are more effective for classification [42]. The SVM involves the separation of objects in an n-dimensional space using a hyperplane. The closest vectors between these categories are referred to as support vectors [54]. The initial n-dimensional spatial domain is thus transformed into a space of a higher degree of complexity, known as a Hilbert space, wherein the dot product is determined by a function designated as the 'kernel'. The SVM is equipped with a variety of kernels, encompassing linear, polynomial, Gaussian, and sigmoidal types [55]. The performance of the SVM model is dependent upon the construction of the hyperplane; if this is executed competently, the model will demonstrate high performance [42]. SVMs are characterized by their strong capacity for generalization, which renders them particularly useful when dealing with many attributes and limited data points [56].

In K-NN classification, all available data are stored and the class of a new instance is predicted based on the similarity measurements from the nearest neighbors in terms of likelihood. K-NN reduces the computational cost of checking and applying the appropriate distance function between the new observation and all k numbers of different data points stored. It then determines the label of the new data point without constructing a mapping function or internal model, in contrast to other classification algorithms [40]. The K-NN classifier is employed to allocate the query into the class that is most prevalent among its K-nearest neighbors in the training set, in accordance with the majority voting rule [54,57]. The K-NN's primary shortcoming lies in the requirement for recalculation of the distance from all $k$ neighbors for each new instance, which results in a significant computational expenditure [42].

The ANN can be defined as a powerful data modeling tool that simulates the cognitive learning process of the human brain system. The key strength of the ANN lies in its capacity to represent both linear and nonlinear relationships and to learn such relationships directly from the data being modeled. The structural composition of an ANN entails interconnected neuron clusters, with the fundamental configuration comprising three layers: the input layer and the output layer, which are employed for the training of the model, and the hidden layer(s), which facilitate the establishment of a connection between the input and output [58]. The structural design of the artificial neural network (ANN) model is determined by the specific characteristics of the problem and the data, and consequently, there is no single standard structure that can be universally applied to all problems [59]. The training of the network can be defined as a process of changing the weights of neurons, where the initial weights of the neurons are randomly determined [60]. The objective of a training algorithm is to identify a decision function that facilitates the modification of the network's weights. A multitude of training algorithms have been documented in the extant literature; however, identifying the most appropriate algorithm is a challenging task. The backpropagation (BP) ANN is extensively utilized in the modeling of nonlinear and complex problem types [61,62]. The BP training algorithm employs a methodology (first-order steepest descent techniques) to adjust the weights of the neurons based on the estimation of the gradient of the sum squared error for each layer. This process is intended to increase the training speed and to avoid local minimum solutions. The error term is defined as the difference between the network response and the expected output. The rectified linear unit (ReLU), as proposed by Nair and Hinton [63], has been shown to exhibit excellent nonlinear properties and is considered to be one of the most widely utilized activation functions in ANNs [64]. For each input element, the ReLU activation function performs a threshold operation. If the argument is negative, the value is zero; if the argument is non-negative, the value is the variable itself. The ReLU activation function ($\sigma$) can be represented by the following Equation (1):

$$\sigma(x) = \max(x, 0), \tag{1}$$

where $x$ represents the input.

The classification tasks in ML models can also be broadly categorized based on the number of outputs and the range of possible values for each output. Binary classification is the process of assigning instances to one of two possible classes for a single output variable. In this context, the functional class requirements are characterized by the presence of distinguishing features that serve to differentiate them from non-functional class requirements [65]. In contrast, multi-class classification extends this by allowing the single output variable to belong to one of several distinct classes, thus offering a more nuanced approach to categorization [66]. In multi-class classification, individual classes of requirements often have few distinguishable features, which can result in challenges in terms of predictor performance [65].

Shapley values, as initially defined by Shapley [67], represent a classical concept in cooperative game theory. These values have recently been applied to the interpretation of ML models' predictions [68]. Shapley values can also be interpreted as representing an equitable or reasonable distribution of feature importance, given a specific model output. Features contribute to the output or prediction of the model to a different degree, both quantitatively and qualitatively. This phenomenon is accommodated by the use of Shapley values. In this manner, the Shapley values can be considered as estimates of feature import, i.e., the magnitude of a feature's contribution to the prediction, as well as the direction of this contribution, i.e., its sign. Features with a positive sign contribute positively to the prediction of activity, whereas features with a negative sign contribute negatively to the prediction of inactivity [69]. The importance of an input $i$ is defined by the Shapley value as in Equation (2):

$$\varphi_i = \frac{1}{|N|!} \sum_{S \in N\{i\}} |S|!(|N| - |S| - 1)![f(S \cup \{i\}) - f(S)], \tag{2}$$

where $f(S)$ corresponds to the output of the ML model to be explained using a set $S$ of inputs, and $N$ is the complete set of all inputs. The Shapley value of input $i$ ($\varphi_i$) is determined as the average of its contributions across all possible permutations of an input set. The performance of ML algorithms is evaluated using a number of different metrics, including accuracy, precision, recall, F1-score, and kappa statistic. Accuracy is the proportion of instances that are correctly classified, precision is the proportion of instances classified as positive that are truly positive, recall is the proportion of positive instances that are correctly classified as positive, and the F1-score combines the precision and recall [55]. The following equations (Equations (3)–(6)) are used for the accuracy, precision, recall, and F1-score metrics:

$$Accuracy = \frac{TP + TN}{TP + FP + TN + FN} \tag{3}$$

$$Precision = \frac{TP}{TP + FP} \tag{4}$$

$$Recall = \frac{TP}{TP + FN} \tag{5}$$

$$F1 - score = \frac{2 \times Precision \times Recall}{Precision + Recall} \tag{6}$$

where true positive ($TP$) and true negative ($TN$) represent the correctly classified instances, and false positive ($FP$) and false negative ($FN$) represent the incorrectly classified instances.

## 4. Results

The company where this study was conducted is a manufacturer of hydraulic and pneumatic motors and pumps for agricultural and industrial vehicles. The company employs cellular manufacturing techniques and has five different product groups, with the selected product group comprising three different assembly lines. It is necessary to pre-assemble certain subcomponents that are employed in three assembly lines. Two pre-assembly stages are identified. One of the three assembly lines is a manual assembly line, which has the longest production lead time. This line was selected as the pilot assembly line for the implementation of the proposed methodology. Prior to the introduction of all components into the pilot assembly line, a number of components are transformed into intermediate products in two pre-assembly lines. This requires the implementation of an appropriate material feeding method.

A total of 2221 unique materials are assembled on the pilot line. Of the total number of materials, 1150 are produced internally, while 1071 are purchased from external suppliers. While 1047 materials are stored next to the assembly line (in Figure 1a), 103 different types of materials are managed in accordance with the Kanban principle with a two-box system (Figure 1b), and 1071 materials are supplied from the central warehouse via a call-out system (Figure 1c) when the relevant material is required on the assembly line.

(a) (b) (c)

**Figure 1.** Material feeding systems in the company (**a**) for line storage, (**b**) for Kanban system, and (**c**) for call-out system.

Different types of materials have different sizes and weights, and product groups have different demand values. The handling of materials should not result in any deterioration in quality. In the current situation, the assembly operator is responsible for preparing the requisite materials for the assembly line in accordance with the production plan received from the logistics unit. The logistics unit disseminates the production plan to the pre-assembly and other assembly lines. The high number of similar types located next to the assembly line results in a considerable investment of time in searching for the requisite materials. This consequently results in an increase in the assembly lead time. In accordance with the established protocol, the assembly operator is obliged to notify the warehouse at least four hours in advance of the materials that are to be supplied from the warehouse. The materials supplied from the warehouse are used as often as required, and the warehouse is informed of the impending delivery, given the lack of available space next to the assembly line. The team leaders, who are responsible for the assembly line, make the decision regarding the material feeding method based on their experience. The organization of material feeding methods is subject to change for a number of reasons, including the performance of non-value-added work by assembly operators, the lack of sufficient space within the company for the introduction of new machines and assembly lines, the objective of increasing the number of assembly line outputs, and the receipt of complaints from customers due to material mix-ups on the assembly line. Given the considerable time required for the team leaders to make decisions regarding materials across the entire company, it was decided that a method should be developed that could be applied to all product groups within the company. Kitting, which is not currently employed as a material feeding method, is proposed as a potential solution given the company's diverse product range and low demand volume. It is anticipated that this approach could address the space constraints next to the line, enhance the assembly line output by reducing the workload of the assembly operator, and improve quality by minimizing the risk of incomplete or incorrect assembly.

Six different classification-based ML algorithms, LR, DT, RF, SVM, K-NN, and ANN, are used for the material feeding method selection problem. LR is a suitable choice for the multi-class material feeding strategy problem due to its simplicity, interpretability, and ability to handle multiple classes [40]. DT models' decision processes are similar to human reasoning and can identify the key features affecting material feeding strategies [70]. RF is attributed to its ensemble nature, leading to enhanced prediction accuracy and reduced overfitting for multi-class problems [71,72]. SVMs are effective for cases with small datasets and valuable for distinguishing between closely related classes, such as when differentiating between similar material feeding strategies [73]. The non-parametric nature of the K-NN model allows it to adapt to complex material feeding patterns [74]. ANNs can learn complex patterns in data with multiple variables and possess practical generalizing ability for multi-class problems [61,62]. A review of the literature revealed a variety of inputs that could be employed in the selection of a material feeding method. These were evaluated in the context of the inputs currently in use within the company, and five input parameters were determined as follows:

- Mode of supply: The supply method employed for the pilot assembly line is a combination of in-house production and external sourcing. Some of the materials used are manufactured on-site in the company's machining facilities, while others are purchased from external suppliers.
- Annual demand: It is crucial to ascertain the extent of demand that the materials will have in a year. In order to reduce the in-plant logistics costs, products with high annual demand volumes may be situated next to the assembly line. Conversely, products

with low annual demand may be supplied from the warehouse when required, thus optimizing the utilization of space in close proximity to the assembly line.

- Finished product reference number (Reference No): The final product produced on the assembly line is composed of between 100 and 150 sub-materials, the precise number depending on the specific type of product. It is possible for each material to be a sub-material of one or more finished products.
- Use case in pre-assembly (Use case): It is possible that the final products may consist of sub-assembled or semi-assembled materials. It is recommended that the pre-assembly step should commence at a specific point in time before the assembly step. It should be noted that feeding material at the same time as the pilot line may cause problems in compliance with the production plan on the line.
- Compatibility of the material size with the kitting vehicle (Compatibility with KV): It should be noted that each material may have disparate dimensional characteristics. Products with dimensions spanning the range from 0.01 mm to 1000 mm are assembled in the pilot line. Given that the volume of the kitting vehicle is designed for a limited range of products, it is crucial to assess the suitability of the products for transportation with the kitting vehicle.

The description of the inputs determined for the material feeding method is given in Table 1.

**Table 1.** Description of input parameters.

| No | Input | Value | Description |
|---|---|---|---|
| 1 | Mode of supply | 0–1 | 1: In-house production<br>0: External sourcing |
| 2 | Annual demand | 1–100 | The demand quantity (×1000 units) |
| 3 | Finished product reference number | 1–45 | The number of finished products(s) that the material belongs to |
| 4 | Use case in pre-assembly | 0–1 | 1: Used only on the relevant assembly line<br>0: Used in pre-assembly line |
| 5 | Compatibility of the material size with the kitting vehicle | 0–1 | 1: Compatible with the kitting vehicle<br>0: Not compatible with the kitting vehicle |

The output parameter comprises four different material feeding systems, including line storage, Kanban, kitting, and a call-out system. The framework of the proposed study can be seen in Figure 2.

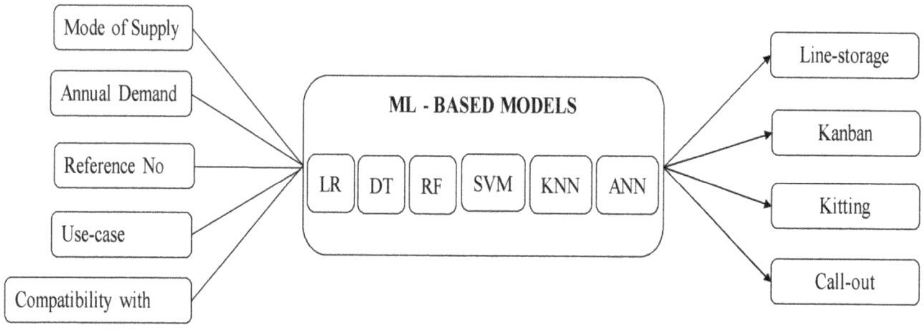


**Figure 2.** The framework of the proposed study.

The dataset contains the material details obtained from the company's enterprise resource planning (ERP) system, production logs, and warehouse inventory records. The data preprocessing applied in the study includes removing duplicate records for the materials listed under more than one product category, correcting missing values for the demand rates by interpolation based on historical production data, and correcting inconsistencies in the material feeding strategy classification labels. Categorical inputs are encoded using binary and one-hot encoding methods to facilitate model interpretation. It was established that annual demand values significantly deviating from production trends were to be identified as outliers and then validated against production schedules to confirm the validity of the data and correct data entry errors. It is imperative to acknowledge the potential for bias inherent in the observed data, which may have originated from historical preferences concerning feeding methods or long-standing practices in the company.

The MRMR algorithm is used to observe the material feeding method for different values of input parameters. The MRMR algorithm, first proposed by Peng et al. [75], measures the redundancies among input parameters and the relevance between input parameters and output class labels for a given set of inputs. The primary function of the MRMR algorithm is to minimize the redundancy of an input set and maximize the relevance of an input set to the output variable [76,77]. The inputs that were ranked highest by MRMR are considered to exhibit an optimal balance between relevance to the output and minimal redundancy. The MRMR method is characterized by its high level of computational efficiency and its capacity for generalization concerning different ML models [78]. In the MRMR algorithm, each input is assigned a weight that signifies its importance or relevance to the output variable, with higher weights deemed more relevant. The MRMR weights for the input parameters have been calculated and are presented in Table 2. The MRMR algorithm results indicated that all selected inputs were relevant to the material feeding method.

**Table 2.** Results of the MRMR algorithm.

| | **Mode of Supply** | **Annual Demand** | **Finished Product Reference Number** | **Use Case in Pre-Assembly** | **Compatibility of the Material Size with the Kitting Vehicle** |
|---|---|---|---|---|---|
| MRMR weights | 0.1390 | 0.6009 | 0.0982 | 0.2930 | 0.0886 |

The training dataset, which consists of 2221 rows, is split into two sets (training and testing) before running the ML algorithms. Cross-validation (CV) is a popular strategy to split the data (one or more times), in which the split part of the data is used to train the algorithm, and the remaining part is used to estimate the risk of the algorithm [59]. CV also helps to prevent overfitting to biased subsets of data and increase generalizability [79].

The ML algorithms are run with the following hyperparameters: a maximal depth of 7; a maximum number of splits of 100, the "Gini index" as a split criterion for the DT algorithm; ridge regularization with the regularization strength (lambda) of 0.00046 and One-vs-One multi-class coding for LR; a kernel scale of 1; a box constraint level of 1 with One-vs-One multi-class coding for SVM; a number of learners (30), number of trees (20), and maximum number of splits (2173) for RF; a number of neighbors (10) and Euclidean distance metric for K-NN; 10 and 12 neurons in two hidden layers; and the ReLU activation function for a bi-layered ANN.

To improve the performance of the ML models, the parameters are optimized using Bayesian optimization (BO). Fundamental principles of BO involve utilizing a surrogate model of a Gaussian process and an acquisition function to determine the subsequent point to be evaluated [80]. BO is an effective search algorithm capable of generating performance results for all values within the user-defined parameter range [81]. Table 3 demonstrates the hyperparameters of the ML models used in the BO hyperparameter optimization procedure.

**Table 3.** The hyperparameters of the ML models used in BO.

| ML Models | Hyperparameter | Range | Optimized Hyperparameters |
|---|---|---|---|
| DT | Maximum number of splits | [1–2173] | 16 |
| | Split criterion | Gini's diversity index, Twoing rule, maximum deviance reduction | Twoing rule |
| | Maximal Depth | [2–16] | 10 |
| LR | Regularization | Ridge, Lasso | Ridge |
| | Lambda | $[10^{-6}–10^{2}]$ | 0.0034389 |
| | Multi-class coding | One-vs.-All, One-vs.-One | One-vs.-One |
| SVM | Kernel scale | [0.001–1000] | 1.1685 |
| | Box constraint level | [0.001–1000] | 551.7341 |
| | Multi-class coding | One-vs.-All, One-vs.-One | One-vs.-One |
| K-NN | Number of neighbors | [1–1087] | 12 |
| | Distance metric | Chebyshev, Euclidean, Minkowski | Euclidean |
| RF | Number of learners | [10–500] | 89 |
| | Maximum number of splits | [1–2173] | 170 |
| ANN | Number of fully connected layers | [1–3] | 2 |
| | Activation function | ReLU, tanh, sigmoid | ReLU |
| | First layer size | [1–300] | 19 |
| | Second layer size | [1–300] | 24 |
| | Third layer size | [1–300] | - |

The performance metrics of the models for the training set can be seen in Table 4. In the context of the training set, the RF model consistently demonstrates optimal performance, both with and without parameter optimization, attaining near-perfect scores of 99.6%. The ANN model also exhibits high performance, exhibiting only a slight decline in performance relative to the RF model. The DT model exhibits lower accuracy than the other ML models. The LR and SVM models demonstrate competitive results, particularly after parameter optimization. The optimization of parameters has been demonstrated to enhance the accuracy of both DT and SVM. The accuracy for DT has increased from 89.8% to 91.27%, and for SVM, from 93.6% to 94.38%. Minimal enhancements in performance metrics are observed for the ANN with parameter optimization; however, a substantial increase in CPU time is evident, rising from 4.47 s to over 528 s.

Heatmaps of the confusion matrices of ML models for the training set can be seen in Figure 3.

Trained ML models are validated with the validation set (including 47 rows), which have not been used during training. The performance metrics of the ML models for the validation set can be seen in Table 5.

**Table 4.** Performance metrics of ML models for the training set.

| | Training Set | | | | |
|---|---|---|---|---|---|
| | **Accuracy** | **Precision** | **Recall** | **F1-Score** | **CPU Time** |
| | Without Parameter Optimization | | | | |
| LR | 93.6 | 93.5 | 93.6 | 93.5 | 4.7772 |
| DT | 89.8 | 92.4 | 89.8 | 89.9 | 8.2123 |
| RF | 99.6 | 99.6 | 99.6 | 99.6 | 6.1206 |
| SVM | 93.6 | 93.6 | 93.6 | 93.6 | 3.5284 |
| K-NN | 97.6 | 97.6 | 97.6 | 97.6 | 4.3682 |
| ANN | 99 | 99 | 99 | 99 | 4.4732 |
| | With Parameter Optimization | | | | |
| LR | 93.79 | 93.28 | 93.66 | 93.47 | 30.253 |
| DT | 91.27 | 90.88 | 91.7 | 91.29 | 16.8544 |
| RF | 99.62 | 99.62 | 99.62 | 99.62 | 49.557 |
| SVM | 94.38 | 94.27 | 94.44 | 94.36 | 190.29 |
| K-NN | 97.65 | 97.49 | 97.69 | 97.69 | 11.118 |
| ANN | 99.17 | 99.11 | 99.06 | 99.08 | 528.01 |

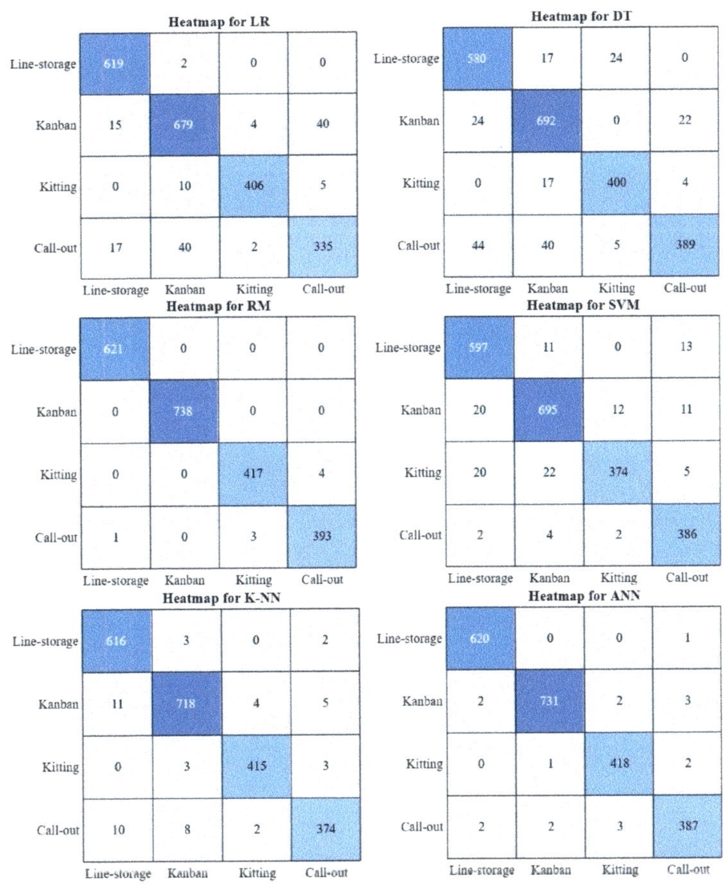


**Figure 3.** Heatmap of the confusion matrices of ML models with parameter optimization for the training set (While the lightest shade of blue indicates a lower quantity, the darkest shade of blue indicates a higher quantity).

**Table 5.** Performance metrics of ML models for the validation set.

| | Validation Set | | | |
|---|---|---|---|---|
| | **Accuracy** | **Precision** | **Recall** | **F1-Score** |
| | Without Parameter Optimization | | | |
| LR | 85.1 | 82.6 | 84.3 | 83.5 |
| DT | 82.4 | 83.7 | 82.4 | 82.1 |
| RF | 94.3 | 94.3 | 94.3 | 94.3 |
| SVM | 81.9 | 82.2 | 81.9 | 81.6 |
| K-NN | 87.2 | 88.4 | 85.8 | 87.1 |
| ANN | 95.6 | 95.1 | 96.6 | 95.8 |
| | With Parameter Optimization | | | |
| LR | 85.11 | 82.61 | 84.36 | 83.5 |
| DT | 82.97 | 82.36 | 81.97 | 82.14 |
| RF | 93.61 | 93.37 | 93.82 | 93.59 |
| SVM | 82.97 | 84.52 | 80.63 | 82.97 |
| K-NN | 89.36 | 90.33 | 88.79 | 89.56 |
| ANN | 97.82 | 98.61 | 98.07 | 98.34 |

As illustrated in Table 5, the ANN model demonstrates superior performance across all metrics when identifying the correct material feeding method for the validation dataset. The RF model demonstrates strong performance with consistent metrics, while the K-NN model performs well but falls short of the RF and ANN models. The LR model is a simple, interpretable model, but it might not capture complex patterns in the validation data compared to the RF or ANN models. The DTs are prone to overfitting and might not generalize well without pruning or ensemble techniques, and the SVM model has the lowest performance metrics compared to the other ML models. In the validation dataset context, the ANN achieves the highest accuracy (95.6%) and superior performance in all performance metrics. The RF model exhibits a noteworthy accuracy of 94.3%. LR and K-NN demonstrate commendable performance, achieving 85.1% and 87.2% accuracy, respectively. In contrast, the performance of the SVM and DT is comparatively lower, with the SVM demonstrating the least optimal results (81.9% accuracy). Notably, the performance of the ANN notably improves to 97.82% accuracy after parameter optimization. K-NN enhances performance (87.2% to 89.36% accuracy), signifying its sensitivity to parameter optimization. On the other hand, the SVM exhibited modest gains in precision but encountered difficulties in maintaining recall, underscoring challenges in classifying certain classes even after parameter optimization. The performance of RF, which reached 94.3% accuracy without parameter optimization, slightly declined to 93.61% accuracy with parameter optimization. Despite the RF model demonstrating optimal performance for the training set, the ANN model exhibits superior performance for the validation set compared to other ML models. The performance of the RF model on the validation set is observed to decrease, and this decline, occurring on the validation data despite robust outcomes on the training set, may suggest the occurrence of overfitting for the RF model.

In order to identify the impact of input parameters on the decision-making process concerning the selection of material feeding methods, a Shapley value analysis of the input parameters was conducted.

Table 6 presents the Shapley values of the input parameters with respect to the material feeding method. Figure 4 illustrates the graphical summary of the Shapley values for the ANN model.

**Table 6.** Shapley values for ANN model.

| | Line Storage | Kanban | Kitting | Call-Out |
|---|---|---|---|---|
| Demand | −0.1142 | 0.6479 | −0.122 | −0.4117 |
| Compatibility with KV | 0 | 0.0029 | −0.122 | 0.1192 |
| Use case | −0.1142 | 0.0481 | 0.0644 | 0.0017 |
| Reference No | −0.0025 | −0.0871 | 0.008 | 0.0817 |
| Supply mode | 0.0008 | −0.0017 | 0.0017 | −0.0008 |

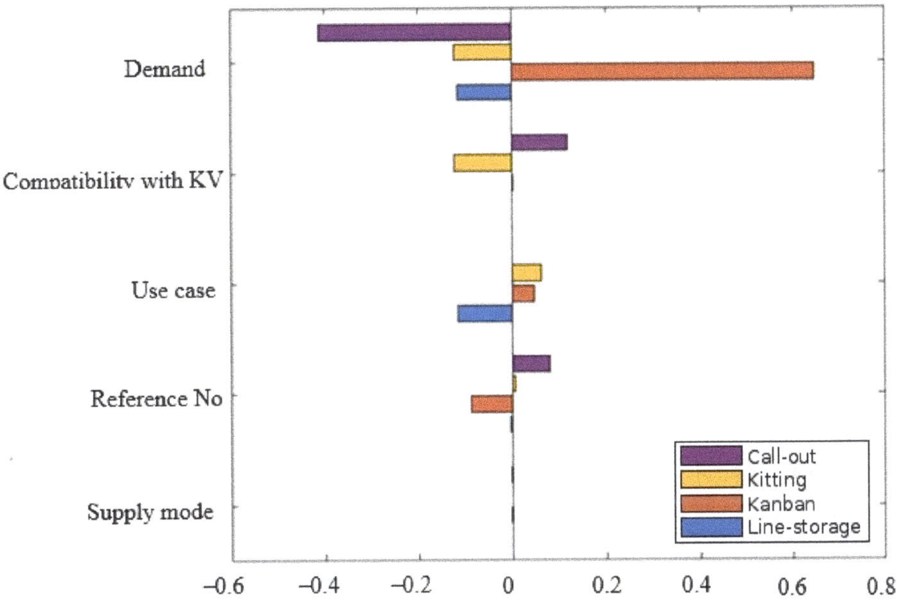


**Figure 4.** Graphical summary of Shapley values for ANN model.

As demonstrated in Table 6 and Figure 4, the application of demand has a substantial positive influence on Kanban (Shapley value = 0.6479), highlighting Kanban's adaptability to varying demand levels and a negative effect on line storage possibly due to inefficiencies or space constraints when handling large quantities, kitting likely due to inefficiencies in preparing kits for high-volume production, and call-out indicating that is not well-suited for high-demand scenarios (most significant negative effect of −0.4117 on call-out). The compatibility with KV has a minor effect on Kanban, with a value of 0.0029, indicating compatibility considerations may favor Kanban, and on call-out, with a value of 0.1192, suggesting compatibility considerations favor call-out. However, it demonstrates a negative impact on kitting, with a value of −0.122, possibly due to the difficulty of integrating kits into existing systems and no significant effect on line storage. Use case has a positive effect on Kanban with a value of 0.0481, showing Kanban's versatility in different production contexts, and kitting with a value of 0.0644, showing kitting works well in specific specialized production scenarios. A negative effect on line storage, with a value of −0.1142, indicates that the specific use-case scenarios do not favor line-storage feeding and have a minimal effect on call-out, with a value of 0.0017 showing minimal impact from specific use-case scenarios. The reference number exhibits a negative effect on Kanban with a value of −0.0871, suggesting reference numbers are less compatible with Kanban strategies; a positive effect on call-out with a value of 0.0817, indicating call-out benefits from specific reference number configurations; a lesser degree of effect on kitting with a value of 0.008, suggesting a minor role in determining kitting suitability; and a minimal effect on line storage with a negative value of −0.0025, indicating that the reference number plays a negligible role. The supply mode has a minimal contribution across all input parameters and has a positive influence on line storage with a value of 0.0008, suggesting that the supply mode plays a minor role in the material feeding method selection process and on kitting, with a value of 0.0017, indicating that it favors kitting to a mild degree. However, it has minor negative impacts on Kanban and call-out systems.

It is imperative to acknowledge that the demand value has the most significant impact on the ANN model, both positively and negatively. Consequently, fluctuations in demand may result in a change to the material feeding method. Due to its continuous supply model and adaptability, the Kanban method is the most influenced by demand, making it suitable for environments with fluctuating or high demand. The implementation of a Kanban material feeding strategy in automotive assembly lines, characterized by frequent demand changes, contributes to the assurance of uninterrupted production flow and the mitigation of overstocking risks. Conversely, line-storage, kitting, and call-out systems are adversely affected by demand due to space constraints, increased preparation times, and inefficiency in handling large quantities, rendering them less optimal for high-volume operations. The compatibility with KV and supply mode parameters exhibits low contributions across material feeding methods. The call-out method demonstrates sensitivity to demand and suggests that compatibility considerations favor call-out. The results indicate that if the company is required to develop a demand-driven material feeding strategy, the implementation of a Kanban system can be advantageous, while the kitting and line-storage processes are streamlined for stable, low-demand operations. This approach is expected to enhance operational efficiency and effective cost management. If the company places emphasis on customization and precision in its material feeding strategy, the call-out system has the potential to be effective in high-variability, high-precision manufacturing environments.

Table 7 presents a comparison of the current application for the material feeding system in the company and the application suggested by the proposed ANN model.

**Table 7.** Comparison of number of materials for current application and suggested application.

| | Current Application | Suggested Application |
|---|---|---|
| Line storage | 1047 | 513 |
| Kanban | 103 | 751 |
| Kitting | 0 | 461 |
| Call-out | 1071 | 496 |

As illustrated in Table 7, the implementation of the proposed ANN-based solution will result in a 48.9% reduction in the number of materials located adjacent to the line, from 1047 to 513 types. This reduction in material types will lead to significant space savings next to the line.

The application indicates a substantial reduction, suggesting that resources are being allocated unnecessarily to line storage and that they could be redirected elsewhere for greater efficiency. Considering the size of the products and the containers in which they are stored, it is expected to result in a 48.9% reduction in the number of material types that need to be placed next to the production line, resulting in the availability of approximately 100 $m^2$ of space in the production area. However, as these materials will be stored in the central warehouse, it was determined that an additional 50 $m^2$ of space would need to be allocated within the central warehouse. The company's inadequate capacity to meet customer demand was a key issue. Consequently, it was imperative to allocate space to introduce new manufacturing equipment. The warehouse space cost was less than the profit from the new machines, thus making the decision appropriate in the context of a feasibility analysis. Prior to the execution of the proposed study, the kitting method had not been employed in the pilot assembly line. However, the kitting application has been proposed for 461 materials within the proposed system. Implementing the kitting application involves assigning a logistics operator to prepare the kit and allocating a designated area within the warehouse for kit preparation. During the preliminary commissioning phase of the application, an emergency material feeding vehicle was allocated to the designated area to ensure the production line's uninterrupted operation, thereby mitigating the risk of material feeding issues. To ensure the system's adaptability, the identification of emerging problems was facilitated by implementing the daily continuous improvement process (CIP) board, action plans were devised, and the transition and adaptation process was successfully completed. Logistics operators were trained in kitting to facilitate employees' adaptation to the kitting system.

Due to the company's production capacity constraints, the utilization of fast production changeover was imperative. In the event of a changeover in production on the assembly line, it was the responsibility of the assembly operators to locate and deliver the necessary materials to the line. The configuration of the production system was characterized by a high number of material types and a low number of units in each type. This resulted in a lack of clearly designated locations for the materials, which led to assembly operators seeking materials in a designated common area. Moreover, material containers were occasionally positioned in a stacked configuration due to limited available space within the production area. It is posited that the implementation of the proposed system will result in a 49.8% reduction in the number of materials located in the assembly line. It is estimated that the relocation of non-essential materials away from the assembly line will result in a reduction of time spent searching for materials. This, in turn, is expected to reduce the amount of production-related stress experienced by the operator. It is also expected that implementing this system will reduce non-ergonomic activities, such as repeatedly moving materials around the production area and taking material containers over each other. As most materials are currently fed to the assembly line in standard material boxes, the remaining materials after production are repackaged and directed to the warehouse. The study proposes increasing the number of materials fed using the Kanban and kitting methods. This will enable the operator to receive the required number of parts from the warehouse with the kit and Kanban system. The elimination of repackaging and subsequent re-dispatch of materials to the warehouse is a key benefit of this system, as is the reduction in warehouse waste. The advantages inherent to this system comprise the elimination of repackaging and the subsequent reshipment of materials to the warehouse, which consequently results in a reduction in warehouse waste and in-company logistics traffic. A reduction in in-house logistics traffic and the consequent reduction in forklift energy consumption will increase energy efficiency.

The increased use of Kanban systems is indicative of a reallocation of resources and tasks to this category, suggesting that the Kanban approach may be a more efficient or effective method for the current operations. The utilization of kitting is not currently employed; however, its implementation is recommended, with the allocation of substantial resources. This suggests a missed opportunity to optimize operations through kitting, which could potentially improve process flow or efficiency. It is evident that the call-out function is currently being used excessively in a manner comparable to line storage. The recommended reduction signifies the over-allocation of resources, which could be streamlined or redirected to underutilized areas such as Kanban or kitting. The presented model posits that there should be a reduction in reliance on line-storage and call-out systems. A substantial augmentation in the utilization of Kanban is imperative, accompanied by the integration of kitting. The implementation of these changes is expected to achieve a balanced utilization of resources, thereby enhancing efficiency and productivity.

The proposed ANN-based system has many advantages, but integrating the model into existing manufacturing systems will be challenging. The model's accuracy depends on the data's accuracy and real-world data quality (which can compromise the model's accuracy due to noise, missing values, inconsistencies, and errors). The ANN is a supervised learning algorithm that requires labeled data. This data may not be readily available or can be costly and time-consuming to generate. Integrating data from multiple sources is challenging due to data formats and protocol heterogeneity. Integration of ANN models requires robust computing resources, which may require hardware or cloud upgrades. Maintaining consistency and integrating multiple production lines or sites is challenging because operators and management often resist new technology. The company should consider a strategic approach to implementation. This could mean introducing ANN-based models to minimize operational disruptions, automating and securing data collection and preprocessing, monitoring the performance of the ANN-based model, encouraging teams to include data scientists, engineers, and operators, and scheduling training to explain the benefits and procedures of the system. This will ensure that the ANN-based model is integrated and used effectively. These solutions will help manufacturers overcome the challenges of integrating ML models and open up new opportunities for efficiency, quality, and innovation.

## 5. Discussion

In the contemporary business environment, manufacturing companies are compelled to enhance their performance in order to maintain their competitive advantage. In order to compete, it is imperative that they enhance their productivity by improving the quality and reducing costs and delivery times. Material feeding systems represent a pivotal dimension that exerts a significant influence on productivity. The selection of appropriate materials feeding systems in manufacturing companies has been shown to result in a decrease in non-value-added work and quality problems, an increase in product output, an improvement in ergonomic conditions, and an enhancement in the ability to respond promptly to customer demands.

A wide range of material feeding methods have been listed in the extant literature, including line-storage, Kanban, kitting, demand-based, just-in-time, and hybrid approaches. Kanban is a material feeding system based on drawing the minimum and maximum stock defined. A notable advantage of this method is that it does not necessitate any additional planning. It is predicated on the assumption that the requisite stock quantity is available at the stipulated location. The line-side feeding method is advantageous in that materials are available next to the assembly line and can be easily accessed in case of any problem; however, it is disadvantageous in that it takes up space next to the line, and the time spent searching for materials is not value added. In contrast, the on-call demand-based feeding method involves the request of materials from a central warehouse when they are to be used in the assembly line. The requested materials are delivered in a box, the required amount of material is consumed, and the remaining material is delivered back to the assembly line. Despite the lack of spatial proximity to the assembly line, this method results in inefficiency due to the movement of materials. Kitting is a material feeding method that ensures that the materials required for the assembly line are placed in a defined quantity in a defined container and delivered to the specified place at the specified time. This method is considered advantageous in enterprises where product variety is high and product demand volume is low. The reduction in material intermediate stocks has been shown to decrease the time spent searching for components. It has been demonstrated that kitting can increase productivity by reducing non-value-added activities. It also helps to prevent incomplete or incorrect assembly by providing a defined and visual management system. However, it is important to note that this method does come with certain disadvantages, including the requirement for dedicated kitting preparation time and labor. Inadequate implementation or a less developed kitting system within the supply chain can result in assembly line downtime.

This study was conducted at a manufacturing company specializing in the production of hydraulic and pneumatic motors and agricultural and industrial vehicles. The company deploys cellular manufacturing techniques and has five distinct product groups, with the selected product group encompassing three separate assembly lines. The company is engaged in the production of motors, characterized by a high degree of product variety and a comparatively low-demand volume. A comprehensive investigation was conducted into hybrid approaches that may be suitable for the company, with a focus on Kanban, line-storage feeding, call-out, and kitting systems. While the requirement for additional space for new machines and assembly lines is acknowledged, there is also a demand to increase the number of outputs through enhanced productivity of assembly operators. Additionally, there is a requirement for a material feeding system that is straightforward to implement, capable of expeditious decision-making, and conducive to assembly lines with diverse value streams within the factory environment.

The material feeding method selection problem is structured based on a multi-class classification problem, with four output parameters and five input parameters being determined. Six different classification-based ML algorithms, LR, DT, RF, SVM, K-NN, and ANN, are used for the material feeding method selection problem. The training dataset, which consists of 2221 materials, is split into two sets (training and testing) before running ML algorithms. In this study, the 8-fold CV technique is applied to the dataset, and random sampling is used to determine the folds. The ANN model demonstrates superior performance across all metrics when identifying the correct material feeding method. The Shapley values of the input parameters are analyzed for the developed ANN model. While the ANN method is commonly referred to as a 'black box' method, the analysis of Shapley values provides actionable insights into the influence of input parameters on material feeding system selection. According to the Shapley value results, fluctuations in demand may result in a change to the material feeding method. The Kanban method is the most influenced by demand and use-case parameters. The compatibility with KV and supply mode parameters exhibits low contributions across the material feeding methods. The call-out method demonstrates sensitivity to demand and compatibility with the KV parameters.

In traditional manufacturing companies, material feeding method selection frequently depends on human decision-making, leading to hidden costs associated with inefficiencies in operational activities, excess inventory, and disruptions in material feeding. In contrast, the proposed ANN-based approach enhances the accuracy of the material feeding method selection, reducing downtime and enhancing productivity. The analysis encompasses implementation costs, including hardware upgrades for data collection, software licenses for ML platforms, and personnel training. These are then weighed against the long-term savings from decreased waste, reduced stock levels, and faster response times to production changeovers. For example, a reduction in incorrect assembly line feeding has been estimated to reduce re-work costs by a significant margin. These comparisons underscore the economic feasibility and strategic value of transitioning to a data-driven, ANN-based material feeding system. It is acknowledged that the ANN model incurs higher initial costs than traditional human-based models; however, it has been demonstrated that the operational savings resulting from reduced labor, inventory, and storage requirements result in favorable long-term cost efficiency. The ANN-driven solution can accommodate additional product lines, different material types, and varying demand levels in contrast to traditional methods. The transition to an ANN-driven material feeding strategy has been shown to deliver significant productivity, efficiency, and cost savings benefits. Despite the substantial initial investment and training costs, the long-term return on investment (ROI) is significant due to the enhanced operational efficiencies, improved decision-making processes, and increased operator productivity.

This study makes a significant contribution to the advancement of knowledge concerning material feeding systems in manufacturing environments, thereby facilitating an improved understanding and enhanced application of such systems. The present study addresses the unique challenges faced by manufacturers operating in high-variety, low-volume production environments. This study was conducted within the context of a manufacturing company specializing in the production of hydraulic and pneumatic motors, along with agricultural and industrial vehicles. The findings of this research endeavor to offer significant real-world relevance, providing practical insights that can be directly applied in industry. The framework of the proposed study is predicated on a range of production-related factors, including, but not limited to, demand fluctuations, product variety, and physical space limitations. The integration of ML models provides a robust and innovative approach to address the complexities of this decision-making process. The integration of six classification-based ML algorithms, including LR, DT, RF, SVM, K-NN, and ANN, by incorporating a multi-class classification system, represents a pioneering advancement in the field, demonstrating the application of advanced computational techniques within the material feeding system selection process. This methodological innovation has been demonstrated to enhance the accuracy, efficiency, and scalability of the decision-making process within dynamic manufacturing environments. The present study establishes a foundation for future investigations into the intersection of advanced analytics and engineering applications by combining ML models with manufacturing operations research. It opens avenues for refining and expanding material feeding systems to meet evolving industry needs. The study's comprehensive and interdisciplinary approach offers both theoretical advancements and practical benefits, thereby establishing itself as a valuable resource for researchers and practitioners in the fields of manufacturing and supply chain management. Overall, this study bridges the gap between theoretical research and practical application, providing a comprehensive and adaptable framework for material feeding system selection in manufacturing. The findings are not only relevant to the specific case study but also serve as a foundation for broader applications and future innovations in engineering and operations management.

This study adopts a comprehensive approach; however, the practical challenges of integrating advanced ML models into existing manufacturing workflows, such as data preparation and system integration, require further exploration. This study utilizes a static dataset for the training and testing of ML models, which does not account for real-time changes in demand, production schedules, or supply chain disruptions. The incorporation of dynamic, real-time data could provide a more adaptive and responsive framework for material feeding system selection. Despite the study's mention of ergonomic conditions, a more detailed analysis is required to ascertain the impact of the proposed material feeding systems on workers' physical demands and environmental considerations, such as waste reduction and energy efficiency. By acknowledging these limitations, future research can build on the study's findings, addressing these gaps and broadening the scope to create more versatile and widely applicable solutions for material feeding in manufacturing systems.

**Author Contributions:** Conceptualization, M.S.Ç.; methodology, M.S.Ç. and A.A.; project administration, M.S.Ç.; supervision, A.A.; writing—original draft preparation, M.S.Ç. and A.A.; writing—review and editing, M.S.Ç. and A.A. All authors have read and agreed to the published version of the manuscript.

**Funding:** This research received no external funding.

**Institutional Review Board Statement:** Not applicable.

**Informed Consent Statement:** Not applicable.

**Data Availability Statement:** The data supporting the findings of this study are available upon request from the corresponding author. Public access is restricted to protect privacy.

**Conflicts of Interest:** Author Müge Sinem Çağlayan was employed by the company Jaguar Land Rover-Solihull. The remaining authors declare that the research was conducted in the absence of any commercial or financial relationships that could be construed as a potential conflict of interest.

## References

1. Faccio, M. The impact of production mix variations and models varities on the parts-feeding policy selection in a product assembly system. *Int. J. Adv. Manuf. Technol.* **2014**, *72*, 543–560. [CrossRef]
2. Bozer, Y.; McGinnis, L. Kitting versus line stocking: A conceptual framework and a descriptive model. *Int. J. Prod. Econ.* **1992**, *28*, 1–19. [CrossRef]
3. Brynzer, H.; Johansson, M. Design and performance of kitting and order picking systems. *Int. J. Prod. Econ.* **1995**, *41*, 115–125. [CrossRef]
4. Choobineh, F.; Mohebbi, E. Material planning for production kits under uncertainty. *Prod. Plan. Control* **2004**, *15*, 63–70. [CrossRef]
5. Sali, M.; Sahin, E.; Patchong, A. An empirical assessment of the performances of three line feeding modes used in the automotive sector: Line stocking vs. kitting vs. sequencing. *Int. J. Prod. Res.* **2015**, *53*, 1439–1459. [CrossRef]
6. Çevikcan, E.; Sol, E.; Satoğlu, Ş.I.; Durmuşoğlu, M.B. Set making based design of in-plant logistics processes and an application. *J. Uludag Univ. Fac. Eng.* **2018**, *23*, 83–98. [CrossRef]
7. Limere, V.; Landeghem, H.V.; Goetshalckx, M. A decision model for kitting and line stocking with variable operator walking distances. *Assem. Autom.* **2015**, *35*, 47–56. [CrossRef]
8. Kilic, H.S.; Durmusoglu, M.B. Advances in assembly line parts feeding policies: A literature review. *Assem. Autom.* **2015**, *35*, 57–68. [CrossRef]
9. Zhou, B.; Zhao, Z. A hybrid fuzzy-neural-based dynamic scheduling method for part feeding of mixed-model assembly lines. *Comput. Ind. Eng.* **2022**, *163*, 107794. [CrossRef]
10. Caputo, A.C.; Pelagagge, P.M.; Salini, P. Selection of assembly lines feeding policies based on parts features and scenario conditions. *Int. J. Prod. Res.* **2018**, *56*, 1208–1232. [CrossRef]
11. Schmid, N.A.; Montreuil, B.; Limere, V. Modeling and solving integrated assembly line balancing, assembly line feeding, and facility sizing problems. *Int. J. Prod. Econ.* **2024**, *277*, 109354. [CrossRef]
12. Tardif, V.; Maaseidvaag, L. An adaptive approach to controlling Kanban systems. *Eur. J. Oper. Res.* **2001**, *132*, 411–424. [CrossRef]
13. Faccio, M.; Gamberi, M.; Persona, A.; Regattieri, A.; Sgarbossa, F. Design and simulation of assembly line feeding system in the automative sector using supermarkets, kanbans and tow trains: A general framework. *J. Manag. Cont.* **2013**, *24*, 187–208. [CrossRef]
14. Kumar, C.S.; Pannerselvam, R. Literature review of JIT-Kanban system. *Int. J. Adv. Manuf. Technol.* **2007**, *32*, 393–408. [CrossRef]
15. Savino, M.M.; Mazza, A. Kanban-driven parts feeding within a semi-automated O-shaped assembly line: A case study in the automotive industry. *Assem. Autom.* **2015**, *35*, 3–15. [CrossRef]
16. Zammori, F.; Braglia, M.; Castellano, D. Just-in-time parts feeding policies for paced assembly lines: Possible solutions for highly constrained layouts. *Int. Trans. Oper. Res.* **2015**, *23*, 691–724. [CrossRef]
17. Ostermeier, F.F.; Jaehnert, J.; Deuse, J. Joint modelling of the order-dependent parts supply strategies sequencing, kitting and batch supply for assembly lines: Insights from industrial practice. *Prod. Manuf. Res.* **2023**, *11*, 2200808. [CrossRef]
18. Baller, R.; Hage, S.; Fontaine, P.; Spinler, S. The assembly line feeding problem: An extended formulation with multiple line feeding policies and a case study. *Int. J. Prod. Econ.* **2020**, *222*, 107489. [CrossRef]

19. Müllerklein, D.; Fontaine, P.; Ostermeier, F. Integrated consideration of assembly line scheduling and feeding: A new model and case study from the automotive industry. *Comput. Ind. Eng.* **2022**, *170*, 108288. [CrossRef]
20. Caputo, A.C.; Pelagagge, P.M. Effects of product design on assembly lines performances: A concurrent engineering approach. *Ind. Manag. Data Syst.* **2008**, *108*, 726–749. [CrossRef]
21. Caputo, A.C.; Pelagagge, P.M. A methodology for selecting assembly systems feeding policy. *Ind. Manag. Data Syst.* **2011**, *111*, 84–112. [CrossRef]
22. Caputo, A.C.; Pelagagge, P.M.; Salini, P. A decision model for selecting parts feeding policies in assembly lines. *Ind. Manag. Data Syst.* **2015**, *155*, 974–1003. [CrossRef]
23. Sali, M.; Sahin, E. Line feeding optimization for just in time assembly lines: An application to the automotive industry. *Int. J. Prod. Econ.* **2016**, *174*, 54–67. [CrossRef]
24. Fedtke, S.; Boysen, N.; Schumacher, P. In-line kitting for part feeding of assembly lines: Workload balancing and storage assignment to reduce the workers' walking effort. *OR Spectr.* **2023**, *45*, 717–758. [CrossRef]
25. Wang, Z.; Hu, H.; Liu, T. Iterated-local-search-based chaotic differential evolution algorithm for hybrid-load part feeding scheduling optimization in mixed-model assembly lines. *Eng. Comput.* **2023**, *40*, 2693–2729. [CrossRef]
26. Wänström, C.; Medbo, L. The impact of materials feeding design on assembly process performance. *J. Manuf. Technol. Manag.* **2008**, *20*, 30–51. [CrossRef]
27. Battini, D.; Faccio, M.; Persona, A.; Sgarbossa, F. Design of the optimal feeding policy in assembly system. *Int. J. Prod. Econ.* **2009**, *121*, 233–254. [CrossRef]
28. Hua, S.; Johnson, D. Research issues on factors influencing the choice of kitting versus line stocking. *Int. J. Prod. Res.* **2010**, *48*, 779–800. [CrossRef]
29. Hanson, R.; Medbo, L.; Medbo, P. Assembly station design: A quantitative comparison of the effects of kitting and continuous supply. *J. Manuf. Technol. Manag.* **2012**, *23*, 315–327. [CrossRef]
30. Limere, V.; Landeghem, H.V.; Goetshalckx, M.; Aghezzaf, E.; McGinnis, L. Optimising part feeding in the automotive assembly industry: Deciding between kitting and line stocking. *Int. J. Prod. Res.* **2012**, *50*, 4046–4060. [CrossRef]
31. Hanson, R.; Brolin, A. A comparison of kitting and continuous supply in in-plant materials supply. *Int. J. Prod. Res.* **2013**, *51*, 979–992. [CrossRef]
32. Zennaro, I.; Finco, S.; Battini, D.; Calzavara, M. A parts feeding model for big size products: The active and idle assembly islands strategy. *Int. J. Adv. Oper. Manag.* **2020**, *12*, 211–236. [CrossRef]
33. Kang, Z.; Çatal, Ç.; Tekinerdogan, B. Machine learning applications in production lines: A systematic literature review. *Comput. Ind. Eng.* **2020**, *149*, 106773. [CrossRef]
34. Bertolini, M.; Mezzogori, D.; Neroni, M.; Zammori, F. Machine Learning for industrial applications: A comprehensive literature review. *Expert Syst. Appl.* **2021**, *175*, 114820. [CrossRef]
35. Moretti, E.; Tappia, E.; Limère, V.; Melacini, M. Exploring the application of machine learning to the assembly line feeding problem. *Oper. Manag. Res.* **2021**, *14*, 403–419. [CrossRef]
36. Zangaro, F.; Minner, S.; Battini, D. A supervised machine learning approach for the optimisation of the assembly line feeding mode selection. *Int. J. Prod. Res.* **2021**, *59*, 4881–4902. [CrossRef]
37. Faccio, M.; Granata, I.; Maretto, L. Modelling and managing "station-sequence" parts feeding in the I4.0 Era: A simulation approach for in-plant logistics. *Appl. Sci.* **2023**, *13*, 1725. [CrossRef]
38. Banerjee, S.; Bhowmik, P.S. A machine learning approach based on decision tree algorithm for classification of transient events in microgrid. *Electr. Eng.* **2023**, *105*, 2083–2093. [CrossRef]
39. Kotsiantis, S.B.; Zaharakis, I.; Pintelas, P. Supervised machine learning: A review of classification techniques. *Emerg. Artif. Intel. Appl. Comput. Eng.* **2007**, *160*, 3–24.
40. Ghasemkhani, B.; Balbal, K.F.; Birant, K.U.; Birant, D. A novel classification method: Neighborhood-based positive unlabeled learning using decision tree (NPULUD). *Entropy* **2024**, *26*, 403. [CrossRef]
41. Aziz, U.; Bradshaw, A.; Lim, J. Classification of defects in additively manufactured nickel alloys using supervised machine learning. *Mat. Sci. Technol.* **2023**, *39*, 2464–2468. [CrossRef]
42. Sen, P.C.; Hajra, M.; Ghosh, M. Supervised classification algorithms in machine learning: A survey and review. In *Emerging Technology in Modelling and Graphics*; Mandal, J., Bhattacharya, D., Eds.; Advances in Intelligent Systems and Computing; Springer: Singapore, 2020; Volume 937, pp. 99–111. [CrossRef]
43. Ho, T.K. The random subspace method for constructing decision forests. *IEEE Trans. Pattern Anal. Mach. Intell.* **1998**, *20*, 832–844. [CrossRef]
44. Breiman, L. Random forests. *Mach. Learn.* **2001**, *45*, 5–32. [CrossRef]
45. Ong, A.K.S.; Cordova, L.N.Z.; Longanilla, F.A.B.; Caprecho, N.L.; Javier, R.A.V.; Borres, R.D.; German, J.D. Purchasing intentions analysis of hybrid cars using random forest classifier and deep learning. *World Electr. Veh. J.* **2023**, *14*, 227. [CrossRef]

46. Jiang, M.; Wang, J.; Hu, L.; He, Z. Random forest clustering for discrete sequences. *Pattern Recognit. Lett.* **2023**, *174*, 145–151. [CrossRef]
47. Sun, M.; Qian, L.; Mukherjee, A.; Xiang, D. An EWMA chart for high dimensional process with multi-class out-of-control information via random forest learning. *Qual. Technol. Quant. Manag.* **2024**, *21*, 722–748. [CrossRef]
48. Zhai, X.; Xu, R.; Wang, Z.; Zheng, Z.; Shou, Y.; Tian, S.; Tian, L.; Hu, X.; Chen, L.; Xu, N. Classification of arctic sea ice type in CFOSAT scatterometer measurements using a random forest classifier. *Remote Sens.* **2023**, *15*, 1310. [CrossRef]
49. Talbot, N.L.C.; Cawley, G.C. The evidence framework applied to sparse kernel logistic regression. *Neurocomputing* **2005**, *64*, 119–135. [CrossRef]
50. Khandezamin, Z.; Naderan, M.; Rashti, M.J. Detection and classification of breast cancer using logistic regression feature selection and GMDH classifier. *J. Biomed. Inf.* **2002**, *111*, 103591. [CrossRef]
51. Wichitaksorn, N.; Kang, Y.; Zhang, F. Random feature selection using random subspace logistic regression. *Expert Syst. Appl.* **2023**, *217*, 119535. [CrossRef]
52. Nusinovici, S.; Tham, Y.C.; Yan, M.Y.C.; Ting, D.S.W.; Li, J.; Sabanayagam, C.; Wong, T.Y.; Cheng, C.-Y. Logistic regression was as good as machine learning for predicting major chronic diseases. *J. Clin. Epidemiol.* **2020**, *122*, 56–69. [CrossRef]
53. Rymarczyk, T.; Kozłowski, E.; Kłosowski, G.; Niderla, K. Logistic Regression for Machine Learning in Process Tomography. *Sensors* **2019**, *19*, 3400. [CrossRef]
54. Luna-Benoso, B.; Martinez-Perales, J.C.; Morales-Rodriguez, U.S.; Flores-Carapia, R.; Silva-Garcia, V.M. A new classification model using a decision tree generated from hyperplanes in dimensional space. *Appl. Artif. Intell.* **2024**, *38*, 2426377. [CrossRef]
55. Gopi, A.P.; Jyothi, R.N.S.; Narayana, V.L.; Sandeep, K.S. Classification of tweets data based on polarity using improved RBF kernel of SVM. *Int. J. Inf. Tecnol.* **2023**, *15*, 965–980. [CrossRef]
56. Azam, Z.; Islam, M.M.; Huda, M.N. Comparative analysis of intrusion detection systems and machine learning-based model analysis through decision tree. *IEEE Access* **2023**, *11*, 80348–80391. [CrossRef]
57. Wang, Y.; Pan, Z.; Dong, J. A new two-layer nearest neighbor selection method for kNN classifier. *Knowl.-Based Syst.* **2022**, *235*, 107604. [CrossRef]
58. Xia, Y. Chapter eleven: Correlation and association analyses in microbiome study integrating multiomics in health and disease. In *Progress Molecular Biology and Translational Science*; Sun, J., Ed.; Academic Press: Cambridge, MA, USA, 2020; Volume 171, pp. 309–491. [CrossRef]
59. Arlot, S.; Celisse, A.A. Survey of cross-validation procedures for model selection. *Stat. Surv.* **2010**, *4*, 40–79. [CrossRef]
60. Marcineková, K.; Janáková Sujová, A. Multi-objective optimization of manufacturing process using artificial neural networks. *Systems* **2024**, *12*, 569. [CrossRef]
61. Bourdeau, M.; Zhai, X.-Q.; Nefzaoui, E.; Guo, X.; Chatellier, P. Modeling and forecasting building energy consumption: A review of data-driven techniques. *Sustain. Cities Soc.* **2019**, *48*, 101533. [CrossRef]
62. Maghraoui, A.E.; Hammouc, F.E.; Ledmaoui, Y.; Chebak, A. Smart energy management system: A comparative study of energy consumption prediction algorithms for a hotel building. In Proceedings of the 4th Global Power, Energy and Communication Conference (GPECOM), Cappadocia, Turkey, 4 June 2022; pp. 529–534. [CrossRef]
63. Nair, V.; Hinton, G.E. Rectified linear units improve restricted boltzmann machines. In Proceedings of the 27th International Conference on International Conference on Machine Learning (ICML'10), Omnipress, Madison, WI, USA, 21–24 June 2010; pp. 807–814.
64. Han, J.; Wang, Z.; Shen, J.; Tang, H. Symmetric-threshold ReLU for fast and nearly lossless ANN-SNN conversion. *Mach. Intell. Res.* **2023**, *20*, 435–446. [CrossRef]
65. Saleem, S.; Asim, M.N.; Van Elst, L.; Junker, M.; Dengel, A. MLR-Predictor: A versatile and efficient computational framework for multi-label requirements classification. *Front. Artif. Intell.* **2024**, *7*, 1481581. [CrossRef]
66. Ghasemkhani, B.; Balbal, K.F.; Birant, D. A new predictive method for classification tasks in machine learning: Multi-class multi-label logistic model tree (MMLMT). *Mathematics* **2024**, *12*, 2825. [CrossRef]
67. Shapley, L.S. A Value for n-Person Games. In *Contributions to the Theory of Games, Volume II*; Kuhn, H.K., Tucker, A.W., Eds.; Princeton University Press: Princeton, NJ, USA, 1953; pp. 307–318. [CrossRef]
68. Smith, M.; Alvarez, F. Identifying mortality factors from machine learning using Shapley values—A case of COVID19. *Expert Syst. Appl.* **2021**, *176*, 114832. [CrossRef]
69. Rodríguez-Pérez, R.; Bajorath, J. Interpretation of machine learning models using shapley values: Application to compound potency and multi-target activity predictions. *J. Comput. Aided Mol. Des.* **2020**, *34*, 1013–1026. [CrossRef]
70. Zhang, S.; Chen, X.; Ran, X.; Li, Z.; Cao, W. Prioritizing causation in decision trees: A framework for interpretable modeling. *Eng. Appl. Artif. Intel.* **2024**, *133*, 108224. [CrossRef]
71. Akinola, O.O.; Ezugwu, A.E.; Agushaka, J.O.; Abu Zitar, R.; Abualigah, L. Multiclass feature selection with metaheuristic optimization algorithms: A review. *Neural Comput. Appl.* **2022**, *34*, 19751–19790. [CrossRef]

72. Mienye, D.; Sun, Y. A survey of ensemble learning: Concepts, algorithms, applications, and prospects. *IEEE Access* **2022**, *10*, 99129–99149. [CrossRef]
73. Del-Pozo-Bueno, D.; Kepaptsoglou, D.; Peiró, F.; Estradé, S. Comparative of machine learning classification strategies for electron energy loss spectroscopy: Support vector machines and artificial neural networks. *Ultramicroscopy* **2023**, *253*, 113828. [CrossRef]
74. Wedagedara, H.; Witharana, C.; Fahey, R.; Cerrai, D.; Parent, J.; Perera, A.S. Non-parametric machine learning modeling of tree-caused power outage risk to overhead distribution powerlines. *Appl. Sci.* **2024**, *14*, 4991. [CrossRef]
75. Peng, H.; Long, F.; Ding, C. Feature selection based on mutual information criteria of max-dependency, max-relevance, and min-redundancy. *IEEE Trans. Pattern Anal. Mach. Int.* **2005**, *27*, 1226–1238. [CrossRef]
76. Jo, I.; Lee, S.; Oh, S. Improved Measures of Redundancy and Relevance for mRMR Feature Selection. *Computers* **2019**, *8*, 42. [CrossRef]
77. Hermo, J.; Bolón-Canedo, V.; Ladra, S. Fed-mRMR: A lossless federated feature selection method. *Inf. Sci.* **2024**, 669. [CrossRef]
78. Mahapatra, M.; Majhi, S.K.; Dhal, S.K. MRMR-SSA: A hybrid approach for optimal feature selection. *Evol. Int.* **2022**, *15*, 2017–2036. [CrossRef]
79. Allgaier, J.; Pryss, R. Cross-Validation visualized: A narrative guide to advanced methods. *Mach. Learn. Knowl. Extr.* **2024**, *6*, 1378–1388. [CrossRef]
80. Kazemi, F.; Asgarkhani, N.; Jankowski, R. Optimization-based stacked machine-learning method for seismic probability and risk assessment of reinforced concrete shear walls. *Expert Syst. Appl.* **2024**, *255*, 124897. [CrossRef]
81. Abdumalikov, S.; Kim, J.; Yoon, Y. Performance analysis and improvement of machine learning with various feature selection methods for EEG-based emotion classification. *Appl. Sci.* **2024**, *14*, 10511. [CrossRef]

MDPI AG
Grosspeteranlage 5
4052 Basel
Switzerland
Tel.: +41 61 683 77 34

*Applied Sciences* Editorial Office
E-mail: applsci@mdpi.com
www.mdpi.com/journal/applsci

www.ingramcontent.com/pod-product-compliance
Lightning Source LLC
Chambersburg PA
CBHW061521210926
51850CB00008B/1988
*9783725872688*